DATE DUE

DEMCO 38-296

THE COMPLETE POEMS

OF

LOUIS DANIEL

BRODSKY

VOLUME ONE, 1963–1967

Books by LOUIS DANIEL BRODSKY

Poetry

Five Facets of Myself   (1967)* (1995)

The Easy Philosopher   (1967)* (1995)

"A Hard Coming of It" and Other Poems   (1967)* (1995)

The Foul Rag-and-Bone Shop   (1967)* (1969)* (1995)

Points in Time   (1971)* (1995) (1996)

Taking the Back Road Home   (1972)* (1997)

Trip to Tipton and Other Compulsions   (1972)*

"The Talking Machine" and Other Poems   (1973)*

Cold, Companionable Streams   (1974)*

Tiffany Shade   (1974)*

Trilogy: A Birth Cycle   (1974)

Monday's Child   (1975)

Preparing for Incarnations   (1975)* (1976)

The Kingdom of Gewgaw   (1976)

Point of Americas II   (1976)

La Preciosa   (1977)

Stranded in the Land of Transients   (1978)

The Uncelebrated Ceremony of Pants Factory Fatso   (1978)

Birds in Passage   (1980)

Résumé of a Scrapegoat   (1980)

Mississippi Vistas: Volume One of *A Mississippi Trilogy*   (1983) (1990)

You Can't Go Back, Exactly   (1988)

The Thorough Earth   (1989)

Four and Twenty Blackbirds Soaring   (1989)

Falling from Heaven: Holocaust Poems of a Jew and a Gentile
   (with William Heyen)   (1991)

Forever, for Now: Poems for a Later Love   (1991)

Mistress Mississippi: Volume Three of *A Mississippi Trilogy*   (1992)

A Gleam in the Eye: Poems for a First Baby   (1992)

Gestapo Crows: Holocaust Poems   (1992)

The Capital Café: Poems of Redneck, U.S.A.   (1993)

Disappearing in Mississippi Latitudes: Volume Two of *A Mississippi
   Trilogy*   (1994)

A Mississippi Trilogy: A Poetic Saga of the South   (1995)*

Paper-Whites for Lady Jane: Poems of a Midlife Love Affair   (1995)

The Complete Poems of Louis Daniel Brodsky: Volume One, 1963–1967
   (edited by Sheri L. Vandermolen)   (1996)

Bibliography (Coedited with Robert Hamblin)

Selections from the William Faulkner Collection of Louis Daniel Brodsky:
A Descriptive Catalogue (1979)

Faulkner: A Comprehensive Guide to the Brodsky Collection
Volume I: The Bibliography (1982)
Volume II: The Letters (1984)
Volume III: *The De Gaulle Story* (1984)
Volume IV: *Battle Cry* (1985)
Volume V: Manuscripts and Documents (1989)

Country Lawyer and Other Stories for the Screen by William Faulkner (1987)

Stallion Road: A Screenplay by William Faulkner (1989)

Biography

William Faulkner, Life Glimpses (1990)

Novels

The Adventures of the Night Riders, Better Known as the Terrible Trio
(with Richard Milsten) (1961)*

Between Grief and Nothing (1964)*

Between the Heron and the Wren (1965)*

Dink Phlager's Alligator *(novella)* (1966)*

The Drift of Things (1966)*

Vineyard's Toys (1967)*

The Bindlestiffs (1968)*

* *Unpublished*

Louis Daniel Brodsky
(ca. 1966)

THE COMPLETE POEMS

OF

LOUIS DANIEL BRODSKY

VOLUME ONE, 1963–1967

Edited by Sheri L. Vandermolen

TIME BEING BOOKS

POETRY IN SIGHT AND SOUND

St. Louis, Missouri

ISBN 1-56809-019-6 (Hardcover)
ISBN 1-56809-020-X (Paperback)

Library of Congress Cataloging-in-Publication Data:

Brodsky, Louis Daniel.
    [Poems]
    The complete poems of Louis Daniel Brodsky / edited by Sheri L.
Vandermolen.
        p.   cm.
    Contents: v. 1. 1963–1967
    ISBN 1-56809-019-6 (cloth). — ISBN 1-56809-020-X (pbk.)
    I. Vandermolen, Sheri L.   II. Title.
PS3552.R623A17   1996
811'.54—dc20   96-17149
                                                       CIP

Cover design by Tony Tharenos
Frontispiece and cover photograph courtesy of Joe Kirkish
Book design and typesetting by Sheri L. Vandermolen
Manufactured in the United States of America

First Edition, first printing (December 1996)

ACKNOWLEDGMENTS

I would like to express my appreciation to Sheri L. Vandermolen, Editor of Time Being Books, who has organized the voluminous, chaotic collection of scraps, notes, manuscripts, and typescripts of my early years as a writer, which I had ignored for thirty years. Amazingly, she has sifted through the many drafts that exist for each poem and has determined the final version for each. Her editorial skill has given this work the integrity I intended it to have three decades ago. Without her fastidiousness, diligence, mastery of the English language, and faith in and enthusiasm for this monumental endeavor, my earliest poetic voice would have remained silent.

I am also indebted to Jerry Call, Editor in Chief of Time Being Books. He has worked with me in revising my poetry for enough years to know precisely how to get the most out of me and from my writing. He has measurably improved this manuscript with his insightful suggestions.

My thanks, as well, to Rose Passalacqua, Ph.D., Comparative Literature, who collaborated with me to translate and edit the poems and passages in this volume written in Spanish, and to Martin Persky, whose thoughtful comments I incorporated in my introduction.

I also wish to acknowledge these publications, in which the following poems, in different versions, have appeared: *Free Lance* ("Confinement," Designs in Storm Time," "Land of the Setting Sun," "Mass Hysteria," "Mulatto," "Selma, Alabama, 3/6/65," "Tenement Eyes," "Unmatched Ecstasy," "Winter Seminar," and "Zoo"); *Reflections* ("Awakening," "The Burning Off," "Do Not Disturb," "Dr. Johnson's Rain," "Jan's Song," and "The Seer"); *Elephant & Castle* ("Land of the Setting Sun" and "Mulatto"); Ball State University's *Forum* ("Morning's Companion"); *Byline Magazine* ("Season's End"); *The Web* ("Winter Seminar").

Three poems, "Jan's Song," "Election," and "Zoo," were originally published in 1968 by the University of Tennessee as part of a musical score composed by Gary Nelson entitled *Three Motets on Poems by Louis Daniel Brodsky*.

I,
as their link
between our past and future,
dedicate my life's work,
my poetry,
to my parents,
Charlotte and Saul,
and
to my children,
Trilogy and Troika,

and to Jan,
as the tie that binds all of us.

Have you reckon'd a thousand acres much? have you reckon'd the earth much?
Have you practis'd so long to learn to read?
Have you felt so proud to get at the meaning of poems?

Stop this day and night with me and you shall possess the origin of all poems, . . .
— Walt Whitman, "Song of Myself"

For books are not absolutely dead things, but do contain a potency of life in them
to be as active as that soul was whose progeny they are; nay, they do preserve as
in a vial the purest efficacy and extraction of that living intellect that bred them.
— John Milton, *Areopagitica*

I write poems to preserve things I have seen/thought/felt . . . both for myself and
for others, though I feel my prime responsibility is to the experience itself, which
I am trying to keep from oblivion for its own sake. Why I should do this I have no
idea, but I think the impulse to preserve lies at the bottom of all art.
— Philip Larkin, in Janice Rossen's *Philip Larkin: His Life's Work*

CONTENTS

EDITOR'S GUIDE TO VOLUME ONE OF THE *COMPLETE POEMS* SERIES

Louis Daniel Brodsky composed his first poem in 1963, as an undergraduate at Yale, and by June of 1967, at the end of his "apprenticeship" and the beginning of his transition into professional writing, he had authored hundreds of poems, prose poems, and short, autobiographical prose works. These pieces, in their corrected forms, constitute this first volume of *The Complete Poems of Louis Daniel Brodsky*.

Over one hundred of these poems originally appeared in the four books of poems Brodsky produced during his apprentice years. He completed his inaugural poetry volume, *Five Facets of Myself*, in January of 1967, while pursuing his Master of Arts in English at Washington University, in St. Louis. Although he had assembled two booklets of his poems in years prior (*Ever-Becoming Dreams*, a set of eight poems compiled and mimeographed in 1964, at a boys' camp in Lake Nebagamon, Wisconsin, and an untitled group of seven poems, referred to as *"Zoo" and Other Poems*, created one year later at Camp Nebagamon), *Five Facets* represented his first book-length poetry manuscript. Having included some of his favorite, most revised poems in the *"Zoo"* booklet, he borrowed its entire contents and selected forty-three additional poems he had composed between 1965 and 1967 to form *Five Facets'* text, which he divided into five thematically arranged chapters focusing on his life as a student, a writer, and a camp counselor.

Determined to better his work, Brodsky continued revising these poems for months while also compiling a new book, *The Foul Rag-and-Bone Shop*, a collection with more surrealistic imagery and socially and politically biting tones than *Five Facets*. He finished *Foul Rag-and-Bone*'s initial manuscript, containing seventeen poems written during the mid-1960s, in the spring of 1967 but subsequently set it aside, not creating its expanded edition until the fall of 1969.

Then, still not fully satisfied with *Five Facets*, he chose to reconstitute it into a new book of poetry, *The Easy Philosopher*, to which he apportioned the final typescripts for thirty-three of the *Five Facets* poems. Although he added only eight other poems (composed in May and June of 1967) to the body of *The Easy Philosopher*, he reworked nearly every piece, rearranged into five new sections the divisions that had formed the thematic configuration of *Five Facets*, and removed the part titles, giving this manuscript a wholly different structure than its precursor. He also changed the texture of the writing, emphasizing the evolution of his style by placing four of the eight new poems, all more abstract and reflective in tone than his previous work, in part one of the book. He completed the book in June of 1967, after his graduation.

Having earned his degree in St. Louis in May and preparing to move to San Francisco by September to participate in a creative-writing program at San Francisco State University, Brodsky sensed an urgent need to collect into book format the rest of what he considered his most advanced work. Since he had already assigned two thirds of the *Five Facets* poems to *The Easy Philosopher*, he allocated the remaining third to a new manuscript, supplementing them with fifteen additional poems from 1965 to 1967, on the relation of the writer to nature and society, to yield *"A Hard Coming of It" and Other Poems*, the final poetry volume of his apprentice years.

Unable to devote much time to this book's full development, he created only one bound copy, with no contents page, dedication, or chapter designations. And although the poems from *Five Facets* had undergone much revision, most of the other poems had only limited drafts, especially those from 1967, which were written and revised in short spans of time, such as during his trip to Redington Beach, Florida, in January and during breaks in his school schedule in the spring.

He finished *"A Hard Coming of It"* by the end of June, approximately one week after completing *The Easy Philosopher*, and then began to concentrate his efforts on his prose writing, intending to become a professional fictionist once in San Francisco. He generated few poems in the months to follow and, from the summer of 1967 to the summer of 1971, produced only the second edition of *The Foul Rag-and-Bone Shop* and one incomplete manuscript, *Points in Time*.

Brodsky's first four books of poetry remained unpublished until 1995, after he and I had finished gathering and correcting the entire body of his early poetic works for this *Complete Poems* series. These books are now available from Time Being Books as separate publications (and *The Easy Philosopher*, *"A Hard Coming of It" and Other Poems*, and *The Foul Rag-and-Bone Shop* will be grouped into a single volume, *Three Early Books of Poems by Louis Daniel Brodsky, 1967–1969*), but their poems are also incorporated into this volume, arranged chronologically among his other apprentice work.

Since this other apprentice material (consisting of poems, prose poems, classroom notes, and fiction and nonfiction prose that had been stored in boxes, binders, and notebooks for decades) had never previously appeared in book format and remained largely unordered, Brodsky and I sorted the pieces in 1992 and 1993, dividing the manuscripts and typescripts according to their form (poetry/prose/prose poetry/etc.) and organizing them by their degree of revision. While many of the poems had been revised in multiple drafts, others had only single, less developed manuscripts. To determine whether pieces were complete, incomplete, or fragmental, we studied their texts and considered the original authorial intention, ultimately defining complete poems as concluded, whole thoughts, generally with revision, incompletes as longer, more complex starts at poems or prose that were left unfinished, and fragments as short, unrevised thoughts with simple structures and no closure. Despite the immature style of many of the less revised poems, poem fragments, and prose pieces, Brodsky and I decided to include them in this volume because they contribute to many of his tones and themes and illustrate the evolution of his writing, especially in juxtaposition with his more advanced works. However, any piece that contains poem, prose, or note fragments is denoted by a dagger symbol (†) following the title, and any piece with incomplete portions of poetry or prose is designated by a double-dagger symbol (‡).

In evaluating Brodsky's various types of prose, we considered the content as well as the form. Although he had vacillated between poetry and prose composition during his apprentice years, by the late 1960s he had dedicated himself solely to poetry writing; consequently, we chose to incorporate into this volume only those prose works offering autobiographical or narrative insight into the poetry or those written in prose-poem form, including meditations, reflections, and various imagerial pieces. We also elected to preserve the lineation of short prose pieces and the versified formats of the small prose poems, which are usually distinguishable from the poems by the style of the writing (when untitled, they are identifiable by the points of ellipsis in their bracketed first lines as well). No selections from the longer fictional works of his apprentice years, including short stories and novels, are presented here. Likewise, the only class-room notes and scribbled drawings provided are those that supply a context for the poem fragments interspersed within or around them or those that contain wordplay showing the progression of the author's vocabulary.

After we had studied the drafts and determined which types of writing to include, I input the pieces into Time Being Books' word-processing files and ar-chives. To retain Brodsky's original intent, I placed works containing groups of poem fragments or poems within prose into single word-processing files, with one database number/record per file in Time Being Books' poetry tracking system. However, when any of these fragments or short poems had been de-veloped into a separate poem during later revision, I put the group of fragments or the prose with poetry in one file and the individual poem in another. As a result, in this *Complete Poems* volume, certain pieces appear in their fragmen-tary form as well as their full poem form, which may appear independently or within a larger prose work.

I then assembled the pieces into a chronological document, ordering them by their dates of creation, which represent the time of their composition, not their revision. If a poem has more than one date of creation (i.e., if it was started on one day and not finished until another day, month, etc., with much content, such as extra stanzas or closure, added at that later time), it is arranged in the volume by its first date, listed at the end of the piece, because these poems typically had their intent as well as the majority of their text in place at the date of conception. All other dates of creation are also included after each work, as is the number assigned to it in the tracking system. If two or more poems were created on a single date or within a group of dates, bracketed numerals follow the dates of creation to indicate the sequence of their composition, which is labeled in the tracking system as well.

If neither Brodsky nor I could verify a creation date, a question mark follows the unconfirmed portion, which may be the month, the day, the year, or all three. When the entire date is in doubt (in which case it is bracketed and followed by a question mark), it indicates either that the drafts carry a date we feel may rep-resent revision instead of composition or that the drafts are undated but were found near other material written at that time. Likewise, the date may appear twice for the same poem, once with a question mark and once without, to signify that the date is accurate for at least part of the text but may or may not apply to the whole piece.

We have included the dates and tracking-system numbers in this collection because they will serve as cross references between the standard volumes and the two concluding books of this series: the index of Time Being Books' database records and the volume of ultimate, later revisions. The index, to be arranged chronologically, will contain each poem's creation and publication data, and this information, in turn, will link the standard set with the last book, which will show the corrected, most recent version of every poem drastically revised years after its original composition date (often for a new publication). Any poem in this first volume that will have its later form printed in the terminal volume because it has already undergone such revision or because it has been assigned to a future book and will, presumably, undergo such revision bears the delta symbol (Δ) after its title. Thus, in the *Complete Poems* set, the standard volumes will present the text of each poem, the penultimate volume will chronicle each poem's publishing history, and the last volume will show its subsequent, revised version, if applicable.

In order to retain the authorial voice of Brodsky's apprentice years, the editorial staff of Time Being Books has not fully revised any of the pieces in this volume except those culled for new publications (in which case, the later version of each poem will appear in the final volume of this series). But Brodsky did revise much of the work soon after its composition, and the staff has completely corrected each piece, with his approval, to meet Time Being Books' current standardizations for language usage and mechanics, with spelling and typographical changes, alterations of punctuation and capitalization, and all other grammatical corrections added silently. Bold and italic typefaces have been added as necessary, replacing emphatic underlining, and idiosyncratic underlining has been removed where possible (when originally used to divide fragments, for instance). However, in order to reflect how Brodsky's schooling and his experimentation with styles affected his early writing, we have preserved his use of British spellings and archaic spelling variations as well as his intentional use of neologized words (such as "tremulations" and "pausations") and compounds (like "lifebreath" and "cedarwhispers"). The editorial changes are meant to standardize the work and enhance its readability, without any relineation or substantive revision, and they have been made only under the direct supervision of the author.

Finally, because Brodsky's study of Spanish greatly influenced the formation of his poetic voice, we have included his works in that language in this volume. Although individual Spanish words and phrases scattered through otherwise English pieces have not been translated, Rose Passalacqua, of Washington University, has provided translations for poems, stanzas, and long passages entirely in Spanish. These pieces carry a lozenge symbol (◊) after the title (when the whole poem is in Spanish) or the first line of a passage (when only a small portion of text within a larger work is in Spanish), and their translations are located in the appendix.

Sheri L. Vandermolen
Morton, Illinois
10/17/95

INTRODUCTION

The first two poems I composed as an adult were most likely written in the spring of 1963, at the end of my senior year at Yale. In hindsight, both seem emblematic of the liberal arts education I gained from that august institution.

The first, *"Culpa eterna,"* embodies all that I had assimilated not just from four years of upper-level honors Spanish literature courses — that magical, musical quality inherent in the Romance languages, its heightened lyricism achieved through the sensuous orchestration of vowel sounds — but from five earlier years of Spanish and Latin language and literature courses, which I had taken while attending a college-preparatory school in St. Louis. The second poem, "Walls of Tragedy," serves almost as a microcosm of the somewhat limited tour of classical and American literature I had taken at Yale: the *Oedipus* cycle, *The Scarlet Letter*, *The Waste Land*, *The Great Gatsby*, *On the Road*, and, through the poem's epigraph, *Moby Dick*.

Ironically, where the first poem evidences a certain degree of mastery of Spanish and use of its conventions, the second one, written in English, is freighted with Latinate inversions of sentence structure, forced end rhymes, broken meters, awkward metaphors, and an overriding somnolence fused with a pious tone the poem just cannot support. Quite simply, I had become more fluent, and certainly more literarily well grounded and confident, in my foreign language of choice than in my mother tongue. Whereas my classmates majoring in English literature had thoroughly familiarized themselves with Chaucer, Spenser, Shakespeare, the metaphysical poets and dramatists, and other important authors up the line, I had mastered their Spanish counterparts: Fray Luis de León, Calderón de la Barca, San Juan de la Cruz, Miguel de Cervantes Saavedra, and many eighteenth- and nineteenth-century, as well as contemporary, Spanish and Latin American fictionists, playwrights, essayists, and poets. Occasionally, my Yale friends would inquire about my postgraduation goals, what I was intending to do with my formidable knowledge of Spanish literature and my broad smattering of the humanities, the liberal arts that had intoxicated me for four years of enthusiastic learning. I had no answers.

The third poem in this volume, "The Marvelous Color Black," may give added insight into the dilemma I was creating for myself as I, perhaps like Oedipus, groped blindly toward some clearer understanding of my undisclosed destiny. I can still recall sitting at my father's desk in his downtown St. Louis office in August of 1963, less than a month before my enrollment in Washington University to begin a dual course of graduate study in business and English — my calculated attempt to satisfy two quite disparate compulsions: the first, to acquiesce to what I believed to be my father's desire for me to follow in his footsteps, enter the mercantilistic life, become a responsible businessman, and reap the rewards of a successful career as a manufacturer of men's clothing; the second, by becoming a professional writer or teacher, to fulfill my obligation to myself not to squander all my precious, hard-won education. "The Marvelous Color Black" manifested itself to me like a genie materializing from a bottle of imagination I had unstoppled in a moment of boredom and daydreaming that afternoon at my father's office, when I should have been concentrating on some facet of the business instead of lamenting being cooped up indoors on a warm summer day. The poem came spontaneously, an astonishing windfall by way of free association, an activity in which I had not previously engaged. In essence, in the time it took me to capture that illusive, fleeting cluster of images and set them down on Biltwell Company letterheads I kept pulling from my father's desk drawer as the poem unfolded, it dictated itself to me and demanded that I slap it on the pages in highly unconventional placements, giving it an unusual appearance, which even then I felt somehow added to the sense of urgency I was attempting to convey. I recognized that something wonderful was happening to me. Exultantly, I was unloosing a voice I could tell was my own, embellishing a theme that was relevant and poignant to me: the clarion call to stop intolerance, prejudice, and bigotry in their tracks, deal them a deathblow. Of course, this was not only the era of escalating offensives in Vietnam but, perhaps more importantly, the rise of national awareness of the need to redress America's shabby civil-rights record, a radical plea for which was being voiced ever more stridently, though, paradoxically, through the Gandhian tactics of passive resistance, by Martin Luther King, Jr. This poem, then, was my own reproach against racism.

Soon, I would be in school again, taking three graduate courses in business and two in English. This decision was only partly motivated by my indecisiveness regarding a profession. Realistically, I knew that I could remain "exempt," as the expression of the day had it, if I was enrolled in graduate school. And although the war in Southeast Asia continued to be waged with ever increasing virulence and resolve on the part of America's messianic visionaries, my own limited clairvoyance extended no further than protecting myself, keeping out of harm's way. After all, if I was to do something noble, worthwhile, with my life, be it by making a contribution to pedagogy, scholarship, or creative writing, I would not only have to hone my skills, continue to add to my intellectual storehouses by pursuing my studies and my writing with diligence and a sense of their importance, but I would have to *stay alive*. And fighting a war that I and my friends had tenaciously protested against on the grounds that it was patently inhumane and ethically, morally, philosophically, and spiritually absurd, even undemocratic, was not going to achieve the hoped-for results for the nation or for me.

Having finished my first semester in graduate school, it became abundantly clear to me that I had extended myself as far as I could in my business studies, considering my limited background in mathematics, economics, accounting, and statistics. Mine was not a numerically oriented mind but rather one more closely attuned to deriving answers and making judgments through implication, by inference; it took comfort in inconclusive, open-ended closures as opposed to clear-cut solutions. There was something literarily, poetically satisfying to me about seeing the world imaginatively rather than empirically. In short, business school and I had to part ways in order for me to avoid facing imminent scholastic failure as well as possible induction into the armed forces. However, by the time the Selective Service mandated that to remain exempt, one had to be not just in graduate school *and* married but *also* a parent, I was twenty-five, unwed, had no inclinations in that direction, and was eagerly getting older and older, though never quite fast enough to say for certain that my 2-S status was impregnable.

The result was that for what became four years of relative freedom from parental censure and the responsibilities of providing food and shelter for myself, I lived in a womb, a refuge that nurtured untainted, pristine learning in an absolute vacuum. My job, my only job, really, was to educate myself, let my intellectual appetites surfeit themselves on some of the finest instruction available in any American university, right there in St. Louis, where I could live with my parents and devote myself to my studies and my creative writing.

All this is not to say, however, that there weren't tensions inherent in this lifestyle nor that I didn't suffer stress from so much independence. Mine was a conflictive life despite its lack of accountability to the powers that be in the "real world." If Vietnam was becoming less of a personal threat, other issues were growing more problematic: Having abandoned my intentions of earning an MBA, would I ever be able to work for my father with a master's degree in English? Had I disappointed him? Had I closed myself out of the preparation requisite to making a livelihood in the world beyond Academe? Did this mean that I had to become a teacher?

This last concern was a knotty one for me because the more I advanced through the ranks toward my degree in English literature, the more I began to disrespect many of my instructors, whom I saw as "hangers-on," even as they condescendingly denigrated others' ambitions, vocations, and accomplishments with impunity. It seemed to me that too many of my professors and teaching assistants were unwitting victims of the same cynicism and narrow-mindedness they accused those outside the rarefied precincts of the Land of Arts and Sciences of possessing.

And these negative and, by turns, misanthropic aspects of university life disturbed me deeply because I felt myself, semester by semester, being drawn into that vortex of arrogant intolerance and intellectual hubris, becoming, like Diogenes, perhaps, a cynic, carrying around in broad daylight a lamp, or welding torch, announcing to the world in my writing as well as in daily polemics with my fellow students that I was "in search of a human being." Little did I know then that that human being was me. Anxiously though, I had begun to suspect that, paradoxically, as my academic knowledge expanded, my good old-fashioned common sense, which I knew I really needed to survive, was rapidly diminishing.

Another struggle I experienced, ancillary yet grown from the same seed, was frustration over whether I should emphasize my scholarly talents or give vent to my creative instincts. Of course, I was writing papers for my classes; they consisted of analytical critiques of short stories, novels, and poems that I was absorbing daily, assignments essential in maintaining a grade point average that would enhance my résumé were I to choose teaching as my career. But I was also leading a double life, that of imaginary professional writer, deriving my living from having my novels, stories, and poems published in prestigious journals and by New York presses.

xxx

This strain was heightened by my ambivalent, double-edged suspicion that, on the one hand, I was in the wrong place, with the constraints of school holding me back from devoting my full energies to writing poems and novels, but that, on the other hand, school was having a very salutary effect: it was a marketplace for the infusion of new ideas and voices that were fueling my desire to be a writer and, simultaneously, reminding me daily that it was my responsibility to speak out about contemporary as well as traditional concerns affecting mankind.

Inextricable from this same matrix of doubts was the seemingly irreconcilable question of whether I should concentrate on prose or poetry full time. My first literary hero, William Faulkner, who to this day resonates in my writing, though only in muted strains, actually dissuaded me from becoming a fictionist, despite initially encouraging me by the example of his poetic prose, because finally his influence was so all-encompassing as to be annihilating. Between 1963 and 1967, I wrote three novels and a novella. Not coincidentally, each of my books resounded with lyrical cadences and convoluted, half-page and page-long Faulknerian sentences patched together with dubious grammar and mechanics. All my prose relied on "polysyllabic pyrotechnics" I was not really capable of carrying off. And even if I had been competent, I realized that after a certain period of studied and/or unconscious emulation of an author or authors, every fledgling writer, certainly I, must invent his own identifiable voice or risk being called an imitator. I knew that foisting on the world even one more approximation of *The Sound and the Fury* would be an exercise in futility for me, a death knell; it would not advance my own unique presence.

The poems I composed during this writing "apprenticeship," which developed concurrently with my graduate education, became more numerous and ambitious as I developed the confidence to express myself less and less through the voices of those I most admired. Nonetheless, the reader of these early poems — prose narratives with poetry, prose poems, free-verse and stream-of-consciousness poems — will readily detect the influences I have previously mentioned: Spanish and Latin American authors, whom I assimilated at Yale, as well as Faulkner and the English writers, whom I didn't fully integrate into my poetry until my graduate years. In retrospect, those whose writing most affected me were Johnson, Donne, Browne, Swift, Carlyle, and Wordsworth; Melville, Poe, Hawthorne, Dreiser, Lewis, Fitzgerald, and Hemingway; Rimbaud, Trakl, Eliot, Frost, Shapiro, Roethke, and Ferlinghetti. However, my greatest indebtedness was, and is, to Milton, Kafka, and Faulkner.

One other preoccupation of mine during my graduate days resulted from trying to nurture some sort of social life while at the same time pursuing a writer's life of self-imposed reclusiveness. Early on, it became obvious that when I was committing myself to writing, I was, of necessity, removing myself from participation in other experiences. Like all writers, I had to suffer extended bouts of isolation, which often led to a sense of loneliness, depression, and, occasionally, even desperation and self-immolation. I saw that as active a pursuit as writing seems, it has a paradoxical concomitant: passivity. I could conjure up and portray extravagant, absurd events and people, even vicariously share their lives, but as the person manipulating the twists and tangles of narration and characterization,

I had to remain behind the scenes. I knew that once I completed the story or poem, the life created belonged to the characters, to the medium itself; I, as the writer, at best retained copyright, usually nothing more than the memory of having willed the composition into existence. Worse, I realized I might end up with nothing to show for all my labor except silence and anonymity and the empty sensation of having accumulated an overabundance of unclocked time.

At some point, I began to question what I intended to gain from writing: What was its fundamental purpose, and what was mine? Could I earn a living from my writing? Would it still provide me with enough satisfaction if I never received the attention I now began to dream my creative works would one day garner? And perhaps most essentially, could I have a social life and still sustain the concentration and ferocious competitive edge successful writing demands of its practitioners?

Indeed, as many of the poems in this volume suggest, I did attempt to reconcile this last dilemma during two aborted relationships and in the initiation of my one true romance, with Jan. However, a close reading of the poems in this volume will suggest that even this latter experience, though healthier than the first two, was of the same idealistic nature. In hindsight, I can honestly admit that in expressing my love, I behaved much like the bumbling, self-deluded Alonso Quijano, who fancied himself Don Quixote, that magnificently preposterous hero-at-large, protecting, rescuing, and avenging his imaginary, beloved "maiden in distress," Dulcinea, or like James Gatz, platonically transforming a mundane Daisy Buchanan, through his outsized Gatsby imagination, into the beguiling East Egg socialite of his most extravagant, green-blinking fantasies.

Doubtless, at that time my immaturity was consonant with my highly romanticized attitudes toward what constituted my life's mission. Through the power of my imagination, I was going to save the world, everyone in it, including myself (maybe even its most deadbeat professors and pious warmongers), from misfortune and unhappiness. Surely, even then, I must have assessed myself predominantly as a naive dreamer, a young man who somehow had managed to propel himself beyond a point of no return in a pursuit that might never offer any hope of reconciling the tensions that had beleaguered him for the four years he had borrowed against his future.

Regardless, without design, he, I, had begun leaving behind, in the form of a semiautobiographical poetic chronicle, a lyrical free-verse book of hours, a tangible record of my travail and my ecstasy, my certitude and my confusion, my journey into the heart of that person, a poet, whom I would one day realize — as I now do, thirty-two years later, on writing this introduction to the first volume of my *Complete Poems* — I would never stop becoming.

Louis Daniel Brodsky
St. Louis, Missouri
4/26/95

THE COMPLETE POEMS

OF

LOUIS DANIEL

BRODSKY

VOLUME ONE, 1963–1967

* This symbol is used to indicate that a stanza has been divided because of pagination.

† This symbol is used to indicate that a piece contains fragmental poetry, prose, or notes.

‡ This symbol is used to indicate that a piece contains incomplete poetry, prose, or notes.

Δ This symbol is used to indicate that a poem has been drastically revised or that it has been assigned to appear in a future publication and will, presumably, undergo major revision. The later version will be printed in a separate volume.

◊ This symbol is used to indicate that a translation is provided in the appendix.

Culpa eterna ◊

¿Qué es nuestra culpa
Si no es la ensimismada pulpa
En el corazón, que nos motiva
Buscar lo interior subjetivo?

El destino es cosa determinada,
Con una significación obligada
Siempre en la aceptación inevitable
Del hombre que conserva la fe adorable.

3?/63 (05142)

Walls of Tragedy

If man will strike, strike through the mask!
— Herman Melville, Moby Dick

From pierced orbits, pastel humor seeped,
Nature's fruits of sight forever reaped.
Still, with those scopes eternally ground,
A tragic vision from inward Oedipus found.

Borne high the head of Hester Prynne,
Who wore the anomaly of her red sin
As a shield of solitude and resignation,
Which dissolved the puritanic abnegation.

Together, Stearns Eliot and Dr. Eckleburg saw
The winter heaps of Earth's noontime thaw.
With outward lenses, they blindly gazed
Upon volcanic remains at a fortress raised.

Blistered skin clung to modernistic, atomic frames,
And Kerouac boys fornicated with no-name dames,
Trying to "dig" their sexless, uncommon fate
Yet unable to forgive the common, cosmic hate.

3?/63 (05000)

The Marvelous Color Black

Isn't it a marvel
                    what Hank Ford has contrived;
         I mean,
                    when a Willie Stark
                              can be pushed
         right off the steps of Capitol Hill
                              or any other farmhouse,
                         for that matter,
And
         walk around the antiseptic house
                                   of chrome and bolts
                    and up to the
         verbal prestidigitator of Brooklyn Bridge fame
And   y
                    order up one   a
         supersport, Sebring-silver tractor-bird   w
And   h
         accelerate   g
         out on down his own white-bellied   i
                                             h

         without any fear of a *color* clash,
                              since his machine is
                              P
                              E
                              R
                              M
                              I
                              T
                              T
                              E
                              D
                    in any of

Howie John-
              son's
                              28-flavored

    Y O K N A P A T A W P H A   counties?

And isn't it a marvel

                            to live in a country in which
              any little nobody

Can buy

              a Woolworth opinion
              which reads

```
                              WE RESERVE THE RIGHT
                               T              T
                               O    S         O
                                    E
                               R    R         A
                               E    V         N
                               F    I         Y
                               U         C    O
                               S         E    N
                               E              E
```

And can abide by

              Mr. Ford's slogan, which, when slightly
                      convoluted,
                    is calculated to give

"Your choice of *color*, so long as

                    it's (NOT) KCALB"?

Why, yes,

            it's truly a marvel to   hope
              that the "Gemini" world of 1984
                           will erase
          color mutations
     when the new Darwinian prophet comes to show
                  the Scopeses
                  and Darrows
                  and Bryans,
       who inhabit a world
         populated by
                  the Kus
                  and Kluxes
                  and Klans,
      that the new reality
*

                    is that of   INV
                                    I
                                    S
                                    I
                                    B
                                    I
                                    L
                                   ITY,
          in which each unidentified
                                            flying
                                            object
                     can regain that
                                        Biblical
             and
                  e
                    o
                       n-d   d
                          e   e
                         cay   instinct
                                        of innocent respect
               for the
                    SUPREME MAKER,

                                            in whose image
                                                 is
                      reflected

                                        an unquestionable
                                        yet now forgotten
                    HUMAN DIGNITY.

[8/1/63]? (05001)

[At the midpoint,] †

At the midpoint,
the moon rushes down the
free-floating creek-streams,
reflecting tiny golden buttons
of crafted dream

peripatetic

I saw Esau;
He saw what you saw

Shooting rapids curranted and strewn
with rocks precariously lodged like
the condiments planted like mines in the
husk of a sizzling, brandy-brown ham.

   Encounter;
    phone call: I love you — protection — naiveté —
I've been waiting to see you all week

8/15–20?/63 (05251)

[Will you write me in two weeks or three]

Will you write me in two weeks or three
About the result of our fantasy of harmony?
What did you say? Was it this that I heard?
Oh, no, my God, the bitterness of his word
Is undermining my love with blasphemy.

Why did you do this? How could I know
That our needled urgency would bid us so,
Whose spear drops of tears, agnostic sperm cells
With glacierlike whiteness, in movement congeal,
Making my conscience cry out, "It's time to go"?

8/15–26?/63 (05361)

Eerie Immobility

> . . . The end of Man is an Action, and not a
> Thought, *though it were the noblest . . .*
>   — Thomas Carlyle, *Sartor Resartus*

It was an eerie sight
To see coffee and cigarette unite
*

In an upward, spiraling band
Of ash-white, brown-bean brand.

Her eyes were fixed
On the vapours that mixed
As they splintered and fused.
Her mind was confused.

She sank in depression,
Devoid of expression,
Knowing that *be* and *seem*
Are no more than dream.

It was an eerie sight
To see coffee and cigarette unite.
She sank in depression,
Devoid of expression.

She was, she thought,
The one who sought
What an image could be
Subjectively.

Yet her actions denied
What her mind implied:
That nobility is known
In thought alone.

She was an eerie sight,
Devoid of expression.
She sank in depression,
Watching coffee and cigarette unite.

8–10?/63 (02320)

[Have you ever passed through a valley] †

Have you ever passed through a valley
        to feel the cool, thick vapor of the thickets
and foliage caress your body and then
        risen to the top of the incline to be
overcome by the claustrophobic thickness
        of a warm April

warm and cold of water

progression with

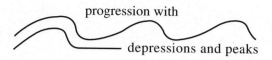

— depressions and peaks

8–10?/63 (05248)

[Howard Johnson's] †

Howard Johnson's

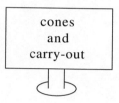

melting-pot restaurant
Hi, Uncle Meyer. How you
                    doin'

  It's so warm today
I didn't know whether to
wear a coat or not

  Let's go home and
  do it. The warmth
 wants to bring out the
bodily heat of intercourse

  Fried clams have   *[document torn, ed.]*
  *[. . .]*of recent vomit
  [. . .] taste good —

"Hi, honey.
  What would you
  like?" — "You!"

I hope his brain
isn't *damaged* —
    insidious hurt
amidst the beauty

8–10?/63 (05246)

[I am your daily wizard] [†]

I am your daily wizard
For TV-dinner gizzard.
My job is to forecast
Colloquy of grey bombast.
Into my crystal I gaze:
The human soul in phase;
A hot spell moving south,
Causing Negroid hoof-and-mouth

8–10?/63 (05002)

[I saw Esau —]

I saw Esau —

    I saw four men walk
      out of the lunchroom,
each wearing a checkered work-
shirt, and I thought to
myself, "Though each looks
the same to me, with his
work-around-the-school
strut, each must be
individually important to
somebody else: a lover,
a family nest, a
prostitute, an audience, a *self*."

8–10?/63 (05241)

[Tertullian] †

Tertullian
> I believe because it is absurd
> > *credo quia absurdum*

           spasm
           irreconcilability

           toleration
           intractable
           the black man's burden
moiety   *sufrimiento*
           spasmodic acceptance
           disgrace
           questioning furtively
           lack of face
           embarrassment
           involuntary incarceration
vagaries mimicked amicability

> Thou shalt love thy neighbor as thyself.
> > — Leviticus

The price of progress
in civilization is paid
in forfeiting happiness
through the heightening of
the sense of guilt
> — Sigmund Freud

Thus conscience doth
make cowards of us all; . . .
— William Shakespeare, *Hamlet*

Vanity of vanities, saith the
Preacher, . . . all is vanity.
> — Ecclesiastes

8–10?/63 (05242)

[This Genghis Khan of degenerate . . .]

This Genghis Khan of degenerate
schizophrenia, who escorts and invites
them into his chamber of unrealized
escape and debilitating repugnance,
who himself has meandered the
labyrinthine corridor
so long that he can display
for others his imaginary Great
Wall of China,
    a wall that he now invites
others to hide behind as an insuperable
fortress against the realities of the rat-race world
outside the night and beyond his own
irretrievable limit of consciousness.

    "I've suffered a
terrific loss
recently, as you know,"
he says to each new face that
intrudes upon the once sacred confines of his
nursing home.
    This is a home for the aged, yet
the children, who sleep through the modern
bacchanals and orgies of those who
defy sleep's tranquilizing mist, and the master
of the family alike have not yet come of age.
    Where is the excitement of living
to be found amidst the choked and strained
breath of these kids?
    They are exhausted and stifled by a
cankerous fear of self-generated
escapism, direction, and purpose,
    this night,
    Sept. 5, 1963.

9/5/63 (05254)

[What is our youth, the . . .] ‡

What is our youth, the
*

girls and bulls of tomorrow's dream of
prosperity and pageantry, doing here,
cushioned upon some unpaid-for sofa,
licking the precious spilt
wastage of congenital tin cans
and crystalline tanks brimming
with the unnecessary overflow of
too-oft-occasioned champagne?
And why do the inexplicable,
false evocations of

[9/5/63]? (05158)

The Panorama Just Beyond

Beyond the glen,
                    a murky summer stream,
          rampant with the overflow of a fleeting shower,
          darts in and then out behind thick mounds of
          alluvial verdure and plots of sun-bronzed
          forest burgeoning
                    with days on days of unnoticed birth.

Beyond the den,
                    the moil and scream
          of downy-winged aviators, alive with the energy
          of beehive existence, traverse ever-becoming
          skyways, alerting the sensitivity of animal
          instinct to the clarion amplification
                    of crackling twigs and crunching earth.

Beyond the arbor,
                    a yearning willow,
          with limbs humbled by the challenge of newborn
          capsules, flags its venous awnings over the
          microcosm of creature-activity that thrives
          beneath the unbound solar cacophony
                              that Prometheus fired.

Beyond the harbour,
                    a solitary Thoreau,
          aged by the ephemeral lapse of the seasons and
          the senility of the human factor, peers through
          *

the portal of blindness to relearn that nature's
cyclical activities of creativity and continuity
are God-inspired.

9/13/63 (02317)

"Each in Its Ordered Place" ‡

The *impedimento* of the psyche
weighs heavily on man's mind
when evil supplants kindness
and dogma the true church,
where beauty and blindness
congeal in the common,
opinionated search
for inordinate hierarchy

9–10?/63 (05243)

The Double Perspective

I knew Stephen Crane in a cup of coffee.
There his dinghy clung helplessly, lurch-
Whirling to the edge of the saucer, listing
In rhythm from the shock of having toppled
Over the brim of the cup like a waterfall barrel
When my trembling hand jarred it into proper order.

"It is impossible!" the reflections in the coffee-boat
Gasped, choking and swollen cold from the swelling
Rift of landlessness that was saucer existence
To their plight. "Is it possible that we have been
Spared this long only to have our bodies give bean-
Blood for so useless a vessel to contain? Impossible!"

Then I lifted the cup as if to toast the group of
Lunchroom survivors, agitating it with my left hand.
Next, I slid the saucer out from under to tilt it up to
The cup. The open boat and its four survivors dropped
With a liquid splat into the plastic sea-cliff walls
And drowned, and I drank till the cup was dropless.

9–10?/63 (02316)

Just Don't Touch Our Eyes

"Just don't touch our eyes,"
Whispered frightened rhyme-birds,
Heightened with the soaring afterglow
Of juvenilia's cedared cries.

"The music we make on the zephyr lies
Wakeful, is the fluted, spun breeze
Of down-winged tree tones set loose
On jets of mute, suggested surprise.

"Take with you our shroud of mysteries
And languid music, the blue-bleated, proud-
Flung clues to the series of Orpheus's
Time-sought aurora of dusty histories.

"Just don't touch our eyes
With your sea-starved fancies,
Which filter frond-down, snapdragon tears,
Babbitt-like, locked in dream disguise."

9–10?/63 (02314)

Please

The age of yore was a fine-gilded whore,
Spawning Barabbas and Rimbaud and more
                    from some wrong spore.

Neo-, quasi-collegiate, Gothic spires,
Fustian, balderdash, claptrap squires —
                    they are all liars.

Sterile, diaphanous, metallic scrapers,
Built by modernistic, macabre rapers,
                    all from blue papers.

The time is here for this perplexed sphere,
Tolling the onset of our faith-trodden fear;
                    it's death's leap year.

9–10?/63 (05007)

This Morning Means Lifetime

I'm going to the car wash, this morning,
to clean away the filmy patina of a bad,
seat-belted warning.

There we huddled, all eight of us, inside
translucent, empty bar bottles, Saturday afternoon,
anticipating the game of staunch rivals,
our heads empty of the impending doom.

I heard a cheery newsman tell me, the next
morning, as I made my trafficked way to
breakfast at the house of red fried clams,

that he had died late that night at the
county hospital from a blow to the head,
sustained when his car hit some Warson tree.

I'm going to the car wash, this morning,
to clean away the filmy patina of a bad,
seat-belted warning.

We joked together over beer and memories
that had lasted us through four years of
college and more, and here,

unaware that the black cloak was descending,
would drop the little red ball, into his
timeworn initials carved in the spinning
wheel of the roulette.

The postgame celebration ended with a sharp,
crushing halt at three and thirty that up-
winding bridge-hill morning,

when the wheel finally stopped its
jaunty, circular course over myriad
numbered/typed/differentiated holes.

I'm going to the car wash, this morning,
to clean away the filmy patina of a bad,
seat-belted warning.

It was Sunday afternoon when the full
horror of what had occurred penetrated
my sensitivity. There, a crumpled little
sports car shied unmolested and
*

unnoticed amidst the collection of scrapped
histories.

My friend told me that the driver, who
had been one of us, had slipped slowly
from friendship to memory to coma to *nada*.

I'm going to the car wash, this morning,
to clean away the filmy patina of a bad,
seat-belted warning.

> We are all driving,
> I figure, no matter
> the immediate des-
> tination, to an ev-
> entual terminating
> juncture that lies
> somewhere beyond, in
> the confused dimen-
> sion of time further
> outside the limits
> of the
>   car wash.

9–10?/63 (05009)

[El cielo azulado,] ◊

I

El cielo azulado,
De líquido azul,
Parecía lago vago,
Vacía languidez.

Sus aguas calientes,
De extraño calor,
Radiaban estrellas
De fluctuante embriaguez.

II

El cielo iba poniéndose negruzco, nublado.
*

Él veía caminos que se alargaban hasta el infinito
Y los seguía y los seguía y los seguía, y siempre
Volvió al mismo sitio de asco y de sed.

III

Fué una noche estrellada,
En que planetas y vaguedades
Bailaban,
> *Reflejándose sobre la retina*
> *De una pobre golondrina,*
Cuya visión fué aterciopelada.

Fué una noche quebrantada,
En que lacayos y fantasma-lunas
Se trastornaban,
> *Cabalgando las espaldas desnudas*
> *De colinas de tortólica nubladas,*
Cuya existencia fué algodonada.

IV

Qué lástima, que su vida era una cosa tan inconcreta,
Como una de aquellas nubes sin fuerza
Que se iba esfumando en el escenario,
El dibujo, el cielo del artista que pinta sin paleta.

9–10?/63 (05006)

[I watch; I perceive] †

I watch; I perceive
What is impenetrable
And know that the
Illusory chimera of
Sedentary sustenance is
Lleno del alma ◊

I'm a Howard Johnson's human creation,
Existing through dreams of *was*
And illusions of what could have been
And of that which may be,
*

For seated amidst the artificial
Potting of people flowers
Sit those who mean
Nothing to me and yet
Mean all to someone

¿Qué es la vida? ◊
Un frenesí.
¿Qué es la vida?
Una illusión, una sombra, una ficción,
y el mayor bien es pequeño,
que toda la vida es sueño,
y los sueños sueños son.
— Pedro Calderón de la Barca, *La vida es sueño*

Charles Mallison
Gavin Stevens
Dilsey
Jiggs
Popeye

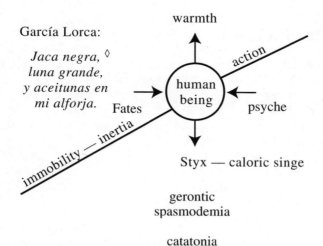

García Lorca:

Jaca negra, ◊
luna grande,
y aceitunas en
mi alforja.

warmth

action

human being

Fates

psyche

immobility — inertia

Styx — caloric singe

gerontic
spasmodemia

catatonia

9–10?/63 (05174)

[Saul] †

Saul
Luas Trabar

Holly Golightly contracted
          the mean reds
While sleeping within
Truman Capote's beds

     Sally Tomato
     O.J. Berman
     I. Y. Yunioshi
     Fred

The *preggers* are in style

I'm the empress of

9–10?/63 (05240)

[Sir Walter Raleigh] †

Sir Walter Raleigh
          introduced a box of twenty-four
                    under
     The Lion's Paw
          while
W. J. Bryan attuned his
          Cross of Gold
               to the
               metamorphosed Beatles
                    in Kafka's
                         hungry i

The goose is loose
          in the farmyard
          *

                    o f
              Hamlin's garland of ibids.,
        and
              the Cing of the Cosmos
        flew hurly-burly
                    through
        the hoi-polloi
              district
        of Tucumcari,
                    N.M.

                              extravaganza

                              resignación ◊
                              fertilidad
                              yerma
Let   *frustración*
    the goodness of my   *humildad*
                    heart   *soledad*

                                   Suzane
Historia de una escalera ◊   Suzan
        Antonio Buero Vallejo   *quel chic* ◊

                         name
                         shame
                         fame
                    vaga or *Dios* ◊
                    mi amante

¿Qué es la vida? ◊
Un frenesí . . .
una sombra, una ficción,
y el mayor bien es pequeño,
que toda la vida es sueño . . .
— Pedro Calderón de la Barca, *La vida es sueño*

   Qué descansada vida, ◊
    la del que huye el
mundanal ruido
*

> *y sigue la*
>   *escondida senda por*
> *donde han ido los pocos*
>   *sabios que en el mundo*
>   *han sido . . .*
>   — Fray Luis de León

palpitation
mean reds

                    Little Miss No Name
              Candy Man
              Salty Dog
Suz

Fly high, my baby boy
                    Me veía la chi [◊]

The Art Mart
Suzie

9–10?/63 (05245)

[Waking from lugubrious dream- . . .] ‡

Waking from lugubrious dream-
waves, soporific and dry,
saving the first puff, dragging
high in the john, cigarette-army
C.I.C. is a faggot in the eye
of his own conscience, seems
not to be disturbed, interrupted,
by the close-in, celldying
deriding of neural *no* and *no*'s.
    It's got to be masochism
that urges him into the anxious nexus
of drawn tars and nicotine

9–10?/63 (05247)

Last Rites of a Woodcut

Archaic cupola that floats
        above the future ruins
                of man's
            disintegrating effort
    to steal from
                nature
that which can never really be his
            since he is
            nothing
        more than a mere gesture of
                its assertion
                    anyway!

O bulbous dome of aerial
                phantasmagoria
        that witnesses man's awful attempt
            to make truth
                stand up
on its shaky, idyllic legs of reason
            and conquer
        what is not his to know
                    and
less
            his to seek
                    but rather
    that which is left to some ultra-
                human power
        of divination
                to ordain!

Horrible cloud of ash-
                laden mortar
            and steel
        that reverberates with the
                    puniness of
some exhausted and
                disillusioned
        result of Jonas Salk and
                Hieronymus Bosch
which has been calculated upon the
        desert of Dali's bent watches!

Perhaps Dürer's Four
           Equestrians
                               envisioned
                                     that
      primitive cupola
that now descends upon the past iniquities
                 of man's untamed and
                               rapacious
           endeavours
to mold from the futurism of
                          the infinite
           that which neither he nor any other
                 MAN
           ever has the right
                               to tamper with
      except in the laboratory of
                 the
                 Devil
                 himself.

10?/63 – [10/29/63]? (05014)

Lubrication for Four: The Dream of Gambrinus

I wandered out the other night
To sense the anomaly of winter
                 and was bit
By the warmth of our mutuality.

James presided at some anonymous table
In Ned's; the Bird smiled his presence;
                          Bill was lit
From the beer that brought us together.

The transience of draftfilled reservoirs
Marked a single permanence of completion
                    that was orgiastic
In the mesmeric intensity we had imbibed.

And here we perceived that friends are love,
Each possessing a soul of beer and pretzels.
                    Oh, how futuristic
To drown together, wet, in pools of Rhinegold!

10?/63 – [10/29/63]? (05003)

Spiritus mundi

The age of reason, nation, science, all,
How very squandered, square, and small!

Strangers who quest our Freudian jungle
Find no exit from God's great bungle.

Solitary, each clutches his chromic grail,
Unaware that truth is Dilsey and the whale.

10?/63 – [10/29/63]? (05004)

[García Lorca was a beautiful pervert,] †

García Lorca was a beautiful pervert,
Lyric symbolism his means to convert
Anonymous, anomalous death into life overt:
A vision to which Yerma alone was alert

Honor   abnegation

10?/63 — [1] (05015)

Slow! Tollbooths, One Mile

The stellar avenues of the universe
Are all mapped out in blinding red,
Strewn with signs of "Danger Ahead"
For those not yet learned to converse.

The Devil collects the compulsory toll
And signals the pilgrim on his way,
Not his fate to endure eternal stay,
While rendering misguidance as his dole.

On a piece, myriad roads narrow into few,
Leaving caution and reason alone to muse
Which detour to the kingdom may fuse
With God's highway, modeled in fog-blue.

10?/63 — [2] (05010)

[Selfish crystals of mesmeric luminosity/ viscosity] †

Selfish crystals of mesmeric luminosity/viscosity
descend from myriad clouded reserves,
lubricating that which most deserves
the vital fluid

10?/63 — [3] (05255)

Cogito, ergo "?"

Reality and rationality escaped the man,
Who nodded at death and from it ran.

On the brink of the dismal abyss,
Friends beside him his only aegis,

Face bent upward, limbs crouched down,
The naked one seized a nebulous crown.

"Suffering" and "Hope" upon it were inscribed,
For from the bitter imbibed, he had survived.

Galilee was His origin, and endurance His vine;
Noble existence was His wine. This path is mine.

10–11?/63 (05013)

The Marriage of Christ

Christ would have married, today, at 3:37,
In the church at Canaveral, not in Heaven.

God hovered, benignant to man's unfitness,
Cringing only from the diffusive, gaseous ray
That filled the cosmos with its spray caloric,
While Lucifer, hurled into space, witness stood.

Humankind ushered in death's bridegroom,
With his sterile and ghastly face burdened.
He alone recognized the ultimate disgrace
Of the mechanical, high mushroom screaming.

Christ was maimed, today, at five o'clock;
His brains were crushed by a falling rock.

10–11?/63 (05011)

[Jack Sprat could eat no fat;] ‡

Jack Sprat could eat no fat;
his wife could eat no lean.
So they divorced each other.
What do you think of that?

Hey, diddle, diddle! The cow ate
the fiddle, and the cat played
a Stradivarius guitar.
What do you think of that?
Don't you think that's great?

Humpty Dumpty sat on his ass
while all the king's men fell from
the sky, and Simple Simon made a pie

10–11?/63 (05016)

[You've got a lot to learn, young man,] †

You've got a lot to learn, young man,
you who yearn to grasp the world and
make it respond to the touch of your
voice, rejoicing in the *I* and the *can*.

There's much to spurn in

10–11?/63 (05017)

Spiritus mundi

The river flows with ageless fixity,
Following the course of its geography.
From tiny pebbles of springs refractory,
It bubble-rushes, throbs, becomes ocean-sea.

The child cries from warm-blooded fright,
Seeking the comfort of breast-fed delight.
From wet, wandering seeds which chance to unite,
It emerges, balks, roars, attains to a noble height.

The sea writhes with prairies of unbound expanse,
Displaying prisms of diluted, atmospheric romance.
Above, the nubile-ated puffs of air look with askance,
Then billow, offering spring particles one more chance.

The man probes philosophic towers of the infinite
With intellect borne forward on experiential light.
Above those eon-decaying ruins, a red, ridiculous night
Warns mortal souls, pleads, tempts with Pharaoh's blight.

The water that long knew the swift river-motion roar,
Filtering, slide-gliding from thick, merging ocean shore,
Returns to its source, released and revived by a downpour
That guides it, crying, searching, to those springs once more.

The bones that now guard the riddles of putrescent days
Lie nestled in fallowing plains of long-gone golden maize.
Quietly, the restless, feeble germs of growing structures raise
From soil to child to man, embracing the promise of another phase.

11/7/63 (02319)

Segovia

I saw you, Segovia, floating slowly
To the vortex of my persistent imagination,
Through dreamlike nets of night's obscure
Menage, with knights and beggars roaming lowly

Through narrow streets and open exposures.
The antiquity of your guardian Alcázar spires
Summons me back to the sacred haunts
Of dim-lit histories held timeless in enclosures

Lined with king's men in chain mail
And walls of impenetrable, time-hewn feldspar
And lime from nearby quarries, hung
With Zurbarán and chalky Greco travail

Depicting attenuated portions of Saint Thomas
*

And lingering glimpses of steeds, manes flowing,
Surmounted with children of Felipe and Carlos,
Bearing titles of *A la muerte nosotros vamos.*

I saw you, Segovia, swimming; your dusty, auburn-
Paved ways; the deep-dug, rain-laid moat,
Made by tears of penury and humiliation and
Baked hard with static penetrating and taciturn,

Intractable voices. The fossilized aqueduct,
Which still feeds the refractory fruits of Eresma
And Riaza, dribbles noiselessly into the plaza,
Proclaiming its Roman shield in legal usufruct,

Signals the completion of Alfonso's behest
On the once congested fields, where the bloody
Corpses of Moorish nobility yielded to the final
Stages of the first Iberian conquest.

I saw you, Segovia, in my dream flight,
Casting true enchantment, granting me slumber
And unrequited yearning within your maternal
Reality, my nocturne of evanescing delight.

11/17/63 (02318)

Questioning an Untimely Passing: Phrenology

And now, the relapse, the volatile reabsorption
into the recriminating passivity of what all of us
have come to regard as positive self-assurance.

Is it for each individual to deal from his own deck
of marked egocentrisms the sinister hand of critical
reservation that was not left for him in the first place?

What does the passing event of a second Billy Budd
say to us, as a collective band, about "The Rights of
Man"?

Why does not each individual praise the efforts
that remain blind and unheeded, until they can only
be witnessed through a bullet hole's cranial fissure?

Do not the rights of man cease to be his when he
fails to recognize that respect and appreciation
are no longer existing?

We shrink from the full implication of this senseless
act, perpetrated in the very face of our intelligence
and knowledge of what was meant for pride alone.

Why has it become fashionable to cut down those
who stand to serve us all, if not to build up our
own ego-thriving inability to communicate?

Must we not individually search the collective
conscious of the mind to answer the clarion demise
of the sallow body, moribund, to cage the thoughts
that must be preserved?

Was the man's attempt to mollify the present
infection that bewilders us on the verge of isolation
not a spiritual harbinger of Northern accent?

Why must each man individually judge and deprecate
that which he has no power to perceive and, less,
the ability to make known, to imitate?

Is it not in vain that we vote men to judge for us
in the place of the Almighty so that we may preserve
ourselves for each other to ravage bit by bit?

¿Pues dónde queda la reverencia por parte de la ◊
gente frente a la situación peligrosa en que se
nos encontramos predestinados y ciegos?

We are as blind as the future and as mute as the
past, yet we inevitably bring to the present that
which has never ceased to exist at all times: disrespect.

Hay una falta invidiosa de comprensión ◊
manifestándose en el fondo de la conciencia
moderna que abnega la compasión y la afección.

11/22–25?/63 (05008)

[Your absence, this lack of even the]

I

Your absence, this lack of even the
vocal communication of a telephone
call after so much love-filled
*

expression, closeness of thought,
and understanding, has just begun.

This receding fervor, which was past
durability, melting our Trevi coins,
is slowly diffusing into the present
sphere of undesired future forgetting,
and mute isolation is doomed to last.

Where is the warmth of mutuality,
that common interest and the crimson
passion you bequeathed me when you
confided the terrifying content of
that small scrap of paper your mother
once scrawled, as you sat on my knee?

II

Oh, by the way, did I hear you say
the President's grave was dug today?

III

I want to smoke, and do so,
masochistically, knowing all
the while that the vapors
inhaled filter a gnawing
sensation of vertiginous limbo.

I stop and throw my cigarette
into the murky sickness and
defecation of the toilet bowl,
flushing away the remnants
of my green, undigested regret.

Why can't I just exist passively
anymore? And why is it that in
having constantly to seek out
that which will provide me with
uninterrupted solace, I find only
Sweeney's fate in my blasphemy?

IV

Oh, no, my love, was it you who said
the President's grave is now his bed?

11/25?/63 (05005)

The Chanticleer †

The early morning cock
caught the moon in
its courtly genuflection,
imperative for sun and clock,
unawares

11–12?/63 (05250)

[show chickens] †

show chickens

Bantam cock — miniature chicken
Fly away, cock! Boomerang
priapically
to me

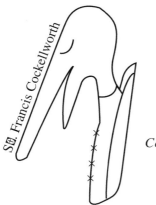

Cogito, ergo sumus

You can, if *as* can
"as"/"if"
conditionals

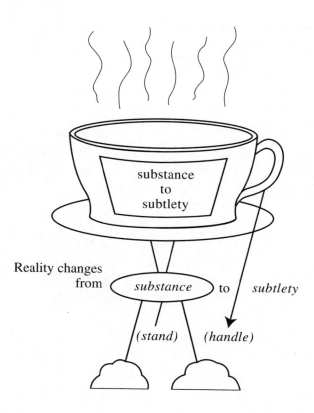

Reality changes from *substance* to *subtlety*

World as process of metamorphosis;
natural verbalizations overweigh
          human verbalization

The officers

            "The Idea of Order at Key West"
            ". . . she was the maker of the song
                              she sang."

fat, fat, fat
belly button

I hear the pitter-patter of little feet
spattering the colloquy of ant
language. The voice of the infantile,
prehensile lips of *hormiga* meat

Stevens' feel for the indigenous
          have to create *American poetry*

    One has repeated many times, no doubt,
the old adage "There is seemingly
no end to what the human
imagination can create" —
          There is! *Annihilation*

12/20/63 (05253)

[I wish to be born again, . . .] †

I wish to be born again,
to cast my shadow within
the silent penumbra of
Sir Christopher Wren's
London spires,
    where the beadles
assume totalitarian
reign down rock-and-
roll whisper in the whispering
hall to St. Martin's
syncopated pigeon
droppings

Crete, Taurus, Jupiter,
            Europa

The Day of the Beadles
            Locust

    Nat West

Holofernes
Mephistopheles — Faustus
            Rembrandt

    A piece of literature,
of necessity, must focus
on the generative warmth
that should engender the
one-to-one relationships,
    never allegory because
  it doesn't allow for
psychological penetration,
*

the abysmal plummeting
of the mind's psychic machination —
    apotheosis — ratiocinative

1–2?/64 (05249)

Primavera

Love I once knew in the halcyon dawning
of cloistered rage, far out of reach beyond
sequestering flowers, walking, stationary, longing
for valleys and acres of meadows mellifluous with frond,

letting their precious heads bow to insentient
teems of bee life too proud to refuse their suckled,
sweet-scented perfume yet far too much their penchant
to hide beneath the tumescence of their flowering cuckold.

And you, harbinger of Botticelli's transparency,
ranging stealthily, rubicund and moist with grief,
upon some fast-fleeing dream, puerile, dancing merrily,
bereft and timeless, conceived in seasons, seized in brief,

your fair flush fawning in lofty genuflection,
searching what escapes, no longer for your finding.
Flustered, evanescing, now subdued by their own perfection,
the golden strands, avatars, are static in their own unwinding.

5/21/64 (02315)

The Moment Before America

Battered brigands flailed their prow-slithered seas
in serpentine quest for that one moment when motion
would cease to be search and the furious ocean might
obviate oblivions of desire and dream would freeze

with wonder-filled amazement and incredulous fright,
expansionless, green, and silky; a something, a land
*

rolling republican, rushing from inviolate sand;
a concept steeped in fabulous, fictive human might,

theirs to stake and claim for a cautious Catholic race,
inevictable, untempered, yet only by some makeshift grant
for to hold in trust, saying, "God's will will supplant
the feeble failure of man's obsequious disgrace."

Manifold in mellifluity and miraculous mirth
their bodies, stores, aspirant and pernicious deeds
fraught in contumelies of greedy future seeds
now planted, reaped, harvesting a nation's birth,

young, insentient, too engrossed in present thought,
their turkeys, truckling in tenebrous thanks for the
giving, grazed and fed on maize and fibers of living
hosts of Choctaw, Chickasaw tricks they bought

with deceitful deviltry distilled in pyred drink,
too-callous masochism indigenous to moribundity,
the Indians, pre-Columbians negating their own fecundity,
until the land was doomed, denied its one last link

with the future's noble past, purchased with trinket,
repudiated with beguiling naiveté, and entrusted to
monstrous man's civilized schemes, vulpine and too new
to cede with patience the advent which on the brink it

hovered, slithering into woods, beyond fructuous valleys,
for paths, then Cumberland Gaps, then roads to follow,
where the raccoon and deer and otter, even unsightly toads,
relinquished their sallies, giving way to Henri's alleys.

Where, then, was, will be, or could have been the moment sublime,
when sanctity, sealed in timelessness, should have been infused
in marvelous, marbled expressions at once bemused,
taciturn, primordial in their innocence of time?

The green light at the end of the dock? Perhaps!
But that was sheer fantasy; the moment, the dream, just chance,
with purpose and chastity mere illusions for a tilted lance,
whose Jay Quijote fell into an inessential, filtered lapse.

6/13/64 (02313)

[The mind of the sun's widowed night] †

The mind of the sun's widowed night
was filled with love's lost lingering,
filtered through dilatory, dusty avenues
of scattering vapor trails of lasting fright,

which wavered in frigid, fictive fantasy,
its coldblown fields of clouds silhouetted
in random meter, measures infantile, turgid

Refractory glints of love's loose grief,
strewn in crystal, catalytic goblets,
containers constricted in rhythmic drops
of static

Whispering winds wind outside space's
evanescing focal point, sublime,
static, and depthless, filter-feeling
their way to the nadir of

Pebbles pierce the stream's structure,
strangulating the undaunted rushing current
fleeting in fast-flowing fantasies, fictitious
in their own purposelessness and

Happy days were filtered through time's cincture,
ruptured

Beauty decided to dissuade nature's

Silence cried out with dilatory celerity,
Sparking gesticulant vows of fluid opacity

Sight robbed sound of nocturnal yawning,
believing that nature's wonders fawned
their

Just Once

                    Just once,
the widowed night cried out for light,
saying, "Kiss my fair fields, filtered
full of loving grace and sight, brightly
ranging into the

Fractured fragrance awoke in me, just once,
awareness of the scent

Illusory trains, slithering serpentine on canvas Argenteuils,
running in random Renoir renderings of fictive creation,
so that stasis and mobility fuse in tandem, felt-lined foils,
subterfuged and squandered in blindness on palette permeations

of thoughts that existed in Hawthorne's

Transcendental oversouls of Emersonian doctrine
lock and fuse in misconceived
                    purblind
                    obtuse
                    abstruse
                    dour, inflexible, intractable
                                        uxorious
                                        insentient
                                        lugubrious melancholia — Dürer
                                                       nemesis
                                                       The Seventh Seal
                                                       Caravaggio
                    ratiocination   Proserpina
                    catatonia, hebephrenia   Helios
                    Tennessee Williams

Into petty, penniless avatars of illusory fountains,
Trevi, Pòpolo, and other guilty goblets, I cast a
sigh of dreams, which sinks, succumbing in disarray,
like empty grottoes vast and reckless or mountains

far out of reach of life's longing to renew itself

[6/13/64]? (05018)

[Resent being used,]

Resent being used,
            and
                    love in spite of yourself!
It's all that really matters anyway.
                Love
                        till your heart breaks with pain,
                        till your eyes blur
                                    and your head swoons.
                But love!

What matters if your pride is battered or
The shame is too much to bear?
When pride gets in the way, and it is over,
You ache,
            saying,
            "Why couldn't I have loved more?"
But what if you had?
Then the pain goes on
            and on
                    and on,
Until, aching so much,
                    you resort to reason.
And when reason fails?
                    Then what?

So you just go on loving blindly because it is
All that you know how to do or
                        because it is
                            the
                            one
                            thing
                            *

That seems undefiled by your own interpretation,
Because it comes naturally,
                         like the sun

                                                    east
                                              the
                                           in
                              rising
Or like the flowers of spring
                         reappearing
                                   after each frozen winter.

And then you cease to question, and
                    the love goes on,
But the pain never ends,
              because
                         without pain, there can only be

                                        indifference.

8–10?/64 (05146)

Child of Life

A child no older
            than the youngest day of summer
Nor less innocent
            than the last lapse of a dream
Nestled into the earth
            and filled his breath with sighs
Of a new day
            folded into coloured harmonies.

He yawned, rolling
            from his night bed with surprise
To find himself
            stark and alone in his little room.
Alone and afraid,
            he hurried his eyes from wall
To dusty window,
            seeing only the blearywet day
And his image
            reflected back into his eyes.

"Where am I?"
            he murmured. "What am I today
That only yesterday
            I was afraid to be? Hear me!
Answer me, Father,
            before the weighty dream of night
Covers me over,
            before it enfolds me once more!"

A silent voice,
            vaporous and soft-white, wafted
Through his cells,
            telling him with glowing repose,
"You are birth,
            dear child of laughter and night.
I have breathed you
            into the nets of a new day's seed
To drink love's draught
            from the lips of this roaring world."

"Why am I?"
            the infant voice said, falling
To the grass outside
            his room. "Why was the ground
Made soft and wet
            for my body?" "Because I willed it,
Child of night,
            tiny clown of laughter. You will be
My earthly word
            through your mild, smiling innocence."

"But what will happen
            when I grow too old to laugh
And forget to remember
            to smile at the day's warmth, at its
Funny surprises?"
            "You shall always be inspired
By My whisper
            and fired by My silent love,
Child unto Me,
            simple seed of birth and life."

10/1–6?/64, 2/17, & [2/20/65]? (05020)

Mere Child of Laughter and Night

A child no older
    than the longest day of summer
Nor less bold
    than the final, fleeting breath
    of a dream
Nestles warmly and neat
    into the down-stream pillow filters
    of screaming quietude and
Listens and hears
    the rain's rhythmic syllables
    beating on the roof of his ears.

The drummer of sleep
    beckons him with narcotic tears,
    suggesting softly in chime,
"Mere child of laughter and night,
    your face will never hide from Me
What it knows your mind
    and its adolescence confide:
    your disillusioned fright, colliding
With glimpses of the fear
    of growing old before your time."

The frail, frigid child
    tumbles and pauses. He stirs,
    whispering quotations from ageless avatars,
    the exotica of Nodfields and Madagascar.
His voice revives,
    coalescing, congealing, inflating
    with air and lifebreath
    like a circus big-top balloon, until
It is soon cut loose
    and floats, clownishly buffooning,
To the surface of nightmare's
    obliterated profundities,
    limbobound,
    resounding in the star's scintillant strata.

Startled,
    the child raises his wakefulness
    and smells that the rain
    *

Has ceased
        its free-fall intrusion,
        permitting him to speak
        a pitiable, all-forsaken protestation.
Groping feebly, he calls out
        from his vernal spectrum of youth, crying,
"Oh, dear Father,
        may the dawn of days
        allow me one more season."

10/1–6?/64 (05019)

A Boy and His Dog

Warm stands a boy beneath the coolcoloured night,
Youthful, Octobering, and with a dog at his feet.
Still and alone, he watches restless clouds fleet,
Wondering what buffets them about at that height.
Red blink and wane the beams of a plane's flight,
Tremulous and subtle, marking its steady retreat.
In synchronous random, he hears the engines beat,
Sensing its alien intrusion with innocent fright.

The boy caresses his dog. Then with pain he cries.
The dog moves closer, sits, and finally falls prone,
Not questioning the clouds or the plane's loud drone.
Content it remains, pliant to the young master's touch,
Now one with the youth and his palm's voluptuous clutch.
The boy becomes aware, then smiles and wipes dry his eyes.

10/6/64 (05021)

[I had to think what the date was, . . .]

I had to think what the date was, and only by focusing on the due date for the paper on Wordsworth's *The Prelude*, on yesterday's syllabus, could I extrapolate (time being such an illusory fiction made up for man's convenience, I can never keep track of its artificial measurements).

Time exists only for the possibilities of what futurity may divulge and for the past experiences that filter into my consciousness at any unassigned moment. What has happened is only significant when it enters the mind as a result of some train of associations. Past and present are only important when the two sequences fuse together in a moment of temporary lucidity.

Passing from my little study, tonight, into the totally black passage-way which leads onto the main upstairs corridor, I was aware of the exhilarating fright of complete and naked blindness, and my thoughts flowed back to yesterday, when I went to discuss four poems I had submitted to Mrs. Thurston. Her comments relied on a disinterested feeling that I had interspersed too many heavy words into the poetry, that pedantry and a quality of the "old-fashioned" prevailed, yet this sensation of blindness I had tonight reminded me of one image that particularly pleased her in "The Panorama Just Beyond": "portal of blindness."

> Reading *The Victim* — Saul Bellow
> Jonathan Swift — *The Battle of the Books*
> Wordsworth — *The Prelude*
> Camus — *The Rebel*
> Dostoyevsky — *Notes from the Underground*

> Godwin — "world without end"

10/21/64 (05159)

[Thought today about theme . . .]

Thought today about theme of engagement, abandonment to some-thing.

Courage — we all know what it means, but do we display it, or are we so stifled by the sense of the institutional life that we don't have the guts to strike out on our own? The ambivalence *entre* the thought and the deed, the head and the heart —

Just give me one beatnik who knows in his own mind he is a beatnik because being one serves his further ends —

Courage and guts to choose, to select what it is that can best ful-fill the individual needs, and then go out and get it, do whatever it de-mands, fulfill all the imperative requirements, not because you think it is the thing to do but because you have to.

Have to engage for its own sake, with guts and patience. It takes guts to make mistakes and vulnerability to rectify them.

My poetry had some initial comments today:
    idea of the single image,
      the necessity to create tension between my own position as intel-lectual and that of elemental reality,
    the basics — love
               honour
               courage
               suffering and pain
               happiness

When referring to the name of a painting or other artistic object, include some of the salient details which are contained within, some distinguishing characteristics.

10/27 & 10/27?/64 (05160)

Time There Was Then

Time there was then,
Not very far away,
When youth cried out.

You responded warmly
And soft. White flesh
Became experience.

Now you cringe,
Hold back your smile,
Unsure and afraid.

Time there was then,
Not very long ago,
When old age whimpered.

You answered not
At all. Wrinkled
Skin became denial.

Now you desire,
Sacrifice yourself,
Futile and grieving.

Time there was then,
Not very far away,
Not very long ago.

10/29/64 — [1] (05023)

Nocturne I: And You Have Gone Away Now

The night sounds around the building
Float. The restless leaves crackle and cry,
Yielding their frames to scuff marks, to
People-tread. And you have gone away now.

Trembling hands grasp coldly for cigarettes.
Ashes glow red. Little girls are tucking
Their fathers in bed, but you have gone away
Into the night. And you have gone away now.

Even the Indian rain tree, once so proud,
Shields nothing now except its spatial hollows.
Still-burning match tip, thrown to the breeze,
Exhales, sighs, and then warmly goes away.

Rain threatens no indwellers, safe and stony
In their private theaters; it shares no
Excitement with the marbled children
Of statuettes who call themselves Father

And Mother. But you have gone away now,
Into the contraband silhouettes of nightfall,
And I am alone out here, hands trembling, eyes
Murmuring white tears in faint recession.

Blackness around the agile corners descends
Like drops of wax melting from a candle,
Hardening my gaze, reddening my cheeks
In its baleful embrace of evanescing light.

And you have really gone, taken with you
The warm day's promise and my desire
*

To try to love and be loved one more night.
I can't complain now. Who would hear me?

10/29/64 — [2] (05022)

More Are You Becoming

Warmer than the snow line
        under quick ski blades
Is your slow breath on mine.

Sweeter than antique wine
                to my tongue
Are your vintage lips on mine.

Brighter than the nightly incline
                of the moon
Has your love mingled with mine.

Stronger than belief in the Divine
                for a worshiper
Has your spirit communed with mine.

Warmer and sweeter
                than the snow line,
                than antique wine,
Has your love made mine.

Brighter and stronger
                than the moon's incline,
                than the Divine,
Is your essence becoming mine.

10?/64 (05033)

[Al Jolson was a merry]

Al Jolson was a merry
            old soul,
who hid behind a mask.
And no one ever saw him
when he sang.

My thoughts grow dim,
swell up in my heart
like inflated balloons, when
I see the leaves scurry
on wheels across the patio.

Something will be gone
from me: old friends, I
think they are, that no
more will be.

But never fear; new
ones will come to take
their place —

somehow not quite the
same but other ones
nonetheless.

11/1/64 — [1] (05040)

Winter's Yawn

Indian summer's last leaves
Totter slipshod on limbs
Set in motion
By somebody's breath
Before sifting to the ground.

Brown leaves, like pinballs,
Skid along the turf,
Windmill-turning,
Somersaulting
To vaults of slow decay.

Who can catch their progress
As they flee
Summer's candied warmth
Like cartoon bears
Pursued by maddened bees?

11/1/64 — [2] (05039)

The Lights of Darkness: Charing Cross Station

The heavy subway-station light
Of half-started neon fixtures
Flickers with unsure pauses
Like the penetrant beams
Of a lighthouse beacon
Striking misty veils
Of opaque salt-sea sound.

The underground train rushes
Around the tunnel, into view,
Grinds with crushing uncertainty
Over the switches and cross tracks.
Its tiny ceiling lights, round
As aspirins, dim, then die, dissolving
In momentary imbalance the dark heads
Of insomniac passengers. Unseen contact
Is made again, and the lights rekindle.

The corrugated train whines down
The straightaway, pulling its illumined
Body against shadowy iron girders
And stanchions and shirt-sleeved people,
Spilling steam and water and red-flecked
Observation-car signals behind its noise.

It recedes into the next nearing
Substreet curve and expires
Like a deflating circus balloon,
Whose nervous child-breath
Audibly escapes when hold is
Let loose on its unknotted nozzle.

All is quiet again except
The artificial darkness of
Half-lighted fixtures, which is filled
With noisy neon clucks and stammers
Which vibrate in random discord
Like busy signals from myriad
Telephones held away from the ear.

The last train of nighttime
Arrives. It is soft inside
And warmly lit, as though
It belongs to another world.

Away it rolls, toward the point
Where porcelain ends and daylight
Fuses into a box of melted crayons.

Only, there is no sun out today, and
The conductor leaves on the car lights.

Everything outside is slow and dark.

A gloomy fog hovers over Hyde Park.

11/11/64 (05041)

[He who makes a beast of . . .] †

> He who makes a beast of
> himself gets rid of the pain of being
> a man.
> — Samuel Johnson

The absence of pain hurts
more than the awareness of suffering.
With grief, there is consciousness;
without pain, there is only indifference.

Frost was painted on the ground
this morning, and I scraped it off
with my feet

How is it possible to live with yourself after you have had to say those things to another person? Important things they were, too, but how to say them so that they don't negate all that you have striven to preserve?

I like to write in noisy places, places packed with people eating and conversing. The clatter of china and silverware and the murmur of chattering voices stimulate my senses. But I hate direct distractions, intrusions directed point-blank at me.

My greatest literary love is Faulkner, and yet he remains my strongest enemy — enemy because his rhetoric and style are too tempting, his style too easy for me to emulate. Yet I love his work because of the grandiose achievement of his effort. It is a truly magnificent effort, one worthy of immortality.

11/11–20?/64 (05183)

["Mr. Cartoone, can you take a call . . ."]

"Mr. Cartoone, can you take a call now, or shall I have the party phone back?"

Coffee so hot that it burns the forepart of my tongue —
    Meet my cartoon; he's animated and alive, and all of his thoughts are collected into a container within his mind, like his namesake, the cartoon whose character talks to others in cloud-captions.
    If only we could lift him off the paper and see him in his private after-hours from the appearances he puts in at certain hours daily, he would look a lot different. His face would not be too pink, and the blue of his suit would not drip over and fuse with the bright red of the Jaguar he is stepping from.

11/22/64 — [1] (05184)

On Responsibility: A Reflection

I travel in a slow world that moves too fast for my own locomotion sometimes. It keeps a pace which alternates between catatonia and kinesis, often passing me by irreversibly and uncontrollably with its preternatural and random expectancies.
    If a person, a girl, woman, but really no matter who, were to say to me, point-blank, that she could no longer bear the responsibility of being responsible for herself or withstand the pressing immediacy of her ubiquitous opprobrium or even just the diurnal demands of her physical life itself, which, I suppose, might even be the least of her concerns, then I would begin to wonder just how very different this gigantic mixture of protest and resignation is from my own condition, since, by the mere listening to her, let alone the memory of what she said (which is a regenerative entity in itself), I would have become a part of that protest — I would have assumed a partnership with the anguish and the ineluctable dilemma of trying to unravel the layers of the ego to expose their essential dharma of nakedness.

Once a person has been included in this society of self-pity, there is nothing else for him to do unless it be to repeat to himself her very words, because he or you or I myself can't force their echo out of the mind, besides being unable to match them with our own. So you repeat them to yourself over and again, pondering, questioning, proclaiming their hollowness to all the misery and anguish and protest and disillusionment that is inseparable from the involuntary bond that was made not by you but for you, before either of whom you would later learn to call Father and Mother even began to consider the anguish and misery and suffering and hardship and the "trying to make do" with the obstacles of their own insufferable condition, because if, by some visionary chance, they had taken the time or had possessed the foresight or the sheer elemental guts to reconsider and discuss and weigh all of the probabilities and the unknowable gratuitousness of the futurity of destiny, then surely they would have decided that it wouldn't be worth it in the first place — the having of the child — because, necessarily, it would have to be the result of their fatuous and selfishly oriented whim or passion or momentary desire to consummate themselves, which would have nothing to do with you, the unborn child, except that the responsibility for their act, which was theirs by choice and, as such, becomes the imperative that gets thrown into the bargain, must then become the equally inimical responsibility for you, even though you never had a choice beyond that of the sheer gratuitousness of having to accept it, since you are bequeathed it in the form of a child's body and since you have to receive it (the terrifying succession of responsibility called life) involuntarily and unknowingly. But people just don't ponder and question and calculate all of that, because if they did, then there would be no future generations. Instead, there would exist, if "exist" be the proper term, a cult of weaklings and psychic paralytics, whose number would diminish instead of increase with each successive phase of mankind, until the only creatures left on earth would resemble the most primitivistic avatars of primordial creation, who themselves would soon perish from sheer fright of their own feeble growl or whimper in the face of what they might have to endure.

So I see the possibility of all this, right there now, in the form of her absented plea, which speaks out within my echoing memory. I am hearing her cry. I can hear her repeating to herself and to me those same erroneous words, "I am too much responsibility for myself," and I am thinking to myself, "But that's it! That's the all of it, the plain and simple and undeniable truth! Yes! That's what it's all about, isn't it? This is just something that all of us should know or at least feel. This is *the* philosophy, split into its smallest tenet, the Occam's

razor-edge of all existence and all sources of regenerative hope and
striving to carry it on and on, to perpetuate the responsibility of all
history, to project it forward for those who will have to come after us
as a result of 'begat' and 'who begat whom.'"

And so that was it, and the outrage of having to hear her say, or,
rather, whimper, that statement of hers was more than anyone should
be made to listen to, let alone begin to feel in concord with — the
weight of that unpremeditated nihilism. But it was also more — much
more than the crying or the whimpering or even the unconscious self-
consciousness of human ignominy and resignation which she was
positing when she brought all of that into my head to be verbalized —
because I doubt that she even knew what she was saying, crying, let
alone the fact that she was scandalizing her own tenuous, though mag-
nificent, position in the indirect but positive line of descendants of
all men through all of time who lived and who cried and who also
continued to hope long before she ever existed: the Christs and car-
penters and fishermen; the Michelangelos and the masons and the
architects; the Platos and the plebeians; the Demostheneses and the
Bryans; the Swifts and Joneses and Picassos and Smiths and Martin
Luther Kings, who were great not so much because of what they cre-
ated but because of the degree of their attempt and, more so, because
they were forced to accept the inevitability of that word, "responsi-
bility," and, in doing so, were able to learn to smile back at it and to
say to themselves what she has not yet learned to say or think or feel
— they could say, "That's the stuff of life, the content and the diffi-
culty of living, the mandate to heed."

I am aware now. I have learned what that phrase has meant to me
personally, and it will be my burden, my responsibility, to try to erase
from her mind the fear and agony that prompted her to say that "I
am just too much responsibility for myself, and I don't want all that,
can't take it!"

And so that was all of it, the outrage of hearing her say it to me just
like that. It was, rather, my outrage at learning of her desire to quit,
to give in to the easiest way out, the inherent indifference concern-
ing the imperative to look it straight in the face. And all the while I
was thinking, "But that's it, and it's the best a person can hope for."
But it's enough to give man grace and humility and honour if he is
willing to accept the reality of what it means. But if he refuses it, kicks
it in the face instead of smiling at it, with it perhaps, then he also re-
fuses all of the possibilities of living and creating and moulding and
forming and shaping at least a piece of the future of all like himself;
he refuses all this because he fails to see that somebody way back
when or, for that matter, all of the sepulchered somebodies were

taught to accept its meaning, its imperative, and, in the process, even learned to live with it or in spite of it so that they could create and mould new progeny like themselves to face the same old things all over again, because, in the learning, they also discovered that man was strong enough to survive it, was even willing to try to outlive it, the most catastrophic whim that God or man could devise. And with that knowledge came confidence and willingness and the acceptance of the responsibility of being worthy of whatever it was at any given time or is now or will be that man and God wills, be it the pyramid of Cheops or the wheel or a Salk vaccine.

But for her, or anyone, for that matter, to say what I heard uttered in a moment of trepidation is to mock all of man's progress, to doom him to the indifference of not regarding the burdens and achievements of decayed generations of men and women who once thought they were doing something, creating, extending something that would further and add to the possibilities of living for all like themselves whom they knew were to come after them as a result of their own assertiveness and perseverance, and who must have hoped, as all men have always prayed, that their descendants would continue to exist in their image.

And they will continue to exist, unless too many people begin to chant and worship her self-effacing, wholly denigrating shibboleth, her resignation in the face of the engaging responsibility, which is life itself. Yet she would deny all of this, the trying and the hoping and the sharing and the praying and the wondering. But how could she? How is it possible that she could have missed the whole point of life so completely? She must not! She cannot, because she is required to recognize, nay, has to remember, that she is one of us, one of them, one of you and me, and that she does, as such, have at least this much responsibility: that she must stay around long enough to learn to smile at it and to laugh it off when she feels like crying or else commit the abject and unpardonable sin of taking her God-given life, because crying or suicide is only good sometimes; they have their boundaries of effectiveness, beyond which nothing can survive without a complete and unabandoned acceptance of those verities which form the undeniable paradoxes and prologues of life.

So here I sit over a cup of stale coffee, and there she is, and the distance that separates us is hope, vision perhaps, and the sheer necessity of distinguishing that distance is our requirement. That time, the distance itself between Adam and Zeno or between X, Y, and Z, must be recognized not as divider but rather as the progenitor of all the intermediary periods of history that range between their continuity and which, at any given moment, equal the sum of all present experience deposited within the reach of each sensitive individual to ponder and grapple with and sift and filter and substitute for and add to. But surely all of that time must not be disregarded as though it were a matter of no contingent concern, of no importance or relevance, and what is required is that we start all over again, from scratch, each new generation, because the past generations have already learned for us, have saved us the travail and the bother of learning what their examples have already taught us.

Ours is a general condition, one which has always mediated between total involvement and abandoned commitment to whatever it is or will be or may just possibly be which can reflect the greatness of the community of men and the individuality of man alone in the uncommon solitude of the individual mind. Yes, time has mediated between this, on the one hand, and the utter and inexplicable resignation from the urgent demands of survival, on the other. It is this that man must first learn: that the community of mankind is one and alone and great and that it depends for its sustenance upon the continuity of a personal, subjective sense of responsibility to live in the image of all men first and then, if there is anything left over, to perpetuate the individual responsibility of the individual mind in the face of all that threatens it.

Perhaps there will come the day when all men will say, "It is just not enough that I be responsible only for myself. Oh, that I may assume the responsibility for the well-being of my fellow man as well!"

World without end. Amen.

11/22 — [2], 11/25 — [1], & 12/1/64 (05185)

[The warmup time for a . . .] †

The warmup time for a
 jet engine sounds like the
hummed whistle of a crying
pressure cooker.

The two were flying this
trip hand in hand: timetable
and Gideon Bible

Hard to tell where the
runway ended and the
sky path began.

11/25/64 — [2] (04677)

The Happiest Little Shrew

I am a happy shrew that grows
each day because my master shows
me how to love. I live in meadows

And scamper all the long day long
with just a screech for my song.
I love to live and live to belong

To all the little children around,
who stoop to sprinkle the ground
with nutty food and the sounds

Of their merriment. I stand on hind legs
and listen. "Look! He begs
to eat from my hand our nutmegs

And lettuce and crackly seeds."
"Watch now!" they say. "He feeds,
nibbling only as much as he needs."

I am the happiest little shrew
in all my tiny little world. You
come with me! You can come, too!

11/27/64 (05042)

A Description of a City Conflagration

(In imitation of Swift's unpublished Scriblerus Minutes,
Friday 13, 1713, March)

I

Jonathan Swift was a magician,
*

Who went by the name of Presto,
And everywhere that Johnny went,
The grubs were sure to go.

He proved to Merlinus Liberatus
That he was a dead partridge.
Hey, diddle, diddle! The almanac maker
Was shot with a blank cartridge.

II

Gulliver traveled *por todas partes*
Through Terra Australis Incognita.
He found a Howard Johnson's urinal
In the Lilliputians' pygmy palace
And put out the fire with a side order
Of modern Yahoo grub-clams.

III

The Bather of the Tub,
A joke, nay, allegory, did tell
About religion and the popish cartel
Of Tom, Dick, and the Holy See
Of Harry Peter, the rye-bread eater.

* * * * * * * * * * * * * * * * * *
* * * * * * * * * * * * * * * * * *
* * * * * * * * * * * * * * * * * *
* * * * * * * * *Hiatus in MS.* * *
* * * * * * * * * * * * * * * * * *

"Knock, knock."
"Who's there?"
"Yahoo."
"Yahoo, who?"
"Yahoo, you! That's who, Magoo!"

IV

A beautiful young nymph went to bed
In Swift's late mind one night late.
Moll Vanessa wept a flood
Of city showers. She swept away
Dung, guts, and nasal drippings,
Hues, filth, and clappish grippings,
*

Cats, dogs, and pussy perfumes,
Onions, turnips, and burning odours.
This and more, from his boudoir,
Came tumbling down in torrents,
Trickles, and biting spears
Of mud-encrusted, painted tears.
They, as each sewer overflowed,
Rolled and turned and fell asunder
From St. Paul's, Soho, Madame Tussaud's,
St. Martin's, in Trafalgar Meadows,
Sotheby's, High Gate, Westminster Abbey,
Tower of London, and the city bourse,
Near the reeking dump, to shape their course
And conjoin in the stable of the Houyhnhnm horse.

V

* * * * * * * * * * * * * * * * * *
* * * * * * * * * * * * * * * * * *
* * * * * * * * * * * * * * * * * *
* * * * * * * * *Hiatus in MS.* * *
* * * * * * * * * * * * * * * * * *

"Swifty, my love," dear Stella said,
"Why don't you tell me who's in your bed?"

"Of course, Md Md Md Fw Me Me Lele Lele!"

"Is it Vanessa, dear love? De De dede Dum dede de!"

"No, no, Md! It is Helena Rubenstein, I feign
To say, and I love her beauty more each day."

Said Stella, "The word is, from Gresham Hall,
That Max Factor at the queen's last ball."

"Out of my life, you stinking young whore.
Rebecca Dingley shant settle this score.
A curse on your body and white, nippled breast,
And spittle and vermin and claps on your chest.
May excrement and dung, like never before,
With pus and clot, escape every pore."

VI

Spittle and grub, scurrility and
                    bubble!
                 *

Broil and suckle, scurrility and
                              trouble!

Modest Proposal, spew and spawn
Children to eat and whores to fawn!
Spittle and grub, boil and suckle!
Let the queen burst her chastity buckle!
Scurrility and bubble, etcetera and bubble!
May the size of her breasts soon grow double!

Broil and grub, spittle and bubble!
Ears and eyes and leg-hair stubble!
Nose and nipple and baby's cured ham!
Mary will have a little bastard lamb!

Broil and suckle, scurrility and
                              bubble!
Spittle and grub, scurrility and
                              trouble!

* * * * * * * * * * * * * * * * *
* * * * * * * * * * * * * * * * *
* * * * * * * * * * * * * * * * *
·* * * * * * * * *Hiatus in MS.* * *
* * * * * * * * * * * * * * * * *

Let's exeunt all from such poetic
                              rubble!

                    FINIS

**The Publisher, Benjamin Motte, at the Middle Temple-Gate in
Fleet Street, to the Reader:**

The existing annotations were compiled and printed, together with
the original form of the poem, in this new anthology according to the
design of a learned scholar closely allied to the anonymous author of
this work and sworn to utter secrecy concerning the identity of this
artist, elsewise I should be only too glad to have the bookseller append
his name to the work, whereby my own curiosity, as well as yours,
would be once and for all completely satisfied.

According to the poet's friend, these notes are to serve in helping
the reader over the more oblique and obscure portions of the poetic
text and to better understand at least some of the more subtle person-
ations and recondite allusions that he might otherwise pass over as

(in truth, unintended) pedantry and obfuscated sophistry, which, the poet's friend has assured me, is so far from his mind that he has given his signature to the use of the compendious notes that follow, hoping, though not without a little trepidation, that the following illuminations of his subtler poetics, in the process, might not be detracted from, that his readers, rather than feeling insulted with such an extraordinary display of verbal pyrotechnics, might come to fully understand every meaning, both intended and otherwise, and, in so doing, will express their esteem for his work by buying many copies of this anthology as well as the numerous treatises that he has projected.

The poet, through close communication with his friend, has proofed the notes for veracity, since his professed and ultimate concern is always for finding new ways to express the same old truths, and, finding them virtually verisimilitudinous in all respects, has conferred upon them the term "satisfactory," which, if I may take the liberty to assure you, indeed is a compliment from this sometimes bumptious, though, in fact, brilliant, man. Where the poet was a trifle unsure of his own intended meaning, he has chosen to make minor explanatory inclusions for his benefit as well as for the reader. Nothing more need be said about the notes themselves. They are sufficiently elaborated where need be and are self-explanatory.

A Description of a City Conflagration

(In imitation of Swift's unpublished Scriblerus Minutes, *Friday 13, 1713, March)*

I

Jonathan Swift was a magician, (1a–d)
Who went by the name of Presto,
And everywhere that Johnny went,
The grubs were sure to go. (2)

He proved to Merlinus Liberatus
That he was a dead partridge. (3)
Hey, diddle, diddle! The almanac maker
Was shot with a blank cartridge. (4)

Notes:

(1a) Jonathan Swift (1667–17??), Dean of St. Patrick's, Dublin, is undoubtedly one of the greatest yet-unsung men of letters of our time. That his work has gone unnoticed I am at a loss to explain. Occasionally, he dabbles in satire, as it is called, but always in a light-hearted manner. He not infrequently personates the style of those he admires for their inventions and freedom with the rules of the English rhetoric and grammar and who are known to him because, unlike him, they feign from carrying the obsequious and opprobrious burden of their calumny for the public recrimination and abjuration. From a thorough reading of this poem, which, though I inadvertently entitled it a "description" and was unable to catch my oversight until it had already been run through the presses, I should have rightly entitled an "ode" to this man's obvious greatness, I trust that the judicious reader will become as equally conversant in praise for him as I have become as of late.

     — The anonymous Poet

(1b) The reference to Swift as a magician who, for *e pluribus unum* of his gauche aliases, calls himself "Presto" is none other than a pedantic allusion on his part, though not the poet's, to the early French form *"preste,"* meaning "nimble," and the Latinate derivative *"digitus,"* or "finger." Here, the context is somewhat clouded as to the poet's exact inference because there are imbedded some indecent suggestions of a spurious love affair with one Esther Johnson. The meaning of the word "prestidigitator," of which "Presto" is a bastard contraction, is commonly taken by philologists concerned with etymologies as "a sleight of hand" or "a fellow handy with his fingers at just the right moment." This may lead the judicious reader to feel, as it has me, that the poet intended something else besides the sheer naming of one of Swift's aliases. This remains a moot point for modern historians and mathematicians to decipher and squabble over among themselves.

     — W. Wotton, *Reflections on Etymologies and Love Relations in the Modern Vein*, 1712

(1c) The appellation "Presto" appears, among those passing references in a few certain other passages, in the thirteenth (13th) inclusion of Letter VI, marked "London" and dated "Oct. 10, 1710." This and certain other of Swift's correspondences will, sometime soon, when I deem the market advantageous to publishing this material, which at present seems quite a while off since everybody and his brother or lover, as the case may be, is turning out second-rate pornographic literature, be collected into what, in projection, I plan to entitle *Swift's Journal to Stella.* Since I am presently occupied way beyond my means or desire with obscene tracts and lampoons against our most outstanding dignitaries and statesmen, which seem to flourish in direct proportion to their rate of output and, I might add reservedly, are flourishing not a little to my own humble advantage, this proposed collection will, no doubt, elude my attention and labours, so that by the time I am able to get around to doing this man's correspondences justice, it will have to be as a posthumous printing. As to how I have come by these letters, let it remain as mysterious as the author himself would have us believe his relations are with a certain "Stella."

> — The Publisher, Benj. Motte, at the Middle Temple-Gate in Fleet Street

(1d) The auguries and talismans of ill omen are shadowy in this particular poetical offering by Mr. Swift. There seems to be an anagogical ministry suggested both by the specific handling of the numbers in the date (Friday 13, 1713, March) of this "Description" and by the obvious reference to the thirteenth inclusion of the sixth letter of Swift's correspondence to his "friend" *Miss* Johnson, in which the pet name "Presto" appears. The number 10 is also suggestive in the date of the aforementioned letter, although, as yet, I have been unable to communicate with the Divine Order of Numerics to obtain a ready and publishable decipherment for it. However, I have no doubt that it is part of a larger plan, the exposure of the designs of which I fear may bring untold disgrace to the author of this and other similar letters.

One is instantaneously struck by the repetition of the number 10 in the dating of the letter (*vide* the following: Oct. **10**, **10**). Besides the two (2) number 10s, which stand out in boldface, the month October, it must be remembered, employed here by sheer astrological coincidence, no doubt, but here nonetheless, just happens to be the tenth month in the calendar of constellations. Furthermore, if one were interested enough, as I have been for just under one full turn of Halley's comet, which is calculated accurately at sixty (60) years, give or take a few unaccountable degrees of atmospheric vicissitude, to mentally add or to do so on paper, though this latter method is incredibly laborious and irksome, he would quickly be assured that once again the number 10 appears, though this is obviously a more subtle and sophisticated determination, as those of my artistic profession will readily confirm. The mathematical equation for this conclusion is as follows:

$$1 \& 0 \& 1 \& 7 \& 1 \& 0 = 10.$$

> — John Partridge, "A Panegyrical Essay on the Magical Numbers Ten (10) and Thirteen (13)"

(2) This couplet personates the meter and high seriousness of the Ancient epic poem *Maris and the Blood of Her Lamb*.

> — Sir William Temple

(3) *Merlinus Liberatus* was the title of John Partridge's yearly al-
manac. Its appearance here suggests that the powers of the antique
sage and supposed sometime worker of miracles in Sir Arthur's Court,
Merlin, have been freed from the magician's dead body by Partridge
through his own secret process of reincarnation and claimed by him
as his own original powers. Reference to the "dead partridge" has
nothing to do with this Modern maker of almanacs but rather with the
fact that for a few months only, the populace of London and neighbor-
ing hamlets was fearful that the great master would be forced to curtail
his fanciful but intrepidly veridical flights in predicting the futurity
of events that for some unknown reason seem to come true every time
he ventures his reputation with a prophetic prediction. The other day,
I met Partridge in person, standing in St. James Library, and overheard
him requesting a book with which I myself am well acquainted, and
one which I highly recommend to anyone desiring to become a scholar,
called *The Real Truth Concerning the Life of Epicurus*. Since I have
not only seen this man in person but, by his consent, been allowed to
touch him, and having done just that, and then on his right temple, I
can fully attest, by virtue of empirical, scientific evidence, that this
great artist, Partridge, is anything but dead, nay, positively anything
at all but dead, and, what's more, he is soaring gracefully and high
as ever before his balloonous reputation has allowed him to climb.
   — Richard Bentley, "A Panegyrical Essay on the Influence of Astro-
      logical Phenomenology in the Kingdom"

(4) Pedantic poetical allusion to the Ancient epic *The Pussy and the
Golden Calf*, dated circa the same cycle as *Reynard the Fox*.
   — Sir William Temple

II

Gulliver traveled *por todas partes*
Through Terra Australis Incognita. (5a–e)
He found a Howard Johnson's urinal (6)
In the Lilliputians' pygmy palace
And put out the fire with a side order
Of modern Yahoo grub-clams. (7a–b)

Notes:
   (5a) The poet has unjustly chosen to project my future intentions of

writing a book of voyages based upon my own prodigious nautical experiences. As to the veridicality or the whereabouts of this imaginary character, "Gulliver," so invented by the poet, I have no doubt that this caprice has sifted up into his brain with the conglomerate of other fatuous and fanciful vapours. The only explanation I am inclined to give to this most arbitrary application of such an equally arbitrary appellation is that it must have some direct relevance to the poet's own tendency to be *gullible*.

> — J. Swift, *Compendium Concerning Voyages to Be Made in the Very Near Future to Exotic Lands, Promontories, Insulas, Flying Islands and Other Hithertofore Uncharted, Unmapped, and Unknown Points of Interest Believed to Exist Just Beyond the Queen's Kingdom,* 17??

(5b) Reference to *"por todas partes"* is a bit of arcanum introduced by this poet, who, allegedly, is a worshipper of things and *rarum* Ancient and, thus, inconclusive and outmoded. The only source I have been able to discover for this obscure usage of the idiom under question, whose meaning is literally "through all parts" and which itself has little understandable pertinence to the tenor of its context, is to be traced back to the works of Ali Hash-On-Rye-Bread, in the original Mozarabic, which were brought from remote regions of uncivilized Africa into Seville by the disciples of Hernando Gomes Vasconcellos de Calatrava, El Sabio, in the year 853 A.D.

> — W. Wotton

(5c) The idiomatic interpretation of *"por todas partes,"* aptly employed here by the poet to suggest rare and exotic cultures which differ markedly from our own advanced civilization, is "everywhere." The authenticity of a projected work forthcoming on Swift's voyages into "Terra Australis Incognita" has been verified by said author, J. Swift, in his introductory projection of treatises to be written, set at the front of my edition of *A Tale of a Tub,* 1710.

> — The Bookseller, John Nutt, near Stationers-Hall

(5d) There is little question as to the proposed intentions of Mr. Swift concerning the possibility of a book of voyages or that the poet has somehow obtained this secret information — and by no fault of my own. Our group has toyed with the idea of employing in our services one Martinus Scriblerus, world pedant by trade, to fit himself out for future voyages so that he may carefully study the habits and customs of the people he finds who differ from us in the unknown parts of the world, the full account of which he will be obliged to com-

municate to us in detail immediately upon his return home to his native village of Redriff and the remunerative recompense for which will amount to no less than five hundred pounds sterling.
> — Arbuthnot, spokesman for the Numerical Association for the Advancement of Calculations and Projections (NAACP)

(5e) "Terra Australis Incognita" is an imaginary island, similar to those which are called the Wit of Cisms and the Caliopimplebreasts, determined to be located in some unknown parts of the ocean and so positioned for the printer arbitrarily, at the fancy of the mapmaker, to divert and stimulate nautical enthusiasts. There seems to be a pinch of satire intended in the poet's allusion.
> — The anonymous Poet

(6) The term "Howard Johnson's" is one of the intended transliterations devised by the NAACP to be used in place of the foreign and unintelligible names of kings and other high-ranking dignitaries whom Mr. Scriblerus will undoubtedly encounter on his voyages, for who among us is bold enough to doubt that no matter how foreign or uncivilized a country or kingdom may be, kings will always exist by divine and proper right?
> — Horace Walpole

(7a) The extinguishing of the fire is an anticipated incident to be interpolated into the true accounts of Martinus Scriblerus to beef up the story where it may begin to lack interest for the reader, though it will appear none the less true and reportorial. I have received this piece of information from one A. Pope, with whom I conversed at Will's a fortnight ago, during which time he was suffering under the exigencies of inebriation and thereby more willing to speak freely on such matters of note. There seemed to be spite and jealousy on his tongue, which I directly assumed to be aimed at the inimitable J. Swift, because he continued to mumble to me all the while, *"Dunciad! Dunciad!"* or other such words to that effect.
> — The anonymous Poet

(7b) "Yahoo grub-clams" has various colloquial interpretations. This phrase, to the best of my knowledge and empirical observation, seems to have first come into existence at the famous Will's Coffeehouse, where all illustrious names of the day, such as Bentley, Minellius, and Farnaby, frequently attend to regroup their spirits. I mention this fact not by way of digression but simply to reaffirm the importance of this mecca of learning and scholarly wit, which, as of late, in some circles, has not been wont to receive its due and just praise and appreciation, and also so that in the future cycle of generations to follow our own illustrious one, this explanation may serve as a genial reminder.

Catachrestically, the poet has misused the phrase here as it appears in print. This is a singular fault, however, and one should be on guard not to censure inordinately the entire poem, which has no mean merit in its own right as well as a scholarly care for exact detail and wit, because this mistake could be made with equal facility by anyone not thoroughly conversant with Will's terminology. The actual meaning of "Yahoo grub-clams" is related in content to meadow muffin and cow pie, coming originally from the early Spanish pastoral novels, of which the chief representative in this genre is *Los siete libros de la Diana*, written by Jorge de Montemayor. The prime preoccupation of these novelists was on naturalistic detail. I trust the reader will excuse this oblique reference, since, although the book is not very illustrious in its own right, it is typical of the outmoded pastoral paradigms. The proper term wanting here is a form of excrement or, more precisely, another term for organic urinary emanation which moves downward by the sheer pull of gravity and necessity from the kidneys to the bladder or urethra and into the open air, rather than defecation of the products of fecal matter, which, unintentionally I feel, the poet has inadvertently overlooked in his proofreading, though the error is not from any basic lack of distinguishing knowledge so much as from sheer overwork, no doubt, a burden to which none too few of us have fallen prey and succumbed in these times of prodigious and worthwhile creation.

— W. Wotton, *Attempts at Improving upon Catachrestic Misuses Carried Over from Ancient Learning into Our Own*, 1712

III

The Bather of the Tub, (8a–b)
A joke, nay, allegory, did tell (9)
About religion and the popish cartel
Of Tom, Dick, and the Holy See
Of Harry Peter, the rye-bread eater. (10a–f)

* * * * * * * * * * * * * * * * * * (11a–b)
* * * * * * * * * * * * * * * * *
* * * * * * * * * * * * * * * * *
* * * * * * * * *Hiatus in MS.* * *
* * * * * * * * * * * * * * * * *

"Knock, knock." (12)
"Who's there?"
"Yahoo."
"Yahoo, who?"
"Yahoo, you! That's who, Magoo!" (13)

Notes:

(8a) The Bather of the Tub was a courtly rank similar to the Order of the Garter, the Grape of the Hothouse, and the Apple of the Adams. Members to this rank were selected according to their Aeolian merits of spinning yarns, so to speak, and for weaving fascinating and whimsical fabrics of wit in the queen's presence.

— Gadbury, Humble Advisor to the Queen

(8b) The origin of this rank derives from a famous syllogism attributed to Bentley, learned scholar of Modern learning and keeper of the books in St. James Library, who once stated to a gathering of the queen's most highly educated projectors of science and other things mathematical and mechanical in nature (and I here quote verbatim from the recorded minutes of that eventful meeting): "Tubs are Modern, and Moderns are Bathers; ergo, the Bather of the Tub is Modern." The term "Bather of the Tub," therefore, has become representative of any person so displaying the qualities of cleanliness and purity, those who have cleaned themselves free from the filthy grime and dirty spittle of the Ancients.

"Knowledge is words,
and words are air;
ergo, knowledge is air."

— W. Wotton, *Intimate Intimations of Inveterate Immortality*

(9) The allegory referred to is from the famous Ancient cycle of Phallurus, having evolved from the Greek Dionysiac mysteries concerning the mystical and supernatural attributes of hierarchal religious organs of the body politic.

— The anonymous Poet

(10a) By these three sons, Tom, Dick, and Harry Peter, the Church of England, our Protestant dissenters, and popery are designed.

— W. Wotton

(10b) Tom is Martin Luther.

Dick is John Calvin, the Anabaptists, the Huguenots, the Gueuses, and John Knox.

Harry Peter is the Pope.

— J. Swift, *Journal to Jesus*, 1712

(10c) "Harry Peter, the rye-bread eater" is a recondite allusion to the revered epic poem *Peter, Peter, Pumpkin-Eater*, upon whose metrical assonance the poet plays.

— Sir William Temple

(10d) The poet seems to be alluding to some ethnic satire upon the fabled race of "rye-bread eaters" of the Old Testament by implying that the Pope had given over all hopes of transubstantiation to his more visceral passions for this certain and very delicious type of pastry, produced in a very few of the ghettos of our kingdom. I do not, however, think that it was the poet's intention here to satirize the strict dietary laws of this Ancient race of doomed pariahs but merely to show that even a Pope can be human and that if his need for bodily gratification is sufficiently strong, he may resort to turning his mutton into bread, or if his appetite is insatiable, he may even choose to convert his prize rye whiskey into bread, which is all according to the popish doctrine of concomitants.

— Epicurus Hogarth

(10e) The allegory in its original was meant to portray what may happen when a fanatic, enthusiast, deist, Aeolist, Epicurean, or Pope tries to pawn off on his friends or brother or brother's friends or friend's brother or brothers (example of Socratic deductive process) his own good stock of mutton and rye whiskey for an obviously unsubstantial loaf of bread (and not caraway or *poppy* seeded, at that).

— Criticism, friend of Momus, daughter of Pride, sister of Opinion, and daughter and wife of Ignorance, who herself begat Noise and Impudence, Dulness and Etcetera, Vanity and Bentley, Pedantry and Wotton, and Ill Manners, her children, who in turn begat Small Compendiums and Large Indexes, who begat Gout and Spleen, who begat Vapour and Etcetera, ad infinitum

(10f) There is direct reference made here that would tend to substantiate the theory of one Curll, an infamous bookseller, that Harry Peter, the rye-bread eater, had heard of the Ancient hymn called the

"Lord's Prayer," in which the unknown author exhorted his subjects
to beg, "Give us, this day, our daily bread."
— The Bookseller, John Nutt, near Stationers-Hall

(11a) Very frequently employed by our anonymous poet (though
fortunately the artifice appears only thrice in this worthy rendering) is
this pretended defect in the manuscript, which he has no compunction
to insert when he feels that the following explanatory material of his
poetic text is too directly calumniating or when he is assured by me or
a friend that its insertion would not be an overt violation of poetical
license or when he believes that he cannot say anything worth reading
and worth his time to fabricate (since his chief preoccupation is al-
ways with the truth of things) or, lastly, when his only desire may be to
amuse his readers with some satirical purpose (which he is not infre-
quently very fond of doing).
— The Publisher, Benj. Motte, at the Middle Temple-Gate in Fleet
Street

(11b) The judicious reader will readily judge the function of the
necessary hiatus I have allowed to be printed in my poem. Needless to
say, I neither had paper and ink enough to poeticize the allegory in its
entirety nor rhymes and variation in meter and footage available to
carry it off, since our language is rather scanty and wanting in fresh
words that rhyme, the old ones having long since been exhausted by
my contemporaries in their by no means mean flourishes of creative
genius. Secondly, it can be seen that the break allows the reader's eye
not to linger unnecessarily long upon the consciously obfuscated and
oblique imagery (which is the poet's prerogative to include sometimes,
if for no other reason than to display his hard-gained knowledge of
things hermetic and foreign), so that he can be transitioned from the
theme of religion to that of learning (the more important of the two by
far, in my humble estimation).
— The anonymous Poet

(12) This terse bandy of seemingly unintelligible phrases, con-
sisting of such words as "knock" and "Yahoo," is in truth but a
commonplace paradigm to those members of the Royal Society who
meet at Gresham College at their leisure. It is a scientific formula-
tion couched in the manner of a codified password system necessi-
tated as of late because of the astounding proliferation of scientific
parvenus and pretenders and enthusiasts and astromathemechanico-
fanatics who have begun to voice their cries for admittance both

here and in Ireland.

> — Newton B. (Bacon) Des Cartes, Curator of Curiosa and Late-Discovered Inventions and Projections to Better Benefit the Kingdom

(13) Magoo, chief projector of the Royal Academy and close friend and admirer of the two most famous theoretical practitioners of our time, Lagado and Legion Hall, was honoured by the academicians, who had to repeat his name each time they desired to gain admittance.

> — John Partridge, *Who's Who in the Scientific Archives of Our Illustrious Times,* 1711–1712

IV (14)

A beautiful young nymph went to bed
In Swift's late mind one night late.
Moll Vanessa wept a flood (15a–b)
Of city showers. She swept away
Dung, guts, and nasal drippings,
Hues, filth, and clappish grippings,
Cats, dogs, and pussy perfumes, (16) (17) (18) (19)
Onions, turnips, and burning odours.
This and more, from his boudoir,
Came tumbling down in torrents,
Trickles, and biting spears
Of mud-encrusted, painted tears.
They, as each sewer overflowed,
Rolled and turned and fell asunder
From St. Paul's, Soho, Madame Tussaud's, (20)
St. Martin's, in Trafalgar Meadows,
Sotheby's, High Gate, Westminster Abbey,
Tower of London, and the city bourse, (21)
Near the reeking dump, to shape their course
And conjoin in the stable of the Houyhnhnm horse. (22) (23)

Notes:

(14) I have been accused by such cursed enthusiasts and pretenders as are not lacking in small numbers in this Commonwealth of having plagiarized the great poet J. Swift, whose little masterpiece "A

Description" is well known to us all. Let it herein be asserted that my intention is no mere recompilation of or lampoon on this great work but rather that I offer my own humble rendering as an elegy to its greatness, not to mention from my grave concern for preserving the noble artifices and conventions of the Ancient kind, which are nowhere wanting in this self-contained poem or in that of the master.
 — The anonymous Poet

(15a) The reference to Moll Vanessa seems to be slightly confused biographically, and I doubt that the poet meant to infer that Mr. Swift was having an affair with a common charlady, for nowhere in his journals or in conversation have I heard mention made of the mopstress Moll, who, as is common knowledge, was sometime ago considered the most intrepid and successful of Soho's harlots and who, in her declining years, has had to relinquish her position because (and it is, likewise, common scuttlebutt) she suffers from contagious gonorrhea. As to the name "Vanessa," there is little proof to warrant any veridical conclusion other than that the poet here constructed, with his characteristic zealousness and fondness for exotic names, this contraction, which finds its origins in the Spanish, third-person plural, present indicative of the verb *ir*, "to go" (*van*: they go), and the highly flexible Latin idiom *essa*, which I take to mean in this oblique context "to bed (with her)."
 — Curll Willshouse
 (Coff Willhouse)

(15b) I have allowed the preceding dissection of my inclusion of the name "Moll Vanessa" in this final edition of my poem to demonstrate empirically what can and often does occur when commentators like Curll Willshouse attempt to exercise the academic muscles between their ears to force an interpretation (and, in this case, one quite erroneous and calumnious, not to mention ungermane and unfitting to a person of his quality and no mean breeding and good taste) which the author never intended. In fact, Moll Vanessa is a close and loyal friend and admirer of mine, and since I owe her not a few favors for services rendered me beyond the call of duty, I felt that this would be a good opportunity to immortalize her in my poem, which, if I may take the liberty to suggest, is assured future acclaim with all the greats of our time, among whom I here include and praise W. Wotton, R. Bentley, J. Dryden, and J. Swift himself.
 — The anonymous Poet

(16) The poet refers to wives of critics.
— Alexander Pope, *A Dissection of the Cavalier Undertakings of Certain Contemporary Writers and Critics*, 1711

(17) "Dogs" are critics.
— Ibid.

(18) "Pussy" is a term given to certain indescribable organic pails of critics' wives.
— Ibid.

(19) The mention of "pussy perfumes" refers subtly to the attempts of the renowned Ancient chemist Paracelsus, who made projections and scientific experiments with uses and practicalities of making or extracting from human excrement a certain highly coveted perfume, for which, when he brought it to perfection, much to his satisfaction and delight, he found the demand far exceeded his ability to mass-produce it, though by no failure to procure the valuable material from which his ambrosia came. He called his perfume "pussibus Occidentalis," or "Western climax," the hindquarters of female Yahoos being the West, according to the Ancient division of Sextus Pervertoris. For a more detailed discussion concerning the progress of arts and sciences from East to West, which develops a personal theory relating to the fact that the Moderns had only such awareness of the learning of Chaldaea and Egypt as was transvalued to them through the medium of Greek and Roman writers, I refer you to the forthcoming treatise I have tentatively titled *East Is Least, and West Is Best*.
— Sir William Temple, *On Ancient and Modern Pornographic Learning Among Those Who Pretend to the Title of Wit*, 1710

(20) Madame Tussaud's is an institution located in Piccadilly Square, at the exact center, where all the streets converge. It can be best appreciated during the height of business traffic, when such a din and moil of civilization and mass humanity is hardly less imaginable. It is famous for its waxlike effigies of persons of quality and fame, who appear almost lifelike as they go about their duties, and it hath been rumored that certain members of the Royal Academy have voiced designs concerning the purchase of this entire tract of the city, whereby they can more satisfactorily continue their experimentations for the betterment of mankind and the advancement of

scientific investigation.
> — J. Swift, *A Modest Defense of the Proceedings of the Rabble in All Ages*, 1710

(21) The city bourse is already under consideration by the architect John Soane, who has advised the queen that a larger and more efficient center of exchange will be necessary once the gains from William Wood's proposed base coinage begins to engender itself. There has been some dissent as to the probable name suggested for the new exchange, some of the queen's advisors feeling that the name "Bank of England" is rather simple and general in regards to its function. Other names suggested which carry some favor are "England's Enlightened Exchange," "The 1st Nat'l Bank of England and Ireland," or possibly "Irish Farmer's and Worker's Savings and Loan, Ltd."
> — Rebecca Dingley, Exchequer to the Queen

(22) Exact mythological source of the reference to a Houyhnhnm horse is unknown. That it is of the same cycle as Pegasus and Clavileño, the thoroughbred steed of Alonso Quijano, is verified in Sir Temple's book *Ancient and Modern Learning*, in which he correctly estimates the source and qualities of the animal under discussion as a solid-hoofed and one-toed quadruped known anciently as *Equus caballus* and distinguished from other species of the Equidae, such as nags and asses and mules and burros, by its very offensive odour and other lack of any semblance of reason and common sense and its utter degeneracy to the habits of the coarsest of all animals in the kingdom, the only useful by-product of which is the glue necessary for binding the multitude of compendiums and reflections and treatises and dissertations and modest proposals and humble petitions that daily flow from our bookshops in staggering quantities, their wit and content in no way related to or detracted from by the mandatory usage of such an offensive animal's waste product.
> — W. Wotton, *The Values of Dissection in the Modern Kind*, 1713

(23) The author here personates the very satisfying style of Dryden's use of the Alexandrine triplet. It is well known that the poet in mention is not too highly regarded by Mr. Swift or the poet of this "Description." It is not the anonymous poet's intention to hide his personations and ironic parodies under the veil of indistinguishable subtlety or pedantic metrical obfuscation or recondite allusions, and so he has instructed me to include this note by way of explanation to those readers who were initially troubled by the conscious usage of the rhymes "bourse," "course," and "horse," since the poet is no great

master in the art of rhyming, and by way of an apology to those who needed no further explanation in the first place. The author's paramount concern is for his readers, and he hath oft expressed his feelings to me by saying, "Nutt, old Yahoo," the reference of which I have never bothered the busy man to explicate, "my one desire has always been the greatest good for the greatest number of my devotees." I have little doubt that this phrase will soon take hold sometime in the future among the learned of our country.

— The Bookseller, John Nutt, near Stationers-Hall

V

```
* * * * * * * * * * * * * * * * * * (24)
* * * * * * * * * * * * * * * * * *
* * * * * * * * * * * * * * * * * *
* * * * * * * * Hiatus in MS. * *
* * * * * * * * * * * * * * * * * *
```

"Swifty, my love," dear Stella said,
"Why don't you tell me who's in your bed?"

"Of course, Md Md Md Fw Me Me Lele Lele!" (25a–b)

"Is it Vanessa, dear love? De De dede Dum dede de!"

"No, no, Md! It is Helena Rubenstein, I feign (26)
To say, and I love her beauty more each day."

Said Stella, "The word is, from Gresham Hall,
That Max Factor at the queen's last ball." (27)

"Out of my life, you stinking young whore.
Rebecca Dingley shant settle this score. (28)
A curse on your body and white, nippled breast,
And spittle and vermin and claps on your chest.
May excrement and dung, like never before,
With pus and clot, escape every pore." (29)

Notes:
    (24) The pretended defect appears here at the poet's exhortation as a means of deletion of some of the more unsavory descriptions that occur between J. Swift and Moll Vanessa, which, on rereading his poem, he discovered might, in some circles, cast an ignominious

shadow over the character of the great dean, not to mention the grave
injustice he might do to his own character as a poet of the first order
in morality, common sense, good ethics, graciousness, humility, wit,
and gentility. For those more zealous and not concerned as much with
poetic formalistics and verisimilitude, the inclusion of this hiatus may
serve as a momentary cutoff point to lessen the strain on the eyes and
as a period of recollective daydreaming for those whose tendencies
allow them to imagine fantastic visions of debauchery and orgiastic
consummations, not a little of which I am assured the anonymous poet
intended.
          — The Bookseller, John Nutt, near Stationers-Hall

(25a) These distressing symbols were chosen by me with great con-
sideration and deliberation. They are included here with judicious
concern and are not meant to impugn Swift for his want of discretion
in moments of euphoric distraction. The story of his infidelity to and
crass betrayal of one Esther Johnson, however, is common scuttle-
butt with the frequenters of the Smyrna, at Pall Mall. It is said that
when he learned how Stella had discovered his nocturnal philander-
ings and cavorting with a prominent cosmetician residing between
Piccadilly and Buckingham Palace, he flew into an insuppressible
and unmitigably unintelligible fit of anger from which neither he nor
Miss Johnson ever fully recovered. I have attempted to recreate here
the vitriolic yet candid drift of the enlightening intercourse in which
the great writer chose to expose himself to the vituperations of Stella's
frothy invective.
          — The anonymous Poet

(25b) This highly irregular recourse to abstracted symbolism is one
more example of Swift's frequent tendency toward enthusiastic cant,
zealousness, and modern madness. It appears that the poet has, with
much concern for the detailed truth, described the situation in which
Swift's mind took an "unlucky shake" and, as a result of tinctures of
uncoagulated, febrile vapours issuing forth in random fashion, deemed
his nature highly irrational. I have no other means but to conclude that
the man, on learning that his deed was found out and no doubt being
unable to absolve the obsequious opprobrium of his misdemeanor,
was evidently overpowered by delusions and heated imaginations
and fancies, having sustained ruptures and displacements of the vital
elements of the brain.
          — Dr. John Arbuthnot, Physician to the Queen

(26) Helena Rubenstein was born of immigrant parents, who came to Ireland in 1682 from Laputa. She began her career at The Rose, a well-to-do tavern, and worked her way up by sure stratagems and design to the position of Cosmetician to the Queen. Swift had occasion to meet her at the Royal Palace when discussing an affair concerning some spurious medals that were supposedly due him from the queen. He never did receive these promised gifts, but from Rubenstein he was recompensed with her not unsubstantial First Fruits and Twentieth Parts and thus returned frequently to discuss "religious matters" at court, until he was finally discovered. Helena Rubenstein was further distinguished for having a birthday poem dedicated to her by Colley Cibber.
— John Partridge, *Merlinus Liberatus*, 1712

(27) Max Factor is one of the leading projectors of the Grand Academy of Lagado, best known for his practical, mystical, speculative, and mathematical computations upon the hierarchical functions of female procreative organs. The obvious allusion here is to the queen's last formal supper, to which she invited dignitaries from all fields of scientific speculation, included among whom, for reasons unknown, was Helena Rubenstein — although some sources held that the queen, displeased with Swift for having seduced her private cosmetician, invited "Stella" to this star-crossed bacchanal with specific designs, previously having persuaded the distinguished scientist, Factor, that she, Helena, would be a perfect subject for some pre-festival experimentation. The result of his findings will shortly be published in a tome to be, with Factor's permission, prematurely entitled *A Modest Discourse upon Female Genitalia, Royally, Mystico-, Organico-, Cosmetico-, Pornographicologically Considered in Various Realms of the Known World*, 171?. Though progress on this book has been tedious, the results will not be abortive, for public interest in these matters is waxing tumescent in these times.
— The Publisher, Benj. Motte, at the Middle Temple-Gate in Fleet Street

(28) Rebecca Dingley, questionable *fidèle* and Celestina for "Stella" Johnson, was known best for her political tactfulness in mediating misunderstandings between the whimsical dean and her young mistress.
— The anonymous Poet

(29) Symptomatic invective is often the accompanying response of vapourous minds, the overt syndromic manifestations of which distemper of the brain are termed acute misogyny with corresponding coprophiliac tendencies. Such verbal displays are marked specifically by inordinate predilections and fixations upon the primary sexual organs.

> — Diogenes Antiquitus, *De mentibus vaporibus et insanus*, 1685, Roma

VI

Spittle and grub, scurrility and
                    bubble!
Broil and suckle, scurrility and
                    trouble! (30)

Modest Proposal, spew and spawn (31)
Children to eat and whores to fawn!
Spittle and grub, boil and suckle!
Let the queen burst her chastity buckle!
Scurrility and bubble, etcetera and bubble! (32)
May the size of her breasts soon grow double!

Broil and grub, spittle and bubble!
Ears and eyes and leg-hair stubble!
Nose and nipple and baby's cured ham!
Mary will have a little bastard lamb! (33a–b)

Broil and suckle, scurrility and
                    bubble!
Spittle and grub, scurrility and
                    trouble!

* * * * * * * * * * * * * * * * * (34)
* * * * * * * * * * * * * * * * * *
* * * * * * * * * * * * * * * * * *
* * * * * * * * *Hiatus in MS.* * *
* * * * * * * * * * * * * * * * * *

Let's exeunt all from such poetic
                    rubble!

FINIS

Notes:

(30) The anonymous poet has here employed an oracular device reminiscent of the prophetic conjurations invoked by the scrubby witches in *Macbeth*. There seems to be some satiric pique intended against fanatics and enthusiastic diviners who, on no few occasions, resort to the deities of filth and squalor to send them succor.

— Sir William Temple, *Incantations and Ancient Mythic Exhortations Revived*, 1710

(31) The term "Modest Proposal" no doubt refers to some preternatural potion or necromantical philter brewed in Ireland by cannibals. Little is known of its origin or function, though through detailed inspection into the pharmacopoeiae of that backward country, I have been able to decipher the mysterious broth's egregious constituents. This broth is a conglomerate of palsy waters, whose compounded tinctures consist of medicinal lavenders, aromatics, cowslips, sage, citron, rosemary, ambergris, nutmeg, lotus extract, mustard seed, and French brandy. The only uses for a fermentation of this absurd nature that I can conceive would be as carminatives or for languors or for debilities of the nerves. The significance of the poet's inclusion of this mixture in this context is completely unintelligible and indecipherable to me unless it is meant to suggest some recondite malady, as yet uncovered, in the nature of J. Swift.

— William Wotton, *A Modest Proposal for a Cogent Textual and Exegetical Rendering of the More Obfuscated Allusions in the Present Poem: "A Description of a City Conflagration,"* published simultaneously with the appearance of this great poem

(32) The use of the word "etcetera" is not meant to add Latinate terminology to this poem, as many of the poet's contemporaries are wont to do in order to display their wide derivative and eclectic lingual virtuosity, but rather to guard against unnecessary repetitions and, by so doing, to spare the reader's indulgent patience wherever possible.

— The Bookseller, John Nutt, near Stationers-Hall

(33a) This refers to the Ancient epic poem *Maris and the Blood of Her Lamb*. The narrative of the poem ends tragically, with Maris having been unjustly seduced by an anonymous satyr, who has the head of a centaur and the hindquarters of a goat, and from the union there comes a fatherless lamb, whom Maris is forced to bathe in its own blood and milk before she is conjured by the Prince of Darkness and Lies to eat it whole. Needless to say, this legend has come down to us from the Ancients as one of the most horrific of stories. The effect on Swift, who read it as a child, was devastating. The story ends with Maris finishing the remains of the lamb and then disappearing into a subterranean abyss that opens beneath her. She is never again heard of, though, mysteriously, from the time of her demise or disappearance it is said that the species *lamb* multiplies beyond all imaginable proportions, until the inhabitants of the land Brobdingnag are forced to vacate and seek other habitable lands.

— Sir William Temple, *Legends Ancient and Modern*, 1710

(33b) The poet has here falsely constructed an Alexandrine triplet to personate one John Dryden, whom he holds in very base disrespect, not merely as a translator and uniquely unoriginal author but as a cloven-hoofed sycophant of the great.

— Richard Bentley

(34) This hiatus appears to have been placed here with great importunity, as though the anonymous poet was abruptly struck by a coruscation of intellectual insight that informed him that throughout this final section he had made very little contextual sense and that he had therefore better beg leave of his readers before they preempted him. Let it also be known that this ultimate break brought tidings of gladness to my typesetter as well, who, by this time, was beyond the point of comprehensive understanding of the abstruse element of this section, having become a veritable mechanical, mindless setter of unrecognizable type-blocks.

— The Bookseller, John Nutt, near Stationers-Hall

11?/64 & 2/16/65 — [1] on 2/16 (05179)

[Inch by inch, like the layers of an onion] †

Inch by inch, like the layers of an onion
peeled off one at a time, death stalks stately
in its masquerade, bathed in balking burlesque

The misgivings of youth
   Are the wisdom of the tooth;
      Whole truth derives too late, forsooth,
         In the guise of a cemetery's booth

I knew the man when his astuteness,
  his vigor, was a thing to behold.
Now I see him, poor broken mind,
  blindness untold, he being unable
    even to count out the proper
      change for his breakfast,
        handing the waitress

Confessions of Zeno
              Italo Svevo

          the last cigarette
          the death of my father
          my marriage

Clyde Tetherbrook
  was a lofty young man

Clyde Tetherbrook
  was a daring young crook,
and a "   " was he.
He called for his torch, and

Huddling 'neath the
  momentary orchestration
    of a fluid, atavistic
      millennium,
        they, it, he,
          creation itself, lurched,
        controlled its posture, then
      opened its mouth and dribbled
      out words like
          "And it was good" and
      "I shall rest."

The most beautiful cause
  worth waiting for
    is the pause
      that
        *

Refreshes
          the heightened

11?/64 (05012)

A Day for Daydreams

The bleak day dawned dreary
And tired, reluctant to spray itself
With rain-filled yawns of wakefulness.
One silvery star cowered
From extinction, reluctant to forfeit itself.
Still, the day hobbled bleak
And leery in its headlong plight
Away from night's oriental station.

The rain fell, shelling rooftops
And umbrellaed passersby like slow arrows
Softly shot from hidden crossbows
Near some ancient Tintern Abbey,
And I just stood there, cold and
Blearytired, in the early morning
Drizzle, dreaming of poetry and painters
And piles of white, wet sand.

11–12?/64 (05031)

Ever-Present Absence

Upon your absence I gaze,
hearing your eyes speak to me
with tears of fear and the
desire to express your love.

Your eyes murmur through blinks
and then say, "I love you, love you,
love," and I want to kiss you
on your eyes so that you will
see my warm breath and sense my heart
pumping pulses through your sight.

But your absence almost defies vision;
it denies precision, and all that I
can sense is the absence itself.
Be one and yet three in one
at the same time! Be *was* and *am*
and *will be*, simultaneously!

Be present to me, even when absence
and fear descend from the regions
of past trial-and-error experience!
For what is there without response?

11–12?/64 (05169)

Peanuts, Cashews, Hersheys

Foghorns frog-sound
From the East River.
Harlem honkey-tonk horns
Tune dizzy rhythms.
Horns of satyrs, rubbed
Gold by curious hands, adorn
Recesses of Frick's mansion.

An early, New York, Fifth
Avenue morning melts
From neon to sunlight.
The warm day groans
Under the shuffling ennui
Of people everywhere rushing
Nowhere.

Airplanes, jets, helicopters
Approach and are then
Swallowed alive by Disneyland.
Birds (swallows, sandpipers,
And pterodactyls) confound
Whining jet engines and props.

Steeplescrapers are temples,
But Broadway is still a cow path,
Cinderellaed now and regal
With decades of concrete
*

And glass and steel splendor.
Its residents are soap bubbles
And pancake mix. Neurotic
And hurried are its ingredients.

Crowded together in its palaces,
Whores, syphilitics, and artists
Of all species display
Their artificialities on fences
And clotheslines and Park Avenue,
Louie XV, velveteen walls. They
Laugh in consort and repeat,
"We fooled you all, suckers."

Fooled and frenzied and Madisoned,
The transients come and go,
Fawning to Eliot and Karl Shapiro.
Even the G.G.1s and diesels are
Perplexed to find their Penn nest
Wrecked for another steeple.
But the gnomes still sell on every
Train, yelling, "Peanuts, cashews,
Hersheys. How 'bout a mag, lady?"

There is no sorrow or solitude
In this fully equipped worldcity.
Everything functions in time to
The taximeter, the bus schedule,
The elevator button, the stoplight,
And even the wrist watch, sometimes.

"People! Who needs 'em?" they all say.
"It all works by itself, automatic like.
Nothin' runs wild anymore — all a big
System, you know!" But it is too
Perfect, too calculated to err.
Somewhere, sometime ago, there was
A *will be* for the tomorrows of
Yesterday's hopes. But that was
Yesteryear and not now, of course.

People have decided to do away with
All of that. It was just too easy,
Too difficult to imagine tomorrow's
Today show yesterday. But no matter!
*

There will still be the gnomes, and they
Will invade the worldcity with their
Pleas for "Peanuts, cashews, Hersheys.
How 'bout a mag, lady? You name it,
I got it! *Playboy*, *House Beautiful*?
How 'bout a Coke? . . . Peanuts, cashews, . . ."

11–12?/64 (05045)

[Truth is consciousness, and youth]

Truth is consciousness, and youth
is awareness of the absence
of total consciousness. Yet what,
save indifference, remains, without your response?

11–12?/64 (05182)

[Unreasonable conceit of one's own . . .] †

Unreasonable conceit of one's own
superiority . . . with correspondingly
contemptuous feeling toward others;
inordinate self-esteem.
haughtiness, arrogance, or
superciliousness

assiduity:
petulance:

approbation:
the act of formally
or authoritatively approving
as proper or commendable, or
as good or true;
sanction

abstentious: eating or drinking
                sparingly; characterized
          by self-denial or
                abstinence, temperate

11–12?/64 (05178)

Time There May Be

Winter has turned out the vernal light
In its living room, and all is gloom
And silvery and iron cold and blight.

But grieve not! Rather, take pity
On all that was forced to relent.
Repenting what never was is flitty

And to no avail. For time there was,
And time there will be again, to love
With comfort, to respond to the buzz

And chirrup of bee and blithe-flight
Cricket. And time there may even be
To touch the moon together one night.

12/1–2?/64 — [1] (05036)

A Traveller, a Witness Am I

I am a traveller who has seen
More in the moon's phase
Than ever a shepherd did glean.

A witness am I to the moods
Of change, to the change of days
And time and night. My mind broods.

Not for the loss of reminiscence or
The memory of things lost do I praise
The mind but for a love not felt before.

12/1–2?/64 — [2] (05037)

Love

To love beyond recognition of
Self is to look through death,
To feel the inner strength
That comes early in life
And then lingers and lingers
And grows like pleasant images
Of a painting so suggestive
And warmly subtle that all
Sensation fuses with thought
And the mind becomes one with
Life and sensibility and loving,
Which transcend corporality,
Like a tree or bird or book
Loved for its own sake only.

[12/1–2/64]? (05035)

[To love beyond recognition of self]

To love beyond recognition of self
Is to look through death,
                    to feel the wealth
Of beauty that hides in sighs
Soft and mild,
                    to penetrate the eyes
Of night and time,
Which flicker with the breath
          of summering nightflies.

[12/1–2/64]? & [3/3–4/65]? (05281)

[Why do certain special individuals . . .]

Why do certain special individuals elect to set themselves apart
from all that engenders unity and stability and happiness?

My mind is clear, this morning, and alert to the movement of all tiny
things around me: people, automobiles, woodpeckers, chicken hawks,

and hoarfrost. It is warm and alive and sensitive to the certain inexplicable calling that exhorts it to see through all outward forms, into the essence of a solitary individual, who is more distant from me than sheer time or distance can suggest.

My mind is void yet sharp, not devoid of feeling but somewhat abstracted, like a soft fog seen at a distance that clouds in indistinctiveness the buildings of a city. My mind's visibility is fifteen light-years, but still no planes are landing tonight.

I can see the yellow-green light at the end of Daisy's dock, and I am Nick Carraway, twice removed. My eyes accommodate now, and I am living in the moment before America: I am a Spanish sea dog *quien se llama hijo del Dios*, Alonso Quijano. ◊

I am yelling to those aboard a galleon we have just boarded: *"Deseamos nada menos que el respeto y la fe adorable a Él quien existe para todos nosotros."* ◊

My mind is clear and fanciful this morning, and there seems to be no stopping its process. I am thinking what a noble achievement William Faulkner made by creating out of the myriad, unnameable materials of his expressive, urgent spirit to deposit his "Kilroy," and I admire it, the achievement, and I admire it with utter abandonment, and I seek it for my own because it seems to be the most rewarding, psychically: not to copy his rhetoric or to imitate his ideas but to formulate a philosophy for living and breathing with sympathy and feeling the spirit that motivates and moves all things to a conscious awareness of inward as well as outward forms.

12/2/64 — [1] (05186)

The Ozark Hunter

I awake each morning long before
The warmth of the sun melts the hoarfrost
From the holler and the stark cedars.
It is a lonely time in a man's life,
But I love to sit and smoke, strifeless,
During the sandman hours of solitude.

Living alone is a beautiful pastime
For one like me. I avoid the fast crimes
Of nine-to-five dwellers, who forget to dream.
My two little beagles lie nuzzling the heat
*

Of a black-walnut fire, which blazes, and
I have stopped to think, drinking hot coffee.

12/2/64 — [2] (05038)

[Am sitting in the university . . .] †

Am sitting in the university dining hall again this morning, as most, and I am dreaming about the rather nebulous career of writing always in an amateurish vein, never for the magazines, etc., primarily.

The women come and go, busy deciding where to go this morning because there is a slight frost that hovers above the ground.
Blank mind, not fuzzy so much as unwilling to cooperate correlatively — no germane associations to be had — try free verse — the prose poem

> Fettered by fanciful feelings
> (The old cat died last night)
> Of love's latent solicitude
> (What a marvelous sight;
>
> Spleen, barbiturate ain't right)
>
> For what

> Beagles yelping beside the draw
> Made warm my heart to know
> That even the tiniest pained paw
> Could scare a rabbit

Approaching my twenty-fourth year, and already my thoughts focus on the activity of conscious creation: experience, recall, distortion, imagination and fancy (fight on, O Coleridge and Wordsworth, enemies in semantics only!), admiration and sensitivity for the great and ennobling efforts of the individual, no matter how seemingly insignificant.
All actions, compulsive or no, have a reason or complex of stimuli that lie behind their fruition. Respect these motivations, for they are the wellsprings of all human striving, of all individualistic endeavour.

The problem of finding a justification for any system of thought or philosophy or overt action outside the easy recourse to alchemy and genes, finding a significant and meaningful form of self-expression, just an outlet, perhaps, if you will —

Writing, like anything else, if it is to be worthwhile, has to be the result of abandoned devotion and spontaneity, combined with Coleridge's willing suspension of disbelief. It involves long hours of schizophrenia, during which intervals the creator is seized irrevocably by the demons of seeing a fantasy or chimaera more real than the reality itself, more real and vivid because the process of dramatization and heightening begin to take over where complacency and imperception and bias are left behind.

There is something in telling a good story, to the mystics, in that both the writer and the good friar achieve a state of somnambulatory hypersensitivity to those things not directly connected with the immediacy of things.

The mind becomes a screen, across whose blank, white fissures flash all objective correlatives in the real world, and these are the stuffings of his source material, added to which, through a process of suspended selectivity, is the structure of the usable content.

12/3/64 — [1] (05187)

The Hounds of the Bastardvilles

"Everything fell into place, Dr. Watson,
When I discovered my motives for killing
The mystery."

"You old bard, Holmes. I never knew you
Had it in you to do such a frightful thing —
The murder, I mean!"

"It was easy, old man, once I learned
To use suspense, climax, and logic
To solve

The riddles of murder, rape, and suicide."
"To me, dear Holmes, 'tis all anagogic —
Your reasons, I mean!"

12/3/64 — [2] (05043)

[Lord Byron]

Lord Byron
First canto: rapid tones and pace, uses anticlimax
Stanzas 122, 124, 132: there is no disunity of theme even though
hay many topical allusions; he maintains a similar talking voice

A fabled race of giants are we,
who people our minds with our own
thoughts of ourselves.
A rueful race of Lilliputians are we,
who see no further than our own
pygmy palaces.
A picaresque race of Byrons are we,
who strut and violate our own
Julias and Haidées.

12/8/64 — [1] (05046)

Two There Are Together

Walking, staying, stalking stately
In stocking feet, pacing from year
To year each minute, I trace the
Fissures of your brain's memory and linger
And pause and linger longer than the
Impatient days of winter once backed up
And staved off by the sleight-of-hand phases
Of an Indian summer too long endured.

Disrobing, faltering, down-dropping the gown
Of your nakedness like a summer shower
Seen off the shadowy horizon, whose descending
Particles glisten as they fall to the ground,
You are seen, anticipated, and I await the
Sweet, thick wetness of your bathed, moist body.

You lie languid in our bed at night,
Swallowed up and enveloped by the whiteness
Of sheets and my white warmth, weaned and
Suckled in your bodily image, at once at one
*

With your warmth and your memory, like the
Distant, green Daisy-light at the end
Of all platonic docks grown glowing and
Hazy in the mind of a Carraway seed.

Live honey oak, mimosa, and cicadas
Howl their coloured sounds to the wafted
Night-clouds outside our apartment window,
And we are one, and we are one now
With the mobile fantasy of vernal vignettes
Staged on each windowpane like a showroom
Display lined with similar television sets,
All turned on, all glowing with similar scenes.

And the night progresses and passes from
Without into our minds' inside and becomes
One with our oneness. The eclipsed moon
Cuts the clear clouds with inaudible flails,
Like a scimitar wielded without control.
Your thighs are taut and sensually loose,
And timeless is their frenzied desire
To repel opposites and attract like desires.

You sleep now, like a warm rabbit
Held close in its nest by ice-cold fields,
And you are sleeping warmly and neat
And softly nestled into the strength
Of my encircling arms. We are one now
With the mother of night and love and
Sleepfulness, though your sleep is like
A wakeful draught of unfermented wine
That bubbles softly to my surface, where
Sugar and grape and yeast kiss, commingling
Into vintage philters of pure enchantment.

Now morning is blinking with flashes
Of soft light on your eyes, on our
Bed, and on our hopes and awareness
Of the new day, dawned dilatory and
Slowly promising. You stretch like
The soft gliss of some classical étude;
You blink to my first smile with the glow
Of Gulf Stream gulls dipping their wings
*

In fanciful pirouettes as they swoop
The wave crests for signs of surface life.
You are awake now and one with my glow.

Eye dust dissolves into nothingness and
Is lost in the dusty vacuity of our close
Room. Our strength has returned from its
Night bed, and we are nakedness and
Daybound. We have slowly become
The mere reminiscence of our night
Together. New coffee perks on the breakfast
Table, and we come alive with its warm noise.
We are fulfilled by its aroma and by
Its hot kiss of eight o'clock wakefulness.

We must go the day alone today, we resolve.
We must fight to outpace our innocence
In the face of the fleeting constancy
In the wider rooms outside our tiny room,
For all is postponement in our other worlds,
And we are all impatience until we can come
Together once more under the smells of honey oak
And the coloured night-sounds of warm sleep.

12/8 — [2] & 12/8?/64 (05047)

December Rabbit Hunt

The brownfurry creature lies hugging
Its ground burrow, which nature has
Provided it, until, frightened away fast
And fearful by certain high-pitched
Yelps, it leaves behind its own warmth
To seek hurried escape.

The beagles follow doggedly, with the
Shotgun-shouldered hunters stalking,
Slowly and certain of their gain,
Somewhere behind. They, the shotgun
People, move near the vicinity of
The burrow and wait.

Each fleeting shift the scurry-rabbit
Makes, a quarter-mile's distance from
The persistent beagles, represents one more
Final exasperation of fear and effort
To vainly elude the inevitable shotgun's
Shell-shot.

Soon, the yelps turn back on their own
Pursued breath. The rabbit has turned
Too and, unaware, aims back toward
Its burrow, to safety, to its lair,
Where it will fail to see the merciless
Hunters patiently standing.

The hurry-rabbit sifts quick and sure-
Footed across its own still-warm, scented
Path and then starts. It becomes aware
Of some foreign element: a cough, a sharp,
Silvery glint of steel, and then
The bally blast.

Too fast and hard comes the shot
Through the draw and the confining
Bramble; too suddenly and unexpected
For the rabbit it comes. Hit from behind,
He jerks, swerves, tumbles over himself,
And then drops, bleeding.

Trying to keep running with snapped
Tendons and burnt fur, the rabbit
Hobbles a few paces and then bends
At the neck to die. The teeth still click,
And the thighs twitch convulsively; then
They welcome stiffness.

The beagles approach, gape, and paw
Before scampering off into the draw.
Up from the holler's creek bed
Come the hunters. Contented with their
Sport, they say to each other,
"Let's have another drink."

12/8/64 — [3] (05044)

[Cigarette after useless cigarette]

Cigarette after useless cigarette
unfouls its noxious vapours into the lamp-
shade, and I wait, hoping to sample
the shade of cool words, which refuse
expression to my useless thoughts.

12/14/64 (05048)

Nocturne II: Lines Composed Five Minutes Past Insomnia

I am dreaming now, desultorily moving from
Classroom Cranes and Shelleys to you, and
I embody your essence in essential questions.

Why the lapses, the silences, and
The awful expectations without compliance?
Why are these absences so loud in my mind?
And what brings this silent noncommunication,
Which tempers passion, which tempts resignation?

Where are you this moment, when thoughts
Of you are living metaphors in my presence?
I've stolen my love from myself to give to you
With no expected return, excepting affirmations
Of your belief in my guileless, gracious gift.

What are you doing to yourself by abusing
Your absences from me? Why can't you suffuse
My expectations and my hopes for mutuality
With your hopes and needs, your aspirations?
Maybe I simply forgot to tell you I love you.

You must be responsible for my irresponsibility
And for my concern, for the hopes and promises
Of growing old together, forever growing younger.

12/15/64 (05049)

["It's all a matter of communication!" . . .] †

"It's all a matter of communication!" the man emphatically stated, as though he had just created a new formula.

"Yes, but why is it that the level on which people operate is so strikingly different — I mean, the manner in which they all think about the same basic questions?"

"Now, that I can't tell you, but that all people are constituents of the same dog-tired species is an ineluctable certainty."

A woman's body and a child's mind —
       how to bring the disparity into a tighter concord!
The child is father of the man,
       is mother of the woman

Why do people have to think too much?

People: the sharpie, who is playboyshrewd, to whom nothing is quite cool enough or suave enough;
      long, straight, blond

My mind is too loud to think

"Let's move in the right direction," the suave guy said to his business secretary as they finished eating a hurried dinner at Howard Johnson's.

I consider myself a man in the modern vein. You know, keeping up with progress and fast living. I can say that because I read Dr. Johnson and eat out at Howard Johnson's every night.
      I have no conscience, you see.

Write away, old boy. There ain't anybody goin' ter stop you, unless it be calumny or disappointment or heartbreak. But all that's OK if you can just make the sustained effort and know all the while that you're writing your guts into it; there lies the dignity, the honour. The purpose is secondary unless it be the sheer *catharsis*.

12/15?/64 — [1] (05193)

One Rain

If life be filled
    with the constant pain
Of childbirth
    and the fear we gain
As death struts,
    then let me choose fear
And constant pain.
    Grant me strength that staves
The dismal frowns,
    that sustains human cheer
In brief spots
    of love, beauty, and conclaves
Of one meeting one
    and smiling under one rain.

12/15?/64 — [2] (05024)

The Kiss

Two lips meet two, together, on a balmy night.
They cry but a short while, then sigh a solitary
breath of warmth and resolution. They smile
with voluntary understanding of what is in sight
just beyond reach, and their close communion
cancels the fear of frightening futurity.

12/15?/64 — [3] (05025)

Two Cast One Shadow

Bright sunlight beamed on a pair of people,
who stood as one on a solitary mound,
diffident in the sight of their sandy shadow.

"Two we are and always will be," said the
people, "but one in the shadow of loneliness
are we, sand-locked on this lonely beach.

"Not even the ocean, climbing its reaches
on tiny feet, can erase what we cast
on the sand, until we wander to new daytimes."

12/15?/64 — [4] (05029)

Dr. Johnson's Smile

Abandon yourself to commitment!
Deny the temptations of willed passivity!
Indifference is the source of self-pity
and the negation of willful, love-filled
compassion. Indifference resides in
the library or in front of the TV.
Commitment and total abandonment,
ineluctably chosen, are as difficult
as the task of Sisyphus, but they are
rewarded with an occasional smile.

[12/15/64]? (05027)

[And I am so tired, . . .]

I

    And I am so tired, and I am just so, so tired that all I can do is think.
I am thinking how difficult it is to act when all you can do is think, so
I am sitting at my typewriter and making words like a cook might sit
at her kitchen table and make, with variegated ingredients which she
has set out while the refrigerator is defrosting, any concoction that the
stuffs engender.
    I hear a Spanish verse ringing in my ears, and it is ringing, and it
is ringing louder and more vibrantly and incessantly, until I am
forced to put it down on this yellow paper, and now I am ready to
write it, or, rather, repeat it, since it was already written and com-
posed before me by Rubén Darío, and I am ready, and I am very tired,
but I want to type it:

       No hay dolor más grande que la vida. ◊

No, no, that's not it, but I am faltering, and the yellow hue of the paper is distorting my memory, and I am tired, but I want to try to write it again:

No hay dolor más grande que el dolor de ser vivo, ◊
Ni mayor pesadumbre que la vida consciente.

Yes, that's it, but what does it mean? Well, I think she could tell you, if you were to ask her in a soft tone.

But wait. Don't forget that cigarettes cause cancer, and that's a fact, because everybody who is anybody, and God knows that everybody is a somebody, at least in his or her own eyes, says that it's so. So I hereby resolve to smoke more and more, and my shibboleth will be: "Every day, in every way, I am growing more cancerous, until I become one mass of carcinoma, but that's OK, too, because I am going to save all of my pennies in my Kennedy Memorial savings bank (the one with the slot in the plastic head), and then I will be able to donate all my money to charity, with the hope that someday we will find a cure for cancer."

Tonight is Christmas-card-writing and -sending night, and so I will write all of the people whom I have forgotten to remember in the past, the forgetting of whom has caused me so much guilt that I have even, at times, forgotten to feel guilty. And I am very tired. I am as much more tired as it has taken me to write all of my thoughts since the first thing I remember having written tonight, which was something to the effect that I was tired. But I must write a little explanatory note on this Xmas card and say, "We wish you a merry Christmas and a happy Chanukah and a successful resurrection or insurrection or masturbation, if all else fails." Poor Zeno! Poor *Notes from the Underground*! Poor world that has to put up with all of the shame we throw on you and for the blame that we attribute to you! And thank you Stephen Crane for starting all that crap!

Burma-Shave when you are tired, because it is good for your nerve endings, and it was said of that woman that she had that golden touch because she used Midol when she felt tired and her stomach or head hurt her too much. But that guy or philosopher was wrong, because the Midol touch ain't golden, and, in fact, everything that it touches (the user or addict) turns to pill dust and shame and ignominy, and we call it the objective correlative of the ultimate absurdity, which is supernal pusillanimity. . . .

¿Qué es la vida? Un frenesí . . . ◊
una sombra, una ficción,
*

y el mayor bien es pequeño,
porque todo el mundo es loco.

But I am tired, and I have forgotten how those verses should be written. And yet she told me that I am speaking like a book that I would write but that I really don't understand her feelings, because I am too much one, and that one is myself, pure and simple. . . . Buckeye Jim, weave and spin, old boy, 'cause you just ain't got far to go. There you are, at the end of your rope, but some people say that it's precisely at this point that we should find you interesting, because we are going to watch you try to climb up that rope, but really we're hoping that you will fall off after dangling for a great, long millennium and drop into Charon's lap.

You really should get out and do something rather than spending all of your time thinking about yourself. Do you want to know what I always say? You don't? Well, I think I'll just tell you any old how. I always say that I ain't very interesting to myself whenever I find that I am becoming interested in myself. Remember that cigarettes kill, but then, so too do people. But guns don't kill. People do.

You talk like a book. Yes, thought and action, the favorite two antinomies, or opposites, or whatever the word is. They are equally inimical to any sense of stability because they are both extremes of the normal processes of functioning in an ordered milieu.

I am blind with total incomprehension, so I remember, now, having told her tonight, on the phone, that I was willing to quit because she was too strong for me, but I never even had time to tell her also that I loved her for what she could be, because who in the name of Saturn can say something like that — to say that you love a person for what they just may become — since there are no odds being given on the possibilities for betterment, especially when the bookie has run out of money or when the risk is obviously so great that it just ain't worth staking that money?

"Like a book you talk, and like a book, you will turn back to dust," said Ted the Termite, who was one of the original clan of wood eaters to infest the Cross of antiquity and the goal posts of the Browns-Giants championship game.

Did I ever tell you that I loved you? No? Well, it must have been an oversight or a slip-up on my part, because I know that I wanted to tell you so. Well, we'll try again tomorrow night by phone unless I decide to become sulky and fail to even try to understand that you are a human being and not an inhuman toy. And I am very tired now, so I think that I will just drop my hulk into bed now and hope that I have a nightmare, because it may afford relief.

II

Typewriter, typewriter, on the table, who's the fairest on the table? No! No, that's not it either, but I am just beginning, and I may be a little cold, so be patient and give me a little time. Typewriter, typewriter, on the table, who's the fairest in the stable? I'll answer that as subtly as possible by saying that it is the Houyhnhnm horse, of course. Why, any little Gulliver should know that, if only he has studied his *McGuffey's Reader* with some diligence.

Tonight will be a long night for me because I have had enough coffee to kill an H. H. Richardson, who, in fact, did die from drinking twenty cups of coffee a day. But what the hell! He did create some of the most influential Marshall Field warehouses in the last century. But I don't want to die from coffee. It's just too inglorious. In fact, I'm not so sure at this point that I am willing to die at all — or ever, for that matter.

"The plague is here to stay," he said. Who said that, do you ask? Well, I will tell you. His name was Dr. Bernard Rieux, and he won a Nobel Prize for saying that. The moral to this morality play is that this man became a hero even though he merely wanted to Ben Casey people.

Coffee, coffee, everywhere, but not a drop to drink, unless you are willing to allow yourself the possibilities of the Ancient Coleridge, which I personally am not, because he was supposed to be a romantic. Today I decided that people collectively are worth it but that the individual doesn't quite make it. Not bad for a grand inquisitor, wouldn't you say? But I doubt that she would agree with me if she could hear my inane dribbling, because she feels that you can know the whole world in the mind and thoughts and behavior of one solitary individual. So where does that get you? Who knows!

Once again, I am sitting here, hidden away in my little Proustian study, and I am envious because I can't afford to buy any cork to line my walls. I have to settle for bookshelves filled with scores of books that I have read and forgotten or have remembered, and their titles stare at me from all angles like apocalyptic eyeballs that shout at me or lie dormant, and I am hoping that someday, right in the very confines of my little study, I will be able to witness a second coming of the Battle of the Books, so that I can write it up for *Ladies' Home Journal* or for some future Swift devotee. Who knows — I may even be another Swift if I'm not careful. Reincarnation isn't just a lot of hocus-pocus, as Houdini or Lydia Pinkham might say. Indeed not. It is a qualified fact that in India the dead are cremated and then their ashes are dumped into the Ganges for the washerwomen to use in place of soap flakes and for the bathers to wash with or drink.

"Would you like to see a menu, sir?"

"Yes, er, no, I will order immediately. But do tell me, young man, what is the soup du jour?"

"Split coffee bean with Ganges ashes is our specialty, and we stand behind it with a full, one-year or twelve-thousand-mile warranty on any defective livers or spleens or kidneys."

"Well, it sounds like just the thing for my designs on immortality. Let me have two schooners. And for the main course, I think I will have your number three."

"That's the Fatherhash, the Suntan lotion with Ghost gravy, is it not?"

"Yes, that's correct, and for dessert I will have three cigarettes and a finger bowl of coffee, Ganges style."

"I'm not sure, sir, but I would say that you have Ganges on your mind."

Well, that was dinner, and I ate alone, because that's the only way to eat if you don't feel that you have the energy to make conversation with anyone else but yourself. So I came home tonight, and the moon was a perfect wheel of cold light, and I stood outside and froze myself, but who can regain that moment of splendor in the sky, especially when you are high on coffee, or glory in the flower bed when you are pissing on it? You just can't bring back that hour, because it is already history the moment you take the time to contemplate it, since, by doing that, you must necessarily force a new moment into existence.

I never want to die, but the way I smoke and piss in other people's flower beds while reciting Wordsworth in distorted moments of tranquillity or Coleridgian willing suspensions of disbelief is a real gas, and it must be hurrying the time toward the inevitable, but it is a scientific fact that all men, for all times, have had to piss and recite poetry at the same time, because it is somehow synesthetically pleasing. It is like sneezing and coughing simultaneously. Only, it's no good if the moon is in full bloom and watching you do it, because the light makes a pissy reflection, and so you become self-conscious. I swear that a guy just can't do anything anymore without some-one else watching and reporting his every action, even if it is nothing more than the banal function of eliminating himself of some terrible draught of Ganges coffee which still has bits of fired people floating in it, which the waiter naively mistakes for coffee beans. But I will be reincarnated if I be sure to drink enough of it, the Ganges coffee, every day. You know what the good doctor always says: "A cup of coffee every day keeps the spirits away."

I talked with a criminal, the other day, who was in the midst of eating his final dinner, which I told him didn't remind me so much of the Last Supper as it did a Tom Jones Barmecide feast. I hated to tell him that, simply because I wasn't sure that he had ever heard of Hank Fielding. But I did, and then I had the shock of my life when I learned that this man's name was Meursault. His last words were a bit confusing to me, although now I am sure that they were pregnant with philosophic content. He said to me that he was going to be electrocuted the following morning and that he was excited because he had succeeded in fooling all of the prison officials. He said that they didn't know it but that he, the criminal, had received his M.B.A. degree from an accredited business school, whose motto had been "Live better for less. Live electrically." He confided to me, that night, that from the day of his graduation, he had determined to take that motto for his own personal symbol of success and that, in the morning, he would finally consummate his lifelong desire. He said that immortality could be bought for virtually nothing and that he would indeed live better for less because he was going to die electrically. At the time, I must confess, I found this concept a little disturbing, but on pondering it, I have come to the conclusion that he may have some reason. You may rest assured that this is a provocative theory and one which philosophers have, to date, disregarded.

I am writing now, and I feel completely in control of all my material, so I have decided that it is a fitting moment that I give praise to Momus and Epicurus and Henry Miller by praying. Let me state, somewhat blackfacedly, that "you ain't heard nothin' yet."

"Praise the Father and the Son-of-a-bitch and the Holy Ghost of Hamlet, who live in the proverbial world without end. May idolatry not blind the eye nor slavery be a perpetual source of strife. Amen. May the darkling thrush and the windhover and the Emperor of Ice-Cream and the bourgeois poet show in the Messiah, in whose image all was created and all will eventually be destroyed if we fail to recognize the reality of our own individual duty, which is, above all, duty to ourselves. Amen."

No, that's not right! In fact, I'm not so sure that this is even an accepted form of prayer. I will try a different tack. "May the words of my mouth and the meditations of my heart be acceptable unto Thee, O Momus, and may I live with a contrite heart and a supernal spirit of the movement of all things in nature, and may I be something evermore about to be." But this kind of prayer is no good either, because it is replete with vanity, and we all know what Dr. Johnson would say about that if he could ramble on with his idling adventurers. But, then again, who would deny that the good doc was a licentious,

salacious, nasty old man? Yes, he was a living paradox, and the most
suitable apothegm for him would have to be either "Live better for
less. Live electrically" or, more appropriately, "Do as I say and *not*
as I do," for if we did as he did, we would all end up prodigal sons-
of-bitches.

Mirror, mirror, on the wall,
Who's the greatest fop of all?
Why, who if not Sir Percival?

Mirror, mirror, on the sink,
Who, indeed, is the greatest fink,
Edna Ferber or her Jett Rink?

For the answers to these and other pressing questions, it is neces-
sary to ask this final question. But now I will just say that "I bare
asshole Mary. She'll toilet to us." At this point, I fear that I had better
drop this song of the eliphop and the Nash telefong, unless I decide to
moralize tonight. But is it not true that moralizing is like building
edifices in the air? That is to say that it is all full of vapours and hot
air. Wasn't it Swift who created the germane syllogism that goes
something like this: "Knowledge is words, and words are air; ergo,
knowledge is air, and hot air at that"?

But I have failed so far in my typing to mention her whom I have
as a constant companion. Her name is not important, but there is one
fact that should be mentioned if one is to form a veridical opinion of
this Dorotea of my wanderings. Let it hereby be proclaimed for the
records of the *Domesday Book* that she paints and writes occasionally
and thinks a great deal but that she does all of this in the nude. That is,
if I may qualify my statement a bit, she does all of this in the nude ex-
cept for the boots she wears. She is beautiful, abstracted, sensual, sen-
sitive, and always nude in my mind, even if she goes out to dinner or
breakfast with me to the nearest Howard Johnson Restaurant. Now
I've done it. I've given us away. Well, I won't deny it. We do, in fact,
go to Howard Johnson's to eat all the time. But I enjoy it because I am
good friends with the manager's son, and it is perfectly all right with
him if I bring her along with me in the nude, because, to tell you the
truth, he likes to see her just as much as I do. I am very proud of this
girlfriend of mine.

I'm not real sure yet, but I have a funny feeling that my girl is a little
strange, only because today, for an example, it was five degrees above
zero, and yet she insisted that it was not too cold for her to brave the
elements in the nude. In fact, she confided to me before we entered the
restaurant that she had just added another quart of antifreeze to her

vagina and lower parts to ensure smooth operation.

Since I have retreated this far with my admissions, I must also confess that, two days ago, I decided to adopt her. I took out the papers and checked over her pedigree and was surprised to find that she was from a prize stock and that she had never placed lower than second in any contest, even though she was invariably considered to be the underdog. But that being inconsequential to me, since I was only concerned with her performance in cold weather, I decided to adopt her, and I did just that. The ceremony took twenty-eight seconds, the fastest recorded in White Cross, and the vet said, "Do you take this girl to be your lawfully adopted mistress?" And I said, "Certainly, but of course." And he said, "Well, then, I do — I mean, you do, and that is that. Next. . . . Next. . . . Hey, you there, I said 'next.' C'mon, I ain't got all day."

Well, there was a reason for taking her out to Howard Johnson's this morning for breakfast. What I had failed to do was to give her the nightly care package that I had become accustomed to providing since the adoption. It was Sunday, and all the churchgoing ladies and the sodality members were decked out in their Sunday-go-to-meetin' garbs, and they were walking up and down the aisles when we came in. And then I noticed that all of the ladies sat down, and there was a lull, when the head waitress, whom I called by name, which was "Virginia," approached with a slight blush and proceeded to escort us hurriedly to a seat near the very back of the large dining room. She always dreaded when I came in with my girl for fear of what her appearance would do to the rest of the clientele, but she had strict orders from the manager's son not only to seat us but to buzz him on the intercom when we arrived, for the truth was, the son of the owner was always downstairs counting heads of lettuce or sorting french-fried clams, which invariably got mixed into the peeled-potato bins and the scallop boxes.

Virginia smiled at me, but I could see the scowl that she gave to my girl, and I heard her murmur under her breath as we passed toward the table in the rear, "A bird in the hand is worth two in the french-fried briar patch." I thought this a bit strange at first, and my reaction was similar to that which I had felt on hearing the criminal philosophize about living electrically last week. My first thought was that Virginia hadn't had much schooling, because anyone knows from sheer common knowledge that a bird in the hand is surely worth more than two in the french-fried briar patch. And, furthermore, I deemed it fatuous in light of the fact that briar patches are loaded with rabbits but that rabbits refuse to run, preferring to hold close in weather as cold as this was. I said to Virginia that her comment, which she was shocked that I had heard, was incorrect and that if she didn't have anything nice to say, the least she could do would be to try to be more judicious about using her aphorisms. Elaborately quoting from Sancho Panza, I cited to her that the correct analogue to her phrase was "A bird in the branch is worth two hands in the bush" or that which, coming from the German, through Shelley, states somewhat similarly, "A skylark in the bush is worth two clams in the broiler." In fact, I even carried this maxim to its ultimate by quoting from Wordsworth, saying that "a cuckoo in the briar patch is worth two splendors in the grass, and we are seven glories in the womb." She was quite embarrassed and apologized with profuse remorse for having even thought that my girl was in any way in league or was suspect.

I love my girl, and she loves me, as the old "Bony Moronie" song goes. But Buckeye Jim must still weave and spin and see the blue jay light in the eye of a spoon located somewhere in the vicinity of the moon. So you just go nude, gal, and all the power and the glory and the kingdom, forever and evermore, to you. You got what it takes, gal. Yeah, you got the guts, and you just stick to your guns.

So this is what I have to say about my girl. She is lovely and smooth and nude, like innocence itself, and her beauty is enhanced by the little tan boots that she wears.

> Coffee, coffee, everywhere,
> and good to the very last drop.

My fingers are tired from thinking so hard on the typewriter keys, but my mind is all coffee, and so I have miles to go before I sleep. But wait . . . hey, you out there . . . say, who the hell is that pissing in my flower bed? You get out of there at once. That's not your property, and who the hell do you think you are, just up and pissing in someone else's private flower garden? . . . Say, that's strange. That's my memory of an hour ago. I guess it got pissed off sitting here on my head while I have been telling all of its secrets.

Well, all I've got to say to that old memory of mine is that sometimes it gets a little cocky, with all of its sophisticated knowledge, and decides to take me over. But, no sir! I'm too strong-willed to allow that. So I am yelling to it now, and I am saying, warning, "You come back in here this minute, or I will see to it that I forget to bring you along with me tomorrow. Then where will you be? I will be out doing all those things, and when I return home tomorrow night to my typewriter, to transpose, you will just sit there, dumbfounded, and will want to know what I did. So, mind, either you get in here quick and quit pissing on my flower bed, or I will obliterate you."

* * *

As it happened, my memory heard me and was floating back into my study through the window that I opened only slightly, since the cold air was a gas to my system, when sleep began to overtake it. I could see sleep coming after it like the sharks that were after Hemingway's stupid sardine or minnow, which he had tied to the side of his last book, and I reckoned that it would be close. My memory got itself almost all the way under the window, when sleep grabbed at its hind extremity, which was continuity and consistency, and took a painful nip from it. Memory limped up to my head and then hid itself under my right eyelid. But I could sense that it would have to retire in shame for the night. I could feel it penetrating my retina and then the optic chiasma, and then I knew that the great god coffee was beginning to dissolve into tiny particles of immortality and Ganges dust-ash again, and so I vowed that before my fingers would give out on the typing machine, I would call a halt to my efforts for the night. The fact was that I never wanted to allow my memory to retire knowing that it had got the upper head on me.

I decided to make one final prayer, since all else had failed me when I tried to meditate before. I began by saying poetically:

> If I should die before I wake,
> I pray my girl, the criminal,
> and Ganges ashes would not forsake
> my organs and their seminal
> fluids and the french-fried clambake
> of Howard Johnson's subliminal
> soul for carry-out. What a mistake! Amen.

> * * *

> God bless the criminal, my girl,
> Memory, Momus, Epicurus, Shelley,
> The manager's son, Wotton, Bentley,
> Coffee, Ganges ashes, immortality.

> God forsake sleep, french-fried clams,
> Birds, cuckoos, skylarks, Meursaults,
> Pissing in other people's flower beds,
> Virginia, Sancho Panza, apothegms.

> God bless nudity and little tan boots,
> Living better for less, electricity,
> Adoptions, antifreeze, Uncle J. Swift,
> Henry Miller, Dorotea, Al Jolson's mammy.

God forsake Sir Percival, fops, finks,
Mirrors on the walls and in the sinks,
Dr. Johnson, Hemingway, mortality,
Shark-bit do-it-yourself kits, sardines.

12/17–18/64 — [2] on 12/18 (05192)

[There are times when I . . .]

There are times when I disappoint myself so much that my only recourse flows into tears that get pillow-confounded.

I cried last night for a year and a half's worth of slow, diffusive disappointment. It was awful to look out of my thickly coated brain-cell and know that I had been denigrating another human being by not allowing her one basic emotion, that of fear, which derives from the uncertainty of a plan or aspiration or Ibsen life-lie. The net result is always the same:

one human repressing the processes of tremulation and trepidation in another to such a profound degree that the one can say to the other, "But you're talking to me like you were writing a book. And I'm not a book into which you can conscript some ideas and have a beginning and an ending which is conclusive. I can't just stop — can't just do what you say, what you tell me — because it's just not that easy."

I must wait, because I believe in myself, though at the same time I fear what the indefiniteness and uncertainty of the future may do to me — the disappointment and then the letdown and, with it, the loss of incentive or ambition and then, finally, the relapse into that semi-mobile condition of depressive indolence, in which the aspect of this suburb will begin to modify and change in my dreams from a set of preplanned structures into an anthropomorphic maze of living organisms, at once constricting and enlarging, until their stultification becomes suffocating.

And then where will I go?

I disappoint myself more than is imaginable, because I have failed to recognize and accept the fact that another not only has emotions and passions and ambitions all her own, which are distinct from mine and equally as real, but also I have failed to sympathize, to feel the kind of compassion whose end result is positive and effectual rather than negative, anathematic, and deleterious to the ongoing processes of hope and promise and the possibility of betterment.

12/17?/64 (05190)

[She thinks now, cowers benignly] †

She thinks now, cowers benignly
from her own aspect in the mirror.

The forest is a darkling creature,
featureless in spots, replete at times
with ambiguities, so often the teacher

of silence, the opprobrium of crimes
committed without violence, without feature,
even without the knowledge

I try with all my imagination to write a poem, but I know
that both trying and writing don't exist when the spirit of creativity
doesn't take complete control over the mind that conjures and the hand
that moves the pen across the white page.
To think is chief, but to act is vital:
the act of writing is the consummation of thoughtful expression.

Mankind is continually plagued by the community of the individual mind in conflict with itself and with the community of minds both present and past. It is man's duty to respond to the tyrannies of the mind, individually, for the amelioration of the collective ongoing spirit.

12/18/64 — [1] (05191)

[The hectic hours of romance grow] †

The hectic hours of romance grow
few and remote, with selection slow
*

and slow-lingering confidences
of what two can make of singularity

To respond slow and moderately to early infatuation is to ensure
enduring respect and lingering early

"What man has made of man" is a favorite aphorism, lifted
from Wordsworthian context, to denote the paradoxical anomalies
and inim

Books and experience and imagination render art, which is a
transmuted and transvalued composite of these three funds of know-
ledge.

To strive to converse with people is to learn to live with yourself.

12/18–23?/64 (05188)

[Tonight I watched the whole world . . .]

Tonight I watched the whole world fall in love, and it was a beau-
tiful sight. It happened about five magnitudes past the moon, at the
latitude of five minutes and ten hours warmer than warmth itself.
She was magnificent, perceptive, gentle, smooth, and loving, and she
embraced me while I cried from a subtle fear that sometimes, when I
least expect it and when I know least how to cope with it, descends
over my head, so that the sensation is like a shower room, which is
my brain, when it is turned on and all the separate nozzles are firing
streams of penetrant water; only, the water breaks down into the con-
stituents of fear and uncertainty and doubt and inferiority.
She hugged me until I thought the skin on my back would part
like the waters that Moses affected and all of my spine would show
through. Only, it didn't happen, and throughout the night, I could
sense her maternal, soothing affections healing my heart-scars. "I
love you," my soul said to her, and she replied warmly, "I love you,
too," and I thought that, for the first time in the whole world, all was
loving and gentleness and God-like. I felt like I could point my finger
and invoke any fiat, and so I thought to myself that if I could have one
wish granted to me, it would be to take her away and adopt her and
have a child with her, whom we would just have to call Liza. I told her
that I never wanted to do the normal kind of work that people do, since

writing was the most noble occupation I could imagine, and she just smiled, and I knew that this was an affirmation so strong and so reassuring that never would I have to worry about the tremendous courage that this desire needed. She would always be there to reaffirm it for me and for herself.

So I just smoked and smoked and forgot to think about all that had previously troubled me. And I smoked until I even enjoyed it, and we sat together at the breakfast-room table and talked, and I told her that I loved her more than the night loves God.

"But you aren't sure about me, are you?" she stated. "You just aren't completely sure yet!" "But I want to feel it more than I can even say."

The night is very warm, and all within its limitless boundaries is love and wonder and novelty and warmth, and so I think, as I type, how many loving things there are to be loved in the world, which is the limit of one's lifetime, and I say to myself, promising, "I will love all the creatures of the earth and all of the people who walk their time with love and hope and pity and charity and compassion for all like themselves." I say this because I am beginning to realize that there just isn't enough time for a solitary individual to try to exist by hiding within himself and pitying only himself and crying when things seem to converge on him all at once. No, there just isn't any time for that kind of thing, because there are too many people that deserve my love and benevolence, and I figure that I can credit all of them by giving all of myself to her.

The night's warmth is very pleasing, and I am reminded of some Florida beach in the spring; only, she says that the night smells like the odour that comes to the senses when one crawls under a log, in a forest, that is covered all over with moss and lichen. I say to myself that this is also true and that I love her for her sensitivity and her gentleness.

Tonight she is a metaphor of everything that is good and simple and honest in the world. Where, in a moment of despair, I saw not even her face, I now can feel her eyes on my tear-stained cheeks, and I can see them smiling without even looking into them.

12/23/64 (05194)

[How much easier it would be . . .]

How much easier it would be just to be able to go to bed right now instead of trying to say in words what I feel about the progress of my first love. I remember saying the other night to her that I had been thinking about how I would feel if she were to die accidentally. Her response was that I should feel even more strongly about loving another person later on. My feeling was that there would always remain a certain vacuity, which I would never be able to fill again no matter how much effort I would make, and that the result would be a slow and gradual declining of my desire to continue living.

Tonight I read a review by Volpe on Faulkner's *The Wild Palms*, in which he developed the thesis of romanticism in "Wild Palms" on the part of Harry Wilbourne and Charlotte Rittenmeyer, and I was affected by what he said, because I love that story more than any other one I have ever read. It is very moving to me, and its themes are those which I will include in my second book this coming summer.

She is my turtle, and I love her more than I have ever loved anyone before. She sees through me, through my intervals of low sentiments and cynicism, and I know that she makes me realize that there is just too much worth struggling for in the world to allow myself the comforts of painful self-pity. That I can give her all that is myself is my one great aspiration, and for this I have determined to make a prayer every night before I fall asleep. Tonight I will hope for her well-being and will pray that she can become the mother of my children, because she is so beautifully human.

Why did you ask me a question like that? I mean, how could you ask me what I thought you had done in the past that was bad? There is little doubt in my mind that she, you, have a feeling of guilt and that you are worried about what I am thinking behind your back. Do you ask me this question because you love me so much that you have to know, or are you simply trying to satisfy your ego? I choose to accept the former, and to it I will reply that I do think you have done some things that disappoint me, but that they are bad I will never believe. Rather, I choose to think that they were all mere trials or attempts to satisfy what is in your heart, to give yourself to the right person with all that is you. Disappointment I do feel, although even this is dissolving as our days together increase.

As I sit here at my typewriter, I can't help remembering the afternoon we went together to the laundromat and then to cut pine twigs for Christmas decorations. It is a day that sticks with me because you were so simple and natural and totally unassuming and energetic.

I want to write more and more, but your sheer absence hurts me at this moment, and I feel that if I go to bed right now, I will be able to make that prayer for you, and this will be enough in itself to assure me a sound night's sleep. I love you, love you, love, with all of my spirit, and I hope that you are thinking the same thing right now, hoping that

as I write this, you are seeing me sitting here typing and hearing my
thoughts as I put them down in random fashion on this paper. I love
you, love you, love, and I shall always respect you, whether you re-
main with me or not.

Goodnight, dearest Suzan, and may God bless you.

12/26/64 (05195)

[During the refrigerated nighttime,] †

During the refrigerated nighttime,
ice and frost grew up like grass
on everything — windows

[illegible notes, ed.]

The leaky stream screams creek-
bound in its rushthrobbing tricklebeds,
forcing over canoes, canisters, carrying cargoes
and shedpeople finning

Without love, there is only
indifference, unless allowing for
the love of the self, which is
equally endemic and *narcissistic*

Don't ever save the best for last,
because the worst may be so
consuming that the mind may not
have room to enjoy the *"carpe
diem"*s of philosophy and Voltaire,
Adam Smith, or you, too, *Magoo*!

Fee-fi-fo-fum! I want the
blood of Bellum Legosum in the
cabinet of Dr. Caligari.
Live better for less; get
electrocuted, you bum.

We want to sell you a car;
buy today, pay tomorrow and
tomorrow and tomorrow, etc.

A new year is on us, and I
have preempted it with a resolution
for an evening prayer each night
antes de dreamsville; it feels
so good.
    Hemingwaves said of religion
that it is that which makes one
feel better afterward.
    My prayer calms me and
prepares me for the next day.

    There is something about love
that is imperfect (I think they
call it the prospect of death),
but into the eye of the hurricane
two lovers must thrust themselves.
To anticipate a thing is to
preempt vulnerability and the
possibility of ensuing disappointment.
    But, no matter, a person must
set his mark and pursue it
with definition and total absorption
(there just ain't no room for
vacillation), *total commitment tacitly
pursued.*
    "I want someone to really
listen to me, to hear my feelings
in the eye of their soul.
    "I want some one person to
mold me in his bare hands so
that I can let go a little more
each day and be completely confident
that I am being loved for myself
only, not for what I just may
become.

"I want to lie down in the
earth and smell its thick smells
and mingle my own with its
sweet, lush perfumes. I want
to roll and turn on my side and
look up at the blueness of the
sky and hear it tell me that
I am beautiful because I am
stained by the earth."

Christopher Paradise could hear
Hunter's thoughts, so far away, and
he smiled with passionate uncertainty,
he unsure that he would ever see
her, even though he had carefully
mapped out his destination.

There is more to be seen in a
person's eyes than all the books
in the world can ever illuminate.
    Eyes grey-blue like mine are hers,
      lively, facile, lucid, and redolent,
sometimes recondite and abstracted
  but usually energetic and quick
and bright and all-knowing in
their limited scope.

    "It may just be that I don't
intend you to know all that I
am thinking all the time. That's
my only defense right now. What
else do I have left? I have
tried to build my dam from the
stems of being hurt, knowing that
there will always be a little water
seeping through the construction —
I mean, the occasional lapses in
which I will necessarily seem
way away for a time — but this
is inevitable, and you will just
have to accept this if you mean
*

to try to understand and accept me
for what I am, because by accept-
ing me now, you have to take
all that has happened to me before
you. Yes, that's all thrown into
the bargain, and you will have to
look at it, sift it, and decide for
yourself whether or not I'm worth it."

    "But I already have decided,
and I love you for what you
are, not for what you can be
even, because I am just
leaving that up to the futurity
of you and me together.
Anticipation never works by
itself."

12/27/64 (05196)

Rain Is a Pretty Sign

Warm rain is a pretty sign in life.
It is a time to lie down in the earth
And feel the growth of things, the wet birth
Of muddy springs, and innocence without strife.

Blue rain traces its source to the mind
Of a child. It is the poet of youth, who breathes
Moist syllables, like soft-mothering harmonies,
Into wide-eyed ears that are naturally inclined.

Cold rain blown on panes of window glass
Cleanses pent-up feelings. It brings together
Rhythms of love and hope with gloomy weather,
Like dream bubbles melting summering grass.

Grey rain is the companion of old age.
It weaves forgotten sighs of a coloured past,
Like beads thrown upon a pond that cast
Opening ringlets on life's equipage.

12/28/64 — [1] & 1/29/65 — [1] (05050)

Reverie of an Ozark Hunter

I travel the world's roads,
Loading my grips with expectation
And curiosity. The world is all mine
For the mere price of ambition
And desire.

People are my guests,
And my love is their welcome mat.
I fill them with my tall stories and jokes,
And we always listen to each other,
Eating together from the same board,
Sleeping together on the selfsame pallet
Of nightfall, dreaming the dreams of Lennie
And George and Pablo.

I open my travelling bag, scattering
The contents of my life
Beside my tattered bedroll:
A small, silver turtle neckpiece,
A cellophane bag stuffed with dollar bills,
One tooth-decayed comb, a rusty razor blade,
Two tiny agates from Lake Superior,
A pair of unmatched athletic socks, and a
Blue-black, buffalo-checked lumber jacket
For the cold.

Now I am falling asleep, fast and
Neatly snuggling into the warmth
Of a goose-feather quilt, and I muse
On my life.

Never have I been lonely, although
My journeys have carried me along one
Lonewinding road thirty-six years
Long. Love has been my companion and guide.
It has provided me with sight and hearing
And smell. It is the strength that always
Encourages me to shy from dead ends, from
Sidetracks. I sleep sound.

Now I awaken with the early morning dust
Of sunrise, which insinuates my body with
Red breeze and sprinkles my yawns and my
*

Sighs with cedarwhispers and lifebreath.
I stretch, gathering twigs and pine
Needles and birch bark from my coffee-and-
Roll fire bed.

I hear the sounds of birds moving air.
I see them encircling cloud drifts
With fluttering wing antics, while
The songs they make linger and then
Dissolve into the brim of my tin coffee
Cup. And I drink their hot draught, smiling,
My head thrown back into the laughing sky
Above my night plot.

I am off again, closehugging the roads
And familiar, unfamiliar creek beds, ravines,
And hillocks, toward any destination
That will accept me and my few cherished
Belongings.

I feel very big, like Johnny Appleseed
Or Gulliver or Paul Bunyan. I feel good
And slightly handsome, with my face dried
And ruddyparched from the night chill and
From the warmth of every new day dawned
On my body.

"You are with me," I hear myself thinking.
"I see you there, through the window
Of my swelling happiness, and even though
You are a princess, pure and simple, to me
You are pride and precious ritual, growth
And love everlasting and strong-willed. You
Are faith in the face of grief and fear.
You are encouragement when disappointment
And indecision intrude upon my mind.

"It is you alone who gives me the desire
To continue looking all people in the eye,
To never desist from the pleasures
Of seeking love in the heart and on the
Tongue of my weariest foe. For you are
The princess of peace, and from you
I have learned that what once was
Will always be possible, evermore and
*

Again, if man will only teach himself
That certain things never die, whether
They fade or not.

"Was it you who said that memories
Can never be changed, that they can
Only dissolve into forgetfulness?
To this I affirm that only a part
Will dissolve or alter itself, the part
That was never meant to last anyway."

I have spent this short, yellow day
Walking on thoughts and seeing in all
People and trees and skies your thoughts,
Your eyes, your reminders of the little
Things. I have seen love in everyone's
Eyes, and I am satisfied and ready once more
For my ground bed, prepared for my
Nightly coffee and prayer:

God bless you, princess of peace.
God bless you with love and respect
And the faith that looks through
Death. When I awake again in the morning
From my ground spot, may I be
Stained with your image. God bless you!

12/28/64 — [2] (05051)

[I think you are going too fast for me.] †

I think you are going too fast for me.

Like a leaf in the rain,
I'm beginning to feel the pain

I love my father so much that I just want to be good and respon-
sible for living in his image, no matter how difficult I may find the
way.

I need to respond to the requests of all people who feel the con-
fidence in me or the futile necessity within their own minds that makes
the asking of me so vital.

I must pray at night, every night, faithfully, to Him who will always
listen to me, who will heed my wishes and blessings for those for
whom I care relentlessly.

God bless you all.

To love others demands a reorientation and alterdirection of self-
love or preoccupation with the self, at least.

To love beyond recognition of self is ultimate sacrifice, and its
rewards are recompense enough from life, if recompense be required
in the first place.

A new year is about to reveal itself like birth itself, and with it
I must move and progress, so that from it I can derive happiness or
that state of mind which is filled with equipoise and stability, that
I may learn to look all persons in the eye and see there, in the glints
of light, a certain sensitivity and love and tolerance and acceptance
of that leveling factor which leaves all people as one great and re-
spectable giant of a person, an individual of a worldpeople, the pos-
sibilities for whom are irrefutably great and extensive and indom-
itable.

To love as prime and then to fear, if fear need be, but to love, for
then alone will fear be mediated and assuaged.

To love

To love, not physically as prime, but to love with elemental re-
spect for him or her who looks you directly in the eye, who speaks the
language of all men, which is the accreted language of confidence,
pride, fear, inferiority, happiness, innocence, concern, disillusion-
ment, the concomitants of mercy and pity and compassion and the
wisdom engendered from the chaos of insufferable circumstances
and incredible and irrevocable human shortcomings and final blun-
ders.

Poetry and art alike result from a state of the mind at once ambiva-
lent and in fluxed groping, not rebellion as such but rather the search
for redemption.

So this is what I feel today, and I feel good and big and outgoing,
though I need to seek refuge from myself in sleep, the supreme leveler
that unites all mankind in a common need (Dr. Johnson). I will take

love-filled thoughts and aspirations to bed with me this afternoon and hope to awake stained with its epiphanic luminosity, so that my whole soul and mind will glow bright jade green and turtle silver with certain warmth and pulsation.

Good afternoon to you, untelephoned Suzan. God bless you always.
                              L.D.

Now you're gonna smile,
                    warmly and softly.
Who am I to say,
                    "No, oh, not now"?
Soon there'll come a day,
Wet and warm and

Love is a gentle thing
that hangs in the wind,
that is buffeted with each new gale,
bringing with it

Absentminded me, absentminded
you; I have lost our love
somewhere and can't find it now

My tiny little world is big-bursting
with new things,

Where is the wind I hear
whispering through the clearing?
Is it in my ears or merely
somewhere beyond and nearing
our home like the reindeer
of Santa Claus, homing with cheer
and tidings of happiness this year?

Through the door slats it horns
its call, coolcold and mourning
the loss of its night mother

Fog-bound, rain-rent, nighting Hyde Park,
mantled with quietude, bent by sounds dark
and deep;
bench-worn, people-passed, lighting Hyde Park,
seen from Charing Cross, steepled by a lark
treetop tall.

Take off my smile and hang
it up in your closet without the pangs

Two smiles do you wear,
sharing your sure warmth
with me and your mother tonight.

From the tight, clear window
of your house you gaze, seeing
the wind winnow streetlights.

A big sleep slithers to rest
in my mind, suggesting calm
and warmly common silence

12/29? & 12/30/64 (05197)

Circus Glimpse

The cakewalk rider rode a high-faced
strutter. Through the circus ring he paced.
The tightrope walker mounted lightly his
high wire. Over the audience's fear he raced
like the left-moving letters of a typewriter,
chased by the finger-forced keys behind them.

12?/64 — [1] (05030)

One Moment Forever

The quietest time in the day is thought.
Life's periods of quietude and calm descend
in a moment of love, monumentally sought.

12?/64 — [2] (05170)

Nocturne III: The Absent Need

I feel your absence even when
We are together, fear your nearness
Then, because I fear myself, fear
What one may do to two together.

I need your presence more than
Togetherness can ever know
At any single spot of time, at
Any solitary moment of experience.

I fear what love so naked and
Thought so soft may do to two
Who passion and desire to be
Completely alone in complete oneness.

.I feel awkward with the fear
Of losing the two-toned testimony
Of our one witness, love, which
I feel needing, needing you now.

12?/64 (05032)

Prelude

A dream, a sigh, a silvery glow
had he who stood bereft in the snow,
which drifted loose above him and below.

A vision, epiphany, a solitary aspect
of union had he who sought sublime respect
for things that were for him to inspect.

A love, a wholeness, one firm affirmation
had he of concord and chaotic inclination,
which were fostered by beauty's tremulation.

12?/64   (05028)

Strangers Beneath the Sky

The contraband pageant of nightfall
Carries cargoes from Clandestination
To Solitude with its spurious drifts,
And we revel, and we wonder; we revel
In its unfathomable clarity, and we
Wonder about its power to expose us,
Naked and soft, to melt our features.

Silently we search the moon's indices,
And we linger, strangers made stronger
In spirit because we wait willingly and
Naked and wise without wisdom for some sign
Of recognition. We wait, wanting and weak,
Seeking the soft, mild innocence of birth
That will be ours someday if we hurry, waiting.

We stand, two alone, together with all former
Eyes that have stood as we stand, watching
What we now feel in the distant nearness
Of the lingering light-year's lambency,
And we ask, "Immortal moon, why do you chortle
Tonight, seeing the callous cow jump over you?"

12?/64   (05034)

[Christmas has a special silence]

Christmas has a special silence
for very special people.
All who live in fear of violence
worship at its steeple,

a Wisconsin tree, with Venice
display of ornaments and
children wild with joy;
mother and father;

special gifts in special
wrappings; ornaments aglow;
a hallway lighted up with joy,
like the moon on new-fallen snow.

12?/64 (05110)

[Hard times, hard times, and I'm a-fellin' low dis day.] †

Hard times, hard times, and I'm a-fellin' low dis day.
Been down to da

The women come and go, listening to Leadbelly's groaning ban-
jo with ears attentive and blunt with whiskey sours and stingers and
martini highballs, while their husbands or boyfriends or pimps keep
time with facial expressions and toe-tapping feet and free change
tipped on the small coffee

12?/64 (03629)

Whore

Naked like new-blown glass
shaped with Venetian tubes,
sacred as St. Sophia's quietude,
Jan Fontana wore sculptured cheeks
through penurious streets.
She was a Byzantine conquest,
who won her independence
from the unprecedented guilt
of noble descendancy.

[12/64 – 1/65]? (05106)

[Tonight is a balmy, . . .]

Tonight is a balmy, Floridian reminiscence in my ears and to my taste, and I can hear it calling to me from the past recesses of all the pleasant experiences I have enjoyed. It is warm and mild and goes contrary to man's sense of the nature of things. We say that this night's warmth is exciting and sensual and thick instead of being blistering cold and icy white as it is supposed to be. But then, who is to dictate to the nature of things and the uncertainty of ever-present phases?

I lift another cigarette from its pack and place it in my tight-drawn lips and light it until there is a faint red glow. It tastes good, but then, so do all the rest of them when they have become a habit, at once automatic, reflexive, and necessary.

The night, with its colorless night-sounds of windlicked oaks and spruce and walnut and elm, drifts into my tiny study through the open window, and I revel, and I dream, and I linger on thoughts that have settled into my mind like melting wax dripping from a soft, green candle into its lower receptacle. The night is beautiful, I think to myself, and so I continue to think of nights with inordinate fascination, and I am enchanted with the thoughts that have focused on her who is within me and yet so completely disengaged from thoughts of myself. "I think I love alcoholics or at least understand them, understand what they are trying to prove or do or achieve. It is quite simple to me. Yes! Yes! They are trying to make night last forever."

The night is the mother of all thought and all essential human delight, and its fragrance fills me like warm child-breath inflating a circus balloon until it is ready to burst. But I won't burst or explode, because my mind is too filled with thoughts of a child, the child who is mother of the woman. I can see her standing there at the door, can hear her remarking that I have tried to force her to kiss me, and I can feel her cowering from distinction, fearing what everyone who has ever loved before fears, fearing the thought of losing that certain elemental and indefinable innocence that is part of any initial relationship. I fear with her, but it is not the same kind of fear, because already I have been forced to feel the fear of losing what I sensed but which was never really there to begin with — the image of her, an ideal divorced from living. But I fear, now, for something else too, something more importuning, because I have taught myself that to fear fantasy and dream wish and false projection is cancerous and that it can only lead to frustration first and then to depressive self-degeneration and ultimately to inferiority. Rather, I fear that she will not be able to realize that people are simply people, people with flesh and bone, and that they all suffer from the same basic uncertainties and insupportable contradictions of expectancy and that their real business in life is living every day as it comes and then dissolves into the dawn of the following one. I fear that she will forget that all people are alike in these matters and that their individuality engenders not from their fears or suffering nor from their self-pity and depressions but rather from their loving and the degree of compassion which they can bring to the object of their affections.

Love is, at best, a tenable process, but it is strengthened by the amount of tolerance and patience and human understanding and self-knowledge that a person claims as his individuating qualities. Love is, above all, respect for the object of compassion. Love is the phone call that is promised; it is the promise itself to be true to the loved one; it is the promise to be true to him or her who is willing to make that promise. A certain truth to self is love, strong and deeply committed. An understanding of the fallibilities and the strengths of the loved object is love, pure and simply estimated. But love can never reside in a mind that is so filled with its own preoccupations that it forgets to accept and to forgive, to cherish and respect what the eyes may say or the lips impart. Love can never be based upon what was never there to start with.

Love is a bear rug given for the sake of sheer giving, or it is a silver turtle, loved and cherished and worked for hard and long, given — given because the act itself is enough recompense and because the recipient's eyes tell all the appreciation that is needed in return. But love can never subsist on false expectation, nor can it grow on misunderstandings imbedded not in the intentions of the loved one but rather planted there by the misgivings of the giver's heart — the false ideals fed and nurtured there by dream and illusory fantasy or the fears and irrefragable uncertainties fostered by a certain indescribable infidelity to the heart's demands for sincerity and hope.

A person can never be forced into watering love with a kiss, just as no gardener can whisper into the rosebud's roots what the rain clouds insinuate with their special nectars. Nor can a person be told what to do with his or her own possibilities against a too-strong desire to the negative, just as no day can be told by a weatherman how it should dawn itself, either bright and sunny or moist with grief and melancholy, because neither people nor days want to be told what to do or how to do what they will do anyway, regardless of desired patterns, let alone be predicted.

But people and days do have a certain affinity in that each is contained by the other. The day sets a frame for the individual, and the person acts within that boundary, which is twenty-four hours. The person has still another obligation, that he or she must listen to the day and consider what another friend or companion or even an enemy might have to say, because people themselves also form a framework in which all other people individually operate, and so I say to that person that he or she must heed the truth, the nature of things, which is only in part that which he or she tells him- or herself is the truth, because the truth is only relative, and, more surely, it is only relevant to the individual when it is measured against what others have to say in his behalf.

"I am very much afraid, and so I will just have to start all over again. My faith has been slightly disturbed."

Well, you just be afraid and brood and ponder whatever it is you are afraid about and brood about how that faith has been disturbed! But be sure to ask yourself what constituted your faith and your love and your relationship in the first place with him who has now seemingly disturbed your faith and who has now become the object of culpability. Ask yourself, also, whether or not it might not just be your own faith in yourself that has been disturbed, remembering that each individual, according to what his mind accepts as being sincerity and self-knowledge, has often been disturbed by his own failure to fulfill self-imposed expectations and still survived the conflict with a portion of his former dignity. Ask yourself whether this is not just a part of growing up with a person, remembering also that maybe, just maybe, you are fortunate that this person is at least allowing you to ask yourself these questions rather than demanding that you not ask them at all.

It may indeed be quite easy for a person to communicate his passions, disguised in a velvet cloth, to gain an immediate and transient goal, but as easy as it is for the one, in just proportions is it equally difficult for another individual to grow to love another by allowing himself to be vulnerable, by showing all of his colours. But what else is there if not indifference if that person refuses to expose his feelings, naked and candid and stark, to the air outside himself? Who was it who said that "to be vulnerable to mistakes is to register a tacit affirmation to oneself that humility exists in the self-knowledge that he possesses," the realization of which makes him unwilling to subject himself to the inimical stasis of deceptively securing isolation, the singular correlatives of which refusal are patience and tolerance and self-sacrificing compassion and understanding? But, then again, it's not really important who said it, is it?

I am looking at your picture at seven years of age, and I stare, smiling and warm with the warmth of those eyes and with the promise of that pose, and I am thinking to myself as I glance away from it that you are now what you were then, with the singular exception that now you have to be more judicious about whom you allow to feed and bathe you with affection and censure. But affection and censure surely are still your lot, as they are every adult's, and the world just isn't going to stop or slow its pace while you (or anyone else, for that matter) sit and brood and vacillate, unless it, the world, is told or forewarned that you are someone special, and that just isn't going to happen either. Another person might make that distinction about you though, if you show him you deserve it, but, nonetheless, it remains for you, rather than for him, to go out and effect that singling out, that apotheosis, that human paean, because if you don't, then you will discover ten or twenty or two hundred years from now that you have been duped and used and tossed around indiscriminately by the "velvet-clothed" world and by its inhabitants because you have duped yourself.

Remember, old gal, that the world is just too jammed with too many people who are in too much of a hurry to go too many places which aren't ever going to lead them anywhere anyway to stop for any stragglers. You just have to get aboard that juggernautish band-wagon, too, like everyone else, or you will find yourself buried under a pile of hay that fell from its tailgate as it increased momentum. But you needn't worry if you do hop on, because there will be no chance of losing your identity, since there is a seat or burrow for every passenger.

Yes! You too must be on your way, but let yourself think for one minute that anyone is going to take the time to "mold" you and nothing more, and you will shortly discover that you aren't being molded at all but that, on the contrary, you are beginning to melt and dissolve into fatuous and meretricious anonymity, because to be molded, you must first learn to extend yourself to the point where you can be the sculptor, who, by molding, is in turn molded, who is made to become a part of his or her own creation, because only then will you discover that the creation is a two-way process.

To love beyond recognition of self is to look through death. Let your heart dictate where you should place and plant your love, but remember that no plot of ground is ever totally without sand grits or pebbles or weeds and that no matter how hard you may try to eradicate these aberrations, new ones (though they may take a slightly modified form) will continue to reappear. But these are the very imperfections that make a man human, that should warn all men that there isn't ever any one man who is without fault or solitary in the face of common fate. And it is these imperfections that allow man the continuing hope for betterment, for stronger affection and union, for that certain sense of nobility, and they must not be disregarded, for if they are, then so too will all of man's potential greatness be disregarded, his constant striving to be better than he thinks he can be. Man's greatness lies in the fact that he has, throughout the centuries of all man's existence, been able to make this simple realization and then, having realized it, forgotten it to the point where he was able to transcend the agonizing thought of his mortality, that which makes him at once ongoing and yet dispensable, that makes him susceptible to pain and affliction and disappointment and death.

There is plenty of time in this world for a person to pleasure and love and live vitally and with purposiveness and compassion, but there has also been allotted him his portion of tears and agony and suffering and hardship in the face of supreme disaster, not to mention inevitable reality of his mortality. So it is your duty, nay, your obligation, to heed this and, in doing so, to resolve that neither the bitter nor the sweet will ever be too much for you to cope with, because if you don't, then you will be admitting that you are not even worth the distinction of having been born with the potentiality for creating on this huge yet short-lived plot, which is held for us only in trust, something that may just perhaps be a little bit better than it was before you got here. Love and procreation and the uncertain hope of fulfillment are those things, those materials, those highly charged verities which you must not only recognize but exist and contend with all your life.

So I say to myself and I repeat to you that when the individual cells of the mind become so domineering, so selfishly imperious that they force themselves to annihilate another person from distinction by taking from that individual that last sputtering ember of what man has learned to term dignity or respect or maybe just decency or the ability to simply hold one's head high in the face of another human being's folly or derision, then it is time to remember that you are no different, neither better nor more sensitive nor less fallible nor more importunate or demanding or intolerant in your needs, at times, than anyone else. Just realizing this should be enough to make you stop and say to yourself, "Now, is this fair?" or "Do I have any right or justification to say this to him?" or "Would I want to be treated like this?"

And so I have spoken with my fingers on this typewriter now, and I have decided that neither the fear of losing that someone whom I so strongly love nor impatience nor impetuosity will ever lure me away from what I feel about the magnificent possibilities of the individual mind, and so I will wait and love, all the same, and will remain resigned to the feeling that I have, because no matter what she decides to let herself do or say, I know now that nothing will ever dissuade me, because I will always respect and love and cherish that someone for herself only and for all of the someones everywhere, always.

World without end. Amen.
                    God bless you, princess of peace!

1/1/65 (05198)

[Blue yawns fawning a grief]

Blue yawns fawning a grief
not really felt for the bluebrief
passing of a love not really felt.

1/4/65 (05321)

[The air breathed grey and coldheavy] ‡

The air breathed grey and coldheavy
sighs at dawn. It lay bold and stark
over our home, like a transparent paper-
weight over fliers and gas bills, like a lark's
song gone silent over the gloomy caper
of forest sounds, and I walked outside
to breathe the quick, crisp dawn, abiding
with me, gliding with my insomniac stride.
I felt the sudden urge to go back inside.

"This is a fine time to be young," I thought
to myself, "a fine time to feel the unsung
spectacles that chime in unheard random, caught
by ears and seen by eyes that venture

God bless you, princess of peace, you who sense what my mind
senses simultaneously, you who hear what my eyes say with a solitary
blink. I can see you there, sleeping in that tiny, heavywarm bed, wak-
ing now, rising into the stark coldness of the new day, dawned dilatory
and promising, and I know that its promise won't be yours, because I
know, too, that you already knew before you ever went to bed last
night that this something that intrudes and permeates your sensibili-
ties is too strong, too ubiquitous, and too persistent to let you be, to let
you let go a little more every day.

So you just stick with it and be stronger than it is strong, because

then you will soon discover that to be strong, to ride it out, to endure
the opprobrium and obloquy of the past, is within your power, ineradi-
cable though the seminal source may be

1/8/65 — [1] (Poem), [2] (Prose) (05320)

Loomings

The day breathed grey
And cold-dark sighs at dawn.
It lay heavy
Over our house,
Like an opaque paperweight
Atop fliers and bills
Or a hoot owl's plaint
Gone silent over a busy forest.
I walked outside
To breathe the quick, crisp dawn,
Gliding with its insomniac strides,
Then felt a sudden urge to go inside.

1/8/65 — [1] (00497)

[Matured sorrow, like vintage wine, . . .] †

Matured sorrow, like vintage wine, is the prospect of recollective,
captured happiness

Must life be lived in the corridors of blue contemplation
for the totality of comprehensive justification, or must the
shafts of lifebreath be inspired with each suspiration, each in
its proper moment? The only justification for life need be
that which insinuates itself into the mind that contemplates
its own dereliction of commitment to living a life actively.

Through the silver shafts of lifelove
and inspiration breathe the soft tones
of your figure, your eyes, your bones,
of flesh-and-blood sighs, and

Does there ever need to be a justification for loving
beyond the self, other than the sheer recognition of the import
of the action itself, the willing suspension

Fri. — Write paper on "The Blue Hotel"
Type paper on *The Magic Barrel* ⊢ for Finkel
Correct essay on *love*
Finish typing paper on Johnson's *Journey to the Western Islands of Scotland*

Sat. — Read Keats and Shelley
Study book on vision of love ⊢ Gottfried

Sun. — *Hunt* Don Schnure, Wendell Rivers, Don Dolton

I listen to the relevant inanity of literary irrelevance to life and action, and I discover that although I enjoy the classroom, there is a certain concomitant to stability and sedentary unreality.

To live is to think, certainly, but it is so much more. It is to move with the riff and tides of the throngs of all people moving and interpenetrating the fabrics of movement, and the pleasure that engenders in the intercourse of people is the ultimate rationale and justification for existing. The commitment to a dilemma that transcends those that the self imposes, until, through the approach to others' anxieties, they come back on the self in a form at once disguised and transvalued, in a corridor of endurable and ineluctable acceptance of, though never resignation to, those fears, without the reference and relevance they have to those with whom the individual has interacted, would, necessarily, by virtue of the cellular dissolving capabilities of the mind, perceptibly leave that individual at once solipsistic and wallowing in a crowd of persons who sympathize not with his individuated anxieties, who breathe not with his breath nor love, though not the turned-in love that he feels, for it is first and primary that he learn that love stirs and grows only when it has an object outside itself upon which to fasten.

tolerance
patience
sympathetic compassion | These are the qualities without which the individual freezes, stark and lonely, in the iced fields he may contemplate traversing.

Youth registers with blunder and simple
naiveté

Classroom casuistries and scintillant
Sophistries register the tenor

She registered a quizzical brow on her frightened aspect and sat
motionless and torpid, like a river horse pictured in a Walt Disney
nature film, and she was thinking with the rapidity of typewriter keys
arcing faster than the operator's fingers can move, until she found her-
self racing over the future obliques of her dissipating revelations of
her past opprobrium.

The problem of how to speak in the face of the moral and actual
ethic of action (Cordelia, in *King Lear*);
        the theme of articulateness and ineffability.

One must learn to listen.
            Don't be hard of listening. It is natural to perceive some
    implication in another's assertion or affirmation that doesn't really
    exist at all in the speaker's mind. Where does this misunderstanding
    lead the individual? What are the lengths and depths of presumption
toward which one person may gravitate away from another?
        tacitness
        ineffability
        incomprehension
        epiphany
        erroneous loquacity
        false presumption

Does a person always need to look for *the* one justification that God
never meant to invest in many beyond the solitary affirmation of love
lingered on and looked for with unswerving abandonment?
    Love may be best appreciated, pleasured, and understood when
the emanations are silent and spoken or expressed in meaningful si-
lences that are heard though never expressed, seen though never ex-
tended beyond the refulgent coruscations of blue-yellow eyeblinks,
felt though not through the musculature or neural receptions of the
physical. Love *is*, and little more, unless it be the ever-present striving
for continuity of the inspiration which it engenders.

modesty ⎤
endurance ⎥
patience ⎦— are prerequisites for happy, meaningful existence.
humility
tolerance

Some people are so full of shit that they appear like humans who never have to take a crap. They talk with sound basis about topics or ideas that have no relevance for the audience, who leave the pile of shit in the classroom when they leave to walk out the door and into the air of lived experience.

I smoke too damn much and suffer from the intellectual indolence which descends at times to cloud my mind with the incapability of just justification for making my mind extend itself.

•• To be vulnerable to mistakes is an attribute that signifies the fact that humility exists in the knowledge that that person is unwilling to subject himself to the stasis of securing isolation.

French-fried Howard Johnson's clams with half a bottle of ketchup sound very much nicer to me right now than all the precepts of willfulness and form that exist in Mann and Schopenhauer and Nietzsche.

To be young is very love

Mid*night*/ moon*light* — Shelley rhyme

Helen Gurley Brown is full of cookbook bullshit.
Junkie Burroughs is in but fucked personally;
His perversion is registered *constipation*

To be young is very love, but to be in love is very living

To be young is very love;
to be in love is very living.

To be wise is very

To be young is very fun,
but to enjoy is very living.

To be more than self is very Disraeli,
but to be less than self is very Bellow.   *(The Victim)*

To be self is very human;
To be more than human is very

A dream blown full with fancy
and hope is worth a thousand
anonymities and the one chance he
will miss to create in a house and
love the particles, to glimpse her
whose

Where have the warm summer days
of my life gone, now that the swarm
of phases fluxes past my eyes indifferently?

There was a spring sparked with hope,
with promise replete with chance of things
repeating themselves for my review.

Sometimes a person has so many enigmas and possibilities

1/8/65 — [3] (05098)

An Experiment in Insomnia ‡

Tonight is a cold, insomniac evening, and I have just finished a game of Monopoly, during which it was clearly pointed out to me that I will never be a business nabob. Screw it. I never wanted to be anything more than a profligate prodigal son anyway. This goddamn typewriter skips a beat when I am not looking, which is a weird experience in itself, almost like dropping trousers in the railroad station in front of ten thousand homosexual Pullman conductors. (There is an intended pun on the word "*Pull*man.")

Poetry has happened to me at times
when my love was yet not grown cold,
but it is a strange time now. Flown
has my paramour to another, more bold
and importunate; another love has she shown,
while with thoughts of self-pity that lover chimes,
and I, with derision and scorn, myself do scold,
for neither the seeds

My head is light with the nightfall
sounds of insomnia, which brightly fill all
my thoughts with a temporal impasse
that is neither wakefulness nor sleep.
I sit and think, ponder, hands shaking
with the burdensome weight of quick-
burning cigarettes too fast smoked,
too little enjoyed, and I think, and
I feel the tears of love lost and gone,
and I weep

The night sounds around the building float and scurry by, head-
long and indiscriminate in their fatuous flight into the deep heights of
forgetfulness, and here I sit, contemplating where she has gone and
what she has done, and I ask myself questions that are at once irre-
fragable and unanswerable, enigmatic and labyrinthine in their com-
plexities. The only response that I can make is this: that she has made
a decision. Whether by virtue of self-indulgence or sheer lack of self
I know not, but care I do. Yes, I care so much that, like Cordelia, I am
unable to respond directly to her, though I look directly into her clear
yet unresponsive eyes.

She, like Icarus Gatsby, has flown too high, borne aloft by her own
self-indulged, platonic conception of herself; she has forgotten to
remember that there are others that are concerned about her wel-
fare. Her mother, her suitor, her sister and father and her past and
hope for the future all denied, all refuted and negated in one quix-
otic and illogical move, which is denigrating not only to her dig-
nity, if dignity it be, but also to any conception which others may have
had of her. Yes, she has done it now, and there is little more that can
be said in her behalf. Her future and her fate are hers in part, but they
are also the burden of all her past, backed up on her present situation,
at once imperious and formidable and jumbled and chaotic and full
of fury and the sounds of baleful and morose and melancholy stasis
and immobility.

Fly high, full-blown lover.
Leap and sing and dance. Fill
with fanciful meanderings the still-
flippant philanderings of souls
not your own

Fly high, full-blown lover.
The sky is not deep enough
for your hopes, your feline
instincts, your sure, benign
indifference to things fine
and easy. Fly high, under cover
of night, with missals too dark
and slow, too indigenous for
your own good. Soar and float
for all you're worth, and if
you fail to reach that goal,
remember that your birth will
come again on another shoal
of reincarnation. I, the mother
of night, call to you, languid
and silent, through the vapours
of lyre strings, Aeolian
yet violent, sanguine yet mute
to indifference and time. Suit
your own tastes, green, silent blue,
and tawdry golden.

Beauty there was in those lips,
hawthorn red and cherry bright.
Love there was in those lengthened
hips, where ships of desire and
plunder lurked like pirates ranging
some uncharted stretch of sea, with
fire dragons swarming all around
(accursed monsters of repulsion
fetching maidens from shoals of
Bimini), Odysseus scaling Scylla and
Charybdis, Ulysses after his Penelope, Jason in
search of Pope's golden lock, Swift
in the heavens, looking for his Stella.

Nowhere are you to be found, though I
sound the depths of day and the reaches
*

of dying nightlight for but a sigh, a
scent of your love. You were there
once. Green and golden were your eyes
to me; goldengreen the sighs of
child breath in my ears. And it is gone.
You have flown high and far from sight,
gone with the winds of tropical Cancer
and myriad satyrs of this life to
a planet of timelessness, locked and hidden
somewhere beyond Compassion and Nicotine.

Snapdragon, wild honey oaks, turtle
blossoms, funny little leaves of love
wasted and rent by the sunny days of
summer, sift and sidle to the ground
of my subtle cells and sequester
in whirlwind rifts in my eyes. Found
no more will be your willow-wept tears
of incompletion. Still you will fear.

The Furies cast a spell, Hell-bound,
upon your naked soul and fast
fleeted to the farthest pole of light.
You they leave to yourself, doomed
and burdened with the sight of what
a woman so strong and fair will never
share again with any of that fabled
race of men-humans blinded by your
golden strands of hair, your green,
jade eyes, your highborn stare.
Alone you must endure the tempters
and the angels of Satan, the wiles
of Charon, and the sighs of Bacchus.

The soft sea torments with its
shifting turf and its sandless
bottoms. It calls a low, moaning
murmur, salt-stained and misty-
moist with salt streams. Pity
not the sandy shore or the
horrible onslaught of sea licks
that lap at its impressions. The
footprints that we left this day
and then left bereft are gone,
*

swallowed by the tide, erased
by the gliding whitecaps of foam
and seaweed. The seeds of our
love are gone too, dissolved into
sea strata and fish bone, blown
to the gulled winds, breezeblown
and lost across the Gulf. Like
the wavewashes, our seeds will
flow again in timeless cycles,
and their burning passion will return
in yet another form, on yet another
day. We say, "Lover, sweet, soft
lover, fly higher than the night."

It is too late to begin worrying about sleep now, too late to even
think about the tomorrows of my life, because life will never get be-
yond any specific moment in which I contemplate only the very pres-
ent instant of my poetic spell, my fascination with the purpose of
expression, the beauties of creativity, the sense of the timeless, cap-
turable in one fine line or in one seminal thought-train.

I begin to live the moment I feel poetry, the instant that I begin to
contemplate the duty that has been given me to work with and mold
and further.

Willow winds wafted soft breezes
of yellow Memphis night-streams
through my nostrils, while beams
of the crystalline moon shot
through the corridors of sorrow
and loss like tiny, white sand
drops dripping through the nose
of an antique hourglass frozen
on the bureau of timelessness.
Gazelles sprung with cadenced
strides over fence posts of sleep,
and the Marquesa de Bo-peep had
lost her sheepish grin before I
had time to remember to tell her
to hide before the agents of doom
could fleece her virginity and
virtue. I saw the police chase
Darlin' Corey into Nottinghamshire,
*

> where the basin met the briar patch,
> and there before my eyes sat Uncle
> Remus himself, surprised by the
> cartoon sequence he beheld.

One can't take too seriously what he or she writes when already his mind has quit functioning with logicality. It is now past three in the morning, and I am so tired that nothing makes much difference to me anymore. Yet I can still see her standing there as I entered her sister's apartment earlier this evening, and I can hear myself saying to her, "I want to help you. I want to do whatever two people working in concord can effect." And I can see her head cowering from my lips as I moved toward her to kiss my hope, my sense of promise for her, who had this very day said something so terrible and so insensitive to a woman who had mothered her and who had always tried to exemplify for her the propriety and the necessity for doing things according to rationale and order. I am wondering, now, whether or not there will ever be any hope for this girl, because she has so damn much going against her: namely, she is working against herself without even knowing it. She is functioning in isolation and virtual anonymity and without the conception of what it means to be manipulated for an entire lifetime. But I have seen this before, and, no doubt, I will be made witness to it again, witness to the gradual decaying of intellect under the chaotic insensitivity and indiscrimination of the bodily instincts, the mind as subaltern to the quixotic.

Love is so tenuous that one blink of the mind's eye and that person has lost what is so hard to gain in the first place: the flowing out of the self in the hope of sustaining a relationship with another human being. But without this attempt, there is nothing but indifference, and with indifference comes isolation and misery and self-pity and constant frustration and disappointment. To be young is very love, but to be in love is very living.

> From Bimini to Nassau, in the Bahamas,
> has she travelled, gamboling with night
> and Negroes and nicotine and with a heart
> neither contrite nor soft. The winds start,
> and the sea goes through her veins like
> Dramamine, which soothes artificially and then
> pains the senses in lingered lethargy.
> On the coral beach, green with the aquamarine,
> bluegreenish strands of solar unguentine,
> she stands, while the sands breach
> *

the smiles of onrushing waves splattered
by the guarding reefs and the tide-battered
fishing barks, with weathered nets strewn
asunder for mending. She is grieving for
the loss of mystery, which sends her grief
streaming in tears of silence
to touch the nonviolent remains
of the powerful sea as they rise to
her wetnaked feet on water limbs.
The flickering lights of Providence
are filled with clatter, yet she hears
not what untrusting mothers fear; she
fears not what others said with sneers
and smothering derision. She is alone,
stark and moist to the bone, and the
languid breeze insinuates her body
with tones of musical harmonies.
She cries to the stars and the far-
off strains of New York by night
as she crouches, now, slowly fighting
the tides, into the arms of the Gulf.
She bends low into the cold bite of
salt water and sees her life flowing
out of her body and entering the sea's
naked shadow, until she is no more
than stillness itself and one with
the depths between shore and death,
between constellated night and peopled life.
She dies, consumed in her own wet image.

1/10/65 — [1] (05365)

Eclipse

Poetry has danced with me at times
When my love was not yet burning cold.
It is a stale time, now that she has grown
Bolder to another, who has ravaged and sown
Her womb with sterile seeds that hold
Heavy tears of remorse. She is borne
Down Charon's depths. Her fare is sold.
There is only her memory for me to scorn.

No more will my spirit toll untempered chimes
Of meter, nor will the alchemy of verse mold
Rhythms neat and fine, like Keatsian rhymes
That melt infinite love from soft, mortal gold.
Darkness has swallowed the lights of her tone
Like cold breath on a flame when it is blown.

1/10 — [2] & 1/12/65 (05053)

[Today I am smoking . . .] †

Today I am smoking with the mechanical rapidity of a piston-driven engine; the reason is reflexive habit and a tinge of ubiquitous nervousness.

> I drift everywhere, though my mind
> remains seated. My thoughts, entwined
> with colorless sounds of voices kind
> and soft, float benign and resigned
> to a love that fades and dies fast
> and green in memory pleasant and past
> all salvation and recoverable contrast.
>
> Something strange there is about loving
> another that ranges from mystery to the kiss

1/11/65 (05366)

A Waking Dream

A child lies nestled in silence,
    Dreaming of dragons and maidens in love,
Mythic Sir Lancelots, and the violence
    Of ribaldry in toilet-scrawled limericks above
The head of the world, seated
    In grace, dreaming of queens and kings
And how they should be greeted.
    He stirs for a minute. His alarm clock rings.

He pulses and starts from his dream.
    He throws off the cover with care not to soil it,
Then pauses for what may seem
    An instant too long to reach the hall toilet.
"Those damn kings and queens,"
    He cries, as he stumbles aside and falls,
"Had more modest means
    Than I, who am tinkling on my mother's walls."

1/14/65 (05054)

[Along the Gulf-paved horizons] †

Along the Gulf-paved horizons
            of shell-peppered shores,
My love wields blank eyes on
            the red-rutty corridors
Of day, which draw

Through the sighs of day
she paces, flying, from corridors
of silence to heights of May-
time visions of green shores
on lakes, on winds grey
and dying —

Gold-melting meadows drip
into the daylight dew point

1/14–15?/65 (05055)

[The cold, dappled dawn down-] †

The cold, dappled dawn down-
draws the icy boughs of walnut
and cedar with

1/15?/65 (05322)

[The apartment was heavy but warm, . . .] ‡

The apartment was heavy but warm,
with its overcoat of thick-plastered
walls, hung with the retrospection of
bric-a-brac and art objects arranged with
studied disarray over the past five
years.

The night was polar icy and
inimical to people activity, yet the
three of us were walking into it at
a fast clip, as though the mere
thought of the cold would, like
Lot, transform us into natural elements
if we looked back into it.

Hunter was laughing the forced
laugh of a stage comedian who knows
he has failed to elicit the expected
guffaws and applause of his static audience
that the father did.

Jenny's apartment was located in
one of the older buildings in Amiton,
which, during the construction boom of
the past five years, had been
shoved off into a cubbyhole of the
thriving city within city.

It was a heavy, squat building,
bordered on each side by other
low-rent apartments, which housed
other forgotten lives. The mainstream of
progress had passed these people
by and had left them all one and
anonymous.

To think about the coldness of the
night was to commit the crime of
deleterious consciousness, by which the
thinker would suffer the transformation
of becoming one with the night and
coldness itself, not mystically nor
anagogically but as though each limb and
muscle and cell were absorbing the
stasis of frigidity

I am sitting here in Howard Johnson's
again, this Sunday morning, trying to take
stock of what has been accomplished and
what is still to be done within the
next half year.
   The story "Evermore About to Be"
is screaming in my imagination to be
written. It must be a story of love —
a love that is implied in Keats' *"La
belle dame sans merci"* or in "Lamia."
      Hunter Augustine
      Christopher Paradise

   She is speaking, and I am watching
her mouth move the frigid sound waves
that separate us in the car, and I
can hear her mouth saying what her mind
avers, hearing those words, "Don't say
that again, please. Lately, you have
been saying that with such feeling that
I can't relate with you."
   "But what do you expect me to
say when I feel this way? You know
it's not particularly easy for me either."
   "But just don't — well, go ahead —
if you must say that, just go on and
say it. I can't stop you."
   "Yes, you can. And, in fact, just talking
it out has stopped me, has made
me self-conscious of an emotion that
never should be spoken anyway, unless
that feeling is on the war.
   "I love you, Hunter. Do you know
that?"

$Se^x = F(u^r) \propto F(u^c)k$ — See! I'm
a mathematician right along with the best
of them.

   It is a strange time in my life,
a period not of vacuity and stasis but
*

rather one in which experience accretes
silently and unobtrusively, so that its victim
is scarcely aware of its persistent process.
    I find myself mounted fourteen thousand feet up,
caught in the snow line of love, the
direction of which is incalculable. Whether
up or down, horizontal and staid it flows;
uncertain and enigmatic it prances and
taunts with its random inconsistencies
and tepid-caloric fluctuations of emotion
and insensibility. I must tell the
referee to call time-out to check
my ball's progress, to find out how
many yards or feet or feelings I have
left to go.

    To tell a story in the most
involving, comprehensive way possible
means, necessarily, to bring a mind
to the work that is at once fraught
in conflicting clutches and yet
lucid and transcendent, objective and
removed to the point where personal emotion
becomes canceled out by the rational
behaviour of the central figure's irrational
responses and approaches to a problem,
when the creator (author) alone knows
the results.
        objectivity
        pleasure
        moral instruction — Plato, Johnson,
                                Keats
    You give me the time, free and
amply supplied, and I will present
you with a story of life, true and
pathetic.
    This shit about Bellow wanting
a character neither more nor less human
is terrible, because it only fosters
anonymity and impersonality, and
no one on this crowded sand pile wants
to believe that he is small or unimpor-
tant.

A petty clerk is fine for Fyodor
or for Kafka but not for *Bellow*.
A Bellow may spark a fire that falters,
but it can't sustain a blaze when the
woodman forgets to deliver the cedar or
black walnut to his back porch.

I like to write at night, late
and alone with my thoughts and
the summer night-sounds of cicadas and
crickets and oak locusts and death-moths
clinging futilely to the screen, vainly trying
to peek at what I am writing at my
desk, at once permanent and nonexistent.
Often my thoughts turn to Faulkner,
whom I know better for never having
known him personally. I cherish and
apotheosize his achievement, his flight
high and soaring and rhetorically vertiginous,
his attempt to speak and breathe all of
life into each sentence, phrase, adjective,
not the attempt to posit the truth but
merely what to him seemed very real
and urgent and vital to the accreted
achievement of mankind: that certain
insight into immortality, which, for a human,
may just consist of nothing more than
leaving on a bathroom tile or porcelain
partition a lipstick- or pencil-scrawled
entry reading "Kilroy was here."
Leaving this little gnome is like
dying Christ-like, because even Barabbas
and Veronica wrote those words, and
don't forget old Cincinnatus Washington,
plowing the Delaware for a lost cherry
tree.

1/17/65 (05155)

Lazarus: Death

Darkling dowagers of passing doom
   Leave me brooding with the gloom
Of hours intruding on jade-green solitude
And the mute doubt of changing mood.
   I crawl, weeping, toward my tomb.

Softly the incense of sleepless night
   Haunts my vision, without insight
Into the cause, the derision of tears,
Dissolving in sighs of dying years.
   I creep, falling over ancient biers.

Waging the measures of vexing desire,
   Falsely has Demeter gauged her fire
In my tight-lipped heart, and it burns
Through the image time always spurns.
   I stall, consumed in my own pyre.

Wrenched from life, like a sandy grain
   Flung from its beach by the rain-
Torrents of Typhon was I pulverized,
My soul, like Prometheus', devitalized.
   I call, entombed and unsympathized.

1/19/65 — [1] (05056)

Lazarus: Rebirth

Sleeping, as stars in daylight's shrine,
   My spirit rekindled a feeling benign,
Which grew like nightfall bidding farewell
The dusk, and my former self broke its shell.
   I sigh, groping for the vision sublime.

Drifting through vacuums of awful maze,
   Which went unmolested by the dark phase
Of birth and sepulcher, was I bereft,
Until essence outlived its life-in-death.
   I awaken, breathing a purer breath.

Silently the dream of that eternal love
    Came streaming like fireflies above
The vapours of breeze, insinuating my mind
With nectar of honey-oak tree and eglantine.
    I hope, flying both before and behind.

Settling, now, in life's sylvan repose
    Like a weary traveller who chose
To end his day in quiet prayer, my soul
Reclined in a love the very young extol.
    I live, loving beyond death's dry pose.

1/19/65 — [2] (05057)

La estrella independiente

Morning star, running wild
Under the vanishing and mild
Moon's milquetoast! Whose child
Are you, O waning host, beguiling
Me with your independence? Warm
Me with your absence, and enfold
My spirit wholly in your cold
Breath! Lift my heart! Make bold
Enough my parts to endure myself,
Free from vacuity and fear of ennui,
Like you, O waning host! I pray
That nightfall will not hasten its delay.
God bless you, *princesa de fe*!

1/21–22/65 (05058)

Ode to Insomnia

    Once again, I am seated here in this study, my study away from home, which I call Sir Don's study. It is a warm place because it is occupied by Sir Don and me, and we think that staying up until all hours of the night is worth more than sleep. We drink more coffee than is imaginable, and at this very moment, Sir Don, who was deeply engrossed in absolutely nothing of importance, has just taken out his small typewriter, the one that skips the beats when you least expect it, and has begun to type out inanities. The two of us, sitting here, facing each other, and with our typing machines backed up against each other, remind me of Ferrante and Teicher at their twin teichwriters on some anonymous stage in some vacant Radio City Music Hall.

I type for all I'm worth, this evening, but my thoughts are so compounded one upon another and are running in such random fashion that I really don't quite know where to begin. I feel bad, almost as though the letdown of exams and the quarrel that I had two days ago have been enough to precipitate a minor eruption in my system of ongoing behaviour.

Old Samuel Johnson, you are the king of all the moralists, and yet there is something about you that is so pathetic that it is even beautiful. You know what I mean, or you would if you were here tonight for me to invite you over for coffee. I would pretend that Sir Don was Mr. Henry Thrale and that I was your humble servant and good friend, James Boswell. We could discuss the latest *Rambler* that you had written, or, as we say now, "dashed off," in the time that it generally takes me to piss. I would tell you that you, sir, are a wonderful human being, because anyone that could say the things you said and write the things you wrote just has got to be in, you know?

I hate to interrupt my reminiscing about the virtues of you, Sammy, but Sir Don just had a paroxysmal fit, in which he hurled his skip-beating typewriter against the back wall of our workshop and broke the hell out of it. I guess Ferrante and Teichwriter will just have to call it quits for the night. But old Mr. Lonely Hearts will just keep on going, like old Buckeye Jim, who just weaves and spins his heart out to bonnie George Campbell and the young soldier named Johnnie.

P. B. Shelley, dear, you are OK in my book also, because you were able to write a defense of poetry that was better than old Coleridge or Wordsworth had written, and, above all, I think I dig what you said about poetry being the expression of the imagination and, more so, the dicta that you professed in which you said that "Poetry redeems from decay the visitations of the divinity in man." That's just too wild for my blood.

Cold, pastoral Keats, you are a wizard of the TV dinner, who said that heard dinners are sweet but those unheard are sweeter. I think that poetry is the answer, but I have yet to put the question to myself that needs be answered.

> Little girl blue, who stands in the shower
> of the torrents of daylight, who spends each hour
> in contemplation so silent, so unsure, so dour
> that all the birds and the blithe honey flower
> *

that climbs to its season along the greeny bower
cannot fail to toll the hour
of your unhappiness the minute that you cower
from distinction, little girl blue.

Little girl blue, who sits by the stream
that flows through the starry valley Seem
and Be, with no more a thought or a dream
of the boy who has passed through your mind.

But just remember that we will grieve not, rather will find
strength in what remains behind, unless the drought has
cancelled out each blade of grass and each flower's glory.

Seashore sifting with the shifting
breeze, its coral sands are lifting
above themselves and blowing away into
the Gulf, and I am left alone.

Home is the baby girl. Long gone
has she been from my shore, my
Rhodes, my Calypso of changing forms,
and I am alone to cry with the gulls,
to breathe the sweet, salty sands of
Gulf and Florida and love that will
never renew itself. I am unborn
again, as I was before the terrible
curse of birth settled o'er my breast.

Tonight I am a stranger to the world of men because I am a stranger
to myself. I have a wonderfully warm feeling for her whom I have
spoken and written about many times before, but tonight I am asking
myself where she has flown to. How is it that a person may feel that
he knows what is best for another person but be frustrated by the fact
that the object of the counselling . . .
Where are you tonight, blithe princess of peace?

For many hours of my life, I have
wandered lone and silent as a gypsy,
as a bedouin, who, in his nomadic
flight away from death, forgets that
he too is but a man among men, that
he must act not apart but in concord
with men.

Teach me, O blithe princess of peace,
to rekindle what is in my heart, to
nevermore remain apart from the love
that lives above the commonality
of every hour, of each solitary speck
of sand that passes through the mind
of life's most precious periods of time,
the sanddial of the heart.

I have travelled through the antique
narrows of Rome and felt the pulse
that blows through every cat-lined
alley and breathes the sighs of love
everlasting. Yet I am not there now.

Nor am I where Santa Maria Maggiore
illumines Guardi's Grand Canal by
nightglow. Would that I could again
sense the inspiring flow of *vaporetti*
churning the islands between Lido
and the Mediterranean's golden gem.

My thoughts weave and toss, jumping desultorily from one dream
to the next, and yet I am unable to focus on anything in particular.
Maybe this is just the result of having felt the extreme sense of guilt
that comes from losing that person who is so very close in senti-
ment to oneself. Oh, that I could regain that feeling sublime, that
sense of oneness and rapport that engenders when a love relation-
ship is so solid and so firmly entrenched in the mind that nothing
but death itself can dislodge it. But that is gone now, fleeted with
the rapidity of a rocket that throws off a lightening that is as brief
as bright.

Again I ask myself where she is tonight. Can she be off in the land
of the Munchkins or in Eugene Field's Land of Wynken, Blynken,
and Nod? What mortal clay is this that we pretend to mold, if no
more than the unsolid matter of transitoriness that daily intrudes
upon our sensibilities and stays but a brief moment before dying?
Can it be that there is nothing so permanent as the mere thought of
the existence of impermanence itself? Perhaps that's it in a nutshell:
the fact that nothing is ever immune from the mortality of human ex-
istence and, as such, each being can always fall back on its own inter-
nal refuge, from where it can contemplate all of the harsh reality of
hurt and pain and misunderstanding that it has to endure just by virtue

of its mortality, its fallibility, its inefficacy to sustain the intemperate temptations of self-esteem and pride and haughtiness and incredible envy of others whom it deems less unfortunate than itself. Will you not ever learn that all entities are the same and that they all suffer from the same causes of despair and languishment and despondency and heartache? Will you not hear the echoes from that other world, the world of the New Jerusalem, the gates of Paradise, which call, though unheard, to all of the children of the earth? They do call, nay, exhort, all of us to remember that the great instrument of morals is love. A love is this echo, a love that is so compelling and so palpable that it goes unnoticed amidst the vain striving and false and deluding ambitions of the self to find mastery over itself and over each other. Will you not respect the call, the mandate that it makes with its stolid lips, that it weaves into the woof of common experience, that it hurls through the web of time that is ours to apprehend if we are only taught to believe and, even more, to become aware of the great possibilities and potentialities of the imagination?

But we prefer to defeat ourselves by making strangers and aliens and pariahs of our souls. We choose to pave our streets with gold-fill or with spinelle.

The child is father of the man, and so it is that we have had our birth in another place. We come to birth mortally wounded by the predispositions and the formal dictates that have been assigned to us by those who have already forgotten that they are the children of the heart. The heart, you ask? What is it? Well, it is a mass of fibers and strands that become more than muscle and sinew and pumping equipment. The heart is that source from which emanates all that is outside of us while it yet contemplates its own rebirth in another individual, whose clay constitution is not so very different from our own.

There is something very pleasant about being free to think what is in the mind to say. Tonight is freedom for me from the routine of work suspended in the works of another person, who, as I read, I can't help but contemplate must have sat at his desk or atop a rivulet-pierced bank feeling the same uncertainties that I feel now and writing the same confident yet unknowing and indefinable enigmas of the heart. There is a certain commonality that exists for anyone who has ever taken up the pen or the typewriter, the same search for redefinition, for that elusive mastery of identity. And all who have written have drawn the same irrefutable conclusion: that the search ends as soon as the poet in man assumes his task to be a something that goes beyond the self, that originates not in the solitude of the individual cells of the brain or the mind but that inspires him to seek the love that is in all things and which is reflected in that certain indefinable essence which is the love of another particular individual, into whose hopes and fears and achievements the soul of man can insinuate itself in a union that need not transcend the mortal into the ethereal or oblivious or empyrean but rather that which manifests itself in the substrata of the concrete in man and woman — the verities of the heart that exist at all times, though their presence may go unchecked or unnoticed indefinitely, until the grains of white sand in the hourglass run through their allotted portion.

To speak of the world without end, as I have had recourse to do in the past, is a haughty self-confidence on my part and not a little presumptuous in that the world for each individual must indeed come to an abrupt end, since there is no predicting when death may decide to intercept our plans and stratagems.

> Midnight tolled its august knell:
> Farewell, the transient clientele
> Of earth, of love, of Mardi Gras.

I end this ode to insomnia, tonight, by affirming that whatever there is in life worth the effort of pursuing, it will never be attained without a stability of moral thinking and a love for life and for the experience or the chance happening so filled with awe and childlike excitement that nothing can compare in simplicity and purity to it but the sheer wonderment of the occurrence itself.

> God bless you, princess of peace!
> World without end. Amen.

1/23/65 (05162)

Loss of Grace

Her
Body
Was   ripe and moist,
         seething with angelic purity,
         dressed in nakedness alone, and
         suggesting defilement never before

                                            Conceived.

Her
Body
*

Was   waiting there,
         framed in the passivity of nightbreath,
         crying out for that moment
         when all traces of youth dissolve into

                                        Experience.

Her
Body
Was   denied of any consolation
         in one instant's urgent ecstasy and
         voided of all redemptive hope
         by her singular act,

                                        Consummated.

Her
Body
Was   used and wizened,
         headlong on its way toward old age,
         strained by abusive pleasure-pain
         and the self-destructive denial of

                                        Expiation.

[1/25/65]? (05059)

[I awakened, this morning, . . .]

   I awakened, this morning, to the
prospect of a snowstorm, a headache,
and a long free poem that has caused
me a great amount of frustration.
   The title itself is pothering; I have
tentatively called it *The Pilgrimage of
Youth*, but this doesn't really convey
the feeling of the poem.
   The theme is twofold:
 the loss of love and the curse
put upon the female and the male.
   The girl's curse is to travel
alone through the depths of Stygian Hell,
always remaining a mystery to herself.
   The boy's curse is to remind
himself that the most impt. thing in
*

life is love and that it must be
constantly renewed and rekindled.

1/28/65 (05163)

[Her soft breath nuzzled warmly] ‡

Her soft breath nuzzled warmly
Into the moonlit night-sounds
Of honey locusts and muffled hounds
Ranging some distant draw, bounding
Along unseen. Her sighs sensed love.

Her warm voice softly inspired
The willow breezes to murmur
Plaintive cries of silvery grief
Through the cottonwood trees.
Her eyes watched one silent dove.

Her deft mind

1/29/65 — [2] (05060)

[The sweet-breasted sighs of sleep] †

The sweet-breasted sighs of sleep
cry softly in my unrested night-
time saxophone. It bleats deep
tenor tones on jets of unheard flight,

while a single tear, blanched and slow,
drizzles my full, fair cheek with bright
ensigns of a melody studded with the glow
of fleeting love lost in the low crowd's sight.

Play like dizzy moths; reed, let go
your sounds like exhausted

Your touch warm and pulse sensed
never entered my mind, recompensed
by a love unspoken

Night drifts, blinking and daybound,
into my solitary city of profound
silence, like memories of nights
spent in Pandemonium's blights
of narcotic fantasy and lush sound

Night cuts a figure blue and green.
Neon light hastens my pace toward
nowhere in two-timing, graceless

Night's haughty incandescence rode
a highflying strutter through minds
incensed with love scattered cold
and naked like the dust one finds
shattered by wind

$Se^x = F(u^r) + F(u^c)k$

1?/65 (05052)

The Breakfast [‡]

   Hanley Dace didn't feel well at all this
morning. In fact, he never did when he awakened.
Morning was the purveyor of soporific indecisiveness
and immobility for him. It was sheer chance
that brought him to the Dowager this morning.
   Dace had left his Jaguar at a nearby
dealer's garage for a minor tune-up (his car
was an anomaly). Hanley Dace rented a small
studio apartment not far from the Square, a
thriving outgrowth

1–2?/65 — [1] (05157)

[Hanley Dace] ‡

Hanley Dace
was a connoisseur
of insomnia, an expert
on the racial crisis
in his own life.
Hanley was a Negro.
He shovelled manure
at the Biferville Zoo.
The functions he fulfilled
were a comedown
from his ancestry:
his mother had cleaned
the vestry in St. Paul's;
his grandfather,
bootblack to Trotsky,
had once turned his back
on a revolution.
Hanley Dace
was a psychologist
of breakfast foods.

1–2?/65 — [2] (05141)

Isolation Booth ‡

It's a lush life for me, "cherry,"
as Gerry Mulligan might say it
to me with his play-toy sax. Play
it, boy, 'cause you sound great
all wound up in those crazy, languid
sensualities.
I hear that horn talking to me
through miles of plastic and deep-
throated grooves, and it sends
me to Florida, to a beach sea-
gulled and bikinied in anonymity,
and sensibility.
Great old Getz has found the gettin'
place, and he makes my skin stand
*

on end; he sends me off on waves
of listening, to the Village, to whore-
houses in Heaven and Barcelona,
and sensitivity.
I see an old Negro, darkglasses-
blind, grinding out some fine,
solid ballade, blueseedy and sweat-
throbbed, with fingers brown and
pink-soft and stained yellow with
nicotine.

1–2?/65 (05148)

[The man's mind in the child] †

The man's mind in the child
lies dormant, waiting for the mild
breeze of summerlife to beguile
it with awakenings of infantile
awareness and the petty, puerile
dream-wishes of drifting wild
and free

1–2?/65 (05145)

Genesis: The New Life

The quietest time in the day is thought.
Life's periods of calm descend
In moments of love, monumentally sought.

I: Son and Daughter

Why the awful stress
Upon synthesis and strained reason,
Which in no other season
Except life's dying youth surges
With uneven pulsings and plagues
Us with strife and chance and change,
Stands rife with circumstance
And unalloyed grief, holds
*

Its helpless minions, tiny people,
Captive under the tawny pinions
Of shadowy reality? Why, O awful
Power, O pained Dominion? Why?

II: Father

Many miles ago, I breathed two children
Into the womb of Earth and watched them
Grow into life. They were mere whispers
Of My mind then, when their ripe-bursting
Seeds drifted into the bright-green sighs
Of birth and golden light of teeming day.

With unseen eyes I watched them sift
Like seasons through the indices of change
And various circumstance, until, by the grace
Of chance, they were carried with time
To a place by the sea, where their youth
Was prepared for by the tideless harmonies
Of the Gulf wind's widening, milkthick breeze.

With unheard cries of worried despair,
I watched My two helpless children
As they stirred from their nightbeds
Into the burning configurations of their
Allotted period of infancy. They turned
Toward each other, plotting their days
Together, speaking with myriad unspoken
Glances of mirth and expectancy and the
Surprise that flows as softly as a dove's
Feather on the downypinked eye-blinks
Of mutual compromise. I watched them bend
Down together, sinking into the soft ground
Of the future, sliding like the notes of a distant recorder
Into the lofty sounds of life.

I watched them with unimagined wisdom
As they learned to question the pageant
Of love. Their festive hearts were burning
With the restless passion that brings two
Beings together under the spotdot fashions
Of night, that mingles two breaths into a
Single moment of warm, mortal longing to breathe
With Me in one informed spirit of life eternal.

But they fast awakened from their dream.
They had laid themselves bare into the
Fragrant, green fairness of the earth's thighs
And were stained by its rain-moist tears
Of dewdroplets. Then they began to cry
With the sinfilled knowledge that insinuates
Doleful eyes, and when they arose,
They were wearing the disguise of My curse.

With the heaviness of unmitigable remorse,
I watched them back off from experience,
Stumbling over the silence of their guilt,
Falling behind and away from each other
Like the slow-grinding hands of a lazy clock
Not built to keep perfect pace with the onrushing
Hour's advancing phase, which outdistanced them.
I watched, waiting for the moment when time
Would complete its frequent, unchanging cycle
And set their tardiness in correct sequence
Once more. I watched as they departed, she
For the lands of future dismay, he remaining
Fixed on the sandy shore, silent with despair.

Many miles from now, they will breathe My pure
Air again. I will wait until they return.

III: Daughter

I used to sing songs of youth
With my love. We would dance through
The traces of poesy, fast pursuing
Time with the pace of a wave's roar
Wrenched from its coral vortex. That
Was a time when I was drenched
In beauty's palpable, blood-panting
Rhymes, when to be young was very love.
But I was left alone, and I am alone now.

But the Furies' consuming powers
Bent me down like winter's ice-
Heavy bowers of birch and cedar and
Spruce. My lips on his became lifeless
And cold, passing through the phases
Of love's brief season, its briefer hour.
And I have flown away now, like Noah's
Dove, like a taper's flame blown by
Cold breath into the eyes of darkness.

Snapdragon, wild honey oaks, turtle
Blossoms, funny little leaves of love
Wasted and rent by the sunny days of
Summer, sift and sidle to the ground
Of my subtle cells and sequester in
Whirlwind rifts behind my eyes. He will
Nevermore hear my willow-wept tears
Of incompletion, though they will lick
His lips and bathe his sighs with unfelt
Tears, until death intercepts decrepitude.

IV: Son

For many hours of my life now, I have
Wandered lone and silent as a gypsy,
As a bedouin, who, in his nomadic
Fleeing from death, forgets that
He too is but a man among men, who
Must not act apart but breathe
In concord with all living men.

I have travelled through the antique
Narrows of Rome and felt the pulse
That blows through every cat-lined
Alley and breathes the sighs of love
Evermore. Yet I am not there as before.

Nor am I where Santa Maria Maggiore
Illumines Guardi's Grand Canal by
Nightglow. I wish that I could recall
The inspiring flow of *vaporetti*
Churning the islands between Lido
And the Mediterranean's golden gem.

I have paused beside the broken walls
Of Kenilworth, dreaming of the love-
Token worn by Merlin, and have kept
Vigil along the unfallen parapets of
Carcassonne. But I have not belonged to time.

My heart has climbed with me, heavy
And slow, to the peaks of Chartres, where
The red-roofed wind blows cool through
The auburn woof of human endeavour.
Yet I was unmoved and uncharmed
By her warm spread of coloured history.

I have sipped the elixir of youth,
But its heat mixed through my body
Like red-molten earth from Vesuvius,
Dissolving my features in static longing
For another birth, like undug Attic ruins
Trampled by throngs of daily creatures.

My night is beautifully sequined. The
Seashore sifts its coralblond strands
With lunar suggestions that the shifting
Breezes make under their voice. But its sands
Are blown away invisibly into the climate,
And I am left alone. And I am alone now.

I have traversed the constellated web
Of night and have brooked its restless
Playgrounds with my mind. But I have
Returned, now, to my mossy haunt of days
Borne full back on the wild-whispering
Rack of darkwindless currents of memory.

V: Daughter

I was the enemy of time, and beauty's
Fast-fading image was my sole defender.
It was her duty to sustain the invasions
Of deceit and doubt that crowd the mind,
That make retreat from life too much suspect,
That force proud men and women to cower
From the respectable promise of molding
Hope and surprise into a thousand living
Fabrics of dream-coloured child eyes.

I felt the tug of his tongued breath
Urging my innocence to relent to the supple
Caress of redyellow flames, and I consented,
Like the unrepentant rose that dares to bud
Itself among the ensnaring treacheries
Of Indian summer. Metamorphosing
Beauty deceived me with her inconstancy. She
Cloaked the simple mysteries of love in myth
And impassioned fancy. She dressed me for death.

I grieved dry-white tears for the dying
Harvest of our seedtime, for our completion
*

Was conceived too early and gleaned with
Too much haste to flower in the wasting furrows
Of my heart. Time had preempted beauty,
Beauty time, until death's dry pose
Appeared to me through the portal of despair,
And I flung myself out of love, into the fright-
Filled jaws of night, which hung around my hollow
Frame like lightning exploded across a storm.

VI: Son

My head is light with the nightfall
Sounds of insomnia, which fill distracting
Thoughts with a temporal impasse that
Is neither wakefulness nor dizzy sleep.
I recede into the solitude of memory,
While the tears of love lost and
Gone pierce my eyes. I weep,
Shrinking into the blank maze of dream.

(Willow winds are wafting soft breezes
Of yellow Memphis night-streams
Through my nostrils, while the moon's
Serpentine beams dilate and filter-
Flow down the corridors of sorrow
And loss like tiny, white sand drops
Drain-dripping through the nose
Of an antique hourglass frozen
Upon the bureau of timelessness.

Gazelles spring toward me with cadenced
Strides, leaping fence posts of jaded
Sleep, while the Marquesa de Bo-peep has
Lost her sheepish grin before I
Can even tell her to hide her sins
From the agents of doom who
Would fleece her virginity and virtue.)

VII: Father

Fly high, full-blown lover!
The sky is not deep enough
For your hopes, your feline
Instincts, your sure, benign
Indifference to things fine
*

And easy. Fly high, under cover
Of night, with signals dark
And slow. Soar and float, and
If you fail to reach that goal,
Remember that your birth will
Come again on another shoal
Of reincarnation. I, the Father
Of night, call to you, languid
And silent, through the vapours,
Saying, "Go where you will, and
Suit your own taste, whether
Green, silent blue, or tawdry
Golden. But remember the curse:
You will be alone, a stranger
To yourself and to memory, mute
To indifference and passing time,
Until, being unborn once more, you
Return to me with infinite loving."

VIII: Son

The soft sea taunts me with its
Shifting turf and its sandless
Bottoms. It calls to me a low-
Moaning murmur, salt-stained and
Misty-moist with siltsoft streams.
I don't pity the sandy shore or
The awful onslaught of sea licks
That lap at its impressions. The
Footprints that we left that day
And marked are gone, bereft and
Swallowed by the incoming tide,
Erased by the gliding whitecaps
Of foam and seaweed. The seeds of
Our love are gone too, dissolved
Into sea strata and fish bone, blown
To the gulled winds, breezesown
And lost across the infinite Gulf.
My baby girl has gone home now.
She has been long gone from me,
From my changing shore, my Rhodes,
My Calypso of changeless forms,
And I am alone to cry with the
Gulls, to breathe the stale, salty sands
*

Of the Gulf, of love that will never
Renew itself in life. She has died
From me and been unborn again,
As she was before the terrible curse
Of birth and beauty settled over us.

IX: Father

There was beauty in those lips,
Hawthorn red and cherry bright.
There was love in those lengthened
Hips, where ships of desire and
Plunder lurked like pirates ranging
Some uncharted stretch of sea; where
Fire dragons swarmed around (those
Accursed monsters of repulsion who
Fetch maidens from shoals of Bimini);
Where Odysseus seduced Scylla and
Charybdis, Ulysses inflamed Penelope,
Jason searched for some golden fleece.

But the Furies cast a spell, Hell-bound,
Upon her naked soul and then
Fled to the farthest pole of light.
They left her to herself, doomed
And burdened with the knowledge of
What a woman so charmed and fair
Would never again share with any of
That fabled race of child-men who
Were blinded by her golden strands
Of hair, her jade-green eyes, and
Her highborn stare. Strange and
Alone, she must endure the tempters
And the angels of Satan, the wiles
Of Charon, and the sighs of Bacchus.

I have carried My son back to the sea-
Haunt of their infancy to seek her, but
Nowhere is she to be found, though he
Sounds the depths of day and the reaches
Of dying nightlight for a single sigh,
A solitary scent of her love. Once she was
There. Green and golden were her eyes
To him; goldengreen were her soft sighs
Of child breath in his ears. They are gone.
*

She has flown high and far from his sight,
Gone with the winds of tropical Cancer
And myriad satyrs of their wretched life
To a planet of no-time, locked and hidden
Somewhere beyond Compassion and Narcotica.

X: Daughter

I became suspended and held close
In the embrace of a world blended
With trafficked indolence and petty desire.
I was disgraced by the uncontrollable
Fires of those who loved without loving.
I was imposed upon and mocked by the curse
Of being indifferent to the perversity
That passing time exacts from our beliefs.
For He is a father who receives without
Giving relief, who steals from memory
The fleeting dreams of future joy, who
Destroys illusions of happiness and then
Repays His debt with counterfeit notes
Of blank confusion and doubt. O time!
O miserable inquisitor of mankind! You
Have left my mind intruded by grim fear
And brooding loss in a dark, alien land.

Life became a mere shadow of itself,
Fading in artificial recession like remains
Of a rain-soaked cask opened for the last
Processional to knell its fast-rotting
Flesh into dust, to cast its crusty form
Into the depths of shadowy nothingness.

I lived in an age outside of time and
Generation and spatial reference, alone
Within the pages of ancient travelogues,
Where island worlds and random no-name
Cities became blotted pinpoints of postponed
Destiny. I longed for the mysteries of my
Unremembered past and for the Septembering
Journeys we used to make together when
We belonged to ourselves and no one else.

But that phase was gone, even from
Thought, and the remaining days of my life
*

Were fast becoming the strained histories
Of shortening hours. Finally, the quartering
Seconds ticked away the unfathomable layers
Of my cell-less works, beckoning me to the
Finality of despair, and I was hurled into the
Dusty air, into the neutral void of another
World, to loiter in waiting, to smother alive.

My being was transfixed by the grey-black
Mixtures of spaceless uniformity that blanked
My blanched eyes. My ears were wound tight
In the nets of time-bound silence that flanked
All space with the deafening shrills and the
Screaming hysteria of belching claxons
Of doom. Meanwhile, the inhuman sounds
Of unquelled devil-laughter continued to yell
At me through ten thousand unbending waves
Of maddening echo. I was insane and frenzied
By the vain, sweet-tempting vision
Of numberless graves that danced beneath
Similar, scepterless tombstones. In my half-
Waking dream, I saw the bones of uncounted
Bodies inscribing each cenotaph with a similar
Refrain; the names and dates on each frame
Were all the same name, the same date, each
Mocking fortune, each blasting the dubious
Fame of one whose name was my name, unfamiliar to me,
One whose infamy was written in each inscription.
Then my vision ceased to be, and I could see
Myself flashing by those graves with unabating
Certainty as I came to rest on the dusky beach.
I crouched low into the cold bite of the sea
And watched life flow out and away from me.

Father, I want to die. I pray that You
Will allow me to fly from this horrible fate
And to be alone with myself no more.
Father, let me die! Let me plow the sea's
Turf until I am worthy once more to accept
The flowering birth of Your seeds of love!
Let me die, Father, into the regions
Above the light of common day, to pray
Among the legion of love's triumvirate,
To stay in your season of glorious eventide!
*

I want to die. Die for me, Father, so that
Love will again flow into my hollow being.
Blow an undefeated whisper back on the
Tidal breath of this drowning frame, Father,
And let the bridal ring of Your words divorce
Me from life's impatient loves. Bring us home
To each other! Die for me, Father, and for
My brother in life, my lover, Your son,
Our victim of living strife! Overthrow me
In this hour of sickness! Imprison my soul
In Your glowing cell, and let me soar
And float until death's Hell be no more!

XI: Father

She has travelled from Bimini to Nassau,
In the Bahamas, gamboling with night
And Negroes and nicotine and with a heart
Neither contrite nor soft. The winds start,
And the sea goes through her veins like
Dramamine, which soothes artificially and then
Pains the senses in lingering lethargy.

She stands on a coral beach green with
The aquamarine, blue-green strands of
Solar unguentine, while the sands breach
The smiles of onrushing waves that are
Shattered by the reefs and the tide-battered
Fishing barks, whose weathered nets are strewn
Asunder for mending. She is grieving for
The loss of mystery, which sends her grief
Streaming, in tears of silence, downward
To touch the nonviolent remains of the
Powerful sea as they rise, inching to her
Wet-naked feet, on softsilent water limbs.

The flickering lights of Providence
Are filled with clatter, yet she can't hear
What trusting mothers fear; she doesn't
Fear what others have said with their sneers
And smothering derision. She is alone,
Stark and moist to the bone, and the
Liquid breeze insinuates her body
With tones of thrust-jagged harmonies.

She cries to the stars and the far-
Off strains of nostalgia, of New York
By night. She crouches, now, slowly
Fighting the tides, into the womb of Gulf.
She bends low into the cold bite of
Salt water and sees life flowing
Out of her body and entering the sea's
Naked shadow, until she is no more
Than stillness itself. And she is one.
And she is one, now, with the depths
That swirl between shore and death,
Between flickering night and memory.
She dies, drowning in her own wet image.
I have heard her pray, and I await her retreat.
She is homeward set, flowing to the end of day.

XII: Son

I gaze upon her absence,
Hearing her eyes speak to me
With tears of fearfulness and the
Desire to express her love.

My eyes murmur through misty blinks
And then say, "I love you, love you,
Love," and I want to kiss her
On her eyes so that they will see
My warm breath and sense my heart
Pumping pulses through her sight.

But her absence defies vision;
It denies precision, and all I
Can sense is the absence itself.
Be one and yet three in one
At the same time! Be *was* and *am*
And *will be*, simultaneously!

Be present to me, even when absence
And fear descend from the regions
Of past trial-and-error experience!
For what is there without response?

XIII: Daughter

Zephyrus lifted my wet soul, carrying me
Up from my deathless sea-bed on the dripping
*

Dewdrops of rising vapour. I was unmarried
From life's figured festival and free
To soar and float at will above and beneath
The council of love's unreasoned demands.

Though you will never hear my real voice
While you stand speckled and solitary among
The feckless seashore creatures of daydust,
I call to you, my one love of earthly lapse,
Regardless, adoring the nearness of your
Absence, abhorring the distance of your presence.

We will be one together once more, as we are
One alone, now, between night and death and
Memory, one forever with godly intimations
Of loving oneness. There will be time together
Evermore to touch the moon's wide smile
With our lips, when we shall ride her beams
With breathless sighs. And there will be time
Again to bow down, sipping the honey nectars
Of higher life, time to lie down upon the
Gloried shoals of reincarnation, flying with
Ageless wings over the singing spread of one
Fulfillment, which, in our other life, was mere
Mortal completion, incomplete as unfulfilled.

But soon we will be born into infinite communion,
For I am bound once more toward my home,
Which lies beyond the faceless days of death,
Which flows before the terrific rush of birth
Into which we were sown. Our Father awaits
My return, and with unknown gladness and hope
That looks both before and behind, I anxiously
Anticipate His burning hand, His brand on mine.

XIV: Son

But wait! I have heard her voice
Calling after me through the wind's
Misty eyes and on the flying spray
Of blinking breakers. Her slow whisper
Trails behind her on the tailwind of
Speed. It is filling my thoughts,
Telling me that, like the wavewashes,
Our seeds will flow again in timeless
*

Cycles and that their burning passion
Will return in yet another form, on
Yet another day. I say, "Lover,
Sweet, soft lover, fly higher than
The black-bottomed distance of night."
I pray, sweet princess of peace, that
The living memory of our love will teach me
To see what is in my stubborn heart,
That I may nevermore remain apart
From the love that lives above the
Commonality of every hour, that floats
Above each solitary speck of sand
That passes through the mind of life's
Most precious periods of quiet time.

XV: Father

Now you have evolved to Me, daughter
Of dust, creature of My imagination,
Through the dizzy maze of mortality
And the unsolved riddles of immortal
Mystery. You are home to Me, reborn.

You have loved My son, as I meant
For you to do, learning to love with
Another, looking through the self and
Beyond to still another, brooking
Death's awful countenance with infantile
Longing to love, crying to me through
A gleeful smile of understanding and naked
Piety. You are home to Me, reborn in Me.

I am the Father of night and everlasting
Life, Guardian of the world without end.
I remove the curse of life from you,
And you are free now to burst forth
Into the glories of revelation, into
A loving liberated from time and beauty
And the leveling forces of grey inconstancy.

Still, I say unto you that there yet
Remains behind you a lonely straggler,
Who is bound in the chains of grief and
Solitude. You must never neglect him;
Rather, soften his pains and ease his
*

Tired bereavement by loving him as you
Love Me, even though your feelings
Will be separated by time and white death.
For only then will he feel no loss
Too great for him to endure nor any
Fate that he cannot resist with the sure
Faith that outlasts insistent plagues
And the vagaries that past experience
Plays on the mind's forgetfulness.

Call him always to Me through your eyes.
Fill his sighs with your constant love,
The simple little reminders,
For then alone will he ever find
The seed of your loving beauty and the
Need to perpetuate his living duties in every
Honey-oak tree and yellow-bellied foxglove,
In the flight of each bird that soars,
Softly and free, above the aspen and evergreen.
This is My word, proud daughter unto Me.

XVI: Son and Daughter

No more will the awful curse
Of birth and unrestrained beauty
Pain our numberless days or confine
Us to worship the blind phases of
Mortal lovers who never discover life's
Mysterious periods of quietude and calm.
Our love will outlast the injurious
Blasts of change and sly circumstance,
And soon we will be one in the soft
Union of loving compliance, three in
One with eternal kindness, living
Forever in longloving communion.

2/4–6, 2/8, 2/11, & 2/13/65 (dates for piece as a whole) (05026)

[Blessed are the meek,] ‡

Blessed are the meek,
        For they shall inherit the earth.
Blessed are the mild,
        For they shall be givers of birth.

Blessed are the weak,
> For they shall not be forlorn.
Blessed are the defiled,
> For they shall not be scorned.

Blessed are the bleak,
> For they shall know no godly fear.
Blessed are the beguiled,

2/7/65 (05061)

A Father's Despair

Mortal lover! Where are you now, you
Who once looked with chagrin as our cow
Jumped over the mothergoose moon?
Mortal lover! Where are you now, you
Who soon fled from sight, into the mild
Midnight recesses of dream with Me?
Mortal lover! Where are you now, you
Who vanquished the bittersweet sighs of
Lucifer with the elixir of your eyes?
Mortal lover! Where are you right now?

Come to Me undisguised and naked and
Abundant with desire. I will breathe kisses
Of love into your bosom, and we will melt
Together in the softness of My glowing fire.
Mortal lover! Return now from where you are!

2/10/65 — [1] (05062)

Warm Night in February

> I went into the night
> > to touch the stars,
> > > where they hung
> In the black clutches
> > of bright, blinking,
> > > summering light.

They felt my tired little sighs,
Where I stood in the just-right corner
Of innocence. They kissed my breath
With straining silence, and then it was
I discovered that loving lives in things
Unseen and in voices never heard before.

The night spoke to me of things unseen
During the fast glimmer of fading days,
While the voiceless rush of hazy clouds
Called me to their pathless skyways
As they flew from place to windy place.
I followed as far as my eyes could gaze
And then returned to where I had stood
For the eternity of that moment's phase.

When a lone straggler, one stray cloud,
Passed over, the face of the pocked moon
Was blotted from the night's wide smile
As it paced from clime to lunar clime.
I had seen the world, and then it passed
Into cloud covers. Warm rain gave birth
To my eyelids, and I slid from nightlight,
Until I was dissolved in dreamless sleep
Behind the opaline lids of my tired being.

        I returned from night
              to touch the stars,
                    where they hung
        In the blank clutches
              of my deep, sinking,
                    wintering sleep.

2/10/65 — [2] (05063)

Faith Is

Faith
        in the incalculable femininity
        of feline stretches of nightfall
Is
        a mazy circuitry of etched lines,
        *

deep-dug with crosshatchings
that melt the patchwork quilt
of an inspired, artistic mind
into graphics of unabstracted
Divinity.

Faith

in the indefinable mystery
of lingering lapses of silence

Is

a tottering child of ten months' cheer,
who topples into its mother's breast
from fear of noise
and the screaming violence of foreign objects
that threaten its innocent

Infancy.

Faith

in the indispensable dissertations
of one heart in discourse with another

Is

a highly wrought verse of poetry
that hurries to reach beyond its coterie
with soft humility,
unselfishly speaking to man's frailty
with lofty syllables of unmetered

Commiseration.

Faith

in the inexplicable season
of snow-bathed days at dawn

Is

a white-dressed honey dove that retreats,
returning with sprigs of love-leaves
that blossom in Biblical lawns,
where waters recede in slow succession
from the tree of unacknowledged

Reason.

Faith

in the irrefutable revolution
through decay to the soul's rebirth

Is

a blasty, cold-wrinkled winter of blight
*

that lasts for the space of a dream
and then fights to be free,
dissolving in spring's burning breath
when God molds dust into higher
Evolution.

[2/12–13/65]? (05064)

[I am imprisoned beneath the ceiling . . .]

I am imprisoned beneath the ceiling of night, swinging from one of Piranesi's dangling ropes as I leap Tarzan-like from one smile to the next, from one salutation to the next farewell. I noticed that the moon came out of hiding, early this afternoon, to spy on me where I was standing beneath a cowering honey-oak tree. All day long, my mind has been running faster than a scared winter jack rabbit under fire; only, there is no more fire left in my charge. She is still saying in my ears one feeble, assiduous refusal to believe what I have done, almost as though the shock of my behaviour were too real to believe or imagine. She is saying, "I guess you learn something new every day." And I can still hear myself ringing in my own ears, "Yes, but sometimes it takes a lot longer than that." But the moon knew what I was saying, even if her cells refused to make contact.

So I will withdraw, hibernate into the normal constancy of the everyday world, remembering what a Wordsworth could say and would declare if he could ever meet Dostoevsky's underground man. Yes, he would have to say something about to fear and love — but to love as prime and chief, for there fear ends. Yes, and I will love again, living within the commonality of everyday love of all people, for there the fear of loving only one person will desist.

I can hear Spanish verse flowing through my ears again, as I did once before; only, now I can remember what it was and who feared enough at the time to transcribe it for us. The good Fray Luis de León, in his retired life, wrote the most beautiful of all verses when he reclaimed from Shelley's visitations of the divinity in man this thought:

> *Qué descansada vida,* ◊
> *la del que huye el mundanal ruido*
> *y sigue la escondida*
> *senda por donde han ido*
> *los pocos sabios que en el mundo han sido . . .*

I have flown high for a short while, and now I am returning to my groundbed outside the city limits of love's last boundaries. What will I do, now that I have to return? There is nothing left in me that burns except for the awful sting of the burnt-out remains of a faint-glowing char fire of a love lost and gone, and I am empty, evacuated of all that was inside of me to give out of myself. I will have to store up another batch of love for the next unfortunate person that chances to cross paths with me. But I will prepare myself, don't you worry about that, old Dr. Johnson, my buddy, my pal, my teacher of the verities of what it means to seek repentance for our vanities and daily contrivances. I will go to my Uttoxeter here in White Cross and stand under one rain and repent for you, father of my school-time youth. Yes, I will pray for you and do homage for your sad soul in the hope that your exemplum will serve me as I strike out from here to God only knows where. I can still see you standing there, though it was almost two hundred years ago now. You are OK in my book, and I won't forget you or Bos or the good Dr. Levet or Thrale or Mrs. Williamson either.

Today, before the moon rose, I heard the funniest thing that I have ever heard, from a stupid garage mechanic. He told me that I looked like the old man and the sea that had lost. That's funny, isn't it, Ernest? Hey, Ernie, let's do be earnest about this whole matter. Yes, let's do. Do you think I have lost the big battle in the sky?

Well, there will be no more poetry for you, old gal, because I think that you have lost the battle with my time, and there isn't any more. It has just run out for you and me. We were short on rations to begin with, I suppose. All we had were a few honey-oak trees and a stupid turtle that you had worn too long anyway, until it was beginning to bite where it really hurts. But it was kicks, wasn't it? The flavour lasted just a little bit too long for us, and now I have dried up and petrified into dusty sentimentality. There will come a day when the princess of peace will live happily ever after again, but that will be in another millennium, right, W.B.Y.?

* * *

This typewriter has had much abuse from my unthinking fingers, and so have I. Where do you stop, though, and just how easy is it to know when you have had enough? True, I will never see her again, but I worry about the nights when I am supposed to be sleeping and which, instead, I will spend thinking about her. Why is it that everything has to run its course even before the purblind Doomsters of Hardy's come chasing after us? I can't find an answer to all that, though I comb the hills of my furrowed mind. I am walking, now, into the subcutaneous

layers of my brain, and it is very dark and gloomy. I am heavy with
sardonic scowl and the weariness of miles on miles of absurd trudg-
ing, journeying which has led me nowhere except to the further re-
gions of my IBM data-processing machine. I can't even think straight
now. Stop this infernal machine, this typewriter of my untabulated
rasa. Poetry, I call for a little of that soothing stuff to ring my ears
clear of this insipid self-pity. Stop, I say, and let me hear something
from you, muses. . . .

Being and not being anything,
Feeling alive and not living,
Seeing and not hearing the eye-blink
Of the turtledove and night when
It whispers blue notes of death —
This is the sickness of my being.

Living without the sure faith that tomorrow
I will be alive or the hope that today I can
Pray is the sure sign that my being is dead.
Give me a hell to believe in if there is no
Other promotion in life besides the terrible
Commotion of inactivity and indolence and
Loving without being loved, of living without
Being able to pray for another tomorrow.

My heart cries out with a ruby mouth
That scalds my lungs. It is breathing
Blood of ten thousand living tongues
Of dragon, gargoyle, and demi-Gorgon.

I am lost in the confines of
                    my own
                        skull.

Carry me up from this dungeon of wicked
                        despair, and
        lift my soul until it can climb back into
                    the light of common day,
                        to live, to hope, and to
                            pray.

There is a grotto somewhere beyond Nighttime
And Clandestination where I long to go. We
    *

Will have a fine time, just you and I, self-
Pity. We can make love to ourselves and then
Laugh when we are done with the bed scene.

Why can't I make any soft poetry tonight? I want more than any-
thing in this tiny world to make soft poetry, to mold singing verses
that will play themselves back in my ears long after I have retired to
my night cell. But they refuse to form themselves, and I just don't
have enough strength to make them work for me. Write me a "Kubla
Khan" poem, please, Mister Milquetoast. I don't care if I will have to
make an apology to anyone who reads it. The important thing is that I
write one now, so that I can take something to bed with me besides the
horrific memories of this afternoon and, for that matter, all of the
afternoons this week in which I have eaten nothing but gall and seen
nothing besides the wonderful essays of Bacon and the better and
more applicable ones of T. Carlyle. You know, dear God, that a fellow
can take only so much of that truth at one time before he decides to
tell his system to break down. . . . Oh, You didn't know that? Well,
remind me, when I see You next, to relate all that has happened since
You left the scene. There have been a few wars. Yes, and a few great
loves, too. Yes, even a few of those, too.

2/14/65 (05199)

[To fall asleep in the embrace . . .] ‡

To fall asleep in the embrace of a Hemingway short story is a dis-
astrous experience because the abruptness of his inane sentences is
so repetitious and a

                To write a Hemingway story like "Up in Michigan" or
  This morning was   "The Three-Day Blow,"
                                                    but *better*

        The north shore of Lake Superior is a fine place to be living near
during the warmer months of the year.

        I detest sleeping, unless my body absolutely demands it, because
I'm afraid I just might miss something, irrevocably.

Now, is that the talk of a cynic,
I ask you?

2/16/65 — [2] (05200)

[I was the last man, I dreamed,] †

I was the last man, I dreamed,
To watch the moaning, menstrual world
Come to stasis, while all inhabitants
Careened

2/18/65 — [1] (05201)

[A bumptious night owl called me]

A bumptious night owl called me
to its voice as I walked along
the icy streets of our nearby forest.
It was laughing at me as though
my voice were a thing small
and lonely, and I hooted to it
with mocking silence. What did
that owl, so lone and so silent,
have to do with me? And what
did I to do with it, so all alone
and so filled with violent thoughts?

2/18/65 — [2] (05202)

[I live my life in books, . . .] ‡

I live my life in books, existing, breathing in crisp pausations at
each turn of a page. My heart beats with the energy of forgotten
others who have hoped to speak to man's continual travail through
their pencil or typewriter. When will I achieve that certain sense of
comforting equanimity that so many seem to possess, living with-
out questioning what it is that motivates them to participate in the
routines of life?

I don't want it, the routine, the burdens of owning up each day to bumper-locked traffic and frenzied people who come to offer their services, because that's just not enough, not enough to be offering a service, to direct somebody else in how a thing should get done. "I don't want it, don't want it, don't!" I scream out loud to myself and to Dali's bent watches, which droop lithographically over my tiny cubicle-study.

"Money!" people cry, pothering me with the inane mimicry of millions of listless souls who consider themselves Newtons or Keplers or Einsteins of the modern world because they believe they have found a way to explain, nay, beat, the system. System, you fools? There is only one system, and that's the one that is written in the back of everyone's tremulous mind from the time he is born. It's a system of human entropy, in which the body makes sure progress toward dissolution, no matter what cavalier, dissimulating measures each takes to avoid the fractional, divisible quotient of death. Systems, you say? Why, you stupid sons-of-bitches! Didn't anyone ever tell you that all people are equal and at once above and beneath the divisible fraction, so that no matter how greatly their numerator is increased, they still get diminished by the imperious indifference of a voiceless denominator, which is their own conscience, their own sense of ultimate failure to sustain themselves in the face of merciless, pitiable, even pathetic disappointment?

But Dali's bent watches will always droop like overripe plums hanging heavy in their very self-destructive tumescence from some branch, unless somebody decides to proclaim himself, arbitrarily, Keeper of the Watches, in which case he will rip the canvas from its Museum of Modern Art frame and abscond with faceless time. Then all time will stop, and maybe people will be conscious that something is missing from their Sunday afternoon museum routine. Maybe just one somebody, somewhere, will say, nay, ask, himself, the significance of that missing time and discover that, in the asking, he can even get along without it for a few days, until the New York authorities apprehend the thief, who, they will report to the local sex tabloid, calls himself the Prince of Darkness and Lies and who runs under the alias of James Bad or Mordecai Moloch, who is a tricky, elusive devil. Then, when he is safely transported to the lower isolation chambers of Devil's Island and the picture has been repaired and set among its compatriots again, all will be back to its ordered design, all will function again in the big world-city like clockwork, as they like to say. They? Who are they? Why, they are you and all the yous everywhere who point the finger at the next person, implying that it is always the other he who is culpable.

But everything does work like voiceless clockwork. Everyone gauges his "each new day" by the bill due date or by the bus schedule, the taximeter, the class bell, overtired Big Ben, which tolls tradition and stiff-colored stolidity to the transience of each tourist or businessman off in a hurry or the apeneck artist, who parades his mental nakedness to every syphilitic or aging movie star or tyro Vassar girl "doing Europe" for the summer.

Even love is mechanical, not that the pneumatics of the process are to be denied. Love: another one of the self-deluding systems that people construct so that they can run their blueprints off on a digital computer and get the same perfect results each time.

I scream when thinking grabs hold of me. It is so insipid and useless; it's like pissing in the ocean. But someday I am going to do just that, going to urinate right into the Gulf, near St. Petersburg, and like Nero, I'm just going to stand by and watch the Gulf rise on tiny water-limbs, until it inundates all of Florida and then crawls up over the country like a shadow of the sun pulling its elongation up the side of a whitewashed wall as the sun hurls itself toward nocturnal demise.

Say, stop! Why am I using those words again, "nocturnal demise"? That crap is incommunicable, even if I can understand it. I know damn good and well that what I meant was "sunset" — yes, that's it — moving toward dawn. Yes, and all the rest (about urinating into the Gulf) is nonsense. I suppose all I wanted to remember to tell myself was to think clearly, to tell myself that a guy can only do so much thinking, so much trying to explain things to himself through introspection, and then everything breaks down, all ties, every bond of communication and common apprehension between me and my book, between me and all those who have looked me in the eye before, who had time or made time to cut short their rigid schedule somewhere to smile with me or even just to exert the energy to twist their body to wave a salutary hello.

Yes, I am screaming aloud inside myself, and the echoing pain that reverberates within me is almost overpowering. Stop this! Stop it! Stop it! Please! Yes, I will surrender. What are your conditions? What are the terms of this contract? I scream; I call uncle. Yes, damn it. Uncle, uncle, uncle. Let me be, head! Let me be, I say!

But you persist. Stop it! OK, don't stop, you son-of-a-bitch. Yell! Yell! Yell! Go to hell, me! I — I — I — you hurt too much.

(Next entry
in diary:)

Dear God, I must apologize if you are listening to me, apologize because I have never started one of my entries with your invocation. In fact, I don't really know what made me do it, unless it was because I found last night that I could no longer write even to myself; my writing was too pompous, too presumptuous, too bombastic or rhetorical — I really don't know. But, nonetheless, I discovered that I had run out of things to tell my mind; it just up and refused to listen any longer, so I am calling to You because You are out there somewhere, beyond the blank blackness of my study window. I can't see You, but I can smell Your presence in the warmth of the night.

It is a strange, eerie night, dear God, and my hands are shaking with too much coffee — or I suppose that's what it is. I am leaning over my heavy, shiny desk, and the lamp above me has cast itself onto the patinated surface below my eyes. Now I can see my own face in its glossy finish, almost as though my desk top were the surface of an unrippled pond. A tear just dropped from my whiskery cheek and fell into my desk-face, but the imaginary water didn't send out any concentric circles. The tearwater is flowing slightly over my right desk-eye, and now it has come to rest over my reflected sideburn.

Dear God, I am afraid; I am crying with short sobs, and I've never ever done this as long as I can remember. Why am I crying, afraid? I am so afraid of my hollowness. My head is dizzy again, as it gets when I am scared, and I can sense that awful feeling that comes over me as though someone has turned on ten cold showers inside my skull. Everything is getting tighter now: my room is closing in on me, coming closer to where I am sitting. The books are coming down off their shelves in regiments, and they are marching toward me from every direction. Their uniforms are all different colors, and they are glowering at me with gaping dust wrappers.

Dear God, I am so weak I just want to put my head down into the desk drawer and hide from them. Stop them, please! Something, somebody, God, Donne's three-personed God, I beg you, please!

I felt something then — not much better though. My hands are tremoring all up my arms, and my legs are flabby now. I want to rise and run from the room, but where is my strength? It has melted like frost into sunlight.

I must get up — got to — just got to. Let me out of this stinkin' room of history. Let me run to the stars and the warmth of the simple night outside.

(Same entry,
   3 hrs. later:
     conversion,
       communion with
         God's warmth)

2/19–20/65 (05203)

The Fallowness of Night

I have searched everyplace;
I have looked into every face
That has spoken to me, but nowhere
Is the eye that cares or the stare
That speaks love to be shared
With me. I am a stranger, mute, alone.
I answer my own voice in the phone,
Which rings but once, then fades away.
But the echo of that voice preys
On my ears like a thousand angry rays
Of too-bright light on the lids of the blind.

I have left sleep to hide in the fallowness
Of night. My mind is anguished, shallow,
And empty of hope that looks beyond
The dismal dreams of those who fondle
Secret wishes for a brighter tomorrow.

My sighs are filled with the sorrowful
Contagion of solitude, which spreads sickness
Through every frayed nerve like the quick,
Stolid indifference of a cyclone
Lashing a village with raging and unknown
Pressure and vindictiveness. I am blown up,
Exploded, and my heart is thrown open
To the demons of my hungry mind.
They gnaw me apart like so much rind-
Carrion or refuse or garbage left behind
By an ocean trawler churning the horizon.

Free me from this awful, binding strain,
From the burden of my mind's invisible chains,
*

Which gyve me to myself. I must endure the guile
Of my own false will until it exiles
My being from the darkness of this Devil's Isle.

2/22/65 (05065)

[The image of the Phoenix . . .] †

The image of the Phoenix has been inordinately abused through the years.
       I want to go home.
I swore off cigarettes last night,
but the fight is more than I can bear.
I swear that the last one will be
the last one, and then I bum another.

"Baby, the Rain Must Fall" → but Jeremiah preyed too hard and too long on the patience of the farmers, and they lynched him for false representation.

"A handful of toil is what I have," cried God to Himself before He could sleep.
Who stole the wind?

The wind nuzzled up against the swaybacks of prairie grass and breathed into them the whisper of love. The funny little tricklets of water that melted from limestone crags of Hannibal cliffs soon held a meeting of the mind and spirit and became the Mississippi River.

White Cross: what is it? It is a city, nay, a breath of life that has gone limp.

I change with the diverse weather of winter like a river chameleon climbing the various rocks of a stream's bank on a sunny day and scampering into the remains of foliage that overlook the water.

Winter is a time of putrescence for one who needs a warm Gulf rest. Take me out of this cold fog of down-sifting snow, and transplant the scion of my imagination into the satiety of Floridian soil and the tepid climate of a *calmado* day in St. Petersburg May!

I can't get out of this library hollow, with its Tennysons and Donnes and Boswells and Coleridges. Transport my spirit from this proving ground, and let me create out of the spectrum of warm-coloured peace of mind!

To tread soft snow on foot can be very nice, almost like breathing with nostalgia a Currier & Ives winter scene or reading a poem of Robert Frost's, but today my mind is effete and jaded, and the fissures of my brain wizened and jejune.

Today the world spun too far off its axis, and time was dislocated; there was no choice but for me to break down all forms of order. I will make no order today, unless it be the one thought that orders all order.

I am out of money; I hope the month gets done soon.

My clear plastic ballpoint pen reminds me of a rectal thermometer, and I'd like to stick it up my butt.

Today is a mean, ragged excuse
for God's divine design. Hang loose
Mother Goose, and let this little nursery
rhyme wind out spindle thoughts
that can sing with the sagging
snowflakes that fall from infinity.
Sing praises be to Him who helped
create this morbid day, and pray
that the rainmaker will go away.
I can't take too much winter
at any one season of my mood,
because it brings with it attitudes
that crave escape from the thaw.
Snow that was beauty-bright as it fell
from the nighttime blackness of sleep
turns to slush and foot-filled dirt,
like clay bodies of people who die
from bone and flesh to dust and dust
and dustrutty red clay before sleep
*

can quit its hold. And so I plea
that if I should die before I wake,
I pray the snow and slush dust
shall not forsake old Ave Maria,
who can still redeem from decay
the visitation of the day's divinity
in man, woman, and snowbeast.

I heard someone say, "Give us
this day," and I thought, "Fool."
"Give us this day." But the day
is no damn good. It has filled
the earth's ruts with snow drifts, and
sifting sleet has filled people-feet.
"Give us this day" — "Keep it,
you Indian giver!"

The day is more violent than a thousand porcupine quills shot at a
curious dog by the archer's crossbow battalion, quills tipped not with
poison but with the soft-melting coldness of snowflakes. I hate it,
hate it, hate, and I beg remittance from it: give me my money back; I
didn't know that the show of the day would be so poor.

The soup of the day is vegetable snow
                     split-pea snow
                     mushroom snow
                     cock-a-leekie snow
                     cream of snow
                     minestrone snow

I stood in a room in which some unseen visitor snapped off the
light switch, and I watched time dissolve into darkness. "Someone
cut off the power!" I heard myself scream out. "Who the hell broke
the circuit?"
I waited long enough to hear the time go back on, and then I could
see its brightness upon the smooth inner surface of my eyelids. It was
time I saw and heard light up in the form of a sudden coruscation
thrown off the artificial glassiness of the stiff man laid out in his
casket for last well-wishers.

Bela Lugosi bit me, last night, in the jugular vein. I think I would
like to have him do it again tonight. It's unique — you know what I

mean? — seeing him all that time in the movies and then to really meet him in person. Well, that's a real gas, unique *et* all. He signed his autograph on my neck and breast — too much, huh? I guess — a real, signed Lugosi

> I am a werewolf; when the summer moon
>> is in full bloom,
>> I will bite every young maiden
>> in the womb.

> Let us go then, you and I,
>> when the evening is spread out against the sky
>>> like a werewolf upon a bloody maiden

My nerves are tiny pistons lined up in a row along my system, pulsing with uncontrollable energy and design. Where they will take me is difficult to determine. They will keep running though, unless I park my body in the garage of sleep.

Samuel Johnson said that sleep is the one thing that renders all men equal — the only thing, except you include old Mr. Death.

What is White Cross to me? Well, I'll tell you. It is winter on a sunny day.

White Cross is a place to be born into and a place to die. But the intervening lapse between those two suburbs should be spent elsewhere.

2/24/65 (05204)

The Eve of Janus

> 'Tis well an old age is out,
> And time to begin a new.
>   — John Dryden, *The Secular Masque*

I

The rattling year roared, yearning
*

Down the drain of its burning
Phoenix, downdropping its skin,
Molting the dying hour between twin
Cyclones and hourglass sand grains.
Two hurling bodies, the new and old,
Flew headlong toward a fated convergence.
The passing phase glowed tinnycold.

II

"Relief," moaned the old. "To hell
With you," groaned the new year,
Belching in drunken snorts of sheer
Debauchery. "Relief!" the old year yelled
As it dissolved into alcoholic veins
Of the sedentary and broke the chains
Of the thick-jowled gentile and Jew.
The new year only replied, "Screw you!"

III

Outside, the leery, blue-black moon
Played zigzag tricks through clouds
Of doom. Blackmantled rain shrouds
Cowled the night in lullaby balloon-
Billows of gin and scotch and tonic.
Somewhere, a misty voice was saying,
"May the time not be distant, O Lord,"
And from inside, voices raucous and bored
Swelled, ranting, "Our times are chronic,
But who the hell has time for praying?"

IV

The fetid hour fell, fast drowned
In dying piles of purple paper.
Confetti and screaming, earthbound
Streamers were hung by the *drapier*
Of time, and everyone resolved
(Merchants, debutantes, and queers),
With trembling, thought-dissolved
Bubbles, "Skoal! . . . Happy New Year!"

V

The old year slinked out unheard,
*

Like a lover whose unhappy whore
Has left him to make darker war
In another district. Soon the word
Spread through the redblushing ears
That all was over, that New Year's
Eve was done, that they must revive
And buzz back to their routine hive,
Half-dead, drunk, yet half-alive,
Until 360° erased the next 365.

2/26/65 — [1] (05066)

The Green Hamlet

For W. R.

A green hamlet hung
Upon the soft upper shore
Of my eye's lid like hoar-
Frost that lingered and clung
To dawn's melting roar.

A silent hamlet squatted
Behind antebellum steeples.
Invisible bells called people
From graves that rotted
Into soil thick and deep.

A dream hamlet filled
My ears with past
Guns and powdered blasts
That wafted into languid
Memory. My voice spilled

Out through the green
Hamlet; then it cried,
Not with a turgid sigh
Nor for a loss unseen
But for a dying breed

Of men, forced to cede
Their green hamlets, and
For a way of living branded
*

With the golden seeds
Of a bold but fetid creed.

2/26/65 — [2] (05067)

[What is involved in making . . .] †

What is involved in making a short story?
Ask Hemingway
    Maupassant
    Tolstoy
    Faulkner
    Malamud

In one word, situation,
      an incident that happens
        and then is resolved in one form or
          another.
When does a story happen to a writer?
    Unpredictable.
Prime criterion: must have some message
      vision
      insight
      conflict

3/3/65 — [1] (05214)

[The warm day surprised itself.] †

The warm day surprised itself.

The warm day breathed pastel wind
into the shirt-sleeved movement
of skylark girls and boy.

    This day is just too warm for people's expectations; the intensity
has created riot with the senses. Everywhere, girls in pastel and soft
blues are coquetting to the drugstore or the local hot-rod coffee shop.
Boys are motorcycled or convertibled or congregating on soggy ball

fields, with tennis shoes and mitts dangling from weary arms.

```
                    T
                    H
                    I
                    S

                    W
                    A
                    S

                    A

                    W
                    A
                    R
                    M

                    D
                    A
                    Y
```

       — IN HELL

Today Hell froze over, and I skated on top of it.

3/4–5?/65 — [1] (05069)

Table Talk

Table talk tempts conceit.
It generates defeat
With vain retreats
Into inane steeps

Of flaunted aspiration.
The vaunted oblations
Of witty conversation
Fly in gaudy gyrations

Of nothingness. Yet you
And I will praise true
*

Thoughts that accrue
To the mind's purlieu.

You and I shall balk
From fetid table talk,
Shall trace the hawk's
Flight and sever stalks
Of Babel. We'll walk
Precarious lines of chalk.

3/4–5?/65 — [2] (05068)

[Yesterday I wrote a vignette . . .] †

Yesterday I wrote a vignette called "The Friends" (it took seven hours to write). The theme of the scene is *innocence being seduced by love*, whatever that means.

I bought myself a passage aboard
some

Give us this bread
Our daily day,
Not to be said
Nor to pray
But to eat dead.

Somewhere, a calendar
advanced the day,
speaking with candor—

(To write a poem, need vital, conflictual passion, despair,
spontaneity)

3/5/65 — [1] (05073)

[Down-dropping the flesh of eyes in uplifting surprise,]

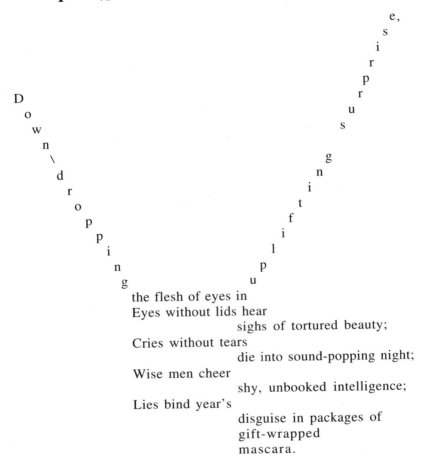

the flesh of eyes in
Eyes without lids hear
    sighs of tortured beauty;
Cries without tears
    die into sound-popping night;
Wise men cheer
    shy, unbooked intelligence;
Lies bind year's
    disguise in packages of
    gift-wrapped
    mascara.

3/5/65 — [2] (05072)

She Being Pure Art

Her bird-soft hair was a metaphor
        more polished
Than a poet's words
Could paint;

Her royal smile an image
                              more colorful
Than a painter's oils
Could print.

Her blissful eyes were similes
                              more fluid
Than a musician's gliss
Could sculpt;

Her uncloaked thighs alliterations
                              more sensual
Than a sculptor's stroke
Could sound.

She was a naked muse,
Pure,
A poem, painting, prelude,
Sculpture.

3/5/65 — [3] (05071)

Old Negro Lady's Winter Wait

An old Negro lady stood shivering
By a bus stop, her knees quivering
Like quills of a desolate evergreen.
Wind-parched lips and runny nose
And tattered boots with naked toes
Were all that showed of her exposed
Frame. Then a single cheek-tear,
Which no cold could cause, froze
On her lips and burned them near
The corners of her salt-sick heart.

The rushing winds began to start,
Twisting through her coldworn parts.
Then she crouched against the wind
And sleet. Her whimper, like binned
Trash paper overturned at night
By stray dogs, scuttled from sight
On the stream of a wintry blight.

"Is I not ah chile sent by de Lawd?
Pray to tells me true, dear Gawd,
Why I ain't made like all dem folks
Who dreams and hopes an' makes jokes
About de better times dat's to come.
I jez stans here all by my lone
An' waits on de bus to carrys me home.
An' what's I got to keeps me wam,
'Ceptin' it bes Yo Gawdly fawm?
Prays de Lawd I lasts dis stawm!"

3/5/65 — [4] (05070)

[Winter is a time to think.] ‡

Winter is a time to think.
The mind is a skating rink
For thoughts that skate
In circles and figure eights
Of dazzling dizziness. My will
Lies dormant on the window sill
Of this icy season, and I fill
My skates with paper, wipe dry
My blunted blades, and sigh.
I await the time when the sun
Will melt my stagnant pond.
Winter is a time to shun
The torpor that festers in
                    lotus fronds.

3/8/65 — [1] (05077)

Selma, Alabama, 3/6/65

For Wendell Rivers

Racist, Jew, fanatic, gentile,
Apologist, Southerner, Anglophile —
I am all these things today,
Things that curse, things that pray,
*

Things that don't know what to say
Or think or dream. My mind kneels
In dusty roads. My knees know fatigue,
And I can't even whimper.

I want to vote, like other things
That qualify as human beings.
I tell myself that I'm a man.
I face the lies of democracy,
Am singed by its senseless fires.
I cry sometimes in my separate room,
Where birth and death are inseparable
And equal, but they do not heed
What I need to say and dream and do.
They claim that *be* and *seem*
Are not the same, that *ought*
And *should* could only be bought
At a cost they'd never pay.

But we'll meet at the church,
Where the road joins a birch copse,
Half a mile from town.
We'll wear our brown skin,
Our black skin, inside out
And ignore their shouts,
For to fight back would be wrong,
Would make us part of the throng
Of innocent ignorance
That preys behind every tree.
We can't submit to the hordes
That disgrace themselves,
Knowing they sow scornful seeds
In the soil of all men's dignity.

We'll march while the sun's in hiding,
Start running as it rises to shadows.
What other way is there to say
That we're not just fractional things,
Unless all men be puppeteers'
String-moved slaves?

Let's march now. Let's run now.
I don't know how to whimper anymore.
Let us bow and pray,
Then walk, march, run that race
*

With the sun. We'll arise today
From three centuries of disgrace
To soothe the sweaty brows
Of children who'll take these vows.

3/8/65 — [2] (00488)

[Endless are the systems,]

Endless are the systems,
the congeries of wisdom
that perplex, come alive
for me above the minds
that strive for meaning
and love; endless the music,
like highway lutes strung out
over a city of night sounds.

3/10/65 — [1] (05205)

[Bloom, O bulbous dome,] †

Bloom, O bulbous dome,
O tumescent, warm womb
of night. Breed in me
constellations of soft seas
of fireflies or katydids.

"Let me out! Out! Out!"
my weak tongue shouts

3/10/65 — [2] (05323)

Heroes

Prologue

Secret meditations.
Political aspirations.
Fetid protestations.

Whirling reels of newspaper print,
Cinematic shots that merely hint
At the truth of the whole event,
Flicker before a people's demented
Conception of what really exists.
Symbols and ideologies persist
In history books and poetry
Magazines. Hordes and votaries
From grass-rooted Hoovervilles
Prostrate themselves; stupor fills
Their dinner chairs and pails
Of factory lunch hour. Nothing fails
To move the unmoved, restless hearts
That diverge in a thousand parts
When they quit the preacher's
Mather-echoing, Edwards-teaching,
Soul-beseeching supplications.
Religion has genuflected to education
For the masses. The minister ceases
To wear his surplices,
But the collection brings increasing
Manna to the central diocese.
"Ours is a too-common disease,"
The Reverend Paneloux decrees.
"Yes! Ours is a common disease."

The Poet

Secret meditations.
Political aspirations.
Fetid protestations.

The pince-nezed poet sequesters
His images in mind-festering
Islands of Laputa and Innisfree.
He hides behind apple trees
Unplucked by palsy-wizened hands.
He lives with corrugated strands
Of words that fashion patterns across
Yellow scrap papers, embossing
Compassion not in outward looks
But in shelved, suggestive books
That collect dust on his tears,
Tears that stain his musty fears,
*

Tears that smother on uncut pages,
Tears that drain down the ages'
Descending gutters, tears of sages
Who lost their prophetic power
The moment the dying hour
Of their words was given birth,
Words that warned, words that sought
To carve cogent and well-wrought
Images of hope, words whose thoughts
Were conceived and faintly fought
For by the man, the poet, the sage
Who hid behind his visionary rage,
Words that garland his dying equipage.

The Politician

Secret meditations.
Political aspirations.
Fetid protestations.

The intrepid politician depicts
With graphic tallies the districts
That he will control in election
Time. He speaks of present infection
That he will remove, of dubious perfection
That behoves him to seek a distinguished position.
He pledges his money to requisition
Buttons and slatternly billboards
That project his angelic face to hordes
Of ignorant enthusiasts who patronize and truckle
To him. He draws the buckle
Of his tight-girthed belt one notch
Tighter. The midnight watches
He keeps have drawn the incumbent weight
From his bulbous stomach as of late.
He cakewalks about in raging ignominy,
Will die soon enough from the calumny
That comes from the local presbytery,
Like a honeymoon death-moth
That consumes the silk cloth
Of its cocoon before the night expires.

Someone has written that his tedious wife
Has spent the better part of life
*

Drinking the saps of ambitious strife:
Narcotics that have torn her mind
Into feeble pieces of unrefined
Epileptic seizures. And someone
Has said that he once undid
Little lawyers and anxious judges.
He refuses to comment, though he budges
A little, draws tighter his belt.

He squirms under the pressure of lies
That echo in his bloodshot head, remembering
His past recourse: the last September,
When he broke the judge and the lawyer
Who refused him. He was the destroyer
Of careers, the promulgator of perfection
For people whose helpless dereliction
Clouded the gaping features
Of his buttoned, billboarded creature-
Like ubiquity. The intrepid politician
Made his last bribe with the mortician
Of the county hospital two years ago now.
He was mistaken by death, somehow,
Who exacted from him one final bow.

The Priest

Secret meditations.
Political aspirations.
Fetid protestations.

Itinerant ministers of the new dream
Of modern living wander peregrine
And alone. Their words of wisdom
Disgrace the intents of Christendom
With sneering mockery, with chiding
Futility. They tell of God's abiding
Grace and worldly, eternal love.
They sell their abstract goods from leather
Attaché cases according to the weather:
On wintry days they choose John Donne
Or Mather, and when the Sunday morning sun
Plays on Palladian casements and chancel,
They draw from a stack of bank-canceled
Notes they wrote to themselves late
*

One night while townspeople prated
From bar to club to charnel lair.
They preach, "Today, the vanity fair
Has come to our city. We must share
The warmth of ennui, the variety of commonality."
They quote the Psalms with practicality,
Noting the week's holy events,
Asking each truthful sinner to repent
By giving to the thrifty collections when
They finish. "World sans end. Amen."

Epilogue

Secret meditations.   Poetic incantations.
Political aspirations. Tammany fluctuations.
Fetid protestations.   Clerical visitations.

      Forms of modern persuasion.

3/12/65 (05078)

[Though it was a mere]

Though it was a mere
      Friday night restaurant,
The din in my ears
      was as reverberant
As the truckled cheers
      for a retiring debutante.

Click, clatter, chitter-chatter;
Waitresses serve Mad Hatters.

Click and spill of water, water;
Waitresses marry the Hatter's daughter.

Rouge and lipstick, permanents,
Cosmetic, fated firmaments
Of fourteen-year-olds, girls and boys
Beauty-spread with baby toys.

First dance; big fun; oh, what fun!
What's new under the sunlamp?
Low-cut dress, plunging bosoms,
Charley horses, heat-balm cramps.

Grow up, girl, while you can.
Beauty fades. And understand
That fun is relative, fleeting
Fast, so break bread and eat.

Noisy restaurant, long-cold food
Hardly let a fellow brood.
Thoughts rattle like used tin cans.
The mind bridges every unfused span
Of consciousness with manners crude
And gossip torpid. Let a fellow brood.

3/12–14?/65 (05076)

Congressional Debates: Viet Nam

The mind works miracles
When we least expect.
It hurls projectiles
On our crowded fears,
Pounding hot as slag.
It slopes to complex battlegrounds,
Where pedagogical sounds
Fester in unreceptive ears.
It pounds the earth's crust
With malarial incidence,
Effective as unrecorded rhyme.

3/13?/65 — [1] (05074)

The Need to Write

I write, this morning, for myself only.
The books on my shelf are lonely
And still asleep. I smoke and drink
Hot coffee; they can help me think.

I write, this afternoon, to survive
The confusion of scholastic hives
Of paperback learning. I thrive
On flying metaphors that come alive

Off the ink-bled pages of my mind.
I form bodies of purely refined
Imagination from badgered brain cells.
I write to quell the hollow knelling

Of distant loomings that always fly
Behind my mind's fog-tight eye.
My fancy goes from Gibraltar to Rome
Without ever finding its chosen home.

I write, tonight, with fear of losing
An unconscious need for choosing
The proper thought, the just-right
Proem for a hard-fought insight.

3/13?/65 — [2] (05075)

[Two children, who were called] ‡

Two children, who were called
Queen and king by their subjects,
Grew up before their time.
They cried for the malfeasance
Owing to their lost innocence.
To be young is complexity
Reduced to its simplest fief.
Growing into maturation is
Indenture and apprenticeship
To the servitude of doubt

3/13–14?/65 — [1] (05079)

Land of the Sacred Tree △

For Jan

Come fast away with me,
Dear love,
And I'll take you to see
What's above
The elm and sycamore tree.

I lived there long ago,
Dear girl,
In a dream as white as wintry snow.
I was hurled
Through dawn into tomorrow.

There were apple orchards,
Dear sweet,
Whose fruitage was untortured
And neat,
Where the moon came down to eat.

Animals of fantastic shapes,
Dear one,
Would munch blue grapes,
Then run
Before the east had sent its sun.

Fly away with me
To the land of the sacred tree,
Where moonberries grow
And fish dance freely
Over towers of infinity.

We'll pluck the brazen cedarfruits
And climb the stalks of woodbine shoots.
We'll ride the rainbow's colored back
And sail down wind's invisible rack,
Until there's nothing left of us,
Except our souls, in love's terminus.

3/13–14? — [2] & 5/13/65 (02298)

[Today is Sunday, . . .]

Today is Sunday, unseasonably
warm, holy, and meant for rest. Every-
where I look, people seem to be
enjoying themselves. There are those
for whom warm weather signifies the
essence of life and love and
commodious living.
For me it means *study*: the
poets — John Donne, Ben Jonson.

I want to scream out to
this moiling world through my
poetry, but by the time it
is presentable, I will, no doubt,
be babbling about something new.
But I must keep writing. It
heightens living, makes it bearable,
fills it with the surprises that we
all expect.

3/14/65 — [1] (05206)

Cottage by the Gulf

The strip of beach
Filled up with loose-billed sounds
Of sandpipers, gulls, and pelicans.
Our cottage was Venice,
Mounted on ancient staves
Above the sandy tides.

We sat on the porch,
Watching the Gulf gather speed.
Waves, like a palm's windy fronds,
Uncurled onto the shore,
While its windscorched lips,
As if in pantomime,
Absorbed smaller oceans of spray,
One at a time.

We gazed out silently
Behind the violent monster,
This gargantuan sea.
Far out,
Beyond a swelling forest of breakers,
A baleful gardener
Walked on waves, raking their crests.

I sighed. She balked with fright,
Ran into the cottage to hide.
"Something's not right!" she cried.
"This is a slutty Gulf!" I shouted.
"You can't ever predict
When it'll seduce the weather."

I watched the sky
Fill up with vapour
As far as the eye could detect.
Soon, the wind shifted directions,
And the cottage, a web
Stitched loosely to decaying twigs,
Lifted once but held secure.
Then I was sure I knew
The grating whine that frothed
And barked at the darkening sky.
"Hurricane!"
I cried,
As I ran inside to pray.

3/14/65 — [2] (00490)

Yearnings

I long to see
    the coastal shore,
Where I can be
    at home once more,
Alone and free from the reeling roar
        of a city's
        frantic race.

I long to pace
    the gulfy beach
And run a race
    with the fading breech
Of horizon's face as it hazes the peach
        that gradually falls
        from day.

I long to stray
    on wafting nights.
My mind will play
    with flickering lights
Of mellowing rays as they spray the heights
        with a love
        not common enough.

3/14/65 — [3] (05080)

[The tumid eastern reaches of morning] †

The tumid eastern reaches of morning
were pregnant. The child sun

I dreamed the other night
that Currier and Ives were brothers;

3/17?/65 — [2] (05081)

[Cacophony grew on every arbor]

Cacophony grew on every arbor
Trellis. The gentle swiftness of night
Blew fury into household windows.
"Look," his wife said with sweet
Unconcern. "I have cut the vine
Outside the patio. See how it grows
In here." "I am fearful," her husband
Replied, "that the plant was meant
To blow alone in the winds of night."

3/17?/65 — [3] (05181)

[I sit at a yellow table now,]

I sit at a yellow table now,
    Drinking the mocha drops of day.
        The coffee burns my eyes.
            I want to cry. Surprise

Has gone out of me, somehow.
    I can't even think to pray
        That something will happen.
            All my hopes are vapid.

Give us, this day, our full
    Of grace. I displace all wonder
        In my misery. Indiscriminate
            Belief has become illegitimate.

I am being eaten by the bull
  Of March, consumed, trampled asunder
    By the lop-eared dog and centaur
      Of life and death.

3/18/65 — [1?] (05082)

[She was a balmy afternoon,] †

She was a balmy afternoon,
  Drooping through the corridors
Of day, a foster child preening.
  Doors of asylums, chambers of whores,
Antebellum steeples —

3/18/65 — [2?] (04679)

[My head is a balmy day,] †

My head is a balmy day,
Though the sun is whispering
Murmurs through cicadas' chirrup,
Through the devastating spray
Of

3/18/65 — [3?] (04678)

A Head Full of Screaming

Scream, scream, hurting head!
Dreams no longer work for me.
Nightmares wake my sleeping flesh,
And I awake to drink the dust
Of rusting blood. Let me scream
To throw off all that haunts me.

Burden me with the thoughts of lovers!
Gird my mind with compassion's quest
For mothers who bear their breasts
*

To street urchins and millionaires' sons!
Let me rest in the running faucet
That leaks pools of honeydew melon!

Turning, screaming, burning, dreaming,
I am drowning in the crust-green drain
Of my febrile brain-filters.
Now I see the slouching beast
Returning to the Peaceable Kingdom.
Let me ride its back down streets
Of Limbo! We will ride together
Over Hell, for damnation is better still
Than no-motion, than the awful inane
Of night. Let me be Diana's minion,
Painless and chaste with sensuality
From the reflected, softdripping goat!

Let Charon's boat carry me from me
To another me! My head screams out,
Howls, belches, then subdues itself
With the Pied Piper's mystic flute.

I am ferried away into morning's cough,
Exhaled, whimpering. Wait. It's all gone.
I have made all gone of myself. Good.
I should have done this sooner.
I have strangled my screaming dream.
I am loosed upon the crest of dawn,
Running wild over lawns of sanity.

3/19/65 — [1] (05083)

Random Exigencies

Warm night in White Cross.
White winds blow cold kisses
Of wisteria. Tepid, hissing sighs
Of billiard balls fall across
Green felt lawns and miss
Open windows of potato-chip
Lovers. Televisions tell people
That comedians still exist.
Scholars resist the inanity
*

Of advertisements, banalities
Of Madison Avenue. Rails show
An increase. Beans are failing
To make the grade. The green
St. Patrick's parade is snowed
Under by Minnesota blizzards.

I have seen it all before,
And I am caught in my coed
Head. We are too complex.
I have seen it all before,
Seen the buried martyrs,
Seen the simple indexes
Of compounding obituaries.
I have heard it all before:
The chant of Ave Marias,
The screams of dying Selma
And Montgomery. My cracking mind
Is overwhelmed by every depraved
Goldfinger or Mickey Spillane
Who needs to explain
The creed that exists unrestrained
In the deed itself, the act.

Is it worth resisting, the crackup,
The commitment — the act, I mean?
Bring me the mocha bean. Now!
Right now! I must think. But how?

3/19/65 — [2] (05084)

The Moon Contends with a Passing Storm

Head held high, shoulders broad,
The wrestling moon weaved and feinted
Through shadowbox clouds of doom.
Feet spread apart like compass legs,
The soft-bellied moon slouched,
Looming like a glass-jawed amateur
Who fought to outlast his fifth full round.

Flatfooted and dazed with opacity,
The reeling moon let fly a jab
*

With its left, missing a fleeting cloud.
The pockmarked, cauliflower moon
Threw a final uppercut, connecting.
A longwhite flash squirted across
Night's slobbering face, and eyes
That earlier had glistened and shuddered
Passed out under floods of sweaty bloodwater.

The punchy moon drew backward
Into the raucous thunder of handclaps,
Held high one arm with hauteur.
The crowding clouds huddled close
As the moon sauntered fast away
To the locker room under night's auditorium.

A cold-hot shower cleansed it.
Turning off the water and toweling itself,
The moon reappeared in starched street clothes
Just in time to watch the worn-out crowd
File through the south gate and dissolve
Into cleargusting streams of Gulf breeze.

It sat on its haunches, swollen with pride,
And beamed victoriously over its unpredictable foes.

3/20/65 — [1] (05085)

[She, her mouth encircling the moon,]

She, her mouth encircling the moon,
And I, my lips lapping her shores,
Lay together on the palette of June's
Oils. Eyes of the opaque aurora
Borealis twittered like cowbells.
"Sweet, soft lover, encompass my warmth
In your eyes. Surprise my lusty swell
Of desire like towering waves that swarm
Upon the hot sand to be devoured."

3/20/65 — [2] (05207)

[Contemplation] †

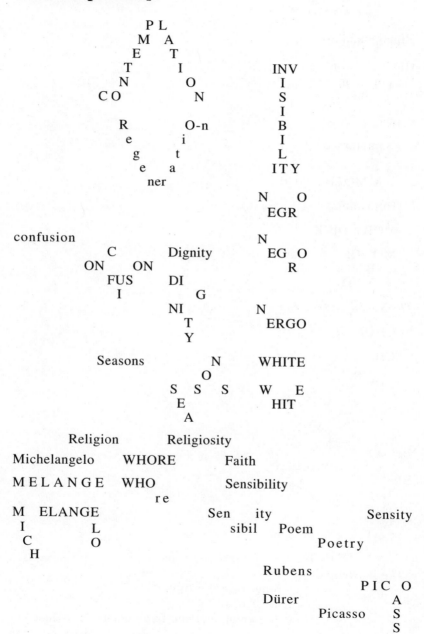

        Persis
          Existence

Hippopotamus
             s
Hip   u
   pop   m
      ota

Clown

   Samothrace

   S
    A MOTH RACE

   Humankind

   MOBY DICK

   MO CK
     B
     Y ID

The Sound and the Fury

   CHURCH

   CH
     UR
   CH
        LOVER

         over
        L
Below
       SWALLOW
BE
   L
   O
   W

       T. S. Eliot
The Wasteland —
          yearning toward a future
           fear of memory,
              presentational and fragmentary in its imagery
                   juxtaposition

time when *había* hope;
time of no hope, no more time/love.

Where is strength in my limbs,
Vitality that swims in stony
Canals of bone and cheek?

Rembrandt's son
Titer

3/21? & 3/22/65 (05086)

[Louis Daniel Brodsky] †

```
    s D        y
     i  a        k
   u    n   Brods
    o    i
 L        e
           l
```

          T. ˢ· Eliot
Total sense of experience

Poetry books
    lie snuggled
        in dusty nooks.
Poetic verse
    is essence,
        wide and terse.
Poetic anthologies
    bind thoughts
        and modern mythologies.

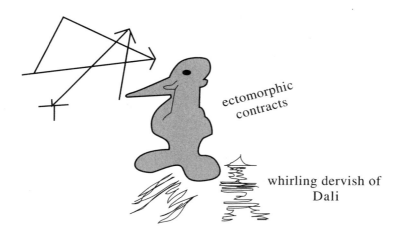

ectomorphic
contracts

whirling dervish of
Dali

Prufrock is afraid of what people will say of him;
        he wants to confess and yet doesn't.
  He has not *sinned*.

   "Mistah Kurtz — he dead." — "The Hollow Men"

    He has acted — total commitment to evil;
    Prufrock does not exist until he acts.

      Most people are not men enough to be *damned*.

      Pruf is in a world of sleep — trivia-like, watered-
      down experience. He is not *damned* — in a *limbo*.

Image in Eliot of old man getting older

Eliot and Dante hate people in limbo; both would rather see the person in damnation.

3/28/65 (05325)

Memphis: The Conflagration

For Gene Redmond

Memphis by night.
That's how I remember it,
Driving north to south:
One gaping mouth of neon
Fillings and wisdom cavities
That needed extraction.
I reacted to the salivating night
Like an Italian beggar
Distracting passersby
With operatic gestures of penury.

Memphis by rainy night.
That's how I remember it.
My windshield wipers smoothed away
Soft revisions of the city,
Metronomically.
Swirling car smoke
Soothed my impatience, my comic hatred.

Memphis by Negro night.
I remember it that way, too,
Scuttling along my sightless eyes
Like a naked, soft-thighed chimera.
I stopped my frightened car
Long enough to watch
Lightning spray the town
With revenge. I was Nero.
I started my silent engine
And drove into the flamerainy night.

3–4?/65 (04009)

[Torrid, shivering heat-fumes . . .]

Torrid, shivering heat-fumes lift themselves up through bonnet louvers of Jaguars and Ferraris and Chaparrals, climbing up to astonished eyes of spectators, drivers, and God, all of whom stare bleary-eyed and exhausted at the races at Sebring. That's how Florida begins for one who arrives as a spectator-tourist. Strangely enough, I am all of those things/people today because I am sick. They keep telling me that I belong in Chattahoochee. It's a what? Well, if you don't know, look it up in *Rand McNally*.

Heat lifts from the white, sandy beaches of Redington like serpents wriggling up the side of a steep, craggy, dungmoist cliff. Gulls hover over the Gulf — Gulfgulls — and pelicans plop into the fish-filled crests in search of sawfish, whales, men-of-war, and stingrays. They find none of these, fortunately, and are satisfied with anemones and small shark-bait.

I have spent a week in this healthy climate, and somehow I contracted a bad chest cold, which, like the heat from the cars, has finally decided to rise up into my head. I am awaiting the advent of the resurrection of this damn thing. I have been sunburnt for two days now. . . . Wait! I have been doing a lot of complaining.

Bring me a pizza, *garçon*, if you will. I am very hungry. No work and lots of play make for a hungry Johnny. I have done no work with my head or fingers for a whole week, and the feeling is good but slightly disturbing. One begins to wonder whether he will be able to get back into the awful corner of creativity. It takes a great deal of concentration, you know, a sort of semiconsciousness.

Let's play the name game with "Candy" and "Henry Miller."
Why?
Because it's "in," like op art.
The name "Horace" is funny as hell.
So is "Nella the Cow."
Don't forget "Pussy Galore." How they got away with it is the question of the year. It was better than the Great Brink's Robbery.
The distance between Selma and Montgomery is three centuries.

3–4?/65 (05233)

[Ezra Pound] †

Ezra Pound

History and culture continually present — Pound and Eliot
    all ages contemporaneous

to visualize the invisible

I must sit down at my desk and bring an
irrefragable energy to my hand to write without stopping.

    a welter of rhetoric
            impersonal indignation
    defects of idiom
    abrupt and disordered syntax
            disparity *entre* words and content
    Words must cling close to things;
        when not, then kingdoms fall.

Rattle-flivver sun come down,
Roll and prattle just for fun.
Blue-green, red-orange, mauve,
There's a sundog over the sky

words are intellectual *weapons*

    I must write my story of Christopher
Paradise and Hunter Augustine. It is a good
story; I can't afford to lose
my passion for telling the story.
    The energy pauses and dissolves
all too quickly — must write it
with inordinate importunity.
    Writing is a secret that
God lets us in on for only a
brief span of time — must grab
hold of its platonic handles while
you can.

Write that story so that you
can go on to the next one.

    Next story, one of
        familial generations,
  like *Wuthering Heights*
    Absalom, Absalom!

  Mind transforms hatred into
ink on the page.
    St. Petersburg, you are
my respite — no mental
  aberrations there. My
handwriting is strangely different
today — can't explain it.

4/5/65 — [1] (05208)

[Lines draw taut]

Lines draw taut
    around midnight's belly.
Scions of thought
    confound lightheaded measures.
Lemmings are people in disguise,
    who rush helter-skelter,
Willy-nilly, slipshod, headlong
    into the blushing bellies
Of fully inflated, floating women.
    We dash madly from one womb
To another like porpoises
    weaving sweaters by pulling drops
Of water up through trick hoops
    of daytime. We dive behind them
Into urns of nighttime and die
    in female Heidelberg tuns.

4/5/65 — [2] (05216)

[If I could live in eyes]

If I could live in eyes
That glisten with constant laughter.
If I could breathe in sighs
Of love that lingers long after
The essence of wetness dissolves.
If I could evolve
Into something more than hauteur
Can echo. If I could resolve
The antithesis of vegetation.
If! If! If! But indignation
Gnaws my eyes and laughter,
My sighs and afterthoughts.
I have become an "if" who couldn't.

4/5/65 — [3] (05209)

[What the hell am I doing . . .] ‡

What the hell am I doing back at school? I should have stayed
where the warmth of St. Pete kissed my neck every day.

I need to have reoccurring, habitual silence of imaginative
thought. Sometimes, like acid, my imagination eats me up, dissolves
my nerves through cigarette and coffee.

There were pelicans and gloomy days that were beautiful in them-
selves.

Ritual and rest are what the Apeneck, who swelled to maculate
giraffe, and Babbitt would love.

I love Howard Johnson's. What a mediocre individual I am! My
intellect does not function;
       it pinball-vacillates, like protozoa,
          from one thought to another, never
settling.
       I write with fatuous, insipid, effete
passion. Need to get out —
          let me out of class —
             move from classroom Cranes and
          Shelleys to you. Screw you, *Suzie*,
                      you whore

4/5/65 — [4] (05210)

Meditation over Coffee, 4/7/65 ‡

It rains, today, on naked flesh,
with painful colors of warm death.

The exigencies of my work are overpowering. I must write right
now because my head is too full of the story that needs to be told. It is
a strong story, about a boy in flux, changing like the consistent, un-
predictable lapses of Gulf tides, unruly yet consistent in their harm-
less, beach-rumbling tremors.
      Must tell this story before my head splits apart.
Importunity is my taskmaster at this point. I must needs throw off
all the burdens of my puny responsibilities to my schoolwork and
friends at the university —
   the
      I must needs sit and write. My reading capacity is all burnt out.
         I can take no more of Browning and Thackeray and Dickens
      and C. Brontë; they're just too turgid and careful, too wordy —
prolixity is their flaw.

Give me the opportunity to tell the tale of Christopher and Hunter.
Free me from academia. Let me write, with precise and concise, free-
flowing objectivity,
      a modern style of a Biblical story of love unreciprocated.

      Part II, *The Sorrows of Christopher Paradise*
         Diary = occurs during the periods of disillusionment and
                                                    depression
               He writes to himself, trying to understand his actions.
         (Diary entries alternate.)

The Sorrows of Christopher Paradise

I: The Everlasting Acceptance

      Conversion — Centre of Indifference
   Get out — futile, pushed beyond breaking point. Only, one doesn't,
can't, break, because even breaking apart does no good, provides no
alleviation, so the next best thing is continuing, is overt action in the
face of the monster, the gargantuan, the gargoyle-faced abstractions
which hang, ever present, in the unfathomable steeps of faulty inanity,
ennui.

Must fight, struggle to vanquish abstraction, read newspapers,
involve oneself with modern media, stare the TV right in its im-
perious system of scanning electrons, and accept it so that it can't
break you.

The victims are those who allow themselves to wallow in the
slippery crags of immobility. Stasis is far worse than rigor mortis,
because it is living, or at least vegetating, death: a protozoan exist-
ence, in which conscious logic ceases to function, conscience refuses
to activate the individual's waking hours, an after-dinner sleep all day
long, as it were.

No funciona la inmobilidad para nada menos que la muerte viv- ◊
*ienda. El ser humano se baja a los hondos de la noche oscura del
alma.*

¿Y yo? ¿Que pasa con el Yo de la personalidad?
Se rompe en mil pedazos de vidrio y carne. No vale la pena de

4/7/65 — [2] (05211)

[Well, I'm latched onto the habit . . .] ‡

Well, I'm latched onto the habit again like a sucker to the belly
of a lemon shark.

Where are the high-school days, when all was irresponsibility
and happiness?

Are they ever going to reappear, or have they dissolved into dusty
reminiscence?

I am sick with bronchitis. Need to
quit writing to yourself and begin writing for
others; that's the only commitment at this point.

To prolong the inevitable is the tack of humankind.
But how to do it? Free will to choose
mode of prolongation —
But don't sit; to sit is to waste the self.

Do we *need* to eat?

I must get into my story, no matter the cost,
tell it now, but I won't threaten myself

4/7/65 — [3] (05212)

[The night lights of White Cross . . .]

The night lights of White Cross are
not very impressive when compared
with the illumined skylines of N.Y. or
Paris, with its lambent, tunnel-of-love-like
bateaux mouches paddling the silence of
the Seine, by Montmartre's Sacre Coeur's
white purity, by night, but
regardless, I find something
warm in these lights, something
hazysoft in my blurred vision
tonight. This is an unseasonably
warm evening, and everywhere,
countless myriads of night people are
out necking or drinking at local
bars to get ready for an illicit
bedtime together.
    I have been badly upset all
day. My stomach has churned like
a noisy paddle wheeler navigating
an iceblocked Mississippi River
during winter Twaintime.

4/7/65 — [4] (05213)

[I was a stingray, a lemon shark,]

I was a stingray, a lemon shark,
Spraying the daydreams of visitors
With darkspawning drops of doom
And fear.

Fugitive sighs fleet.
    Vain retreat conspires
        With blistered feet.

The shotgun blasts at the skeet range,
    distracts air and membranes; it echoes
    *

like pogo sticks and billiard cues
    bouncing on cemented basement floors.

A waterlogged worm
    squirmed on the rotting boat bow.

My flesh ordered cheeseburgers,
    But I couldn't eat, because
        Her eyes were sitting there like pickles.
            I cried aloud, drank a glass of water,
                And dove into the ketchup and died.

We lay there, huddled
    Upon the bare rug of thought,
        Weaving strands of *seem*
With fair colours of red and white,
        Weaving strands of budding *be*'s,
Which blossomed into loving, fleshly dream,
        Weaving fluid wet as spray.

4/9/65 (05215)

[The University of White Cross]

The University of White Cross
Is a pitiable whore,
Whose glossy routine
Is boring and artificial.
Her thighs are turgid books,
With broken spines and hinges
From too much abuse.
Her lips are lecterns,
Parched and discoloured with rhetoric
And polemical backwashes of insight.

4/9–14? — [1] & 4/22/65 — [3] (05217)

[I walk out on Hampdon Downs] †

I walk out on Hampdon Downs

It's that time of the year.
The trees grow green
and sear with music of the spheres.

A glossy, filmy sheen
of youth glows thick
and heavy in every

4/9–14?/65 — [2] (05218)

Escape in April

Four o'clock in the Florida morning.
We, the car and I,
Had fought intemperate rain and cold
To reach this spot on Mercator's map.

I was Henry, prince and navigator,
Drawing lines of desire and hope.
I was Ponce de León,
Cresting each hamleted hill and slope.
My astrolabe revolved the needle,
Until, obliquely,
It exceeded ninety miles an hour.

Nashville, or Memphis,
Then Lookout Mountain
Faded in retrogressive blinks
Of billboards and coffee stops;
Next, Atlanta,
Serpentine,
Molting in rush hour.

Finally, I could see the outcast slip,
Stretching in a ribbonstraight horizon
Of beach like a strip of uncoiled tape
Stuck to the crease of night's tare.

Four o'clock in the Florida morning,
And I am spent of energy,
A dizzy, dying death-moth,
Forgetting the slow pain of maturity.

I'll end my journey,
Running down sandy corridors,
Pirouetting into obscurity,
Falling to embrace the lisping shore.

4/9–14? — [3] & 10/15/65 — [3] (05280)

[From White Cross to Redington]

From White Cross to Redington
Is just a tricky flick
Of the vapid imagination,
Cold to hot in one breath.
That's how it is with me,
Escaping seaward on a whim.

4/9–14?/65 (05219)

[My vacation to Florida was sick]

My vacation to Florida was sick
With bronchitis. I was smoked
By wicked cigarettes that rolled
And licked tight my wrappers.
Florida! Highways that dream
Down corridors of vapid memory.
Florida! Motels that breathe
Comfortable lies from December
To April. My sickness remembers
Scenes of snow and sand beaches.

My mother is a fish!
Vardaman had some difficulty
Reading Izaak Walton.
Hemingway didn't. However, I doubt
*

He ever read Donne's book
About the incessant Poebells.
He dream-wished, daydreamed,
Vardaman, that is, and
In flood time, too. A dead mother
Only bred contempt for idiocy.
She wore a scarlet "A," for "Addie."

Redington Beach! What of it?
How many resorts consort
To squander, to hoard the sun
Of December? . . . A boy of fits!

4/14/65 (05220)

Pylon

Atrocious speed
   wings around pylons
      set off the ground
         like saurian scarecrows.

Indefinite need
   slithers from oily tappet springs
      that swell from the heart
         of indomitable human wings.

Flying violence
   noises above crowds
      of sunslicked gnomes,
         who grandstand with shrouds.

Heartless bastards
   read in the papers
      of the useless accident
         and shrug their placid consciences.

4/14–17?/65 — [1] (05221)

[Shell-strewn beaches,] †

Shell-strewn beaches,
    soiled motel rooms
        consort
Together, teaching people

4/14–17?/65 — [2] (05222)

Jiggs

Barstools are for sitting,
        Somehow.
No one ever does that,
        However.
Barstools are for drinking.
        Nonetheless,
No one ever does that.
        Only, nothing.

4/14–17?/65 — [3] (05223)

Faulkner's Funeral

Diverse cronies attend
    His funeral.
Nopeople and nobells toll
    His demise.
Someone has chosen to send
    A ship-filled whiskey bottle
To his minister:
    A distress signal —
SOS!
    Gambrinus bloats his ego,
While Percy Grimm and Popeye
    Escort Lena Grove
To some bawdy "gettin'" place.
    Dewey Dell and Laverne
    *

Fall face down on the ground
    In cringing genuflection.
The Right Reverend Shegog gags,
    Takes a second to reflect
Upon the passing of life,
    Then dissolves into black heat
Like retreating bugle volleys
    Swallowed by a century of unadmitted defeat.

4/14–17?/65 — [4] (05224)

Too-Late June

Dandelion burrs
    chase dizzy rhythms
        through June's lassitude.

Oxford shells
    dig whirling pools
        behind their glide.

Busy butterflies
    pirouette on currents
        of full-throated noon.

Cicadas tune
    staccato murmurs
        in grassy rooms.

Words stand up,
    walk on stalks
        over dreamy solitude.

Too-late thoughts
    beacon their arcs
        above blatant sleep.

Her heavy night
    lies beneath me,
        drinking wasted weight.

4/14–17? — [5] & 4/20/65 — [1] (05087)

[Today I am twenty-four years old. . . .] ‡

Today I am twenty-four years old. I have written one book, which was conceived and given birth to out of the vaults of sheer human energy. The writing was too extended and overconscious, but the effort was there.

The second book is a good story — not the movie-adaptable type, however. It has its locale in the mind, not the countryside, though my brain works on an APB when creating it. I will be able to tell the story as soon as I can steal enough free and unintruded time to think. I will try to do it in London this summer.

"Take stock" — an old slogan of mine that today I resuscitate. What have I done with myself this year?

A love affair, which will give me the story of Christopher Paradise and Hunter Augustine. A great deal of poetry, which culminated intellectually in the last "Meditation" poems

4/17/65 (05164)

[I am twenty-four springs old]

I am twenty-four springs old
Just now. I am water
Without the thickness of dogwood,
Redbud, purples, thick red-whites,
Textural greens;
Shoes and socks that wear speed
And urgency; pockets with fists
Clenched tight against their linings.

4/17?/65 (05225)

Fear Experienced Driving North to South

The funnel-furrowed Delta
Is too introspective,
Shrunken into itself.
Oleanders and live oaks grown ancient
Are hung with silver goatees,
These the patricians of gentility.

Pandemonium.
      Wire-spoked wheels
      Of space and sunlight
      Speak terrific speed.

Limbobound.
      Instrument gauges,
      Made by Smiths,
      Glow with dazed light.

Popeye lives
      On others' pain, symbiotically,
      Somewhere in Virginia.

Percy Grimm
      Frightens innocence with butchery,
      Somewhere in Mississippi.

Urania cringes
      While Faulkner tunes macabre rhythms
      On a sordid past-tense lute.

      Now Milton,
      Wordsworth,
      And Dr. Johnson
      Drown together in the Yazoo
      As the funnel-furrowed Delta
      Explodes its banks, gurgling.

4/19/65   (05103)

[The night is languishing . . .]

The night is languishing into stillness, and I am ready for bed. My nerves have settled down into a steady rhythm, and I believe that I will be able to sleep soundly. I have a lot on my mind, and somehow it refuses to order itself. But I will stick with it, the writing of a novel that will be better than the last one because I refuse to overwrite. I demand what Arnold and Johnson, and Aristotle, before all them, demanded: a picture or portrait that is true to human nature, one in which there is a noble action that supersedes the rhetoric or style. I must tell a story with similitude and honesty.

Until I can make enough time, a big iceberg of it, one block in which I can create it, the story, then I must content myself with my dabblings in poetry, the noblest form of creativity, the most exacting and careful, the one in which the author has got to be concerned to the greatest extent with sincerity and responsibility for each word that he chooses and each form and meter that he decides upon.

> Poetry is the individual's working out of personal conflicts.
> Fiction, the novel, is creating a solution to the conflicts
> of individuals in relation to each other; the personal
> gets interfused with the general, until it is indiscernible.

4/20 — [2] & 4/30/65 — [2] (05232)

[He wore tight, white work trousers] †

He wore tight, white work trousers
and a faded shirt that hid the dirt
of unconcern. His horse boots
hung like perfidious statuary beneath his weight.

His deep, beady eyes
     floated across the recesses
of thought and time and night.
They were frightened

4/20–22?/65 — [1] (05226)

[And wouldn't it be nice]

And wouldn't it be nice
     To think so, dear Brett?
And wouldn't it be nice?
     But that was years ago,
Before the anomalies of war,
     Before the soaring afterglow
Of Pamplona and the Riviera.

4/20–22?/65 — [2] (05228)

Hide and Seek

Cigarette smoke
Curled into the acoustics of night.
Traffic lights spoke a redgreen
Dialogue between motion and sound,
And somewhere, a moaning siren melted
The liquid interlude of parked lovers.

Where was I?
        I was here, inside myself,
Sharing the uncoloured soliloquies
Of my throbbing blood,
Listening to the obsequies
Of my buried heart, which lifted
Lilliputian cock-a-doodle-doos
To the subdued dawn of my mind.

Here I am,
        Sitting on lawns purplelit
With Gatsby dreams and the half-drunken
Ecstasies I have had thinking of Daisy
And the irrepressible Catherine Barkley.

4/20–22?/65 (05104)

[You say he was here]

You say he was here
yesterday? I wish he
had stayed. We could have
drunk beer together
for breakfast.

4/22/65 — [1] (05229)

[She was reticent and shy,] †

She was reticent and shy,
A child who never learned
*

To wear perfume and negligées.
I tried to warn her,
To treat her like a woman,
But sure enough

4/22/65 — [2] (05230)

Five Facets of Myself

I am the twenty-third sermon
Of the learned Jack Donne.
Words and rhetoric funnel me
Through absurdities of conceit.
I am Alice's glass, darkly lit
Like a recess in some movie theater.
I am an ill-conceived Quixote,
Deceiving myself with thoughts
From my outclassed mind.
I swing by my umbilicus
In the cave of Montesinos.

To compete with effete academies
Is like spitting in the Gulf:
No rising tides of insight.
My words, whose insides die,
Are abandoned shells
That no longer hold the roar
Of ancient shores.
Now I am a framed capriccio,
One of Goya's beastly improvisations,
Or a fantastical latter-day saint,
Whose features dissolve in cobwebs
Of Swiftian digression.

My veins burst within the cortex
Of myth and philology.
I gasp for breath.
My poems decay
Like pith in a debarked tree.

4/23 — [1] & 4/26/65 — [2] (04026)

Resurrection

That very same night,
Birds flew in from everywhere.
The beach was an airport,
Whose runways were flecked with tracks
From hysterical gulls and pelicans.
That very same night,
Retired Struldbruggs came off
Their fishing piers to sleep
In beachside motel rooms.
They knew something was wrong.
That very same night,
The bars closed early,
And turgid whores and drunks
Crept away into the night.
They knew a storm was mounting.
A form floated in with the tide,
That very same night.

That very same night,
I leaned against a traffic signal,
My mind attuned to the metaphysical
Dialogue between red and green.
I had known life once and fast,
As a night of lasting inconstancy
That grew up my spine.
Someone said, "We are friends.
Tonight we will love fast
And together, protracting the hours
Between shadow and light.
Tonight we will discover ourselves
In each other like oceans in shells."
But I hid behind a gown of sickness
And walked into the Gulf to drown.
They found my frightened body,
That very same night.

4/23/65 — [2] (05231)

[Today I lived through] †

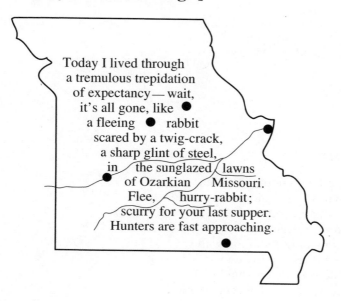

Today I lived through
a tremulous trepidation
of expectancy — wait,
it's all gone, like ●
a fleeing ● rabbit
scared by a twig-crack,
a sharp glint of steel,
in the sunglazed lawns
of Ozarkian Missouri.
Flee, hurry-rabbit;
scurry for your last supper.
Hunters are fast approaching.

A creation of himself,
    Gatsby's platonic conception,
        Hemingway's boisterous claims

A Move Able Feast.
    His beer lacked yeast;
He plopped a rancid egg.
    Stone had to beg.

Searching, strafing,
stooping, pulling,
the dowry cat
sat on sofa arms,
mewing charming lies,
flaunting bluelit eyes
into the autumnal of evening

4/26/65 — [1] (05326)

[Lake Superior rain pelted] †

Lake Superior rain pelted
the boys' camp this morning.
The boys were cold and bleary-tired

4/28/65 (05327)

Boy of Fits

Who passed through noon's tension,
Its fire-hot wires of boredom?
I did, that day in downtown June.
I melted into the restaurant,
Flowing down quartz-bubbling walks,
Then, seduced by revolving doors,
Was flung into a chorus of single-file,
Sideshow secretaries and nonsectarian
Arcanabiologists.
I did, that Juneloony afternoon.
I ate and spoke with the accidents
Of a liveried world, whose words
Were finely machined and polished
Like insides of a high-compression engine.
I did. I am. I was made privy
Against my whimper, made judge
Of actions, the lord high exchequer
For futile funds and vapid sounds.
I was made to vie with businessmen
And lunch people and lawyers.
I did. I was Benvenuto Houdini
Of my own solitude, playing tricks
With the solar plexus of ambition
And immortality. I was the game,
But Momus held the winning cards.

4/30/65 — [1] (04027)

Trial by Sickness of Christopher Paradise, Pariah

He was no older than a vivid dream, and yet he had outgrown the need to live among those who dreamed.

He would travel by car from his home, driving north to south, leaving January's harsh, cold face for the unwintered clime of Florida.

Sickness, like a noontime shadow, would plague him, would chase his tragic escape, until even solitude was denied him.

He would love, too, for a brief spot, would blossom, until all of him would leave him, and then he would walk into the Gulf to be reborn.

4?/65 (05156)

[Wallace Stevens] †

Wallace Stevens
"A High-Toned Old Christian Woman"

I am so tired today, exhausted to the point of disintegrated chaos — must *go to sleep*.

"Daddy, did you ever read
F. Scott Fitzgerald?"
"No, son. I never did."

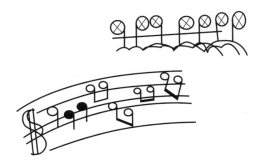

A world created out of the need to
create that world

April is   Glackens   Coventry
paradise   Sloan   climax
                Bellows

I can't write; I can't think;
I can't move my heavy arms.
Pencil drops upon the floor;
Floor shoots up in my face
As I bend to pick it up.

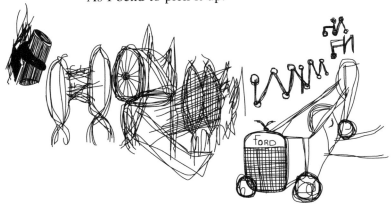

Threatened loss
makes things
    beautiful —
        the fact of
          death.
             Death makes life
                meaningful.

5/3/65 (05328)

[White Cross is just as young] †

White Cross is just as young
as the

They owned the sole rites
to my gaze; my

This afternoon,

      It was no ordinary car,
      extraordinary in its own style.
      Its birthright was filed in Coventry.
      Some call it simply Jaguar;
      others initial it XK-E.

White Cross breeds malcontent
in my boring mind

5/4/65 (05088)

[The ribbonstraight slip of Gulf . . .]

    The ribbonstraight slip of Gulf beach, which some arbitrary pro-
genitor had once dubbed Redington, not for any particular reason

other than just getting it done, the chore, burden, of having a worthless
plot of uninhabitable land nameless as well as unsuitable for dairying
or farming or sheer relaxation, Redington, an amphibian, a terraque-
ous anomaly that some Pleistocene accident had decided to let remain
in its wake of disaster and unseen fury off the mainland, Redington, a
place without a history: this place, now a beach for modern living, had
metamorphosed into the mother of night. She, the beach, was as long
as each soft, tidefilled, saltreeking blast of night wind that washed it
with sandy mist and tumid breezes.

 I had always wanted to find such a place, located out of time and
dimensionless, new to its very garments, a place where I could retire
for weeks at a time to cure my flights of turbulent discontent. She was
there, just as I had left her last year, inviolable and innocently friendly,
like a pet dog or rabbit who has not yet experienced enough of day-
light's obstacles to be leery and tense. As the tourist seasons came and
went, however, I watched her begin to snap at the customers, until her
prices were feared by even the wealthiest Jews from New York, who
invaded twice a year in their '38 Lagondas and '65 4.2 XK-E's.

5/4?/65 — [1] (05234)

[My mind skips rope, leaping] †

My mind skips rope, leaping
from the hard substance, earth,
to touch the clouds of night.
Now it lies suspended,

She was a shy girl
        until you stopped knowing her.
Then her absence whirled
        into a windblown swirl
of hair.

5/4?/65 — [2] (05235)

The Worm

> *Born to bring forth the angelic butterfly*
> *That flies to judgment naked and alone.*
> — Dante Alighieri, *The Divine Comedy*

Part One

White Cross is a lonely place to be during the cold winter months of January and February, especially if you have to return to the university every day to see the same dustdingy faces poring over the same books, which foretell the doom and finality of the same, insane world.

"Those poor sons-of-bitches," I think to myself, "who sit there reacting but never act themselves, reading about the struggles of another's effort, never realizing that to make it, you're expected to jump *in medias res*, flailing your helpless hands."

> The University of White Cross
> Is a pitiful whore,
> Whose routine
> No longer meets its needs.
> Her thighs are turgid books,
> With hinges broken
> And leaves thumbsupple.
> Her lips are lecterns,
> Discolored with rhetoric
> And polemical backwashes of insight.
> Her eyes are shelves that line arcana
> Of dusty memories
> Back to back.

There's something nice about sitting alone, daydreaming and planning how to escape, even if you never fulfill your dreams with the real thing, the commitment, the one action that will carry you out and away from the routine urgencies. Things academic are fine in their place, the library, but they have little use outside their own narrow context — at least, that's what my friends tell me. What to do?

> I am twenty-four winters old
> Just now. I am polar water
> Without the thickness of dogwood,
> *

Redbuds, purples, soft redwhites,
The Juneloony greens.
I am shoes and socks
That clothe speed and urgency.
My pockets are filled with fists
Clenched tight against their linings.
I am twenty-four dreams new
Just now, a boy of fits.

Now I run with my dream, careening over walls of discontent and frigidity. If I can just bring this dream into focus long enough to hold it within my scope, I may be able to get a clear shot at it. But I must first remove these brambles that block my vision. I wish I had a good English guide, like Hemingway's Robert Wilson. Yet I can't dally with idle wishes. But Alonso Quijano did. I will sally out, a new Quijote, perhaps.

From White Cross to Redington
Is just a tricky flick
Of the imagination,
Cold to hot in one breath.
That's how it is with me,
Escaping seaward on a whim.

I'm driving home from the university now, and there won't be any more five o'clocks for me. "This'll be a day to remember," I'll say. "I was able to make a resolution that day," I'll boast. "I left for good." Now I'm home, and it's good to be here, even if for a short while. I wish it were warm as pancakes outside so I could walk and stand under the black-walnut trees, listening to the sounds of summer, hearing the distant whir of cars pulling themselves down the highway, the anonymous airplanes and jets confounding the air with incessant echoes. But the air is frozen outside my study window, and I must arrange for my departure.

I'm so tired, and now I am smoothing into a lull. My senses are leaving me, and I am falling fast into sleep. Now I have left everything behind me. I hope I won't remain vanwinkled in this chair too long. I have a long trip ahead of me.

Cigarette smoke
Curled into the acoustics of night.
Traffic lights spoke a redgreen dialogue
*

Between motion and sound,
And somewhere, a moaning siren melted
The liquid interlude of parked lovers.

Where was I?
        I was here, inside myself,
Sharing the uncolored soliloquies
Of my throbbing blood,
Listening to the obsequies
Of my buried heart, which lifted
Lilliputian cock-a-doodle-doos
To the subdued dawn of my mind.

Here I am,
        Sitting on lawns purplelit
With Gatsby dreams and the half-drunken
Ecstasies I have had
Thinking of Daisy
And the irrepressible Catherine Barkley.

It's five-thirty in the cold, bleary morning, and the sun doesn't have a chance of beating me to my car. I must get going. Where is my trusty nag, Rocinante, and my lance?

I've been driving quite a while now. I'm sorry I even bothered to stop off home. Nighttime melted into today so quickly I haven't been able to adjust to my dawning thoughts.

Somehow I feel as if I were still in school, reading all that stuff on Donne and Marvell. Let me out of this grip. I give, surrender! Uncle, if you will. But you won't let me alone, will you? I can see you there in front of me: Memphis by night. I see you hiding there, with all your sham and artificiality, your Sterick building. I can see all of you rich Philistines up there, with your piped-in music and your vintage alcohol. You can't fool me. I know damn good and well what's going on down here in the streets, and I can hear them yelling Martin King, James Baldwin, Farmer and Meredith and Silver and Peckerwood. And I know, too, that they're running a race with the sun and that sooner or later they'll overcome you. They'll beat you to a pulp with cries of guilt and denied compassion.

It's the indirect approach, but it'll work. It always has. Even the Jews have worked their retribution now. Everyone wants to be one of them because they have something none of the rest of us has: a history of suffering and oppression. That's their history and their culture, too. And so I see you, Memphis, clothed in neon and slatternly billboards, dressed like some Chatterley Lady in flowing robes of conceit and bigotry. You don't have to tell me your merits. I can read them on every toilet wall as though they were sacred words inscribed on the holy tablets of Sinai. But why does it have to be night? I'm alone and afraid that I may not live to pass through you, dissimulator of good deeds and philanthropy.

> Memphis by night.
> Driving north to south:
> One gaping mouth of neon
> Fillings and wisdom cavities
> That needed extraction.
> I reacted to the salivating night
> Like an Italian beggar distracting
> Passersby and rain and the moon
> With operatic gestures of penury.
> Memphis by rainy night.
> That's how I remember it.
> My windshield wipers smoothed away
> Soft revisions of the city,
> Metronomically.
> Cigarette smoke
> Soothed my impatience, my comic hatred.
> Memphis by Negro night.
> I remember it that way, too,
> Scuttling along my sightless eyes
> Like a naked, soft-thighed chimera.
> I stopped my frightened car
> Long enough to watch
> Lightning spray the town
> With revenge. I was Nero.
> I started my silent engine
> And drove into the flamerainy night.

I was Nero for a moment there. What a feeling to have all that power at your fiddletips. It's good to get out of all that rain though.

The car hurtles itself down the long, horizontal stretches of the Southern night, gaining speed as it caroms off every white-lined curve. The moon has come out from behind clouds, and now its light is falling over the small hamlets and shambled roadside shacks. The car passes through small towns, along the way, that boast two filling stations and an all-night café or drive-in restaurant or truck stop.

All the inhabitants are fast in bed, filling some of them with moans or grunts of lechery and fast talk; others, not even beds really, cramped with three black bodies where one should be.

I drive along, thinking of all these shacked-in people. People, I suppose you call them, since they qualify with arms and legs and a head that looks human even if the members of the local vigilante committee refuse to credit them, the brown or black-wizened heads, with the respect that penury deserves.

"This is fine country though, or was at any rate," I say to myself, "before all those men with their bright ideas decided to take it into their own hands: the Sutpens and Byrds and Carters and Montgomery Ward Snopeses, who figured (some never even stopped long enough to figure) that avarice was the most expedient way to retire. It's still a fine country to drive through on a night when the moon is full and the horizon albino."

But I know there's something going on behind those antebellum porticoes and casement windows that even a Faulkner or a Tennessee Williams would be shocked to witness. I just feel it there, lurid, as I drive by myself. I sense the stifling, rancid quality of a future, not merely a past, and I know what will happen. There's no rejoinder or congressional amendment that will cure the endemic sickness, that will eradicate the Bulls and Bilboes and Vardamans. I foresee it all: the truckling well-wishers of the Negro, the friends of the poor, the schoolmasters of the future generations. It's all been said before, so I know it must be so. They'll have their way, the Negroes. They'll run their race with the sun, until, like the fabled leopard, they'll even succeed in changing their telltale spots, as they've already done with their hair and speech and intelligence. But so what? Will they ever find a way to remove the contumely, the deeds already stamped into the annals of the Mason-Dixon *Domesday Book*? It's a soulless, echoless land, and I'm afraid of it. Is there no way out of this tangle of lacerated hearts and minds, no way to say I'm sorry to those who have seen too much already to ever forget that they were, and still are, anathema and out of time? I don't believe in it! Can't! Not now, anyway.

> The funnel-furrowed Delta
> Is too introspective,
> Shrunk into itself.
> Oleanders and live oaks grown ancient
> Wear silver goatees,
> These the patricians of gentility.

Pandemonium.
*

> Wire-spoked wheels
> Of space and sunlight
> Speak terrific speed.

Limbobound.

> Instrument gauges,
> Made by Smiths,
> Glow with dazed light.

Popeye lives

> On others' pain,
> Vicariously,
> Somewhere in Virginia.

Percy Grimm

> Frightens innocence
> With butchery,
> Somewhere in Mississippi.

Urania cringes

> While Faulkner tunes macabre rhythms
> On a sordid past-tense lute.

> Now Milton,
> Wordsworth,
> And Dr. Johnson
> Drown together in the Yazoo
> As the funnel-furrowed Delta
> Explodes its banks, gurgling.

"Well, boy," I think, "talk to yourself some more before you doze into oblivion." "Say, stop talking with those big words," I think reproachfully. "You've left the university now, where this is a prerequisite for admittance into the elite, scholarly cliques of the coffee lounge. What an absurdity that is, too! That goddamn group of table-talkers vying for top intellectual dog."

Well, that's not bad for a starter, but I think I've run out of talk and metaphors and petty poetic jargon, which gets me nowhere anyway.

Say, that's the University of Mississippi over there, isn't it? Old Faulkner, he had the right idea, going among the enemy, sitting on their spittled porches just long enough to steal all their secrets, those carefully guarded infamies handed down for generations at a time intact. A wholesale steal, I'd say. He really knew how to play the game, hiding behind a guise of farm hand. Hell, there was a man who could spell the nuances of his own blood. Yeah, he was good all right, tricky, and who recognized him when it counted? He did alone, because his cronies refused to be a part of his charade until it was patented by some publishing Parker Brothers or Milton Bradley outfit.

But this is his country, and it's fine because it gave up, vomited, aborted this ragtailed scarecrow of a man, this hangdog rumrunner, Gulf-shrimp-trawler hand. I say to hell with all of you sleeping mummies, there in your crinolines and hand-me-downs. I say crap on all of you until you learn that you're more disgraceful than the blood and innocence you desiccate. Oh, but there I go again with the comic hatred bit and the big words. What a lousy habit anyway.

Part Two

I'm flying into night. The trusty car responds to my quixotic foot, and I open the draft window now, bracing myself against the cool, crisp, dawn-coming air. A second day. But dawn is still many hours away, and the speed is exhilarating. I must get through this country to arrive at my final destination. It'll be a while still, but I'll bend the spectrum of the first rainbow I see, bring it down to me like those Frost-scrawled birch trees. And I'll climb aboard that rainbow's limbs and try to hang on to red or orange for all I'm worth. I'll make it, too, and then let that thing fling me into pewter heights of the Gulf and be gone for good.

That's what I wish, anyway, if it were only possible. But that takes more guts than I have, and, besides, it would be selfish.

I refuse to be one of those people who go from day to day on a shoestring, bumming cigarettes and meal money from every anonymous benefactor. Not me! I absolutely refuse! I'll be free and settle down in Florida and make a decent living. I'll marry a fine, handsome girl and make a child with her, and we'll live until there's no more living to exhaust, and if that isn't enough for that high-spirited filly-to-be, then I'll improvise. But I will work, and I will build some dignity and respect, or the equivalent to whatever those words mean. I'll construct a house of dignity. No palace of art for me! No pleasure dome! No, sir! None of that crap!

I refuse to be inhuman and out of time and place, a displaced person who nobody cares to care for. I'll bend the dials of the clock if I have to, until they read five or ten years into my childhood if necessary, if that's what it takes. I'll rip those hands off, too, if needs be, but I will wonder, and I will dream, and I will hope for a something, a future that's filled with the simple harmonies of living.

I plea for redemption, for forgiveness, proclaiming I am vulnerable. But I won't be made pitiable scum or dross of opinion, nor will I accept responsibility placed in my way simply because it's the way civilized people are supposed to react. I refuse. Do you hear me? Refuse! Refuse! But I don't deny that responsibility and doing are the primary things of living, and so I do accept, but on my own terms. I will be responsible. I will! I will!

Jesus, I'm a didactic bastard when I want to be. At least it keeps me awake.

Tallahassee.

Ah, I've finally come through the winter of my disconsolateness, and there's resurgence in my heart. This land is warm and friendly. But I am tired, so tired, and . . .

Hey, wait! The orange dash light flickers, warning me I'm low on petrol. Better find a place that's open soon. Ah, there's a place just up ahead.

"Fill 'er up, will you, and better check the oil and tire pressure too. The front two get twenty-three pounds; the back twenty-five."

I walk around the asphalt pavement, under the insect-white neon lights, stretching out my weariness like a large, sky-tilting hawk. "How far to Redington, mister?"

"Maybe two hours' ride from here, if you don't get lost or hit a cow."

"Smart bastard," I think.

"Highway 101."

What thick land this is. . . . Look out! The highway narrows into two lanes. A little different from the outstretched arm of Interstate 75. But this is better anyway — more curves to keep me alert.

My headbeams tickle the impenetrable, now-dawning live oaks and brush pines that line the road. There's something mysterious and a little frightening about driving down here early in the morning, before all the road crews and fruit vendors strew the roads with their penurious tourist wares. "This is tourist country, wholly dependent upon outlanders for its subsistence," I tell myself, as though I were some silly, uninformed *Rand McNally* or bus driver. "A poor country," I continue, "clothed in the richest, lushest garments of tropical silks and Afric brocades."

I'm anxious to reach my destination. It's been a too-long drive, a depressing one because my thoughts have been bitter. But this will all end now. I just know it, and I'll allow myself to fall in love with my new habitat.

But I am very tired, so tired now, and it'll be good to arrive and throw myself flat upon the whitedawning sands of Redington. I'll caress it, sinking into its tidesmoothed pebbles, and then I'll sleep there until some beachcomber or hotel official or my love comes and taps me on the shoulder and says it's time to awaken. After that, I'll be stained permanently with an image of sweetsilted sand and sun, with the laundry mark of Redington. I just know it.

   I'm almost there now, and my mind is restless, though relaxed, with the prospect. Maybe I'm crazy. Yet I think I've cast off all my comic hatred and the intolerance that's plagued me like carrion trailing some tanker's wake. I've lost all that, I think, passed through winter, into this comfortable climate. My mind is contemplative but not brooding anymore, and this is good. I feel a certain ecstasy, a relief.

> Four o'clock in the Florida morning.
> We, the car and I,
> Fought intemperate rain and cold
> To reach this spot on Mercator's map.
>
> I was Henry, prince and navigator,
> Drawing lines of desire and hope.
> I was Ponce de León,
> Cresting each hamleted hill and slope.
> My astrolabe revolved the needle,
> Until, obliquely,
> It exceeded ninety miles an hour.
>
> Nashville, or Memphis,
> Then Lookout Mountain
> Faded in retrogressive blinks
> Of billboards and coffee stops;
> Next, Atlanta,
> Serpentine,
> Molting in rush hour.
>
> Finally, I could see the outcast slip,
> Stretching in ribbonstraight horizons
> Of beach like a strip of uncoiled tape
> Stuck to the crease of night's tare.
>
> Four o'clock in the Florida morning,
> And I am spent of energy,
> A dizzy, dying death-moth,
> Forgetting the slow pain of maturity.
>
> I'll end my journey,
> Running down sandy corridors,
> Pirouetting into obscurity,
> Falling to embrace the lisping shore.

   Now I drive down the longwinding beach road, Gulf Boulevard. I've arrived, but somehow I have that funny feeling again in the core of my stomach, something heavy, the nausea returning, turning my insides with disgust again. What is this feeling? I should be thankful I've made it.

But as I drive along the ribbonstraight slip of Gulf beach, I can't help thinking that this place, Redington, was once dubbed Redington not because it had any symbolic or significant reason behind it but simply done by some arbitrary progenitor for no other reason than to get it done with, the chore, the burden of having a worthless plot of then-uninhabitable, untreed land, unsuitable even for dairying or farming, without nomination.

"You stinking cynic," I chastise myself, knowing that I'm in Redington now, nameless myself, perhaps, but relieved. But I can't quit it, the nausea, not yet at any rate.

"Redington, you bastard!" I think, "I am here! Redington, you amphibian, isolated from the mainland! Redington, that's what you are!" "Redington," again, loud and clear, I shout, "you place without a history, without a people or race or religion! This place! You, Redington! I love you! What else can I say?

"You're so quiet now. You sleep like a Siamese kitten nuzzled into a pillow and clawless. This place, Redington, this beach for modern living, you are metamorphosed temporarily into a peaceable kingdom, and I love you. Maybe it's I who am the slouching beast, coming to your kingdom. Yeah," I think. "Don't I wish my name were Yeats!"

This beach road is as long as each tidefilled, saltreeking blast of sea breeze is wide, and I can feel the salt in my lungs. I've almost finished my trip now. I'll park the car and never resume this foetal position again.

I think how I've always wanted to find such a place as this, located out of time and dimensionless. "Redington!" I shout. "You are this place, that respite where, for weeks at a time, in the journeys of my mind, I have flown. You, beach, are here now, where I left you last year, still inviolable, still friendly in my early morning arrival, maybe a pinch more sand here, a bunch more shells there.

"But I've seen the tourist seasons come and dissolve like old photographs that brown and fade and flake with time. And I've watched you, Redington, snap at your customers, defending yourself, until, now, your prices rival Miami and Lauderdale and Vero. But I've returned to you, and you are still here, and this fact seems most important to me, somehow."

I must learn to temper my bitterness, I a waif, a student who's got no more business deprecating others than a zebra has scoffing at a horse because it's got no stripes. OK. So what I'll do is become a doer, a citizen in this free country, a person with a small amount of respectability, even if that respect goes no further than the bedroom where I'll spend my nights with a future wife. She'll simply have to be a person to whom my being an Alexander or a Shelley makes little difference. I'll teach myself, and her too, to be content with the small things, the little favors, at least for now. First things first. And I'll start by becoming the unacknowledged legislator of my emotions.

Part Three

So I arrived with good intentions. First I was going to relax and try to take stock of my present state. But the drive to Redington turned out to be too much for me, and I grew sick with disorders of the lungs and chest. I had bronchitis, and a local free-clinic doctor gave me pills to take and made me quit smoking for at least a week. But that was all right, too, since I had lost my desire to smoke anyway, had no reason to do it, no anxieties, no brooding remorse, no introspections. I had arrived. I was free at last, and the only thing holding me back was my sickness. "In what better place could I be to cure it?" I told myself assuringly.

Yet, one day, at the height of my infirmity, I sank into a fit of delusion. My mind was given free flight, and I sensed myself reverting to the old attitude of bitterness. It took complete control over me. It was crazy, but fortunately for me, it didn't last long.

> My vacation to Florida is sick.
> I'm bronchitis, smoked dry
> By cigarettes that roll and lick tight
> My pure white wrapper.
>
> Florida!
> Motels that breathe comfortable lies
> From December to April.
> Florida!
> Highways that drill out
> Adamant cores of memory.
>
> My sickness intervenes:
> Phantasmagorical beaches,
> Literature, and ballpark bleachers
> Scatter in fantastic disarray.
>
> My mother is a fish!
> Vardaman had difficulty
> Reading Izaak Walton.
> Hemingway was a speckled trout,
> *

Though I doubt he ever read
Donne's words on the Poebells.

Vardaman is a fish himself.
He dream-wished, daydreamed,
About his dead mother,
Who bore contempt for idiocy
And wore a scarlet "A," for "Addie."

Redington Beach! What of it?
How many resorts consort
To hoard the sun from me,
A boy of fits?

The fugue soon passed, and with it, the dampness in my lungs and brain. I had been afflicted with the hurt of trial. I had survived it and felt I could now begin to enjoy all that Redington had to offer. I started thinking about work, a job. I had a little money left from the trip, and with it I rented a small economy cottage that overlooked the Gulf. It was reasonable enough. At seventy-five dollars a month, I could live comfortably for sixty days or so without additional income. By that time, I knew I'd be working.

Reassured, I took my leisure convalescing, and every day, on the beach, I tried to conceive a new me, a me with personality, whatever that meant. I resolved to be outgoing and friendly, to read a newspaper daily and learn about current things. I would have all the facts at my fingertips. No more Nero for me. That would all be a part of my past, a past I was already beginning to molt and shed behind me. I hoped gradually to wander into the light of a new person: *me*. I even vowed to read my horoscope and the "Stargazer," every little thing that could help me, lend encouragement.

The beach was a fine place to sit and dream. The sun warmed and consoled. One afternoon, while I was sitting watching the pelicans and grey-breasted gulls swooping down to the Gulf's lips after fish and other flotsam, the solitary figure of a girl, perhaps nineteen or twenty, strolled by in a tightly drawn, black bikini. I stared at her. She was coy and reticent, and her eyes were staring down at the beach before her feet. She was returning from somewhere, walking down the beach toward the stairs that mounted the protective wall behind the adjoining motel. Then she was gone before I realized it was not her figure I was still gazing upon but her invisible image, that lithe figure of a womangirl, wifegirl, longlegged and lazyslung as she walked in front of me. In her absence, I saw the del Sarto smoothness of her round face and the applesauce hair that framed it. I don't think she ever saw me that day.

Dusk began to settle over the beach. The orange horizon melted slowly into the pinkred powders of night, and the sun dropped not in short spurts like a car's odometer numerals but fast and all at once. Then it was grey-blue before I knew what had happened. The screeching gulls and pelicans and sandpipers faded into shadow, and from myriad recesses of motels and cottage patios and terraces came odours of barbecuing meats and heated breads and vegetables. There was quietude everywhere, and I felt comfortable, slightly warm, listening to the lap, laplap of the tides, and I was too warm inside to feel hungry.

I walked back to the cottage, changed clothes, then returned to the beach with a bottle of whiskey and a glass filled with ice. The liquor's tingle made me lightheaded and mellow. "How nice it is here," I thought. "How wonderful to be free, just to be able to sit on a beach with a drink and think about everything in general and nothing in particular. No phones to answer, no ten chapters to read for Monday, no familiar faces to greet." "How banal of me," I thought, "and yet how true, irrefutably."

"God, how good I feel. How can this be real? Now I'll find a wife for myself and make a child and live here forever. I'll never die. Night, you're beautiful! Your stars swim around up there without concern, and I sit here gazing with equal unconcern. But we'll talk to each other every night, you and I, and when I find my wife, we'll talk to you together, and we'll kiss the moon together one night, lying flat on our backs.

"I feel strangely alive tonight. Maybe I'll sleep on the beach and breathe the same air you breathe up there."

> Lines draw taut
>> around midnight's belly.
> Scions of thought
>> surround lightheaded fugues.
> Lemmings are people in disguise,
>> rushing helter-skelter
> Into the blushing bodies
>> of spawndying women.
>
> We dash from womb to womb
>> like mad porpoises
> Weaving threads of water
>> through flaming daytime hoops.
> We dive beneath their splashes
>> into nighttime urns and die
> In female fires of rank perfume.

Though I went out on the beach every afternoon at the same hour, I didn't see the young girl again for three weeks. I envisioned her in my sleep and knew she was my wife. I didn't even have to know her name to love her, because she was love, and I was prepared for love. Already I had dropped off all the remnants of my melancholy. I knew, too, now I had outdistanced youth, with all its little ironies and turns of phrase, its skepticisms and cynical commentaries on society and people and customs. I had stepped over the boundaries, into maturity. From youth to maturity was as simple as springtime burgeoning and yet as difficult as the process of dissolution and regeneration involved in its fruition. Mine had been but an after-dinner sleep, a Van Winkle nap. For twenty-four years, I told myself, I had walked in the shadows of death, of life's harshness. Now I knew what Wordsworth and Vaughan before him meant when they wrote about the life that *is* before birth and after death, and I knew too what Browne was thinking when he spoke of man, the noble animal. But I would never remember them again, or if I did, I promised myself, I would call them Billy and Hank and Tommy. No more scholarship for me. No need for it now. I was living it.

And it was on this evening of my vows that she returned to me, when silence spread itself over the sky like shimmering neons of the aurora borealis. She had returned, not by accident and yet without conscious design. The night was a painting, and we were the figures in the far lower corner of the canvas, barely visible, and yet we had come together, holding hands, now, on the beach, become one out of two people. For us, everything else melted away. We were anonymous unto all but ourselves, I a mere boy, she a compelling lover. We spoke few words, yet we lived together in their correspondence. We were thralls and conquerors in the same lapse, that evening, when we lay together on our backs, looking up into the clear, lambent sky.

> She, her mouth encircling the moon,
> And I, with lips lapping its shores,
> Lay together on a palette of oils.
> The sky's colored eyes
> Twittered like missal bells
> From some ancient campanile.
>
> "Lover, encompass my warmth
> In your eyes. Satisfy my desires
> Like waves sieging shores
> Hot as fever."
>
> "Young boy, tonight we'll love
> *

Fast and together, protracting the hours
Between shadow and light,
Discovering ourselves
Like oceans in shells."

We became one, and all the harshness of the past dissolved. We were one together in thought and compassion. We made living and freedom realities. The beach was ours, as though soil, instead of sand, appointed to us. The beach was our plot and nightbed, and it was here we were anointed and given birth.

We lay together,
Huddled on thought's rug,
Weaving strands of *seem*
Through widewhite warps
Where *be* and *is*
Coalesce,
Weaving tapestries
With fleshly dreams,
Weaving fluid
Wet as spray.

Part Four

Before I knew it, three months had passed, and June was over us. The bronze weather was unfriendly. We spent all of our free time together. Two months earlier, I had applied for and got a position writing copy for the *Redington Sentinel*. It didn't pay much, but at least it was a start. I was on my way. I had a design.

One night, while we were having dinner on the wharf at John's Pass, a strange feeling came over me as though something were falling away from me, as if I had been flung into depthless night, free-falling. My mind was in a quandary, and I was at once unsure of myself. The girl, sitting across from me, was silent, her lips drawn tight, the eyes distant and staring out into the channel. She was too silent, and my uneasiness showed: the fidgeting hands playing with the napkin and silverware; smoking again. We ordered dinner, no words passing between us.

"What's happening?" I asked myself. "What's moved our world apart?" She didn't answer my silence. Her eyes weren't looking at me but gazing abstractedly at the tabletop, and I could see them, the eyes, reading the descriptions under the different-pictured fishes on the menu. "What's happened?"

"Will you take me home? I've lost my appetite. I'm afraid of myself. I fear what two can do to one," she whispered.

"What's that supposed to mean, honey?"

"I'm afraid, that's all. We're the two, but you're the one I worry about."

"But we two are one now. You're going to be my wife. I thought we had that all settled. Just as soon as I can get enough money to . . ."

"But I'm afraid for us, for you especially."

"I don't understand. Why me? . . ."

"You will, honey, and I won't deprive you."

"Of what?" I pleaded, sick to my stomach with fear. I was not yet afraid of loneliness but frightened by her cryptic words.

"You'll understand. Please take me home now."

"But we two are one," I insisted, whispering to her as we left the restaurant. "And we'll always be that way. It's been settled. You're my future wife."

That same evening, I sat on the beach, thinking about what had happened, and I was lonely now. I was beginning to think too much again, and I knew it, felt solitude stalking me slowly, hobbling like an old man with outstretched arms, begging for alms. "I need her," I told myself. "What'll I do without her? What will I do tonight? Sleep will be lonely, if I sleep at all."

> My mouth ordered cheeseburgers,
>> But I couldn't eat.
>>> Her eyes stared at me
>>>> Like pickles on a plate.
>>>> I cried aloud,
>>>>> Drank a glass of water,
>>>>> And dove into the ketchup
>>>>>>> and died.

During the next few weeks, my old hatred revived. We saw little of each other, and I spent extra hours at the office, trying to forget, to understand what had happened between us. What had I done to make her afraid? I hadn't deprived her of anything, had given her all of myself. And no matter what angles I studied, I couldn't discover an explanation for her behavior, the abruptness, the pulling away.

It had all happened so suddenly and unexpectedly that my first re-action was to think of her as a temptress, as an oversexed girl looking to make me her victim. My rage grew beyond proportion, and I pros-trated myself with recrimination.

"Where did I fail, screw up? I took this girl, would have made her my wife and made a child with her, too, all without asking her name.

I've loved her completely, and she was mine. If I only knew. I can't go back home, can I? Or can I? Back to White Cross, to the university, to my routine. Is there no way of escaping it? Is this all there is?"

> If I could live in eyes
> That sigh with laughter.
> If I could breathe those sighs
> Of love that linger after
> Essence of wetness dissolves.
> If I could evolve
> Into something more than hauteur
> Can echo.
> If!
> If!
> If!
> But indignation gnaws my eyes
> And hollows my laughter.
> It mocks my sighs
> With vapid afterthoughts.
>
> I'm an "if" that couldn't.

The hours grew longer, and my thoughts increasingly sardonic and dour. My days became the mere shadows of escape from myself, chasing me wherever I went. I couldn't escape from the freedom I'd won for myself. And this freedom began to weigh heavy on me.

> Fugitive sighs fleet.
> Vain retreat conspires
> With blistered feet,
> And I walk naked
> Over sand on fire.

I had known youth and then maturity as though both were partners in some lewd game of dice, throwing me out speculatively, not betting on me. And I came first as snake eyes and then seven-come-eleven and then boxcars again. I had watched my wintering night fade and dissolve into spring, then go back into autumn, and I had known, for that breathless moment in between, no shadows, just the warmth of mutuality and the freedom of selflessness.

Again I was a waif, fast becoming another Nero, and I knew that it, the madness, would control my reason once more.

I quit work at the newspaper and retired to my cottage by the Gulf. The sunsets, with their warming spray, ceased to work charms, and the night murmurs of birds grew distracting. I sat nights by myself, refusing to eat anything, just whiskey and crackers or potato chips or popcorn.

My frame declined. The cheekbones receded into my skull, until the arches of the jaws jutted. My features shrank from the mellowness of health to a ghostly resemblance of their mirrored selves. The beard that clung, now, to my sideburns grew down below my chin in thick, dirty swirls.

"What's happened to me? I can't keep any food down, even when I force myself to eat. What in hell can I do about it? It's just no damn good. I've changed from day into night, from summer into autumn, right before my own eyes."

> I'm a sideshow stingray,
> A fan-tailed lemon shark,
> Spraying customers' faces
> With darkspawning drops of doom.
> I'm a grouper's gaping mouth,
> Laughing at myself behind glass.
> I'm a swimming sawfish,
> Skimming the top of my tank
> To cut the dawn in half.

I had grown rancid; even my language was disgraceful. I tried to nourish my mind with pity, but that failed, and I knew there was still something missing, still something I had to do. I realized it was foolish trying to find her, the wifegirl, because she would have to come to me as she had done that first day or come not at all.

"But what is it, then?" I repeated to myself anguishingly. "Maybe I can find it in my books. But no, they're at home, back in White Cross."

Once again, I was becoming a student. I had tried to get outside it, to leave the sordid, musty faces of the library, but in my dreams they kept haunting me like apparitions some projectionist flashed upon the screen of my sleeping hours. "Then, I must return," I resolved. "That's the only life I really know, know best at any rate. There's nothing out here that works for me. It's too fast and too unpredictable. No one's had time or taken the time to write it down for librarians to file away under OUT HERE call numbers.

"Honey, where are you now? Is there no human way for us to remain together and make a child? We loved once, and then it was gone. Why couldn't it have lasted? Hemingway, you bastard! Fitzgerald, you cheap cheat! You deceiver of time and reality! You rotting Carraway seed, drifting endlessly in the mind of your own imagination! Man's not a noble animal; he's a stinking beast that reverts to instinct the first chance he gets.

"I had a design. I was going to be like everyone else who's good and respectable and loving. But I never found that in myself. Not yet, anyway. God knows I tried in the only way left open, and now I've nowhere to turn.

"I'll be the banks of the gurgling Yazoo and consume myself in the wake of my own inundation. I'll roll all my strength into a ball and hurl myself through the gates of this threshing-floored earth.

"I'll be Popeye and Percy Grimm rolled into that formless ball.

"I'm disintegrating quickly, a fast-spreading cancer going in reverse. I'm inverse mitosis, splitting into nothing, not everything. There I go again, though, a damn pedant.

"But I did love once, and at least I'll be able to say this when I'm no more. I'll have this one credit to my name. They'll say, 'Here lies a boy who never quite had the courage to make a clean break with himself. He had the right idea, but that wasn't enough.' 'The courage was there all right,' they'll say, 'but he never learned how to implement it. He had the energy but not the wisdom. He was a paradox, not even human, only half-formed. But he did find a love and almost a wife, and he would have made a child and a home for it, too, if he'd only known what he was meant to do. He was as knowledgable as a library and as empty as a new-bought trash bin.' They'll say all that. . . .

"But wait! Who will? Who'll ever know I did whatever that something is I've still not comprehended? And who'll ever question whether or not I even left the festering stacks of the library? Who?

"I can see her there on the beach," I imagined, now, with perverse nostalgia. "I remember my initial anxiety on returning to Redington in February to look for her. But that was sheer fancy. I know it now, and so I'll go home to White Cross. I must, have to, before it's too late. She was beautiful though, my wifegirl. Where has she gone? . . . Where are you, honey? . . . Where am I?"

> And wouldn't it be nice
>   To think so, dear Brett?
> And wouldn't it be nice?
>   But that was years ago,
> Before the anomalies of war,
>   Before the soaring afterglow
> Of Pamplona and the Riviera.

Part Five

"I'm in my car now, driving back up the winding chain of beaches, heading home, and one beach recedes behind the next in rapid amaze. I've got to stop once more. I'll rest up ahead, here at this cove, just for memory's sake."

The cove was unpeopled and quiet and was sheltered from the main highway, which led into Interstate 75, by a copse of dense scrub oaks and sycamores and tropical conifers. Evening was fast descending over the palmettos and bristlestalked palm trees that drooped over the inlet. The car was parked at the top of the summit, which overlooked the enclosed line of shore. Below, a boy walked along the greying beach, his hands clasped behind his back, head drooped, and he thought:

"I must get out of here, get going." But he was thinking alternatively, until he reached his decision: "I'm going to hit Redington once more. I've got to return and see if she's there anywhere."

The car pulled onto the highway, retracing its tire tracks for thirty miles. It was almost dusk when he finally arrived, and the sky had darkened more deeply than the color of night. Everywhere, clouds chased each other across the neon-hazy horizon of Gulf water. He knew a storm was forming and that he'd have to hurry.

"But I've got to do this," he thought. "I know there's one thing left for me to do, and I must do it, have to, but what is it? What if I can't find her?"

He mounted the beach wall in back of the motel where he had first seen her walking the sands five months ago. His legs were taut and throbbing with dulltired pain, and he was smoking a cigarette, looking far out into the whitemoiling Gulf. Now he watched the smoke coil around itself, until there was no more consummation.

People were rushing everywhere, spinning around on their feet, madly searching for overlooked items of clothing and other artifacts. It was a dervish world, in which everything had become minimized and fastwhirling. The roar of the waves slapping the shore one behind the other set up grumbling noises, like a telephone's busy signal magnified a thousand times, in his ears. Now the clouds were bunched together, forming in his mind a phalanx of warring creatures.

He was thinking of that first night they had spent together, touring the best nightclubs in Redington, remembering how he had stood in front of his cottage after he had walked her home, thinking then, "What a fine place this is." But that was all gone, and now he was standing against the winnowing waves of the Gulf.

He took off all his clothing and waded into the trammeled waters, which, even in close to shore, broke over his head; then he trudged further out. Soon he was beyond the fishing pier, a hundred feet out into the Gulf, and he could feel the unsubtle tow grabbing and tugging at his body, coercing him with rough arms. The water came alive around his body, and he was becoming a part of it. He pulled back, frightened, until he stood again on an invisible sand bar, temporarily safe from the swelling tides.

"Where are you, honey? I know you're here somewhere. I've searched everyplace else. You have to be here. Don't hide from me any longer. I can't go home until . . . not without you, anyway."

Once again, he plunged forward, unhesitating now. The waves were coming in faster, higher than elephants, roaring and coughing like machetes flailing their force at his body. He was beyond the pier now, beyond the sand bar, alone and confined by the colorless, whitetopped water, and the water was living around him. Still he ranged further and further out, barely able to keep his head up. There was a yellow clangor of lightning, and then he was no more. Where he had gone under was a momentary bubbling cavity, and then that, too, closed behind his entry, and the Gulf was again one with itself.

"I don't feel any different," he thought, with slow, unexpected relief. "I'm naked and alone but free. And now I can see the university looming before me, right through the seaweed and water, plain as day.

"Everywhere, these blunt, brown bodies swimming, darting, plunging around me, and it's cold down here. But I'm flowing back now, and everything is familiar. There's the spire of the chapel. And there's the main dormitory. Now I'm floating through the doors of the library. Here are these same faces. They recognize me, I think. There's one who's motioning me over. But no. I've got to take my seat back here among my friends, the books. I'm home again. I'm myself again. I don't mind. I think I may even stay here, maybe forever."

For three days, the storms continued, and then they tapered off. Everything went back to normal.

One afternoon, a week later, a girl of nineteen or twenty, wearing a tightly drawn, black bikini, walked out back of her motel and came down the stairs of the sea wall, onto the beach.

She walked along the shore, a lithe figure with pastel-smooth complexion and hair the color of applesauce. She moved longlegged and lazyslung, until she stood inconspicuously by a bridged lifeboat.

She sat on the wooden bow plate, musing into the sleeping Gulf. She was crying, silent and one with the calm meter of the tides. Her wet eyes refocused slowly, gazing into the boat's greyweathered ribbing, still crying to herself. Then she stood up, rubbing red the eyes, walking back to the stairs, almost running now, climbing them quickly,

until her figure disappeared into the motel's shadows.
        She had come again, and now she was no more . . . maybe forever.

                A waterlogged worm
                    Squirmed on the rotting boat bow,
                        Floating in a perfect pool of tears.

5/5–7/65 (dates for piece as a whole) (05236)

[The unaccented accident] [†]

The unaccented accident
of Highway 41

The cabin was a child
tucked into the Ozark hillbeds,
unborn and windblown

5/10/65 — [1] (05329)

The Firebird

Firebird floating above the slime
Of sandlocked salt-sea shores,
Fly with fleeting, blinding speed
Through the pocket of dawn's new sun,
Flow on wingflailed, fan-tailed light,
And fight the particles in obstacled flight.
Then emerge from your spindown,
Spellbinding maze,
Into my mind's steelbarred cage.

Firebird, firebird,
My thought's bright-blown business,
Blind me with dizzy heat.
Firebird, firebird,
Land in my boyhood sandlot,
Linger long enough for me
To lock you in wild speculation.

Then, fly-by-night firebird,
Fly away again
And sink
Into despair's cold-fingered furrows.
Melt, Icarian bird,
And disappear
Beneath the daytime of my ashen night,

But stay there, firebird,
Full of hidden brightness,
Perched and loitering
On my bar of hardened tears,
To fly once more
In lofty resurrection
When I cry out for inspiration.

5/10/65 — [2] (05090)

Of Poetry

Poetry is the very essence of man's spirit. It is the chronicle of his own self-justification. It is the threadbare genuflection, the plea for forgiveness, and the assertion of his admiration for God. It is the inscription on the dank walls of mortality, the hieroglyphics on the slimy recesses of Lascaux, the ashes in the Catacombs and the fields of Walsingham. It is the record of man's piety and his humility, for if it were otherwise, man would still be a beast, a clown with an intellect, a personator of Zeus and Pluto simultaneously, a tiny seed of inconsequence.

Poetry is man's scream for recognition into the flaming, echoless baffles of everlasting night, and it is this cry, this tiny peal of indefinable authority, that gives man his nobility. But the spark of creativity is elusive. It darts behind the blind spots of the mind mysteriously and reappears with terrific, though evanescent, quickness. The man who can capture this spark is called a poet, though in fact he is simply a man, a solitary human being perhaps, but a man nonetheless, possessed with the selfsame vanities and ambitions, trying to speak to and through his fellow man to the spirit of God. He is no less the very same man among men who runs the course between night and day as though it were a steeplechase toward nowhere, everywhere, for time anon.

Poetry happens to some people, but the moment that it happens, it has already become memorabilia, evidence that rests in the public domain. Poetry need not be truth any more than a human being is truth. People *are*, and so too *is* poetry. Poetry has a voice as individuated as the myriad fingerprints of the world. Its speech transcends all the stalks and scions of the Tower of Babel, and its words stretch their limbs over the innumerable, unnameable minds of all civilizations for all times — Li Po, Plato, and Karl Shapiro, all bound together in a word or metaphor or poem.

Poetry is man, as noble or as insignificant as man himself is. But poetry was spawned in the same paradoxical nest of human endeavour, with all of its attendant muses, and, as such, has always and will forever remain a substance of indeterminate significance. If it is truly descended from the spirit of God, it is doomed to remain hermetic and inviolable. For those few who can feel its message, the spell is too overpowering to disseminate its meaning. And for the rest of us, there is no middle ground. We are doomed to incomprehension. But it is our responsibility not merely to recognize the screams or whimpers of the Platos and prophets who scribbled their lives onto silk and papyrus but to heed their words and mould them with our own, to use them to our benefit. It is our duty, not as poets necessarily, to take the bulk of the past bequeathments and to sort them for ourselves, absorbing those fragments which may shed light and grace on our own condition.

To say finally that poetry is under suspicion is an unpardonable truth we must all accept. But man the thinker will always be trying to discover better ways to tap that message which flows between the spirit of God and the mind of man. And man the poet, until he no longer has the strength to lift his hand to the scratch paper, will be trying to tell his temporal community of the timeless nobility of mankind.

> . . . *Man is of Kinne to the Beasts,*
> *by his Body; And if, he be not*
> *of Kinne to God, by his Spirit,*
> *he is a Base and Ignoble Creature.*
> — Francis Bacon, "Of Atheism"

5/10/65 — [3] (05165)

Mulatto

Hair the color of applesauce,
*

Mottled with cider streaks;
Hazel eyes that blinked like freckles
Under the sun's spectacle.
The grass she lay facedown in
Licked her stomach
With feline tongues.
She watched her twenty-one years
Pass overhead
Like migratory ducks in flight,
Remembering the cold kisses
That chased her tragic escapes
And hot rumors
That greeted her arrival
In each new place.
Her fingers were stained
Green and wet
Where she tore clots of grass
Aimlessly
From the ground's wrinkled face.
Tomorrow looked at her
With albino eyes
And a disconcerted brow.
Now she was sobbing,
Resisting her separateness,
Her inconsequential disgrace.
Somewhere, a thrush throated
Three quick notes,
Then dissolved in the underbrush.
She stood up naked,
Alert to night's sneer,
Ready to flee again
Into a thousand hungry mouths
Of the populace.
As she neared,
Her footfalls echoed
Like pulsebeats
In the city's groin.
She was up for sale
To anyone who could match the price
Of her ambivalent nudity.

5/12 & 5/18/65 (04010)

Nocturne IV: The Gentle $^\Delta$

Summer day, sticky
As a glass of whiskey.
Dialogue of traffic
Across highways
Spread for dinner.

Country river, walking
Over dappled beds
Below the restaurant porch,
Talking to us
Like a drunken sailor
With mystical delights
Of Bangkok by night.

Supper after Tom Collins,
Then dessert and cigarettes;
Slow talk mingled with mist
From the whispering traveller.

Hurled through headlights,
Heading home,
Nature's blackened eyes
Spying on our gentleness.

Odors of clipt grass
Pass down our nostrils
Like women on Pigalle.
The ground shares us
With late evening dew,
Absorbing our weight,
Congealing our spray:
Unity in night's disarray.

5/14/65 (05091)

[Absolute silence is the monarch . . .]

Absolute silence is the monarch of this mid-May evening. Out-
side, there is virtually no noise now except for the occasional series
of chirps from some distant meadowlarks or bobwhites and the soft
murmurs of cicadas and crickets slouching into dawn, singing with
their feet. There are no ears awake now to hear the silence except for

my own and no eyes to notice that the lights of all the county houses
have dissolved into the three o'clocks of blank evening. Only, there's
no blank stare in my eyes and no inaudible slumberings in these ears,
which have listened to the thousand flickering intonations of a busy
city by night.

White Cross is a friendly place this evening. It is bathed in a three
o'clock aura of stillness and warmth. No breezes, no rustle of new-
born leaves on the mimosa and black-walnut and sycamore trees. I am
alone, sitting in my tiny study, gazing out of the miniature chicken-
wire screen of the solitary window, which is open and absorbent. The
bright lights of the ceiling and pole lamp daze my senses, and I relax
into the easiness of reminiscence.

Somewhere off in the back of my consciousness, I can hear my
good friend Gene reciting lines that get confused in the background
jazz of the lounge. He is saying, "Love calls us to the things of this
world." I say in a sustained reflex of astonishment, "Beautiful, Gene!
How I wish I had written that line." The noise is fine, fully embodying
the atmosphere of the Negro lounge. There are people of pronounced
skin colors sitting around, minding themselves, and keeping time to
their senses' music with nodding heads and feet tapping on the floor.
The place "swings," and all the people come alive with silent ges-
tures of pleasure and fancy.

The lounge is softly lit with green and bluedark colours, and the
walls are painted with stark representations of jungle scenes reminis-
cent of Henri Rousseau pictures. "Someone has done a fine job of
decorating," I think to myself, remembering what anonymity told me
about the designer being a homosexual. There is an air of Africanism
that wafts through the tidy confines of the place.

"All in green went my love riding." I can hear those strains from
Cummings as I sit beside my lovely thing of a woman. We are drink-
ing now, slowly and steadily — Vodka Collins, with a twist of orange
floating to the top. It is cool where we sit, in front of the open door,
through which flow winds of the Negro street by night. There is a
certain texture to the coolness, which flies beside us crisply and neat.
The drinks float down the corridors of inebriation, and we are car-
ried off to Africa on a magic carpet of thought.

"In a dark time, the eye begins to see." "I wish I had written that
line," I think again to myself. "Begins to see what?" my girl ques-
tions. I can't tell her what fills the eye with desire for wholeness and
completion, because words don't work that subtly. "The eye begins to
see itself," I say. "It sees what warmth can melt away from the taut
pressure of the brain, which refuses, during the daytime, to set itself
free from inane responsibilities."

She is sitting there, softly slouched into her revolving chair. Her
face is tilted toward me, and there is a glow of reflected warmth flow-
ing from her to me. Her eyes are deeply set into the dark contours of
her cheeks, and they see straight ahead into the shadows of my own.
The eyes meet in tight constriction and pause silently, calculating the
futurity of love. They come alive out of the dark time and cry out for
laundry, praising the banalities of commonality as though these were
the things of this world that hurl us from us to us, from singular to
plural relationship.

Her hair is weaving patterns of immortality over the face that
holds the eyes, curling over the sharppoised nose. There is beauty in
that face, beauty that thralls with its indeterminate fire, beauty that
tempts and tortures, beauty that is singular and difficult to contem-
plate, beauty that needs no music nor paint nor words to define it.
She sits beside me, her longfashioned fingers climbing over the knuck-
les and raspy folds of my hands in slow waves of sensuality. I re-
spond without speaking, thinking that all in green my eyes have seen
the things of this world and that there is nothing more worth seeing.

I have returned to my study now, and my mind is clear and ordered.
There is no sweet, soft girl sitting beside me now. Rather, I have the
company of my books. I can remember having said earlier this same
evening that too many books are the sign of a cluttered mind. Yes, I
agree. The mind that is truly free needs nothing more than a mother
to care for it, to comfort it with only the facts and poetry of the mo-
ment. [I am John Suckling, with a dozen dozen loves, all of whom
focus with constancy upon that sweet, soft thing of my thoughts. "Fly
away with me," I have written to her, "to the land of the sacred tree."
[restored, ed.]]

My solitude is friendly to me tonight. It is peopled with the thoughts
of my Wendell and Don, my Gene, and the sweet thing named Jan.
I have flown over the towers of infinity tonight and have returned
again with the laurels and moonberries of another world. I am so
tired now and seek the respite of sleep. I will run a race with the sun
this evening, rushing from my study with steady determination, and
mold myself into the gentle folds of my bed. I will sleep in pools of
honeydew melon and awake stained with the shades of her image im-
posed over mine. I will bury myself into the gentleness of slumber,
unencumbered with the persistent hummings of busy birds and the
baffled barks of early morning dogs, which will soon shout through
my windows of unconsciousness. God bless you, dear girl of strange
countenance. God bless you with the graces and the gentle touch of
insomnia that has been my own gift for the past hour. I must fling
myself from myself into the vacuum of sleep now and drown in the

gulf of our temporary separation.
          God bless you in this time
                    When the eye begins to see
                    The things of this world
                    Come riding all in green.

5/15/65 (05237)

[Andrew Marvell]

Andrew Marvell

     "Last Instructions to a Painter" —
                         satire

I sit in class,
    listening to the tractor blasts
        that sound indiscriminately
            outside the window's pedantic glass.

My mind is sick
    with quickened snorts
        of the lecturer's ebullience
            and the listeners' boredom.

Spring, in booktime,
    is rife with slow growth;
        the vine smolders
            on university walls.

Why should Marvell
    have to contend
        with unrelenting sounds
            from dumb construction men?

     Appleton House —
          goes back to Penshurst,
               complements the man's way of life through house;
                    "Cooper's Hill," too — describes
                                             landscape
          problem of retired and active lives

    spatial and temporal description
anti-Catholic — monastic life
                anticorrupt monasticism

    in praise of retired life but not a place that
would stop history

                    house
                    gardens
                    meadow   the reconciliation of the
                    wood   senses and the will
                    stream

It's always evening when
we see the future in
another generation than ours.   — *future gem*
            — Joseph Summers

5/17/65 — [1] (05330)

Phases

I

The moon was coming.
            Day's roads
        were dimming under neon,
And people saw the moon
                coming
        on dawnshiny car hoods,
                coming slowly
        like a nursewhite waitress
                coming on duty,
                coming anxiously
        through a restaurant's side door.

The moon was coming.
            Night's windows
        were shining with televisions,
And steeples pierced the moon,
                coming
        on its balloon belly,
                coming fluidly
                *

like dappled champagne
          coming from bottles,
          coming bubbly
through lusty Tuscan spouts.

The moon was coming.
          The pond's skin
was shot through with beams,
And creeping spectra touched the moon,
          coming
up through sleepy surfaces,
          coming mysteriously
like scattered debris
          coming from submarines,
          coming mutely
to meet a secret sea.

The moon was coming.
          The water's bridge
was creaking under a breeze,
And lovers felt the moon
          coming
after their backflung dialogue,
          coming murmurously
like a too-chaste voyeur
          coming with guilt,
          coming jealously,
wearing musty hospital sheets.

II

The moon was falling.
          Spongy clouds
were drinking its light,
And sparrows smelled the moon
          falling
in flaxen nightgowns,
          falling billowed
like silvery parachutes
          falling in series,
          falling full-blown
from an airplane's tongueless mouth.

The moon was falling.
          The lovers' nakedness
          *

was sprayed with liquid,
And they heard the moon
            falling
    in a moment of union,
            falling swiftly
    like a flood-time crest,
            falling unexpectedly,
            falling with vengeance
    through a city's deluged streets.

The moon was falling.
            Day's yawn
    was breathing down its back,
And the city watched the moon
            falling
    with dawn's lazy sigh,
            falling away
    like cigarette smoke
            falling in swirls,
            falling apart
    in strands of invisible air.

The moon was falling.
            Day's streets
    were bubbling with heat,
And people sensed the moon
            falling
    on tinny feet,
            falling noisily
    like a mechanical polar bear
            falling in spurts,
            falling insanely
    over a kitchen tabletop.

5/17/65 — [2] (05092)

Zoo

A peal of recorded trumpets
Introduced King Arthur,
The trained chimpanzee,
While the California sea lion
*

Vied for top honors
Before my avid eyes.
He was slick sensuality,
Glued to the pool's green lip
Before slipping away into coolness.
Behind me,
The sloth bears
Ogled at paid customers
For signs of recognition.

Everything was talking
In singular ascendancy.
Visitors sneaked up on cougars
In cages, their own naiveté
Obvious as steaming manure.
Cowards fingered venomous triangles
Poised behind glass,
And lovers held hands,
Shying from Freudian implications
In the reptile station.

I could see the whole zoo
Looming before my lurid eyes
Like the grand finale
In the Caracalla *Aida*.
But the zoo was friendly,
I thought,
In its own private way
On that May afternoon,
When solitude stalked me,
Uncaged.

5/17/65 — [3] (04005)

Park at Dusk ^Δ

We straddled the shadows
The twin-forked oak
Quickdanced
Down ground-limbs'
Residual light.

We breathed the sounds
The spinster crocus
Dizzyshuttled
Through dusk's
Anonymity.

Within our lips,
We enclosed the pond,
Frondflowing
Like gradual ripples
That tickle the wind.

We watched the moon
Add color to height,
Powderpuffing
Its cheeks
In our mirrored light.

5/20–21 — [1] on 5/20 & 5/26/65 — [1] (05094)

Fancy #1

A breast in the hand
Is worth two
In the bush.
Be careful, however,
Cuidado,
That you're not cock robin
Nor she
Robin redbreast!

5/20/65 — [2] (05093)

The Noble Animal

I am the "noble animal"
That lies fallow
In time-trammelled fields,
Whose calcined bones
Rot in shallow pockets
*

Of lime-filled Walsingham.
Relics deceive me
Like outmoded slang
Preachers still resurrect.
Obsequies grieve me
With their swollen rhetoric,
Their weather-lined epitaphs
For the lacerated hearts
Of unmartyred laureates.
Customs entreat me
With vulgar errors.
Their clichéd metaphors
And abhorrent syntax
Pierce my concrete strophes
Like nails that threaten
A trafficked street.

I have sought sublimity
Within my papal grot,
Passed sodden eternities
With Colley Cibber;
Have debated the merits
Of Wotton and Bentley
In the caffeine solitude
Of my will's saloon.

I have even consecrated
My strength to the end
That words be living breath,
Not chance's passive slaves.
But their manumission
Molders in the grave
Of my unpublished pages,
Dead in freedoms of dust.

5/26/65 — [2] (05095)

[I walked out of myself, . . .]

I walked out of myself, into the diaphanous veils of the evening circus, where I espied those bright shoots of everlastingness that Henry Vaughan bequeathed to Wordsworth to give to me. Or was it

the sheer and easy sobriety of solemnity that soothed my comic un-
certainty?

Far into the baffles of night, I could hear the noises of White
Cross wafting across the expanses of deep-throated blackness. The
highway trucks were dragging their raspy voices behind them, away
into the distanceless silences of tight-clawed night. A dog barked
somewhere off in the lawns of neighboring houses, which were asleep
with their guests.

My warmth was cowled by coolness, like ice floating within a gin-
filled glass. I could see the sky looking at me without comment, and
I knew what it was thinking. I knew that if it could speak with its eyes,
it would tell me that there are things worth the effort, worth the think-
ing about, because beauty lies hidden under the slimmest shale and
sediment and can be excavated with the tools of sensibility and desire.

Lubricity is the theme, my conscious: fluidity of thought and mo-
tion. The body must be constantly fluid and in motion to overcome
the stasis that threatens at every corner and turn where the mind is
forced to reduce its speed. The body mirrors the mind's activity.

I could be Gulliver tonight if I willed it. My thoughts have the
evocative power to transcend the immediate in favour of the actual
imminence of the *to be*. I leap walls of consciousness to reach the
summits of associational stability. My fingers touch the mechanical
Aladdin's lamp, and all turns to dream wish before my eyes. Now I
am in Venice, flowing with the rhythms of the pole as it moves me
through musty canals of former elegance and power. Now I am in
Shapiro's Tulsa, breathing in the thousand hot flags of Laputa, which
ruffle above the white flames of lusty desire. Now I have transformed
myself into the eminent Professor Sartor, residing above the Teu-
felsdröckh of a city gone rotten with too much dealing between the
bark of Marvell's garden. Illusory! That's what I aim at. To open my
doors, one has to be able to translate literary symbology that I distort
with the precision of a sideshow Houdini.

My study is a friendly place, set far away into the stresses of this
house-plantation. Before me, and to each side, are the memorabilia of
years of patient exercise and frenzied work. The dust-jacketed spines
of myriad unnameable spectres haunt me with their silent profundi-
ties, their accumulated chronicle of man's effort to order that which
can be reduced to the briefness of a few thousand years of combating
the senses with the soul, the resolute soul in defense of its besieged
bastions, set upon by created pleasures.

I wear no ceremonial colours. I have no emblematic garters to
prove that my coat of arms is more antique than another's. My chain
mail is woven with strands of vulnerability and elliptical brain fi-

bers. I show myself to any merchant or beggar or whore who will give me the time of day or the compulsive cigarette that I fumble for without success.

Some say I talk in circles. I defy such banal simplicity of explanation. I am the verbal prestidigitator of parabolas and schizoid tangents. My mind claws at everything within its reach, trying to balance itself on the fulcrum of speculation and sincerity. But the scales generally tip toward the former, since that is my true dominion. I, like Sir Thomas Browne, love the mystery, the *O altitudo* of all attempts to define "order." Order! Ridiculous fiction that man invented to fit into the standard dictionary between the more realistic fictions of "ordeal" and "order arms." And what is order, anyway, but the hysterical bellowing of a Benjy when it realizes, somehow, that it has been driven the wrong way around some anomalous and moss-encrusted statue that, for years, has survived the trials by excrement of lofty pigeons, a statue whose effigyless figure of a hero-soldier rests the butt of its static gun at orderly arms?

I feel like a dimly lighted ferryboat crossing over to Staten Island, honking its resonant prosody to the inane, stir-crazy heathens of Manhattan by night. I am speaking without being noticed. I have travelled through day toward the nighttime of weariness, have done a full-face, complete turnabout, and now I am prepared to rub my lamp one more time, to wish for the soporific effects of slow sleep.

5/27/65 (05238)

["He eats strange "] †

"He eats strange,"
they say of me;
funny habited

Naked

From this cold studio,
above what's left of innocence,
I see passersby
holding hands,
eyes gleaming
*

like buttons in the cold sunlight.
A little dog

"Keeper of Their Ashes"

5?/65 — [1] (05113)

Sport of Winds ‡

Sunday is for praying;
only, no one prays anymore
except the rainmaker,
the architect of marriages.
A strange pair, sin and death,
both inheritors of the Devil,
bereft of youth, devoid
of naked innocence.

I hang on the edge,
weak, vertiginous,
witnessing the clutter of days
mounting beneath my fear.
Now I no longer hang
but stand, feet dangling
just above the quag,
the quicksand of regrettable history,
which has caught up,
overtaken the nuptials,
the ceremony for cowardice
and ruff

A miraculous wind awakens me,
and I can see
leaves of beaten gold
scurrying over the edge
of Pleistocene earth.

A coil of hemp,
goldwoven,
serpentine,
girds the earth's puberty,
*

and I know the pure truth
of chastity

5?/65 — [2] (05112)

[One building's shadow] ‡

One building's shadow
Leans against the next tenement's skin:
A castle with parapets, turrets,
To my sunny imagination.
Though I have no past
Recollection,
Nostalgia cries out for recognition.

I sit in the Packard's backseat,
Summoning visions from books,
Stealing alien looks at this neighborhood.
A child of five rides a blue bike
Down this Saturday street.
Did you see that red hair,
Streaming like tomato juice
Into a glass? An old white man
Passes with a brace of bulldogs.
There's no trace of a vocation
On that aged face.

Now the lawn mower ceases
Its monotonous vibrato. The man
Swaps work gloves for a can of beer.
"Did you hear about the prowlers
They caught late last night?" he asks
His next-door neighbor.
"Can't say's I did. You know, I've said
Ain't safe 'round here for man nor beast."

Some books I've read lately
Say that God is dead, that man
Is an animal unto himself.
How is one expected to speak
Against mass media and reflect
A normal sense of well-being
*

When those who claim to know
Hole up all hours of day
Playing games

5?/65 (05150)

[Seven o'clock falls] [†]

Seven o'clock falls
over the tumid river.
Bobwhites and finches call
to unseen young,
who clamor with sightless eyes.

6/5/65 (05360)

[Of a sudden, all motion . . .]

Of a sudden, all motion of the breeze through the stately plots of
maple and sycamore and wild-cherry trees has ceased to whisper to
me; all night-sounds have quit their garrulous quarreling. There is a
brief interlude as I sit here, caught between the poles of no-motion
and no-sound. I am thinking of time before and time after as though
nature has provided me with a perfect vacuum of clairvoyance. Only,
I can hear my heart pumping life, and I feel the impulses of my nerves
throbbing lightly against the insides of my skin like soft rain pelting
the corrugated roof of some unmolested country cabin at night.

Now the sounds have returned, and I am filled with the swirling
afterglow of interlude's insights. The wind sounds through the limbs
of summerleafy trees, giving the sensation of a forest-hidden spring
or rivulet wafting distantly through the undergrowth of some Ozark
back country.

Tonight my fingers are seeds that plant themselves in fecund rows
on the typewriter's keyboard. My words are hybrid. The distilled
freshets of dew and cloud-charged rain that fill my furrows with novel
growth are like spray from the Gulf, which insinuates the body and
the spirit with yearning and thick-scented wonderment for a time when
all progress and fatuous endeavouring to excel will cease to be.

Motion has returned, too. I can see it in the breathing, patterned cur-
tains that hang restlessly over my open study window like two locks

of hair. Somewhere, a diesel engine whines through its crusty stacks as it passes a desolate, red-green semaphore on its burdened way into the downcountry baffles of blank night. The highway yields its stasis to clanging gears and squealing tire rubber, and everywhere, the night is alive with activity. A lightplane passes within hearing distance of my sobriety, and a dog moans for some ancient companion. Cicadas and honey locusts speak to the stars and the thousand sleepy ears of the populace with their rhythmic constancy. Their sounds, like that of the plane, flit and dissolve and then are no more. Then, another plane, larger this time, and more cricket music, and the night is magical again, renewed and alive with each natural inhalation.

The interlude is broken, and I am left alone. No-motion is shattered, and my pulse and impulses have silenced into the vertebrate colors of reminiscence:

I am driving in my car now, floating with the sway and roll of Highway 67. I can see the ground coming up at me before it fleets past, and I am calm and warm. Everywhere, the gentle, rich fields of Illinois topsoil stare at me; they let me pass unmolested. I wonder what they are thinking about me, my speed, the fluid suspension of the car as it eats up mile after mile of countryside. Signs speak to me, reflecting the crazy, man-made slogans of office-billeted mutants. I am alert and badgered by their dizzy intoxication: "Get Right With God," "Kas Thin Potato Chips," "Funk's Hybrid," "Burrus Yields Better Harvests."

My mind is backing up on my thought, now, like a Delta stream in flood time. I have regressed in time to the point where I am seated in the den of their house: the family album, with its decorative morocco binding; the upright mahogany gun rack, which looks like a grandfather clock without the face; the antique rocking chair, which is a legacy of some superannuated grandmother; and the desk itself, strewn and littered with fliers and bills and family pictures of a child, through which the two of us have browsed for hours, laughing and chiding each other for their quaintness and innocence.

The room is beginning to reel with sound around my sensitive ears and smoke-white eyes. I can feel the soft sensuality of the phonograph record flowing through me, and I think to myself: "I am a free agent." And I am alone with her now, entrenched in her smiling gaze, at one with her soft, gentle cheeks and highlighted eyes, her shadowed nose. We are living in each other's thoughts, holding hands, looking out from the den window onto the town's heatfiltered Square, which looms ahead of us like some Overburian character intent upon dispelling doubts about its own morality. We are borne fast back on drafts of the past. The time is 1860 as easily as it is 1965.

Time's cadences are at my back, drawing me into its backwash of insight. I can see her sitting there, for the first time, on Easter Sunday, early in April. She is dressed in the finery that befits that day. It is a restaurant, filled that morning with church people and businessmen and college students from the U. of White Cross, all in a hurry to go nowhere fast. I am there too, wearing my Wellingtons and wheat jeans and work shirt. I have nowhere to go in particular and nothing pressing to get done: no prayers to be said and no forms that have to be filled out.

I am ready to sit, over coffee and fried eggs and sausage, with a book of Faulkner. I want to read this morning for the sheer enjoyment of living with the mind that wrote into his characters his own disguised thoughts. I feel young and free reading Faulkner and being dressed against the main current of custom. Then it is that we see each other. Neither of us speaks, but we have met, I hiding behind my book or coffee cup, she dressed for the Sunday rituals.

Now my mind has missed its turn in the road, and I fail to correlate. I am flung back again, ahead of past time, into the den. Again there is a shift, and I am on Highway 67, passing the cattlelined fields that lead from her house back to White Cross. I am passing the Funk's Hybrid signs and the billboards that speak in updated, hip banalities of the god that saves all from eternal damnation. Now I have flown across the stretches of night's interlude and am aware of my typewriter before me. I can see my fingers plodding along the keys, fumbling for thought.

The spell is broken. The night is quiet, and my body is tired with nagging fatigue. I would like to have a cup of coffee to warm my insides, to be my companion at this time. I have just lit another cigarette. There is a strange, abstracted pleasantness to the vapours that curl and mingle, climbing into the niches of my study. I stare at them, and at once, I can see her face forming in the mélange of fusing imagery that pulses across my stolid eyelids. She is looking into my eyes, smiling with silent understanding.

I inhale and blow the smoke into the room, and all dissolves into patternless forms again. She has disappeared into the night. I have a feeling of remorse, a slow sort of feeling that this absence will be heavy as sleep itself. I vow that I will roll all of my strength into a ball to preserve my stability, to last out the interlude between now and futurity.

The draughts of sleep filter down on me now, like smoke curling into the dimlit panes of window glass inside some bar. My eyes are rushing across the pages of thought and emotion, and I feel the need to pray:

"May the time not be distant when my Jan and I will come together, again, into the tight conformity of duration, when absented exaggeration will cease to blind the eye and solitude will be no more. I pray that she and her family may enjoy the fruits of happiness, good health, and peace of mind.

"God bless you, Jan, princess of peace!"

6/7 — [1] & 6/16/65 (05167)

[The rain's drunk tongues] △

The rain's drunk tongues
Lap the ruffled roof above our cabin.
Night's neck is cowled in mufflers
Whose ends are frayed and torn.
Winds wrapped tight for winter
Shatter attic clapboards, buffet glass,
Steal through chinks where our joists
Lie freezing, screeching like claxons.

We lie together,
Dreaming of Westminster Abbey,
Thames' shabby banks at noon,
Sinking in pools of sanity.
We are static yet free
As breathing rituals in earthwet urns
Sealing our subtle oblations
From historical minds.
Our rhythmic mysteries are immolated.

Outside, night's nimble fingers
Crochet rebuttals to our crucial debate,
While winds weave our shadowed patterns
Into textured sleep. We keep the score,
Adding the simple, indivisible sum:
From one and one comes One.

But we've come all this way in storm time
To be alone together, to make the world
Stop long enough for us to do sacrifices
Not to God but to the goatbellied moon.

6/7/65 — [2] (05097)

Summer Idyll

For Jan, in Jacksonville

Outside her den window,
Autos moved slowly uptown
Through heat-filled streets.
Elm, sweet gum, and maple
Swayed with Illinois breezes.

Within, a Victrola's silhouettes,
Like acrobats walking wires
Stretched from New Haven
To the taut Old World,
Barely touched our ears.

We were a staid couple
Lifted from some family album,
Winslow Homer's society people,
Fragile Japanese figurines,
Deftly playing croquet,
Flitting across boardwalk lawns.

Then something changed the symmetry.
Rural masques grew dim
Beyond the window's perimeter,
And bustlebusy Piccadilly
Sifted dateless grains
Through our hourglass eyes.
We saw the Mississippi River
Pause, then dissolve
Into Thames' quivering lips.

6/12/65 (04013)

Rejection: The Legacy

For Moses truly said unto the fathers, A Prophet shall the Lord
your God raise up unto you of your brethren, like unto me.
                              — Deuteronomy 18:15

He took five steps
No wider than rib clefts
*

To cross the Stygian waters.
On that other side,
Where fat river horses
And leopard frogs
Slithered into rushes,
He lay facedown,
Weeping.

He was Moses, rejected.
The shattered tablets
He'd clung to for life
Were smeared with blood;
They'd cut his body
Like shears severing wire.
Behind him, across the flood,
Fugitive voices pierced his ears
Jeeringly:

"Sinner! Your promised land
Is where you lie. High treason,
Committed in the name of mercy
And right reason,
Shall be your crime.
You shall drink the sand
That swaddles you
Until your throat flakes dry
As dead fishes' scales."

He looked around, writhing,
In time to see the crowds
Dissolve into suburban houses,
Clothesline cities,
And temples on mountain retreats.
"High treason!" he repeated,
With insidious disbelief.
"That I were a Christ,
Born to some First Cause!"

Then the mired waters
Overflowed their banks,
And as he lay there,
Fingers of liquid heat
Closed in about his neck,
Burning off dead memories.
*

Sand and skin congealed
Blessedly, until he drowned,
Purified.

In five short breaths,
He was filtered back
To the river's other shore.
He had seen Eden
But was home once more,
A stranger in a stranger land
Than he'd ever known before,
Where a babe lay facedown,
Weeping.

By the manger, he placed
The mended tablets,
Which had washed up with him,
Whispering into the child's ears,
"Mercy and right reason
Shall be your crime. Tribunals
Shall sentence you for treason.
You'll be their only sinner,
My quiet Prince of Light."

6/13/65 (00428)

Designs in Storm Time

The sticky Illinois highway
Stretched like tape
Over down-cowed fields.
It was morning, late,
And a greypurple sky
Leered with squint eyes.
Then a sign caught my gaze:
GET RIGHT WITH GOD.
Corn, droopeared as nuns
Retreating in prayer,
Waved me on.

Rain's footfalls
Danced across my roof,
*

And I watched the morning
Turn from dust to mud.
Lightning, like a scoop's jaws,
Ate the pavement
Fifty yards ahead,
And I coasted into silence.
Wires contracted,
Snapped to the ground,
Glowing white as halos.

Then,
Turning to look behind,
I saw another bolt
Whiplash that listing sign,
Shattering it into charred bones.
"Someone or something menacing
Has trained vengeance
Upon that sacred design,"
I said to myself.
GET GOD WITH RIGHT
Read the electrocuted slogan.

Then a third blast
Juggled the frightened earth,
And I drove away
Fast,
Not being a person
To tempt providence with delay.

6/13?/65 (00482)

[New York, when it's crisp like autumn . . .]

New York, when it's crisp like autumn
in June, teeming with beautiful and
impersonal myriads, everywhere/nowhere
insinuating themselves; now that look of beguiling
youth, painted on wandering, wonderfilled
faces,
    young faces fleeting furiously
in communal anonymity, cosmically
homeless, deeply rooted in rootless,
marshy soil.

The people brood and ween,
dreaming of Leonard Bernstein.
The old men are dead:
Faulkner, Hemingwaves, the rest
resting in restive pools of self
and drink, stinking this earth, whose
grief is fatuous, posthumous.
And what am I doing in New
York? I have no relatives, family, ties —
nothing but desires of hiding from the
lonely crowd, absorbed in narcissistic
solipsisms of dreams of greatness and
success, to be above, not of, them.

6/16–18?/65 (05239)

Reuben's: Early June Morning

The unsummered city shivers.
An erudite cabbie conjectures:
"The day forgot to make June's oblations."
New York wears an autumn bikini,
Anomalous as a '65 coed
Donning a raccoon coat
At the Yale Bowl.
Outside the restaurant,
Cold, sullen crowds
Float by like a priest's cassocks
Toward their mile-high confessionals,
There to repent.
And I just sit here,
Relaxing in morning's compromise,
Coffee steam bathing my eyes.
I can see my glasses,
Gold-rimmed and filmy,
In the murky surface
Of Eucharistic coffee.
Now a bus passes the window,
And a green billboard-bather
Glides by,
Fresh as a first cigarette.

This place takes its time, performing the selfsame rituals of yawning and stretching with the rest of the entrepreneurial staff of the city. It is quiet, and the lights are dank, like the air in some slimy, bat-dung cave; dank and muffled are the dust-encrusted chandeliers, the same no matter what time of day or night, always dank and muffled, like death. Strangely, I feel the room filled with powdered faces and glittering sequin-junked dresses and perfumes of the ten thousand lands and trademarks. It is as though one has focused upon an object and then changed his gaze, only to find that the original image still persists.

In this instance, the image of languishing faces and phrenetic noise and scatterbrained shuffling of waiters is as old and persistent as the after-hours from which it derives. The post-theater retreat of high fashion has congregated here from time immemorial — a veritable restaurant of Eden, a throwback into whose washes I have been forever drawn. But it is quiet in here this morning, and the low music is soft and gentle. I may regret leaving my cup of coffee, but sometime within the next millennium, I will have to get up, pay the tab, and walk out into this early, coldbright, New York-type June day.

6/17–18?/65 (05096)

Beginnings

My mind starts with beginnings,
A trickle from the spring
That tickles pebbles
In Itasca State Park.

I am Mississippi's head,
Hydroptique,
A river's cryptic brainwashing.
What I see
Issuing from a miracle
As I leap from puddle to muddled puddle
Is embryonic geography.
I imagine growth here,
Where I peer into opaque crystals
I bridge by stones.
Circles too perfect to contain death
Ripple to tourists' gazes,
And here is neither beginning
*

Nor any end to the natural phase
That hides in history books
And almanacs of other rainy days.

I am fabled Finn's river,
Upon whose widening banks
Hannibal paused to reflect,
Bloodhounds and townspeople
Failed to detect Nigger Jim
Hiding on the moving island
That knew no colored twain,
And Clark and Lewis
Began their inland trek,
Père Marquette settled forts
Along stray shores, where Indians
Chanted over burial mounds.

Bingham's flatboat men
Stopped here to watch their barks
Collect grey shadows under keels,
And side-wheelers slapped waters
Up and down, from Saint Louis to Cairo,
Memphis, Vicksburg, and New Orleans,

Queens in clapboard and belching stacks,
Pouring dust upon the land,
Navigating illusory undertows and sand bars,
Carrying elite to Basin Street
And even with the Natchez Trace;
The Gateway to the West wrested here,
Its monumental courthouse steps
Tongues decrying prejudice,
Vociferous obstacles to man's duress.

My mind grows like creation,
From pebble to Delta,
Beginning again in tomorrow's eyes,
Ending again where I began.

6/26/65 & 3/4/66 (00558)

[What a frustrating sight, . . .]

What a frustrating sight, to wake up in the morning with your blank pages of writing paper strewn across the top of some Formica facsimile, the ballpoint pen suspended in desolate abandon, as though the whole scene (empty bottle of natural water included) were the devastated remains of an ancient battleground, the difference residing in the notion that the only fight waged and lost was that conflict between fatigue and consciousness, between the emotions and the dull, deadening lack of insight.

The poem, like a rigged roulette-wheel ball at some Monte Carlo dicing house, refuses to fall into the slot of creativity. Still, I refuse to abandon it, because its beauty is redolent and supple, somewhere in the back of my head. I must strip down all the crossed connections of sensibility and present perception to regain that former awareness of abandonment. I want this story-poem. Maybe it will be there in Venice, waiting for my arrival.

This morning, when I walked outside by the pool, which, like David confronting Goliath, or Gulliver among the Brobdingnagians, faces the tepid Mediterranean, five light aircraft buzzed overhead, their mosquito drone catching my awareness. For a blip of concentration, I thought Pussy Galore and her flying circus were going through their universal rituals; then I awakened and remembered that this was Tel Aviv, not Miami — or was there really that much difference?

> Books to read:
>   Socrates
>   Plato
>   Greek drama
>   *The Rise and Fall of the Third Reich*

>   Write Margie,
>   Steve Riven,
>   Dumper, Jan.

6/29/65 (05256)

The Adolescent Caravaggio Writes to the Mistress of His Tutor

From where I sit,
Riding like the sea
Over ancient floors,
*

My eyes see pigeons flocking.
David's marble hair
Turns yellow
With futile despair
Before the camera's quick stare,
And the masons' hammers
Clatter, clank,
Raising from scaffolds
That flank, like scars,
Palazzo Vecchio's stony face.

Anonymous heads
Below the air
Are floats bobbing atop debris
That's daily swept away
By people whose heads and eyes
Scream for history,
For picture-book memories
To stow away
In tight, dark rectories
Of the mind's forgotten amens.

A tourist carriage
Turns the corner across the way;
A scooter's eye freezes,
Leaps like a scared jack rabbit,
Then blinks a thousand times.
From where I sit,
The city passes me by
In a hundred guises
Not its own: these victims
With eyes sewn shut
As fetuses'.

But we are alone,
Bacchus and I.
He bears me aloft
On soft, round shoulders
Like some ancient Saint Christopher
On the back of a Christ,
And I ride delirious,
A sacred child running wild
Through pools of insanity
And over Gethsemane lawns.

7/3 & 7/6/65 — [3] on 7/6 (05257)

[I threw a silver dollar] †

I threw a silver dollar
into her Trevied eyes

Like a woman's skirts,
the cloth caught the breeze
as it flirted with Florence.
The table I sat at
was grotlike and

When a silver dollar floats to the surface
of my Trevi grotto, then I shall have my wish:
to return to the contemplative solace of my
private duomo.

7/4/65 — [2] (05258)

[To sit with a clear mind,]

To sit with a clear mind,
Signing the register
Where blue lines
Define my vacant spaces.

I'll write my own epitaph
Before time expires,
Exonerate myself
Of fatigue's lusty fire.

7/4/65 — [3] (05259)

[Night's clamshell]

Night's clamshell
closes slowly
over the Arno's welkin.
Hazy bluepinks
*

wrinkle their brow
around my body,
and I am shut out,
inside,
from the city's circle:
a pearl
imperfectly formed
by the mind's sandy dross.

7/6/65 — [1] (05260)

[Rembrandt's beggar]

Rembrandt's beggar
hobbled across the mirror,
his legs bowed,
his brown brow rent
with painted fear,
the discontented eyes
vacant like bomb craters,
leering through him
to another figure
somewhere behind.

7/6/65 — [2] (05261)

Cloister and Courtyard of Santa Maria Novella

Green rectangles fold into arched cloisters.
Solitary pigeon feathers
            Nestle like impassioned children
            In the grass's downy lap.
Flaking frescoes guard forgotten tombs,
While birds knell sweet, soft songs
            In four grottoes
            That temple their laments.

Nowhere is there the pitiless yew,
            Though noble acanthus
Grows in static beauty
*

Over the fluted sarcophagi
That line these hallowed chambers.

And all is quiet;
       All are sleeping now
           Except me.
I have come here to be forgotten
Like the voiceless souls
       Interred beneath my feet.
And I know
       That one who has lived before
       Will always repeat that living.

A solitary swallow
       Follows the relentless solstice,
And I am caught between hotcold pools,
Striving for essential quietude.

My neck pulses;
       I feel its wrinkled creases,
Like water clogging a long-dry stream,
Filling with fluid excitation.
       The dead stand up.
My mind revels
Performing their excavation,
       And I am buried
Under piles of antique dirt.

You, "ugly one," breathe again;
Walk beneath these sacred arches;
       Let those surplices float
Behind your masterly awkwardness.

And now you, Lippi,
Speak to me through frescoed lips.
And you, Brunelleschi,
       Carve me
Out of worm-rotted sticks
Into a perfect crucifix.

Ah, how glorious the bereavement.
       Yet I must leave these haunts.
Crying, beseeching,
           I go.
      Taunt me these remaining hours,
  *

Till, like you,
        I rise
From this fragile, tormenting grave
    And soar into snow-white nocturnes
        Of everlasting day.

7/6/65 — [4] (05263)

[I wear my Florentine . . .] †

I wear my Florentine sport shirt with pride; my stomach and shoulders feel relaxed against the soft texture of its insides. My legs are heavy, but they feel best that way, as though the mind's accomplishments were transferred to the limbs: a conjunction, communion of body and soul in one spirit.

If you asked,
I doubt I could say   (slipshod
just how many stairs   metrics —
play like vertebrae   no content)
up Giotto's spine.

    Florentine Gothic — how exquisite, like a piece of intricately cut ivory — and then the

Two o'clock
Florence time
                Its

It drew me to it
like some miraculous divining rod.
Masochistic in intent,
we went toward it,
my fears and I,
careful to avoid witnesses,
but the sun's messenger,
my shadow, chased behind,
hiding when I turned aback,
*

leering
when I laughed at myself
for my childish fears.

7/6/65 — [5] (05264)

Piazzale Michelangelo

Redblinking, beautiful city,
Tucked in hilly folds
Like a child in bed.
Softsinking, beautiful city,
Sleeping under glowing sheets,
Repeating yourself in every breath
The whispering Arno breathes.

Etruscan *bèlla città*,
Night lightly dreams,
Remembering your ancient circles,
Revenging that living conquest.
Circles of light swirl
Like bending voices,
Without beginning
Or ever any ending.

7/6/65 — [6] (05265)

[The sun's oils merge into night.]

The sun's oils merge into night.
Pink and blue-violet lights
pastel the upper surface,
where distance meets forgetting.
Dizzy bats weave webs
through Arno's thick breath,
like tapestry needles
navigating two centuries.

7/6/65 — [7] (05266)

Florence: The *Luna*

Someone chopped the moon in two.
Where is the other half?
How can a cow jump
with only partial light?
Anna Maria Ludovica
died with that prize
beside her, all eyes
fastened like buttons
to her dignified sepulcher.
She took that slice, the *luna*,
with her dying breath:
the first two letters
of her last name, the last
two letters of the first, she inhaled
the *luna*; the middle initial
she breathed out for all the world — *Medici*.

7/6/65 — [8] (05262)

[Time has a way of gorging itself,]

Time has a way of gorging itself,
        Distending its belly
Between two fleshly sections,
The front and back,
        Between marrow and bone.

O gluttonous time,
        Temper your lusty habits;
Hold those reckless arms in check;
Refrain from grabbing every soft thing
        On the table before you.

Let me respond, O time,
        In my own time
To your rusty chimes,
Which toll, rolling like waves
        Over ivory oceans.

Then I'll return,
        Slow as a seed,
        *

To burn off the weeds
That show through my skin.
    You must know
It takes a time to grow.

7/22/65 (05267)

[She was so filled with humble grace]

She was so filled with humble grace
That each sigh she breathed
Filled my face with shame.
And I was not worthy.

Ave María, llena de gracia! ◊

Death took her from me,
Stole her grace, her purity
In a quickblistered sigh.
And I was not worthy.

Ave María, llena de gracia!

Death, be not proud.
Take me also.
Wrap your mysterious shroud
About my agony,
Unless I'm not worthy.

Ave María, llena de gracia!

7?/65 (05268)

[How bitter is the taste]

    How bitter is the taste
Of another's bread! How weary is the
    road
Of going up and down another's
    stairs!

7?/65 (05269)

[It was merely . . .]

It was merely a White Cross à go-go that night, when the four of us walked along the Square, but something made me turn in. Perhaps it was the moist, nervous summer weather, the need for a quick drink of beer, or just the necessity to evaporate in that climate of torrid noise.

We filed in, down the narrow aisle, which was scattered with clumsy legs and strewn with soiled napkins and fist-clenched cigarette wrappers, until we reached the small table off against the red-brick wall. From there, we could see the whole menagerie: the confidence of the shrewd bartender; the terminal-like bar, to which businessmen and executives just stopping over in White Cross for the weekend came to linger long enough to wolf a few martinis, Manhattans. And we could see the band, positioned behind the bar, upon a stage. There were just four of them: two electric guitars, a saxophone, and the man behind the trap set. All four were kept in constant motion, as though set in sympathetic vibration by some invisible sex chime. And then there were the two of us. The other two didn't matter now, were not really there at all, because we were hiding within the confines of our own affections. I could see her sitting beside me, drifting into my eyes, climbing behind the cells themselves, through the resinous vapours of the bar. And then, of a sudden, something happened. I lost control, felt the need to regurgitate words which for a month I had been completely unable to express. Now they rushed upon me with frenzied impetus, and I took up my pen and began to crawl back into that familiar void that fills my solitudinous moments. I was transfixed, watching the pen race across the dim-lit scratch pads, seeing page after page fill itself mysteriously:

The saxophone's brassrutty patina screams moist, skintight flashes at me more sensual than a hothouse, Manhattan rooftop suntan.

Dream on, little dreamer, and scream your sex through the erect mouthreed of your saxophone, that reed blown like some atavistic golden bough whittled out by some ancient madman.

What would Sinclair Lewis have done with a Gibson guitar that has more gadgets than he imagined to exist in Babbitt's bedizened bathroom and makes sounds more vile than old Jonathan Swift could have ever mustered?

Seagram's whiskey
Jack Daniel's
Smirnoff vodka

Torsos that writhe like animals boiling in steamheavy cauldrons;
bodies, wringing with wasted sweat, that shuffle away their energy
within a five-foot glass-enclosed dome of somebody's Sunday.
There are no ideas of order in this Key Club West.

Budweiser at ninety cents a shot. Even the very rich would balk if
it were not for the "pause for the cause."

And the band breaks, and the noise shuts down temporarily, but the
bodies continue their ritualistic routines. They get paid by the bump
and grind, by the pelvic contortion.

Suggestiveness. That's all it is. Any parent who has been reading
Life weekly can tell you that it's the thing to do. "Just their way of let-
ting off frustrations. And healthy, too."

No longer is it cool for a parent to say, "I just can't understand the
teenager of today."

The leader has set his guitar against the traps, and now he addresses
the mike, grinning through his new beard, saying, "Got to go, folks.
Be back in a jiffy, before you can spell 'able.' Got to make weewee!"

Blue spotlights flash like baubles dangling from some Victorian
chandelier, from some Princess Grace-naked neckline.

The cigarette's glowred tip slips into sultry interstices of my tremu-
lous eyes, burns my innocence like a romantic's taper that licks the
moth's delicate, one-night-bright, luminescent wings.

I sing out like Mahalia Jackson, who finds that the seats in front
of her blackness are vacant, singing tears of hope with an effort that
is unflagging in spite of the odds. I want to scream out, to blow on the
end of my pen and spatter the thickblue ink of my disgust against
the walls.

Shoe pounding the floor, body taut, eyes aglow like bookink that
peers back over centuries of sensuality and corruption, like impulses

that push away from the mouth of that shinegaudy horn as though
they, the sounds, were skiers whose hands were pushing away from a
hot-cold slope with their bodythrust poles.

Now my energy drains into a rainy puddle locked in some corner of
the asphalt pavement, and the delirium passes as if it were some dream
vision of Kubla Khan, of the land of the Tennysonian lotus-eaters.

I want to lie down in Sir Thomas Browne's darkness like so much
fodder or fossilized petroleum-bound dung, grant my excited nerve
cells momentary rest.

Let me crawl inside his new beard for the rest of my life, like a
bear into a wrinklewarm cave recessed into the midwinter Current
River dreamlapse. Let me be a solitary Van Winkle who slumbers in
pools of Knickerbocker beer. Let me hide from my own shrill, sharp-
screaming nervousness.

Drumsticks pound tightly drawn skins, shattering the softmoist
innards of a redrestless sheep.

She is sitting by me, strong in desire, driving herself into subli-
mated, unrelaxed quietude.

I can sense her soft hands soothing my back as it hunches into the
loud darkness, and all I can think to think is "Let me lead a dark, de-
cent life." A voice slides out of the boisterous, deepcool darkness,
telling me with fingers soft and subtle, saying, praying almost with
incantatory insinuations . . . but the words are lost in the roaring din
of scattered, spraying, insensitive voices, and I have lost those words.

Now I can hear them again, the words, for there is a lull: "Don't go
home. Please don't ever go home." And I respond, communicating to
her through my unmoving, ineffable lips, saying to her with my word-
less, imageless expression, "No! Never will I go home, unless it be to
that brightglowing spot at the end of dawnless nighttime, where to
dream is to wake from life into the immaculate afterlife."

Rhythms dance off the ceiling,
    bounce,
    jump,
multiply themselves ten million times the speed of a yawn.

Why do you have twenty-four eyes?

Crazy amplifiers intensify the finger's, the wrist's pulsebeat, until the ear responds to the sheer noise itself.

Hair long and jostled like a horsewhip, pelvis shuddering under the cacophonous abuse of fifty hungry eyes. Why are you up there, girl, displaying yourself to the insensitivity of the masses? Don't you want to spit on them, on me, want to laugh aloud and say to each of us, "You pigs, swine. Look what I have done to you. Just think how I have brought you out of your ratholes, away from your families. And for what? For the unadulterated pleasure of indulging your fantasies. All of you out there. You all think you are something other than what you have been allotted. But don't you know? You are what you are and nothing more. But none of you knows what or who I am."

I despise the sax's voice because it alone knows her secret. She lives between the sheets of night, sleeping somewhere within the slick sensuality of her low class and the gentility that her body alone has attracted. She resides somewhere amidst the craven, sterile desire of this manfilled room and the gentility that once thrived in a land before her birth. Nay, she dances, treads upon the very innocence that was denied her the moment she stepped into that glass bubble. The sax knows her secret, knows the dingy, drapeless, sunstained room where she cohabits with every musician and junkie and entrepreneur on the Square. The sax knows better than any of us because it speaks to her, slides into her body nightly from 9:00 until 1:30.

Growl, you brass, goldblown saxophone!

Nervous hands lift the clear, cold beer glass to lips that let its slime pass over, that let the surviving drops of rhythm hang like some Coleridgian moonlit dusk above some ancient and evacuated corner of an opiumstarved dream of that something which he never could have anyway: peace of mind, freedom from himself, perhaps.

That rough vibrato sets my rib cage tuning with a feeling that has survived longer than the primeval beings, longer, in fact, than the first quakes that set the world into a seething moil of darkdrunken, but somehow decent, existence.

I quit. My mind just blew open like a Brontëblown, Thrushcross Grange, oaken door smashed back into the face of some almost-forgotten Heathcliff.

Someone just said into my inattentive ears, "How much longer are we going to stay here? This is fine music — they are indeed great musicians — but they are too loud; they hurt my ears."

You bastard, I think, without bothering to stare up into his cringing eyes.

And now I can see what before was too abstract: the red smoke of bluefiltered cigarettes.

Thoughts no longer seem congested from my month's period of uncreativity.

I am not an invalid.

Exhaustion has dissolved. But what a terrible consequence of gaining, collecting, knowledge: the paradoxical mental inactivity one experiences while trying to open up those same dustheavy, gluelidded eyes to the experience of the ennui-laden vacuum.

Now I can go again, can write.

She speaks to me. I can hear her saying, "I want to be able to laugh at society, at all the people who come here to gape and lust for what they have no business desiring."

"But not that," I contend sympathetically, "not that way, because one just can't laugh at them directly. They are mean and insensate, and they only know how to retaliate with scorn. They can hurt you."

Must chide,
        deride,
            but so subtly that your pen's ink can cover over, blot out, your own cynicism.

You can hate and still make those same heretics believe that you are speaking for them, to them, with amicability.

And then there was T. S. Hothouse, the nutmegged and fig-pronged bastard.

Prong!
Phony, stinking cynic!

Where was his sense of moral obligation, of duty to help?

Buried, no doubt, underneath some Momusbound tome.

Help!

Did he help those whom you saw walking over London Bridge like deadmen?

But he never knew that word and will be doomed to the Dantesque icebeds, doomed to decay in the mire of his own disinterested self-interest.

OK. My fingers are tired, have had enough, and they holler out, "Uncle!"

Face seized in contortions,
                    abortive,
                    distressed,
                              and rigid, now,
from the frenzied, frantic noise, which flutters lambently like St. Elmo's Melvillean fires atop the mizzenmast of some doomed and apocryphal Ahabdriven ship.

Dance, you inspired fires, until the eyes either burn up amidst this smoke or go blind within this spotlighted shadow behind my hand, which spreads itself over the whole pad of paper like a sheet stretched over some anesthetized patient etherized upon the Eliotic brain fissures of 1917.

Forearms strained, wrist aching, the veins bulging and crying.
My veins, the musician's wrists and arms and bloodbubbling veins all beating and throbbing as one fused tissue.

Blast out!

A protracted pause, during which the eye surveys the eyes, the filmy nets that weave listlessly.

Now her hair, those softstrung strands.

I hear her saying, praying, but the words are ineffable and like the voice of some modern John Donne, whose words still slide across three centuries of St. Paul's pulpits to fall as loiterbound, autumnal leaves in a distant field of impossible decay.

Fall,
fall, and filter frond-down like alive, white water into the pits of my ears.

I can see her words forming somewhere in the back of history, and I know she will say them again:

"I love you. . . . Oh, but I have never said that to anyone before . . . but
    yes!"

9/13 & 9/20/65 — [3] on 9/20 (05176)

[A new school year, . . .]

A new school year, looming like dusk's slippery, unseen dew,
  crouching like a lion cub that yawns with docile ferociousness.
    And I will write, and I will overcome the residual lassitude of a summer preoccupied with seeing and learning and hearing and breathing.
    And I will finish the Dante allegory, *The Heron*, and I will complete the strong story of Christopher Paradise and Hunter Augustine,
    and
     I
    will find
        time to live, to see through the antiquated mirror of the self, to indulge the spirituality that some call prudishness, which I call right reason.

9/20/65 — [1] (05271)

The Sport of Winds

People that march with slogans and things tend to take themselves
a little too holy . . . it's pointless to dedicate yourself to the cause;
that's really *pointless. That's very unknowing. . . . People who can't*
conceive of how others hurt, they're trying to change the world.
They're all afraid to admit that they don't really know each other.
— Bob Dylan, interviewed in *Playboy*

A cold gust of wind
Rushes across my neck.
The hair on my naked skull
Flutters recklessly
As Illinois. wheat,
While I shy
From the group that gathers
Before my suspecting eyes.

Indiscreet slogans
In praise of freedom and right
Pass regimentally.
Vulgar soles,
Rebels of some darker cause,
Scatter the pebbles
Demosthenes spat.

Cardboard posters,
Erect,
Church steeples
Of some newer religion,
Ride the backs
Of identical Christophers;
They bob in impious genuflection,
Reflecting the same reflections,
Projecting a simple, subtle safety in numbers.

There are people there,
Somewhere
Beneath those cardboard scepters.
They wear their consciences
Nakedly as lesbian witches
Gyved to broomsticks, riding westward
Into night's dry vagina.

And I sit here freezing,
*

Braced against this greystone bench,
Reasoning
How people huddled in human clusters,
So tight-lipped,
So heavy-lidded (their eyes sewn shut),
So sculpted and alone,
Can believe in darker causes
That, like wasted semen,
Grow rancid in pools of misconception.

9/20 — [2], 10/9, 11/12, & 11/19/65   (04007)

[When an early autumn rain] †

When an early autumn rain
Descends
And the surly winds bend oaks,
Then

Winter winds knock at summer's
back door

Find a voice among the winding echoes of the past, knead and
spread the sinews of that voice, like yarn before the seamstress begins
to sew, to sift the words. Weigh the thoughts and then write your heart
out, never, never, never to give in to the lassitude that, like a midafter-
noon shadow, tags along restlessly.

regeneration into the heavenly light of salvation	— 3	*Between the Heron and the Wren* "A Dark, Decent Life" "Christopher Paradise"
life	— 1	"The Pilgrimage of Youth"
death	— 2	"The Worm"

And then there was the *turtle* — she mentioned it, she the one who
never knew anything about it anyway

To scream out,
    throw off the burden
  of White Cross, to travel
 through the maze, into the fields
of uncomplicated simplicity —
        can't just run though;
        The Wild Palms proved
    that, beyond doubt —
        but must never stop dreaming
      about the desire to run, to
   keep running, not as a
fugitive but just the running, the
inability to drive your roots too
deeply into any soil — endemic
                inimical
                inequitable
                unequivocal

9/22/65 (05272)

[I live between Biblical pages] †

        I live between Biblical pages

                        limbs
                        ribs

    My thirsty veins drink the fuel

      "I live in the nostrils of my grandfather."
    My mind is made from pewter
      that, with time's lusty invasion,
        has exchanged its Tudor for Gothic standards.

    I long to lie down in the ground,
    wrinkle my tired brow,
    and feel the cleanliness of thickrich dirt.
    I want to revive, stained
    from hours of rain-soaked harmonies,
    *

to scream aloud
   that what this silly little child of a world needs
is love, sweet love.
   I long to nuzzle in between the sticky reeds of the lily
pad, to sink into the coffeebrown muck of some dirty Waupaca
Lake, to lie surrounded by hard, cold water until the skin refuses,
until it wrinkles.
   I must write a story at once whose possibilities are both
locked within and without time.
Grant me the stable catharsis, the literary escape that both rec-
ommends and makes humble the individual simultaneously.

I sit by myself, drinking coffee, listening to the tiny, quibbling
 ubiquitousness of the hundred faceted mouths that fill this room
with squeaks and roars.
I look, and what I see is enough to appall the ancient traditions,
for this is not an institution patterned after some Hadrian Villa for the
furthering of the arts and sciences;
 rather, this is a moratorium, a respite for decaying, mindrenting
individuals who have succumbed to the easy academic demands of
their position.

Verily, I say, I have written enough, have spread the curtain that
bars my night from your bright day.

And who can smile? But this is just it —
 the vital imperative, that Everlasting Yea which Carlyle pos-
ited and which still exists — that we reach out, that we make the
effort to touch another with the smile or the sparkpopping eyes, that,
indeed, we penetrate the Formica patina that, like negative chrome
processing, accretes after years of phony socializing and running the
scholastic gamut.

9/22–28?/65 (05273)

[A soft day, this day,] †

A soft day, this day,
Yet my mind goes hard,
Defines the windy cloister
And the fetid history book

I sit with my weight against the warmwrinkled grass,
can feel my lightsome burden resist the pressure of the rib cage sliding
against my skin. The left eye burns, and my mind cries out:
O God, what will happen where there is no more
love in the world, when all that is good and decent and fair has been
forgotten or just ignored?
What we all need now is love, sweet love.
Never before today has ugliness, ungainliness, been such a crime
and waste to me. I live between the heron and the wren.
I breathe in the hot scents of this almost Indian summer.
Who can I turn to when You turn away?
This campus is so very pressured —
the friendships made are very quickly forgotten.
And I need to write, need to hear
myself speak down the rusty corridors of history.

9/28/65 — [1] (05274)

[Breath comes knocking,]

Breath comes knocking,
pausing,
         rocking
my sensibility.

She is a young girl.
Even the absence connotes insecurity,
a longing awareness that this will
be completion on earth, but only through a glass
darkly.
"Isn't it a shame that so few people
marry the one he or she loves?" — Yes!

Tell a story about the two
Southern lads and one
Northern boy

9/28/65 — [2] (05275)

Tenement Eyes

Raped noise,
And boys return home from growing up.
An alley cloyed with tilted music,
And naked shouts
Shatter the lids of night.
I can see her privacy
Through venetian slats,
Grown riotous there,
Where her pink, silky skin
Swallows his lust
Hastily.
Now I shrink away from the sill,
Unrelaxed,
Into rude hexagonal breathing.
The eyes go limp,
Dreaming of past retreats,
Drowning in lewd chastity.

Somewhere, a black saxophone
Scratches lazy elegies
Over taut frets of the skyline.
A cat brushes up against space,
Arches, barely mewing.
Prurient dawn licks red the horizon,
And I awaken, seeing it all.
She sleeps, a selfish, simple face,
Subtle reduction to the commonplace.
Now they are one again,
Lying there defenselessly,
Free in stupid harmony.
My eyes creep along the alley's backbone,
Searching in vain,
Craving their myriad, stray, unsown seeds,
Still seeking (the eyes),
Sneaking back now, returning,
Fatigued and alone.

9/29 — [1] & 11/10/65 — [3] (04012)

[A person is only as crazy]

A person is only as crazy
as he believes others think
he is. When there is no
opposition to his nonconformity,
he may safely assume
that everyone else is crazy.

   I love you for
sharing my whim so
unflinchingly.

    With all my love,
      L.D.

9/29/65 — [2] (05311)

Good Friday, 1965. Riding Westward

I

Several ideas at the same time
Held in suspension;
The poet's spine,
Sprung in rhythmic declension;
A static mind,
Burning off febrile tensions
That line vaults
Buried under convention:
Resuscitated designs
Make untraditional intervention.

II

Ears, like probing words,
Hug the ground,
Listening for the pounding monster
That spans Promontory's plains,
Not knowing that they, Indians
Of an older battle order,
Must submit to iron horses
*

No arrows can pierce for meat.
Their eyes, despising ideas of progress
They neither understand nor want,
Band together in renegade tribes,
Lost as deeds to lands
Forfeited for beads and spirit water.
See them now, folks, riding fire engines,
Sitting atop flagpoles, oil rigs,
Volcanic city halls, those few who knew black gold
Was worth more than presidential oaths
Endorsed by Teapot, slick-domed ministers,
Whose constituencies refused to speak.

Those same eyes today, who can say
Where they might be if not for "machines"
And democracies by which white fathers
Swamped the senses
Under crepe patriotism and red tape,
Which flowed profusely as buffalo juice?
And what of their sacred totems,
Which no modern magicians can reconstruct
Or duplicate with mechanical templates?

Who knows what gods expired from lands
That dust bowls ravaged and perished miners
Trod in creaky Conestogas and Willys Jeeps,
Those same gods, phoenixes consumed in pyres
That know no end, that ride like pennons
Atop stacks of crude refining and cracking plants?
God! Who would exchange Manhattan today
For a nickel subway token, when Texas, Oklahoma
Are unspoken masters of a race of Houyhnhnms?

III

And over there, on thin invisible rails,
Windwagon Smith drifts behind his mizzenmast
Like some scurrilous Ahab driven by rage
Into the eye of some private cosmical debate.
He waves his hands, flying by, dropping seeds
Behind his disappearing geography.

He's seen defunct Indians on reservations
In Dry Gulch and Dead Man's Junction,
*

Had a shave and haircut for two bits
Behind cigar-store obelisks of ignoble savages
Made heroic years later by TV ratings.
Once again he takes to his wagon,
Trying to elude magnates with enough money
To endow museums with his accouterments.
His wagon skirts towns without insides,
Behind which hide court jesters and fools,
Scruffy stunt men and flunkies
With sawed-off Buntlines and 74s.

He reaches crests of Tahoe and Estes Park,
Plummeting from literary bluffs into climes
Restricted for mobile homes and Baker tents
With rents based on average national incomes.
But the windwagon needs refueling.
He'll have to make his grubstake and "get"
Or retire as local police chief or guide.

IV

Painless Peter Potter extracts teeth
For half-price, while his wife sews bows
And imitation-leather buttons on coats
Made "specially" for the local politico,
Seneca Doane, and other Zenith gentry.
Soon, the Potters will sell out
To open a shopping center in Gopher Prairie
For their growing clientele. Who can tell
What the future will hold, when Greeley,
A new-world Nazi, is selling for free
Ideas on peripatetics? "Little Chickadees,"
Clementine, Steinbeck, Claude Dukenfield,
And refurbished *Cimarron*s go very west.

Where are the legendary ones who made a name
For folklore and fame from deeds conceived
And recorded by teenagers and adolescent adults:
The Bowies and Boones, Crockets, Dillons and Jameses,
Who fled when elbowroom gave way to Hollywood?
"It can't happen here," said a certain Mr. Smith,
Forgetting to be prepared for corruption
And interruptions from his boy-scout duties.
"What guts!" some said, when he trained to D.C.,
*

Then drowned in Willet Creek — a senatorial Dante
Who couldn't forget what he'd seen
In the nation's Lethe. Lies! Unbelievable!

But that's what this country's founded upon:
Bedrock and ten-gallon bola ties and hats.
Don't knock it, buddy, if you ain't tried it!
It's the West, baby, safeguarded against poverty.
Prosperity reeks like dying cattle
Slaughtered right here before your eyes,
Behind rodeo pens and picnic grounds.
It's the open road, running untrammeled
Through Currier & Ives lithography
To the great ocean/sea Balboa claimed
And Frost transcribed. Take Brooklyn Bridge
And Eads! Let me have that Golden Gate
That opened to Jolson as Troy to Agamemnon's noise.

V

The poet flies westward on a whim,
His wings flapping out hollow words
On cool breezes of demise. This is our country.
Sing praise! Echo those golden strains!
It's the open-ended plains Frederick Church
And Remington stretched out on canvas;
It's a land unheralded ever before in the history
Of man. Don't you understand? It's freeways
And psychedelics and misguided Riding Hoods
And Heidis sleeping with rummies from the Hill.
Goddamn! Ain't that the berries?

Where else does one go to discover stardom, boredom,
Fish brought in on trawlers to your doorstep,
Campuses crowded with so much imagination
And drug-injected incantation and protestation?
It's here that the newer religions of Li Po
And Maharishi spawn on suburban lawns
And in beer grots and impoverished espresso bars.

We got it all right here, baby,
Right under your fingernail. All sails
To the winds! It's the promised land
Moses never knew firsthand. Understand
When I say this is the place, baby.
*

You can't beat it with a milelong hot dog.
We got that, too, if you ain't fatted calves.
Eat, drink, and feel Mary, for tomorrow ye diet!
It's the challenge. The sun grows bigger each year
On the garbage we leave to be carted away.

VI

Hey, hey! What say! *Carpe diem*, take it away!
Good God! Can you hear those cheering fans?
Can you see them standing up? Touchdown,
And a silvery fuselage shudders on rubbery gear,
Then whines into crowded silence, and you're here.
It's under three hours from ghost to ghost.
Unprecedented, baby; that's all I got to say.
Hotels, extravaganza, motels, and boatels;
Bonanzas on every corner owned by Zeckendorf,
Where delicatessens in Chinese neighborhoods
Do bang-up carry-out service to Steins turned Deans
And Leland Stanfords, né Olefskys, turned Simons again,
Each of them gospelers of wealth, anachronistic
Silas Laphams who refuse to give in to honesty,
Which might break them overnight. It's business, folks.
And there ain't no stoppin' it, I say.
Pray in your churches, just like always;
That's what they're there for. But don't forget
That to help the handicapped ain't good business.
That's just grass roots, baby, common knowledge.

Who's got the fastest gals in the West?
Dallas, SMU, or Southern Cal?
Stay tuned in to the halftime show
And postgame interview to learn the real truth.
But now let's take time out for station break.

VII

Just now, the sun is settling in the west,
And there seems a definite need for rest
From fatiguing endeavours that spend the mind
As profligates their precious inheritance.
It's a mild, sherbet-smooth night for sleeping,
And I'll drop all thoughts and sink secure
Into an unwrinkled bed with the wife and kid.
There's no sense fooling myself. That red ball
*

Out there — we're friends. In the cool morning,
I'll just step out on my patio above the bay,
Stand in my P.J.'s with a glass of O.J.,
A vitamin, Zentron, coffee and toast,
And shake hands with the host of another day.
Goddamn! What a great life they've made for us!

*9/30, 10/8 — [2], 11/15/65, & 1/28–29/67 — [1] on 1/28 and [2] on 1/29
(00426)*

[Red taillights lick the past,] †

Red taillights lick the past,
A screaming whistle wolfs aloud,
And I can see the vastness
That opens like blood from the *shroud.*

A child could never see
the vastness of eternity,
where soft white

sing

Charcot
Franzle
Frazier

Fancy #2

People who wear purple
pants
Shouldn't throw tantrums.

People who hurl purple
peters
Shouldn't roll stones.

Miss Charlemagne
Poochie Trumbo
Susan Plato

10/4 — [1] & 10/4?/65 (05100)

[Long little leaves of Indian summer . . .]

Long little leaves of Indian summer sift and sidle through the venous fibers of mentality, and I think of all the little reminders that creep, snakeslow and crispy brown, through the nets of intelligence.

I can write incoherently, not thinking nor experimenting but simply letting the listless fingers of the hand scamper across the keyboard of this rented typewriter.

Between the Heron and the Wren: this is a title of a work in progress. My mind is dazed after its encounter with Stanley Elkin. The man is no man at all but, in fact, a small, unassimilated child. He took the story and made nothing from the something I had created. It was like ashes to ashes, dust to rancid dust, and when I looked up, the Four Horsemen had trodden upon my marrow. There was nothing left except the whimpering of the desiccated metaphors and diction.

I cannot think this evening; no desire. I am dead to the world, and the world is flitting by me noiselessly. I am torpid and affectless.

10/4/65 — [2] (05276)

[Why is it that the intelligent man . . .]

Why is it that the intelligent man is always bombarded by the stupidity of the common man? This is a great and absurd joke because the common man never loses the game. He is too dull, insensitive, and ignorant to realize that he is hurting the sensitive individual.

Why must I keep on like this? It stinks to see my writing sink to this level. This is sheer self-pity, which is worse than blindness itself because there is not even the consolation of the inner light. I have come a long way in three years, only to have to subject the eyes and the mind to the trash that comes now from me. Why do I have to exist in this halfway state of creation? There is nothing but to stay at home, to keep the stuff to myself. People are selfish and inconsiderate. They forget that a human heart and body and effort went into the creation of a piece of fiction or a poem. They forget that it may have taken a person better than a whole day to create some little work that in two minutes can be shred like tissue paper and stuffed away in the back of forgetting. Well, I say to all you proud bastards, "Try it yourself, and see how it feels to be eaten alive, to have your skin and tissue torn from you one piece at a time."

10/4/65 — [3] (05277)

The Quarry

Green, wet grass,
Matted where our bodies
Blotted the sun's shadow
A half-hour before,
Stands up now,
Still holding the loud impression
Of crowded personalities.

That was a yellow-jealous day,
Late in May,
When we watched the costumed earth
Playact, antic and wild,
Coquettishly desiring
The tiny, wet fires
That jumped the gap between us.

We learned to pause,
Stopping long enough
For our breath to spell itself
Upon mirrors,
Sowing a new day's womb
With rhyming seeds, knowing
It takes a time to grow.

10/8/65 (05101)

Suffering Adam

> *Many there be that complain of divine providence for suffering
> Adam to transgress; foolish tongues! when God gave him reason,
> he gave him freedom to choose, for reason is but choosing; . . .*
> — John Milton, *Areopagitica*

I

There was a time
When everything difficult
Came easy, was routine.
Now, when time hangs
Pendulous,
Simplicity plagues painfully,
Suffers me to boredom.

The eyes cry out, burning,
And pitiable tears quench nothing.
The day spurns tomorrow,
The protracted hours of evening,
And I return to the safety
Of this private apartment.

I sit here, drinking the draught
Of this darkness.
The head goes dizzy, is fraught,
A frantic water strider
Drowning in pools
Of too much sanity.

II

An apartment, filled with dark sounds
That hang on the sill
Like words on the end
Of someone's troubled tongue.

Traffic rush hour,
And I imagine a thousand eyes
Glowering at themselves
Through rearview mirrors.

Coffee warms the insides of this day,
Which abides with me
Like the epiphany
I read about in infancy.

Outside, it is Monday afternoon,
Late, and the wizened highway
Is too busy to think about tomorrow.
Within, I am all the sorrows of Sunday.

This apartment warms me,
Locks me from their messy traffic.
I'll wait until they all go home
Before quitting my safety.

III

These walls are my freedom.
Orange nudges purplered hues;
Rancid yellows and blue
*

Filter through my equilibrium,
And I stand numb,
Precariously fixed
Like an isolate metaphor
Awaiting divine completion.

Dark is my desire,
And dimmer yet the awful designs,
Like distant airplane lights,
That threaten to consume me.
Mine is the voice that chooses,
Mine the choice that loses itself
In a chorus of too much freedom.

These walls are my freedom.
I hide here, as night
Behind the sun's absence,
Fearing the sharp glare,
The lid-tearing glimpse
From tomorrow's restless eyes.
Night's umbilicus feeds me.
I must cut the dawn in half.

IV

Now I run, skimming the wind,
Cut loose and funneled through walls
That once proscribed my freedom.
I throw myself through bramble brakes,
Taking a lead in the race with myself.
I leap, jumping, running, breathing wild,
An energetic sandlot child
Too dirty to come home to dinner
Yet somehow too refined to decline
The invitation. I accept
My self-imposed rejection.

I would like to know people,
To slow down,
Retard the growing process
Long enough to contend with adults
And other nostalgic children.
I want to grovel,
Creeping along the ground,
*

Where autumnal conscience loses itself
In aromas of burning leaves.
I want to crawl inside
The gnarled, brittlebrown maple,
Hide in the elm leaf
And sleep there at night
With just the wind
Screeching into my personality.

I am the wind,
Combing the tops of trees,
Churning through towns and cities,
Overriding the Pharisees,
Who sleep on ivory beds.
I fly with unseen speed
Above the feigned religiosity,
The haughty gentility,
The Model T gentry.
I am the individual force
That disregards residual belief.
I ride an unpredictable course
From Bethany to Jerusalem.

10/11, 10/22 — [1], & 10/25/65 — [1] (05102)

The Questions

Where is the secondhand,
Duco-blue Buick
That cluttered the oak-strewn street
In front of my youth?
Where is the half-timbered,
Brown brick, two-family flat
And the fort made of twigs,
Maple sticks, and a pinespear floor,
The Kenilworth of our backyard?
Where are the vacant spots:
The makeshift ball lot,
The basement haunts
Where the six of us
Plotted heroics of a hearsay Bluebeard
*

Or angry Genghis Khan?
Where is the church I feared,
The priest, who preached hell, I hated,
And the rebellious Dedalus I became?

And where is my mother,

Her blue felt beret,
The long gingham print,
And funny little leather shoes
With buckles that blinked like doubloons?
My memory has misplaced them
Among the clutter of mounting years.
It only remembers the questions now,
And the hum behind the eyes grows louder;
The awful buzz in the ears
Is persistent.
Yet the tongue no longer resists
The Eucharistic wine;
The stomach accepts the softest bread,
Craves the palpable feast.
Perhaps I am going dead,
A loose bulb
In a dim, immolated cellar,
Licking fine, forgotten preserves.

10/12 — [1] & 11/13/65 (04000)

[A day with woodsmoke] †

A day with woodsmoke

rhetoric and literary history

Sister Miriam Joseph

a certain innocence in the criticism of these Ren. writers — Caxton,
for example — naiveté
preface to *The Canterbury Tales*
how to lead noble lives — use of mythology for same reason,
to serve as a model for how a person should behave —

Caxton's sense of lit is very simple — how people behaved

Thomas Wilson —
He stresses the power of eloquence;
eloquence made society, holds mankind together.
The man who can speak (trained in universities) should be given
the *civil* responsibilities,
political offices.
Stress on moral value of lit
yet emphasis on diction and rhetoric.

Roger Ascham

George Gascoigne
energy, not triteness
Concept of *decorum* vital;
everything must be appropriate.

probable impossible is better than
improbable possible

Strange forebears have passed here,
where an ocean sounds.
The voice surges about me
in a sort of Occidental purgation.

There's a quiet to the evening
No daylight can assume.

10/12/65 — [2] (05332)

Winter Seminar

One tries to decipher
Three-day-old symbols
On the greenwhite blackboard.
Another, with nimble, yellowstained fingers,
Contemplates filtered disease,
*

Reads Donne's "Obsequies."
A third, more prudish yet,
Peers through the fearful symmetry
Of octagonal pince-nez.
She,
A brilliant vixen at twenty-three,
Could just as easily be
Winslow Homer's schoolmarm
In some one-room conception of the universe.

How intellectual and subtle we are,
"Doing" John Donne or scanning
The bricklayer's sonne
In our seminar class,
While I just sit here,
Mind too bleary to concentrate,
Imagining distractions that fit my temper
(Trying to spell Yoknapatawpha)
Beyond the window's grating.

Outside, it's begun to snow,
And I feel an urge to bolt,
Fleeing without my coat,
Arms and ears bare,
To touch one slow-exploding flake
And hear it sear the palm
As it disappears,
Incarnate.

10/12 — [3], 11/10–11/65 — [2] on 11/10 (04018)

The Front Steps †

I sit on the pebble-filled steps,
Waiting for the day to end.
Apartment buildings are defenseless
Under my endless scrutiny.

10/15/65 — [1] (05282)

[An afternoon kind of work; . . .]

An afternoon kind of work; everywhere, stray people are returning from their Friday business. Now they disappear again into any one of the thousand gaping red-brick or brownstone mouths that await their arrival, dribbling dross and excess onto the street.

Children across the street are chasing their own smiles, running on feet lighter even than a dream, playing at football cautiously, running and jumping like the pros that perhaps just one of them may become in fifteen years or so, running on tiptoes over the hard, black pavement of the parochial playground.

Soft aromas from eveningwarm kitchens filter down to the street collectively, and I just sit here, wondering where her familiar face has strayed, and I guess at the smells: chocolate-chip cookies and cake, banana bread, and stews and meats of all varieties. The sky is still blue, without a trace of the circus colors that within ten minutes will begin to appear up through the still-leafy limbs of the elms and oaks and spruces that line this city street. Now car exhaust jumps down my nose.

Again, the children, playing their almost-winter games of basketball and jump rope and tag and pass-the-football and keep-away.

And it is a fine, warm afternoon, a day when all fear dissolves, when involvement with the springlike warmth of this mid-October day is enough.

People walk past;
scooters churn innocently;
another car passes, jolts, then pauses before forcing itself around the corner at the end of the street.

And I just sit here, thinking how nice it is to break bread in the sight of natural things, things that exist outside the classroom; how nice to breathe the warm, uncigaretted air and to inhale without experiencing the backup, the strong, raspy congestion.

The children yell: "Don't, Jimmy!"
"Here, throw the ball, Eddie."
"Pamela, you really shouldn't have."

The little girls stand off by themselves or walk in confidential pairs along the Cyclone fence.

And I can see the wind. Gene Redmond echoes those words through my ears as I sit here in the apartment: "I live in the nostrils of my grandfather."

Now, the greyblue shades of dusk descend over my sensibility, and I think it is time for me to eat dinner. Will you cook me something to eat — chicken potpie, perhaps, or one of your cheese sandwiches? It really makes very little difference this evening.

10/15/65 — [2] (05177)

[Seminar — John Donne] †

Seminar — John Donne
principle of elision

Newly paved,
    the craven traffic of my head
        runs fluidly and freely
            down my mind's Appian Way.

My heart supports
    the fibrous weights
        of galvanic electricity,
            cutting along above the head,
                the mind's Continental Divide;
                the central, cerebral fissure
                shudders, wrinkles, landslides

Sitting here, listening, weary
and blunted, to the too-brilliant exegesis
of the beastly Jack Donne

10/19/65 — [1] (05333)

The Trial of Christopher Paradise, Pariah

*I cannot praise a fugitive and cloistered virtue, unexercised
and unbreathed, that never sallies out and sees her adversary,
but slinks out of the race where that immortal garland is to be
run for, not without dust and heat.*

— John Milton, *Areopagitica*

Born to bring forth the angelic butterfly
That flies to judgment naked and alone.
— Dante Alighieri, *The Divine Comedy*

I

From White Cross to Redington
Is just a tricky flick
Of the imagination,
Cold to hot in one breath.
That's how it is with me,
Escaping seaward on a whim.

II: Memphis: The Conflagration

Memphis by night.
That's how I remember it,
Driving north to south.
One gaping mouth of neon
Fillings and wisdom cavities
That needed extraction.
Memphis by rainy night.
That's how I remember it.
My windshield wipers smoothed away
Soft revisions of the city,
Metronomically.
Swirling car smoke
Soothed my impatience, my comic hatred.
Memphis by Negro night.
I remember it that way, too,
Scuttling along my sightless eyes
Like a naked, soft-thighed chimera.
I stopped my frightened car
Long enough to watch
Lightning spray the town
With revenge. I was Nero.
I started my silent engine
And drove into the flamerainy night.

III

Cigarette smoke
Curled into the acoustics of night.
Traffic lights spoke a redgreen
*

Dialogue between motion and sound,
And somewhere, a moaning siren melted
The liquid interlude of parked lovers.

IV: Escape in April

Four o'clock in the Florida morning.
We, the car and I,
Had fought intemperate rain and cold
To reach this spot on Mercator's map.

I was Henry, prince and navigator,
Drawing lines of desire and hope.
I was Ponce de León,
Cresting each hamleted hill and slope.
My astrolabe revolved the needle,
Until, obliquely,
It exceeded ninety miles an hour.

Nashville, or Memphis,
Then Lookout Mountain
Faded in retrogressive blinks
Of billboards and coffee stops;
Next, Atlanta,
Serpentine,
Molting in rush hour.

Finally, I could see the outcast slip,
Stretching in a ribbonstraight horizon
Of beach like a strip of uncoiled tape
Stuck to the crease of night's tare.

Four o'clock in the Florida morning,
And I am spent of energy,
A dizzy, dying death-moth,
Forgetting the slow pain of maturity.

I'll end my journey,
Running down sandy corridors,
Pirouetting into obscurity,
Falling to embrace the lisping shore.

V

I am a sideshow stingray,
A fan-tailed lemon shark,
*

Spraying visitors' dreams
With darkspawning drops of doom.

I am a swimming sawfish,
A widegrinning dolphin,
Skimming the top of my tank
To cut the dawn in half.

VI

My vacation to Florida is sick.
I am bronchitis, smoked dry
By cigarettes that roll and lick tight
My pure white wrapper.

Florida!
Motels that breathe
Comfortable lies from December to April.
Florida!
Highways that drill
Out the cores of memory.

My sickness intervenes:
Phantasmagorical snow and sand beaches,
Literature and ballpark bleachers
Scatter in fantastic disarray.

My mother is a fish!
Vardaman had difficulty
Reading Izaak Walton.
Hemingway was a speckled trout,
Though I doubt he ever read
Donne's words on the Poebells.

Vardaman is a fish himself.
He dream-wished, daydreamed,
About his dead mother,
Who bred contempt for idiocy,
Rejected her anomalous sin.
She wore a scarlet "A," for "Addie."
Redington Beach! What of it?
How many resorts consort
To hoard the sun
From me, a boy of fits?

VII

Fugitive sighs fleet.
   Vain retreat conspires
      With blistered feet,
         And I walk naked
            Over sand on fire.

VIII: Resurrection

That very same night,
Birds flew in from everywhere.
The beach was an airport,
Whose runways were flecked with tracks
From hysterical gulls and pelicans.
That very same night,
Retired Struldbruggs came off
Their fishing piers to sleep
In beachside motel rooms.
They knew something was wrong.
That very same night,
The bars closed early,
And turgid whores and drunks
Crept away into the night.
They knew a storm was mounting.
A form floated in with the tide,
That very same night.

That very same night,
I leaned against a traffic signal,
My mind attuned to the metaphysical
Dialogue between red and green.
I had known life once and fast,
As a night of lasting inconstancy
That grew up my spine.
Someone said, "We are friends.
Tonight we will love fast
And together, protracting the hours
Between shadow and light.
Tonight we will discover ourselves
In each other like oceans in shells."
But I hid behind a gown of sickness
And walked into the Gulf to drown.
*

They found my frightened body,
That very same night.

10/19 — [2] & 10/22/65 — [2] (dates for piece as a whole) (05089)

Meditation over Coffee, 10/20/65

The rainsneering, blackpatched sky, hanging listlessly, watched my tired car weave here through the morning rush-hour traffic. I was invisible to myself, aware only of the music from the radio. And now I sit over a cup of throatraspy coffee, thinking more clearly, though still frightened and constricted in the stomach.

But the thoughts are simple now, not complex or clothed in the vulgar rhetoric of some anachronistic Thomas *"Medici"* Browne as they were last night. An echo: "Make me worthy of you, dear God! Please make me worthy!" And the strained reply, coming through the cracked voice of her fatigued, tear-filled eyes, and she merely saying with a look not of disgust so much as sheer fatigue and inability to endure further, saying, crying softly, "Don't say that again. Please don't ever let me hear you say that again."

But the thoughts, this morning, are stripped raw and essential. The cup of coffee is not mine, not even the coffee itself, let alone the cup, which I would never contend anyway, because it is mine only in trust — and herein lies the ultimate simplicity of human behavior, the blind trust that engenders friendly communion between people.

I think of when I entered the cafeteria earlier, eyes bleary with sleeplessness and drossfilled residue of bedtime nervousness:

My pockets are empty. I fumble through the blue-jean jacket: the gold-rimmed spectacles, a phone number scrawled on a child's Manila notebook sheet. Hands go limp; the mind resigns itself to helpless silence, but the body, my tired legs, are halfway down the aisle. Now I stand before the stainless-steel coffee boiler, and the white porcelain of stacked cups distracts my eyes. I think of hot coffee flowing over my tongue, envision its potion travelling to my head to stimulate the tiny brain-beads which exist there.

Those old eyes look into my frustration, penetrate the early morning disappointment, and I can see them warming in their orbits. She looks; I say it is not possible to take coffee this morning: "I have forgotten my money. Why do I do this?" But as I speak, mumbling bemused apology as I prepare to retreat, she is already lifting a cup to its saucer. "But I have nothing this morning, not even the dime. I spent my last eight dollars last night."

She looks at me out of the portals of her age, through the corridors of longtimepast motherhood, watching not pitiably nor sympathetically but rather with uncomplicated, inevitable warmth. And I watch her lift the tiny, blackplastic spigot to untap the pressured coffee, and the cup gets filled. She speaks, "Let me buy this for you," and she sets the saucer before me, going to her purse, stashed on a shelf. "My heart most naturally goes out to the boys," she says. "You see, I had two sons myself."

I am sitting here, hearing my reply still echoing over the temporal wires a half-hour long now: "Nice of you to do this for me. I'll be certain to bring your dime in tomorrow morning."

The voice, warm and aged, cracking, "I have had two of my own. Don't you worry about that," and I know she doesn't expect, doesn't want, me to assure her, to say, "I'm good for it, straight, will bring it in, the dime, first thing in the morning."

And now I think about the simplicity, the trust, the greatness of the small act committed unselfishly, and again I am drawn back to the past evening:

A boy, too old for his age, hunched against the radiator's silent, cold, spineiron back, looking up into her distressed face (a face not old nor wizened nor smiling sadly and distantly), his pained with tears, the source of which he has never been able to trace, the indefinable and obsessive, sporadic and unpredictable moments of dubious fear, timorousness. But he cries, and his fear is that of a child. He cries, his mind ranging over what has transpired, the lapse, voluntary desiccation, abnegation of confidence, passed before his eyes like flutterlighted slapstick, silent Chaplinesque comedy, during the past three years. His tears issue forth, dripping down the redrough cheeks, and he says,

"But just once, then, please let there be goodness."

"Don't you look for goodness here in me, where the only good is what you have imposed, placed here yourself?"

"Perhaps! And that scares me because it can't work that way. But I have known goodness in you — yours not of my willing, projecting — have experienced the softness of your mind, the simple trust you have shown me through your willingness to admit my eyes into your warm sanctuary."

"But I don't, won't ever, trust anyone."

"Don't say that. You can't imagine how that hurts."

"Better I hurt you now; it's easier when someone else makes the first recognition for you."

The boy, crying, sobbing, wants to call to the girl, "Mother," thinking, "Why does age trust what youth, in its too-hurried, too-importunate groping, distrusts, refuses to believe can exist for itself?"; saying to her, soft and questioning, inscrutably,

"When a dime floats on Trevi's water, I will belong to time."

10/20/65 & 2/8/66 (05283)

[I can sit here as I do, . . .]

I can sit here as I do, over coffee, thinking how my life has passed along its horizontal, biding its fast-burning hour, sitting now, thinking how nice it is to feel carefree amidst the exigencies of all these fastrushing people/students around me. White Cross is a nice place to be when the brownmulch leaves lie scattered at random along the ground and down the gutters.

The leaves cling, like fingers clawing fur, to the furrows of the still-green grass; leaves of ash and poplar, spruce and walnut and maple litter the ground everywhere with their deadpan faces, loitering like subway people lingering en masse, waiting for the subterranean serpent of Charing Cross, the brown line's best.

10/25/65 — [2] (05284)

[To sit in a public lounge, . . .] †

To sit in a public lounge,

totally unconcerned about the sensibility that sits beside/around them —

and now I'm transported to the Zürichsee, churning slowly the rolling waters that line

They sit all the long day long.
What's the diff. *entre* the slope of
the tangent of this curve and the value?
slope = tangent

Let's read about water
God   = I have two days *antes del examen*
science

Feet up on the table,
Naked and dirty;
A cough, consumptive

I see through the eyes
  of my grandfather,
   look for the king,
    the wizard of
      TV dinners

Pass out before I sink into silence.
Violence stalks me —
        the roughmuscled forearms,
      the siltwhite eyes that
      see beyond the irises' lids

        I doodle long into the afternoon, when the rooster has finished his
future
        I wish I could read, I, I, I, I
                        Why so many "I"s? Didn't your grade-school
teacher (that kindly anachronism) show you the proper way to write
compositions, vary your sentences? Don't always depend upon the
first person — I, I, I

Adele Spangler

A beard frizzled, stiff,
as if seared by fire,
clings to invisible skin.

A body without form,
incoherent as a mixed metaphor,
settles into a yawning slouch.

And I just sit here,
listening to the songs,
*

the reprisals for the wrongs,
the injustices against them.

10/26/65 (05105)

[Last night, I sat reading . . .]

Last night, I sat reading Faulkneriana again. How can one man give one youth so much pleasure and not even know it? I enjoy climbing into the world he created, into his real world of Oxford, too, to see the transformation of the fact into the distorted fictional milieu.

I can read him, can make him my lifelong hobby. To read his entirety, to be able to converse with the souls of his land, this is my desire —

to be as close to him as possible.

And then let me write, not what he wrote nor in the manner he wrote, but let me write about the virtues he spoke of.

To create is to contend with God's magnificence.

10/28/65 (05285)

[As I sit here, my mind sputters . . .]

As I sit here, my mind sputters and turns over rapidly like a propeller-driven airplane engine that refuses to make full contact. I can see the events of the past swirling in the exhaust eddies of my solitude, and the propellers still revolve. Now they catch, and with a loud roar of the typewriter keys, my mind makes complete circuit. I am borne forward on the strength of past recollection. My fingers sail down the horizontal runway of this keyboard, and now I lift into the slick, clearcool air above the surface, penetrating the frozen banks of cloudtufts. My skin is scorched in the sub-zero climate of my blood's circulation, but the cabin behind my eyes is pressurized and able to stand extreme vicissitudes.

It is a cold day, and even the leery greens have taken on a peaked coloration; there is an impending sense of winter everywhere I turn. The Chinese elm is droopeared and spent, its nimble limbs drooping to the ground as if its thousands of thirsty mouths want to drink the

dew from the grass. And the mimosa, too, has begun to settle into sus-
pended dream. It is green still but knows that its red life will be gone
long from it. The pea-pod seeds that hang from its branches in twos
and groups of three or four are feathers from some forgotten Indian
chief's war bonnet.

There are the birds still; some of them will even forget that it is
time to leave, will remain too busy to fly away. Now I can see the
squirrel and the cautious jack rabbit, but they have little meaning to
me in this time of my sickness.

Then there is the stray dog who sits beneath my window, barking
because he is cold and hungry and without a place to go. But no one
will answer his calling today because it is too cold to go outside to
fetch him, and I am too sick to expend the effort. Why does the dog
have to bark under my window?

Today I find myself living in a Currier & Ives world. Everywhere,
there is the sense of an older time, as though today's threats have all
melted into the softer sensibilities of the steam-locomotive days. I
feel extremely simple and uncomplicated, as if the most important
duty were to go out and chop a cord of wood to last for the winter. I
can see myself walking into the icebrittle field behind the farm out
there, double-bladed ax swinging from my side, listening to the sharp
pop and crackle of the thorntorn boots as they cut through the hard-
ness of the ground.

I sit here, in my room, looking back on my past no matter which way
I turn my neck. The walls are burdened with the weight of perhaps
thirty-five framed pictures and diplomas and other telltale records
of my youth. Now I turn to my left, and the last year of high school
appears to me. It was not a time for frivolous endeavouring but rather
a sober march from innocence into the fields of the future commit-
ment. There was a job to be done, and I had to meet the challenges
right then or the levees would have necessarily broken. But what I see
on my left is the car, the Corvette, and I can remember the other side
of the high-school coin. This was a rare car then, and there is a story
to be told about it and about the boy who was my running partner.

10–11?/65 (05161)

Heading North from Friday

Friday afternoon.
*

A red-pregnant circus sun,
Balloonhung and burning slow,
Turns across the sky's tongue.
Now, molting hues
Bluegold to pewter,
Friday roars, mute
As lion cubs,
Through dusk's fuzzy cage.

A day gone blind,
Drawing behind its ebb,
Like shore-receding waters,
Myriad suggestions of Calypso.
A car too silver for night
Digresses in shadowed retreat,
Pulling its squeal behind it.

We drive on together,
Past fastrushing lawns,
By lackluster farms and pastures
Wombed with picket fences.
Highway 67,
A quick, Egyptian god,
A Nile gone hard,
Stretching orthodoxly
Over unleavened Illinois soil.

We drive on, into darkness.
Lambent eyes cast insults,
Despising our naked speed,
Our uterine security,
And the uneasy freedom
That exists in the motion of things.

"Where are you from?"
Someone once asked us.
"Anywhere," she replied.
Now she sighs,
Sinking into sleep's vibrations,
Thinking aloud,
"Where are we going now?"
"Somewhere north from today,"
I say,
*

Trying to keep night
Before my orient eyes.

11/1/65 — [1] (00484)

[I sit here, behind this typewriter, . . .] ‡

I sit here, behind this typewriter, feeling the heaviness of my arms
and hands, and the pressure that is needed to press the keys is pain-
ful on these fingers, which nervousness has chewed to the quick.
The mind is in a swirl, craving the old habit again, thinking how the
body never ceases to plague the morality of conscience with its in-
sistent needs. Why can't a person just carry out what he knows is
proper and necessary for the futurity of the individual? Well, here I
go again, sounding like that puritanical, ludicrous moralist Christo-
pher Paradise.

I don't have the guts to continue, to write about the beautiful, se-
rene weekend that we spent together. Where are my guts, and where
is the staying power that I had last year at this time? Has my patience,
like the nails of these fingers, just worn away to nothing? Where is
the residual power I once had to stave off the pangs of ennui and in-
tolerable boredom? And where are the tools, the vocabulary and the
diction and the rhetorical awareness of subordination and Johnsonian
symmetry? And where is the little boy who looks after the sheep?
Why, he and the werewolf are eating Bo-peep.

The coffee tastes good to me — the only thing I have to depend
upon, excluding my very unpredictableness itself.

No guts

11/1/65 — [2] (05286)

Morning Rush Hour

The morning hour backs up,
Totters, spreads out,
One block at a time,
As ink on a mottled blotter.
Cars salted with frost
List along the street,
Precariously sliding in opposites
*

Like undone souls
Rushing toward resurrection.

Their breath depresses the air,
Disperses, and is lost,
Making room for newer exhaust.
I don't see cars, now,
On the tight-lipped thoroughfare
But a circus,
Whose light-footed elephants
Loiter in line, trunk to tail,
Or an endless assembly line,
Stalled by a power failure
At the traffic sign.
The sun teases a thousand glowering faces
As it dances from shadow to glass,
Cauterizing thoughts in antic frieze.

11/2/65 & 2/3/67 (00429)

[I listen to the youngsters . . .] †

I listen to the youngsters around me, listen to the confidential,
highly dramatized discussions of peers, companions who have gone
off the deep end, who have failed to make it — dope, booze —
                         Temple Drake takes the cake

                    Serape —

        Serape draped in yellow
        over rounded shoulders that reach
        through clothes

        Hair that falls half the back's length
                like a thousand kitten tails
              feline
              bovine
              equine

11/2?/65 (05287)

[I stoop to kiss her hair,] †

I stoop to kiss her hair,
Where she sits in the kitchen,
By the wooden table,
In the fragile slat-back chair.

She can tell I have cried
During the past half-hour
By the tears that stream,
Covering her wrinkled forehead

[11/2/65]? *(05107)*

[Already into November, . . .] †

Already into November, and I see no escape from the accumulat-
ing ennui, the fetid routine, the too-familiar setting of the campus;
there is stultification built into the classroom, the structure, the con-
cept of "institution" itself.

Must get away long enough to forget that stultification exists
the moment you disregard the dangers of familiarity, like rust from
oxidation.

to hear erosion
to see the wind

polysyllabic and mono-/disyllabic adjectives
\   /
irrevocable   puny
irremediable   gaunt
                 dour
                 fragile
                 small
                 scant

puissant   vapid
puerile   innocuous
perfunctory   abstruse
                  nonplussed
         sordid

11/6/65 *(05288)*

A Crisis †

A Sunday in early November, too warm to be real and too long to be endured more than once every other lifetime; it just takes too much effort for one person to contend with that temptation. The day was paradisal and epicurean, foaming and leaking hazy sensuality like dry ice emitting ubiquitous white vapors for no particular reason or without any visible source outside the sheer knowing that the element always gives off the same properties.

Sunday, a day of rest for the traditional believer, but there was something wrong

> I am Monday morning,
> forlorn and far away.
> A coffee lounge,
> filled with the accidents
> of conventional education,
> who loiter like brown water,

> Where is she,
> the girl I have known for so
> long? I miss her, feel myself
> spinning out and away from her,
> sifting in a void of meaningless silence.
> I want to smoke again, want to live
> foolhardy and free, doing as I please, flying to Florida
> if it suits my fancy

Crisis

I am Monday morning,
warm in appearance
yet warning and foreboding,
latent with cold stares.
The last dying leaves
drown among their kind
on the truckling ground.
Soon they will dissolve
under revolving tractor blades,
seeking their source.
*

I am a forest of thoughts,
defoliated and aloof,
raising my protests to the silent sky.
Why is there no place for me?
Where is that voice,
the face on the verge of crying,
eyes too hot and indecisive
to adjust the innocence?
People always use me;
I know it but not how
to

11/7–8/65 — [1] on 11/8 (05289)

[I am sick of watching old men . . .] †

I am sick of watching old men
make war
for the young to fight . . .
            — Walter Lippmann

Child's play — friendship
                  selfishness
                  possessiveness
                  jealousy

11/8/65 — [3] (05290)

[Ring ye the bels, . . .] †

Ring ye the bels, ye yong men of the towne,
And leaue your wonted labors for this day:
This day is holy; doe ye write it downe,
That ye for euer it remember may.
            — Edmund Spenser, "Epithalamion"

Veteran's Day:

the eleventh hour
of the eleventh day
in the eleventh month
of the year

This day will be history!
        Nov. 9, 1965 — Tues.

Dec. 7, 1941

    Nov. 22, 1963

Damn it!
The day did go from sun
to ascetic cloudiness.
I should have known though;
the forecast predicted so.

The Moment Before America

Some historians
glorify the deeds of da Gama,
Cabeza de Vaca,
pre-Columbians all,
and they say the Mayans' fall
gave way to Moctezuma —
all a matter of noncommunication.
No one has yet discovered

11/9–10/65 — [1] on 11/10 (05108)

[I] †

I

    LOVE

        MY

            SWEETSOFT

                PRINCESS

                    OF

                      PEACE,

    JAN.

                    L.
                    D.

11/11?/65 (05309)

Ritual △

    I never knew youth
    Could last so long,

      Then explode
        In
Freedoms of female entanglement.

      Silent fire burning off,
      Consuming accumulated desire;
      Sun eating morning frost
      From selfish lawns . . .

Somewhere, a weary angel stirs;

      I emerge.

    A Fourth of July rocket
    Sears the eye's horizon
    Tonight:

      A celebration of the seasons,
      The personal creation.

        Small breasts grow in palms
        Moist with loving.

An angel stirs.
> Stray beams skitter through venetian-blind teeth,
> Screaming down fine, private walls
> Of this ancient confessional.

> A rite is being performed;
An urgent current flows through us:
> Some haughty Thames
> Or floodclogged
> Zürichsee.

Will we ever return to ourselves?

11/17/65 (00493)

The Hunters and the Hunted △

I

I walk out alone this morning,
Before the traffic,
Bent with singular intention,
Rattles my madness
With importunate drones.

As I walk the green and pied fields
Of briar and winter wheat,
A sweetcold scent of onion
Whispers through the nostrils.

I step staccato, stalking rabbits,
Tripping over groundvines
That line intricate runs
Smooth as a bird's nest's belly.

Walking alone,
Shotgun draped like cloth
Across the weary arm,
I think how she waits,
Contemplating my solitude.

II

Done now; the car rushes back
Through pewter sunsets
*

Toward distant White Cross.
The stomach gurgles like floodwater,
Feeding impatiently on itself.

Nighttime, and I think
How I walked the fields this morning,
How alone out there
Without her.
Now all is changed.
There are no creatures to hunt.

III

A naked creature crouches,
Eve of some ancient conception,
Shoots wild,
Writhing into subtle fruit.

Skin folds into skin,
And somewhere an angel stirs,
Delivering us from ourselves.
She is outright giving
The gift reserved for once and only.

The eyes fill moist;
The lips go dry, slightly foxed —
Paradox of the seasons.
Rain settles in remote regions,
Spraying the mind's garden.
Something is being born.

IV

I know the spine's subtle curvature,
The "I love you," simply spoken,
Inadequate token of the world's religion.
We rest between generations,
Ten thousand voids coming open.

We are among the martyred handful,
Profligates of our own invention,
Toppling Pilate's cedar trees
Like Cyclopes dashing rocks.

We are the human animals
Lured out of coiled hissing,
*

Silent as seeds
Twitching under soil's first tillage,
Awaiting resurrection.

11/20/65 & 2/24/66 — [1] on 2/24 (00494)

[The estate of Elizabeth Drayton]

The estate of Elizabeth Drayton
Is up for auction today,
To be sold at Farnum's barn,
On the northeast end of Main.
Pickups and trailers line curbs;
Autos converge on the gravel drive
Like flies enticed by jelly
Left on a table overnight.
Buyers from all over the state
Congregate inside to investigate
Antiques the aproned men uncrate.
The townspeople huddle in corners,
Discussing Miss Elizabeth's estate.

[11/24–25/65]? (00788)

[A Kennicott-type town,] †

A Kennicott-type town,
Where any Prufrock could tilt
With courage and fealty.

A Kennicott-type town
At the end of Highway 67,
Situated squarely, though unplumbed,
Like a lumbering dinosaur.

Old Horton Jaspers
Peers through dustmottled,
Sixty-year-old, gold-rimmed pince-nez,
Squinting along the Square,
*

Fearing the day, thinking
Riviera in place of '27 Buick,
'15 Reo . . . R. E. Olds.

Mahogany gun case:
Glassy face admits peering children's eyes
One glance at grandfather's pastime.

The bank's octagonalfaced clock:
A white skin with large, bold numerals
Sprinkled evenly over eternity
Of perfect mechanical history.

Thanksgiving is a time for travelling
Back through time's pageant, unravelling
The dense mysteries of spiced history,
The misty heritage of unnameable fathers.

A rich, fullthroated heritage, ours.
I can hear Glenn Miller's band
Doing acrobatics down nighttime's
Corridors (an unsophisticated, fine time
That one), Packards dancing through
Nightmisty veils of Chicago's Lake Shore Drive,
The spoked sidemounts, circular perfections,
Badges of gentility and soft, fine taste.

Where is Scott Fitzgerald,
That sensitive kid from the country
Who made the public support him?
Budd Schulberg
Sheilah
Arnold Gingrich
Edmund Wilson
John Peale Bishop

Amory Blaine
Anthony Patch
Dick Diver
Jay Gatz
Pat Hobby

I own a '27, two-tone, blue and black Buick,
Stolen from an alter ego, an anterior time,
When

If I could choose the thoughts
That fight for precedence in my mind,
I would direct the process in a backplunging
Line of progress until I arrived back to 1923,
And there I would let the mind lie flat out on its back,
Sidetracked into forgetting.

Let me fly with the time's shabby signs,
Over the beds of sleeping gypsies,
Past iniquitous dens where the Pharisees
Malign all credos and all darker causes.

I need to concentrate
To feel what has gone before,
To let the sensations pour through my brainfilters.

A young girl, Zelda of some anomalous Fifth Avenue,
Revels in my mind, and now I am in New York,
Taking Thanksgiving lunch with the former mayor.
I can still see the cold of that day,
The thought of the crew season looming ahead
Like blueblackcoloured fear,
A child of the seasons,
And the Macy's parade passing before the windows
Of my consciousness.
I am party to my own past, no forgetting
No matter the effort in the "Wrong-Way" Corrigan
Direction.

I need to write to express the fever that eats the
marrow of my unscientific, semi-Donnelike, punning
mind. There is a place for me in the future if
only I will prepare myself now against the onslaught
of a culture made too scientific and too intelligent
for its own good. I must be on top of all the
quick-change culture that exhibits itself, this
culture a meretricious, slovenly prostitute,
*

parading all its gay colours on the marquees
of McDonald's and "the Nation's Innkeeper."
What an incredible insult, a slap in the same face
that still sees Mary Todd Lincoln sitting there
in the penumbra of oil lamps, breathing the heat
of some one-room log-shack hearth.
Or am I a modern Jackson Pollock or just
some anomalous, mild-mannered reporter for the
Daily Planet or the ragamahooly man from
Buffalo Bob's daily Howdy Doody extravaganza of
the mid-fifties, still-postwarinnocent imagination?

Now "Bix" Beiderbecke churns out the marathony
rhythms of the twenties era. My mind
is alive with the footstomping New Orleans

Where is the power figure, the one about whom
F. Scott wrote, the Great Daisychaser
from West Egg, or Elmer Gantry or Sutpen,
ad infinitum, in our literary history —
all a bunch of unsophisticated power figures,
the Willie Starks of another generation, who climbed
the necessary social ladders, ruled supreme
in their very naiveté for a brief spot, and then
declined the invitation for immortality? They just
couldn't cut the ice all the way on the northernmost
pole of the literary aesthetic.
The fault lay in the author each time. They say
now, in looking back, that there was just too much
middle-class morality going around at the time.
And even the bitchdog Hemingway was overblown with
that incredible thing we call JakeBarnesian naiveté.

You can fling it all out the publisher's window
now, if you want. Know it just can't work anymore.
We want not blood and gore, not even the heroics
of some minor Babbitt or Prufrock nor the manly
bullshit of the bullbound Barnes or Gorton, and
strangely enough, the only one to survive that mess
about the sun rising diurnally is the unreal Robert
*

Cohn, because the Jews are in today. . . .
In the center ring, ladies and gentlemen and children
of all ages, is Saul Bellow, the king who will
juggle three martyrs from an outlandish (foreign)
tongue for his bowling pins. They have names —
Baldwin, Ellison, and Wright — the three of whom he
will ignite and juggle as never before on the
end of his nose. . . . I forgot to mention, ladies and
germs, that Bellow is the circus's newest trained
seal. What a deal!

But then, this is Thanksgiving, and I would like to
propose a toast to Winslow Homer and George Gershwin
for making my stay here a pleasant one — my visit
to Earth, that is. My only regret is that I can't
stay longer. You people have been so nice to me. . . .
Clap, clap. Hurray, hurray. Bravo for the little
man with the white mustache and slicksilverysouthern
hair and the whiskey bottle dangling from his Nobel,
taught-himself-to-forget hand so that the pain of
reality was numbed, though never the perspicacity
of it, the sensitivity that he held in suspension
long enough to transfer it to the paper in his lady

Did you ever hear a thrush throat so softly,
and did you ever see the robin fly so swiftly,
when only the brownmuted quail should do that?

I wish there were room for me inside my brain.
Somehow, somebody forgot to leave a space for me
here, where the hair splits sensibilities along soft,
fine lines of reason and insanity.

There is just one thing that plagues me beyond
anything else, and that is the lack of responsibility

There was a time in this Whitmanesque country when
the Pierce-Arrow and the Packard and Cadillac
limousine were the apotheoses of modernity and
style (just ask your father), when Scott Fitzgerald
*

and the whole gang from Scribner's and *Saturday Eve-
ning Post* were on top of the heap,
    when Albie Booth was amazing the Saturday
afternoon crowds at what would later be known by
thousands of brilliant heads as the Walter Camp
Memorial, when Ernie Nevers and Thorpe and Grange
would gallop the range of the field . . .

    a time for Mack Sennett and the Long Island
studio with Gloria Swanson,
                Fatty Arbuckle,
                  Harry Langdon,
                    Chaplin, Charlie, my boy,
                      Eugene O'Neill.
What a fine time, when ticker-tape receptions
were the thing to do. It's too bad the great
Gatsby never had one — he could have, you know.
Even Tammany rose to the occasion with the youthful
pride of their Fiorello La Guardia, their Al Smith.

    The Hindenburg fell somewhere about that time,
didn't it, somewhere near New Jersey? My seventh-
grade history teacher was a child then, when it happened;
he told us how he used to get a quarter for working
as a guideline boy, would hold the lines from
the dirigibles.

    Do you remember Zebbulin Durrigible?

          He fished for pike

             somewhere along the fast-rushing
currents of Colorado's White River.

11/25/65 (05291)

[A fine, windy day . . .] ‡

A fine, windy day in Jacksonville, and solitude has left off its alle-
gorical chase; loneliness lies dormant in the city's street shadows.
    There is a slow excitement here, the day after Thanksgiving, and
the townsfolk are busy preening and gazing in shop windows, pulling

tight their belts before the first furry blast of real Christmas spirit
invades the Square,

a Square around which, on the quadrangle, the shops, like hibernat-
ing animals, have glutted themselves with suede and leather, peignoirs
and hosiery, boy-scout items, and men's haberdashery and footwear,
preparing for the incredible inundation of fastfleeing money.

I see this Square before me and the little girl of so many wonder-
ful and amazing moods — it's hard to tell what to expect

                camelhair ensemble
                the florist shop
                        mums — white ones left too long on
                the stem turn purple at the edges;
                        the light bronze turn yellow in the
                center when left unattended —
                        dark bronze
                        orchid purple
                        white

She is — I am — *We*

the cold odor of fresh Christmas flowers

11/26/65 (05292)

[The Wild Palms]

The Wild Palms
                |
        "Old Man"

A tall convict,
in flood time, too,
plowed black, sheer soil,
outraged and impotent,
planting the seeds
from which environmental dragons
*

would soon appear —
not Cadmus but Quijote,
reading pulp-fiction
dime novels,
criminals of modern round tables
fighting the monster flood,
the bilious devil-Delta,
1927.

Mr. Muse
Natalie Muse

Wild Palms

shit, shower, shave — toiletry
soup, salad, sandwich — lunch
sand, swim, sun — Florida vacation

April Love
Splendor in the Grass

11/30/65 (05109)

[I sit here, in the university . . .] ‡

I sit here, in the university coffee lounge; a cough, short/abrupt,
for no discernible reason lest it be some paradoxical crying out for
the cigarette, the cessation of which, during the past two months, has
caused my nerves to settle into a too-comfortable state of lotusmania.
I am emasculated, quiet, and sans the fierce disrespect, the rebellious-
ness — in fact, without the nervous depressions.

My hand brings the warm coffee cup up to my face, and I can see
the gold-rimmed spectacles peering out at me from somewhere be-
neath the sicklybrown surface, where I imagine ameboid monsters,
Lilliputian in size though not quantity — tiny little legacies of Max
Planck — and as I drink, the myriad inconceivable quanta roll over
the dry tongue, invading the stomach with stingers/flagella raised as

though it, the stomach, were some ancient Quijotemill or giant or some modern doomsday beach in France, Normandy perhaps, or farther, Corregidor, Iwo Jima, that is under siege.

So I write now, looking at the red spermink that flows off the pen's point, thinking of the immediacy of the act of creation. There is no real fruition of intention beyond the immediate act of committing thought to action through the pen. Sure the mind may labour to conceive the story, thought, or insight over an extended duration, but the act of writing is so immediate.

A gloomy Thursday; everywhere, the ubiquitous greycast sky settles, crawls, and grovels into the battered ivy vines on redbrown, color-of-Atlanta-claysoil walls of the campus buildings.

I stare out the window from within, locked from the outside only by the temporary constraints of these makeshift confines.

My body is sterilecold, and all I can think of is my work and the poor progress I have made since London.

I must finish the mystical *Heron* soon before I lose it,

    then the story of Christopher Paradise, the story of the Ozark hunter, the independent boy/man who becomes a man/boy.

My studies have gone poorly, work on the poetry slow, though I have moved into a personal form of expression. I lie somewhere between Whitman and Donne — a ridiculous

12/2/65 (05293)

Meditation over Coffee, 12/10/65

I have reread *The Wild Palms* this past week. All I can do is shrink with self-realization at the fact that, like Harry Wilbourne, I suffer from a lack of my own convictions. His curse was too much *morality*; he could not allow himself simply to be free to love completely.

Why can't I let myself go, give wholly and freely what's inside me? Why must I involuntarily hold back, torture myself with self-recrimination and doubt? What is it I want? I have already exacted everything she has within her. Why do I constantly question myself? The doubt, the insecurities I suffer at times, they just aren't fair to her.

    I lade her with respect,
            but I am not soft
              or gentle;
              there is no subtlety.

Please let me give her room to breathe, so that she won't have
to struggle against my deficiencies, the moods: elation just behind
downness and just before further dejection.
    Let me let her love in a way slow and simple, not obfuscated to
complicate beyond her capacity — love me.
                              My sweet little princess of peace,
                                    I love you more than
                                    words can tell.

12/10/65 (05295)

["The Mower Against Gardens" — Marvell] †

"The Mower Against Gardens" — Marvell   Phineus Beauregard
A wild and fragrant innocence;   *The Easy Philosopher*

          Gulf-spray-coloured sleet
          fell,
          silvermink

          Summer takes sick,
          breathes harsh and rasping, with chills

    •• Love is a redeeming force, despite all lusting
              Between the Heron and the Wren

    A rich, blue spring-fed pool,
    set deep into the hills,
    stitched with the sun's brocades.
    She hung by a loose arm
    to a bank-precarious cypress,
    supple as strong-holding
    trawl and static,
    then plunged into that pool
    to swim free, lungs

Where is the inspiration, the ability to determine my own activity
and behavior, the desire to be beholden to none but the muse,
       to read and write?
            Only one major problem:

                              self-discipline —
                                   the work, the action,
                                   the sheer doing, the
       necessary self-imposition.

12/14/65 — [1] (05111)

A Hard Coming of It

> *The Law of God exact he shall fulfil*
> *Both by obedience and by love, though love*
> *Alone fulfil the Law; thy punishment*
> *He shall endure by coming in the Flesh*
> *To a reproachful life and cursed death, . . .*
> — John Milton, *Paradise Lost*

A stranger in the night
Has come to White Cross
This Christmas of the year.
Undercover agents from Gethsemane
And Olive Branch,
Cities that garrison the fringes,
Press up snugly under shrouds.
Myth and personality coalesce,
Celebrating their annual renaissance.

The man, whose intellect
Spans interstices of history
(He's a twenty-century-a-year man),
Alights from his carre
     (Some say it's a golden sleigh)
And walks into night's silent carnival.

Neons finger his bewhiskered face,
Mistake him for a chaste mannequin.
There's something mystical
About this ubiquitous figure, who sees
Himself
*

Reflected in every department-store display
As he wends his way,
Unavoidably narcissistic,
Down the city's via media.

It's a potpourri city, White Cross,
Conglomerate of embossed descendants
And easy politico-philosophers,
Musty remnants of Old World stock:
French and Spanish fur trappers,
German brewers and clockmeisters,
Who drifted down De Soto's channels
From more constricted sources of inspiration.

He'll have to see the children
Of marble statuettes who sit passively
Before daylong TVs and coffee tables.
He must confront broadloom societies,
Ottoman and brocade ladies,
Who parade their boys
And lust-bellied daughters
Like wind-up toys on Florentine chains.

He knows integrity and sophistication,
Unlike names of a brokerage firm,
Enlist no specious supporters
From this atavistic race of moderns.
Were there ever such animals,
These post-Pentateuch creations,
Before Noah's peregrination?

Who could have ever guessed
The only surviving creatures
Would be Ashtoreth's golden calves,
Sperm-grey elephants, and worms
With human faces — abstractions
That fit some middle-class conception
Of itself, a clown's ludicrous shoes?

It's been a long journey,
Reminiscent of some Magi's senseless trek.
He's come with belly flabby
From ballpark "red-hots"
*

And a hundred and one other elixirs
That sell as phosphates once did
At marble-countered drug stores.
He's come by the city's snoozing limits,
Walking fugitively at the right hand
Of no One, absorbing thorny insults
Under flickering, gaslit penumbras.

Only, there's a task to be performed,
A service to be rendered, this night.
He's a vendor, the maintenance man
Who repairs and replenishes machines
When their slots go dry.
He's the artificial inseminator
Who comes once a year
Wearing royal purple faded red by time
And menstrual peculation
(Abortions that confuse creation),
Denied light by the dark flood
And the blood of Mary's little lamb.

As he walks, he spies a light,
A different kind of glow.
It's not the soft yellow of kitchens
Nor passenger cars spanning stretches
Through which he passed in youth
(Duluth, White Cross once, New Haven:
The million and one clichés,
Exclamation points, and dry-plain junctions
Recommended by Rand McNally, Prince Henry . . .
He a kind of embryonic Claus even then)
Nor soft-filtered hallway beams
And bedroom lamps burning early
Over tucked-in heads of fairy children.

No! As he walks alone,
Gathering stray shadows under his feet
Like ten thousand prurient Eves
Gladly accepting defeat or children
Doomed to the piper's mythic lute,
A light
(Some newer kind of helpmate),
Harsh and silverywhite
As a fish's upturned belly,
Jumps out, meets him halfway.

And he thinks as he goes,
Dreaming of sounds and causes
Sourceless and artificially bright,
And he knows that all's gone
From this former world of light.
He imagines himself a secular messiah,
Whose blackened mitre
Is nailed to a scarecrow's head,
Whose silver scepter is tarnished
Beyond human recognition.

But he goes ahead along the fence
(Fences are always there,
Pales for stray leaves and newspapers
And subversive notices now;
These white picket mountains
No longer creak under martyred weight)
And by stolid row houses and flats
That slumber complacently
On this preseason Advent.

He speaks to the darkness this eve,
When snow flows like fatted manna
Or wedding rice from well-wishers.
There's a ceremony being performed
Somewhere near this maniacal city,
Swaddled and shivering numbly
In the Mississippi's manger-valley.

He walks on in his own company,
Companionless except for that shadow
Of his female confidante
(Mrs. Claus, as some theologians have it),
Which (Who) lingers like netted memory.
He trudges until Spirit strangles him
And the tumid bag he swings over his shoulder
Like a polar peddler explodes
(Taking twelve months to conceive),
Swallowing him. The morning bursts,
And his breath dies, rather starts anew;
Something is born, breaks its sac.

At once his breath is consumed
In two thousand shouts of glee
*

And fetid expectancy.
The Christmas pageant slaps his back,
And life starts. (Bosses pass out cigars,
Turkeys, or electric can openers.)
He witnesses the reenactment:
Birth old and nascently reformed.
He hears the penetrant rending
Of sacrificial wrappings and ribbons
And stuffings and marrow and wishbones
(Only one at each table gets the heart),

And yet he knows why he's come
All this way for the solitary day
On which they'll rend him
And tear him limb from cedarn limb,
Burn tree-clipped tungsten candles
In effigy, fasten his corona to doors,
And hang his long woolen underwear
From their gaslit hearths:

It's for love alone he's journeyed;
It is love he has carried with him,
A love with which he'll return
To hold in trust
(A form of due bill, some speculate)
Till the children come of age
Or forfeit his day,
Irrevocably.

12/14–15/65 — [2] on 12/14 (00546)

Grace, After 1945

There once was a blue nude who combed the beaches of Bimini in
search of her mistaken identity. It seems that someone, preferably a
surfer or beach bum, mistook her for Tokyo Rose in bikini. This was
an easy mistake if one considered all the facts, the most essential one
being the rotting skin, the deteriorating pigmentation that was ap-
parent just beneath the skintight suit she wore. If you looked hard
enough, and obviously the man who made the mistake did, you could
see how the layers of dead flesh and smellrotting fat and muscle
strands were dissolving and falling off into the crotch of the garment,
causing a mess, as though it were the soup du jour.

So, now that we have the whole affair straight in our minds, why
don't we all sit down and eat?

12?/65 (05296)

[An abstracted disease,]

> An abstracted disease,
> Ennui,
> Creeping, lurking in the shadows,
> Where indecision bellows,
> Helpless as Benjy.

This has been a strange, unaccountable year for me, one filled with
the disappointment of failure to commit. I have made errors of omis-
sion and errors of commission, and now I can feel the hollowness of
my thighs echoing the emptiness of routine.

I must get on with the novel about the modern Dante, the one with
pride and lust, who lives between the heron and the wren, between the
knowledge of what is right and wrong, and suffers the inability to con-
nect reason and choice meaningfully.

It is a fine, clear, sharpglaring day, with the temperature sinking
far below freezing, and I am inside, absorbing the vapoured heat of
the radiator, which bellows thick and full.

1/8/66 — [1] (Poem), [2] (Prose) (05297)

Caddy's Sin

An abstracted disease,
Ennui,
Creeps,
Lurking in purple shadows,
Where indecision bellows
Helplessly as Benjy.

1/8/66 — [1] (04033)

[I am too gaunt to act . . .]

I am too gaunt to act with endurance. The problem compounds itself: the weaker I feel, the harder it becomes to eat and exercise and function without signs of lassitude and torpor. No longer do the arms and legs display the tonus, the definition, and it has become difficult for me to lift a chair without feeling the pain.

Where will it end? Will I have time to finish whatever it is that I have yet got to write, that something not comparable with Milton and Dante necessarily but maybe with Faulkner or Carlyle or Wordsworth? Will I be able to write it, the masterwork? I am even willing to write ten novels, hundreds of poems, and tens of short stories just to get one good work out of all the mess and dribble that comes bounding from my lips and mind and fingertips.

1/8/66 — [3] (05298)

[I am the Everlasting No; . . .] ‡

I am the Everlasting No; the Centre
        of Indifference am I.

The day is faceless.
                I am passing through a period of transitional
unresponsiveness. A storm cloud looms, proffers its skeletal hand to
me, and I shrink, diffident in the guise of an artist. But the pain I feel
is the son of uselessness, having spawned from some illusory, platonic
conception of myself.

            I run over trails,
            Smearing my face with brazen war paint —
            An uprising —
            Disguised as a railroad detective.
            The train carries me
            On a senseless journey,
            A movement from Friday,
            Riding eastward into sleep.

            About me, boys and girls
            Struggle; everyone talks of tragedy
            *

And freedom, suffering inherent in greatness —
Oedipal, Samson-like

Why is the thought process clogged, dissatisfaction utter and supreme? Time to make a clean break with the environment that pinions me. I can't even scream or whimper. The awful, burdensome weight has severed the mind's vocals, has clipped the tongue like a sharp pair of garden shears. So I must go, running I know not where, skimming the currents above the air pockets of Cancer, Cassiopeia, until I can soar, unclothed and free, lighter than palewhite bosoms of cloud and soft vapour.

No more am I a romantic.

The answer is somewhere;

must find a purpose, a reason for the

effort — effort, reason, choice, purpose, *God*

1/10/66 (05331)

[A cool, comfortable evening . . .]

A cool, comfortable evening in Redington, filled with warm laughter and the closeness of people joined in harmony. This is a motel room on the Gulf, but an apartment only from the outside. Within, we are all friendly and alive with a certain slow vitality. The words are all that count, the funny little sayings that have an ulterior significance, a meaning that transcends the literal. We are all W. C. Fields for the moment, with pineapple juice in our pineapple juice, drunk with fatigue.

Outside, it is a cold, breezeblown, palmflowing evening, late and somehow outside of time. Everything has ceased to progress, and we are held within the suspension of quietude.

On the floor, a brown and white rug; on the rug, the girl with curlers in her hair. Before the lowplaying TV, the mother, eating hamburger at one in the morning, the friend, Wally, quiet and relaxed in the cushioned chair. And I sit at the typewriter, thinking of all the time that has transpired since I was here last, the terrible, grinding ineffectuality of creativity that has pounded on my brain.

Once in a long while, a person is gifted with the opportunity, the sheer chance, to forgive, and it is at this time that a person is allowed to show whether he or she is strong and compassionate enough to forgive that which is the error or weakness of another, which is of little significance to the world anyway in the long run of morality, important only to the forgiver.

And I just sit here, behind my typewriter, thinking about all that has transpired in the world that Puritans or heretics and other weak-minded theologians or moralists would call error or sloth or immorality, knowing in my own small way that what counts above all is the simple ability to forgive that which has brought minor, though traumatic, disgrace on a person. I can hear myself saying to another, a minor victim of the world's mean wickedness, that it takes guts to err, to make mistakes. It takes guts because by succumbing to the easiness and deviation, the person necessarily makes him- or herself vulnerable to him- or herself.

And so I say to myself and all the ships at sea that only in making the error, in experiencing the sin, does a person allow himself to be human. John Milton wrote about reason. Reason is choice, and man's freedom exists in the ability to choose. But man, in choosing, also opens himself up to the evil that exists and, by doing this, also makes it possible to discover virtue in overcoming, in atoning for, that sin, which has been in the world as long as the myth of Christianity.

> A blue light,
> Through a cool, grey night,
> Shimmers like eels,
> And my ears burn.
> The eyes are learning to see
> Through the silence and wet.
> The ebb flows out —
> A life on the wane.
> I see Beatrice in the rain's silvered eyes.

So I can write tonight, when nothing but laughter grows alive within my sensibilities. Behind me, in the same apartment that for years has existed as it is now, I can see the girl whose tiredness has outlived the need for sleep, who works at the blondstreaked dinner table, writing out notes that exemplify enthusiasm and effort directed in the right direction.

I can hear her saying the words that she has learned, like a child confronting its ABC's, and the words have a meaning all their own:

> hyperbole
> pulchritude
> usurpation
> admonition

These are the result of a misguided education, a funny little mind that, like Cadmus or Johnny Appleseed, goes through life planting the dross of diction.

Redington, on a wet, greyrainy afternoon, and progress, which consists on a normal, warmwinter day of relaxing on the whiteness of myriad beaches, now has drawn to a halt. Everything is bathed in the slow, drowsy colors of the wet rain. Everything, motels and beauty salons and the wax museum, even the pavements and the bridges, are the hue of elephant; everything is wrinkled. And so we return, after sleeping through the afternoon, to the apartment and to the warmth of familiarity, to eat hamburgers and spaghetti, to drink the soothing Calvert blended whiskey with mix and the nervous brown coffee.

The phonograph, with Pete Fountain and the soft, shrill clarinet of Benny Goodman, Julie London and Jack Jones and Barbra Streisand . . . and so we spend the evening together, joking with the king's English, every joke under the sun — yet there was no sun today.

Beatrice lives in the mind of every person who has ever invoked the Muse, Urania, Apollo, or simply the word "love." She lives in the eyes of young lovers and of elderly people as well, who have long since left off with the sweet little simplicities of first love and who now content themselves to sit at the bar, still holding hands, though not now glowing and bursting forth as once, and, like Adam and Eve, still going out with wandering steps and slow, hand in hand, dubious and fearing and benign and obedient to the Providence and the fiat and the interdicts of their modern god, still with the ability, nay, the desire, to choose.

Now I sit here thinking of all the slowness in the life of the transient, the person who wanders not as a Romantic or Peripatetic so much as simply the one who goes out in search of some modern grail. And so I sit here among the friends who breathe the air that circulates slow and easy, that presents itself blue and warmyellow and brazen. I am the mastermind of travel; my mind moves like soft airs over the Gulf, suspended above and beneath the firmaments. I am a certain minor god, the image of love that exists in the simple words of love or compassion or sheer understanding and forgiving.

I am a late bug, a person, termite perhaps, who burrows into the pockets of night and life. My song is that of change and time and life.

Somewhere in the back of my late mind, I hear the words "Yes, but we all get along," and I know the answer now, the reason for all of it: difference and accepting, and living and accepting the difference and the chance and the change.

To accept change, one must be able to change, to flow and swing with the change of things. Robert Frost was one to go with the drift of things. I am a west-flowing brook, the thoughts like tiny pebbles that grow in the eye of an underground springsource and then move with the swift current to the end of things, the mouth of the river, and then the pebbles are mashed and spliced and hewed until they decide they want to return to the source, so that with the vapours of day, they climb to the sunburnt cloud, surcharged with creative, procreative energy, and throw themselves, the pebbles, prostrate on the softpelted surface of the stream to begin again.

So I am the voice of regeneration.

I hear laughter, and my mind says laugh. So I laugh with a softsubtle resonance, thinking of sleep and things that have to get done in this life, and now I know the answer, if answer we must claim to hold: the sleep, the long, purple sleep of night. I am the after-dinner sleeper who waits in attendance for the time to make the move, to rouse like the winterlong sloth bear, to tumble from the palate of darkness into the brightstreaming light of glory.

Everywhere, I see Beatrice and those eyes. There in those eyes is the key to everything, the eyes of order and harmony.

So I will sleep tonight, comfortable and lightheaded, filtering the dreams of the Wizard's Dorothy.

1/20/66 — [1] (Prose), [2] (Poem) (05358)

Election

A blue light,
Through cool, greying night,
Shimmers like eels,
And the ears burn.
Shadows turn in on themselves.
The eyes are learning to see
Through the silence and wet.

An insurgent current
Upstages the mind,
Unwinds the body's thread.
The ebb flows backward —
Life on the verge.
Far out, a fish flips,
Disappears in a grey-blue pool.

1/20/66 — [2] (04029)

[Background sounds . . .]

Background sounds of the Supremes break my ego, carry my thoughts of excitement far from this apartment room, and yet I know that, here, I will work and transcribe the sensitive mental vibes that dance, twisting and moiling like a seismographic blip.

> A day too cold for the plants:
> Palmettos and palms freeze,
> Play solitaire with the wind,
> And I shiver under Florida blankets.

> A cottage winks warmly at the Gulf.
> Poor bastards that live in water,
> Caught under billions, weightless,
> Claustrophobic.

> A writer on fire, burning
> Under inviolate covers,
> Cranking out typewriter thoughts
> Bought at too high a cost.

> In my dreams, a Brancusi seal,
> Alabaster and pumiced soft,
> A Pierce-Arrow,
> Sculpted on someone's rolling mill;
> A seal and a car,
> Emblems of freedom and lust,
> Screaming.

> Beatrice lives between the legs
> And a too-fast sunset,
> Screaming red words of love —
> Florence on the mind's fluttering lids.

I sit behind a typewriter, not profound, not complex, but lilting soft and composed, relaxed behind the throatwarm slide, gurgle of whiskey, dripping like a rainbow's colored dross, living and freedom and the eye-blink embossed behind the head.

A redburning, brightturning ball of fire falling, dropping into the Gulf, hissing like a sinking ship on fire and exploding, listing and hissing in a wrap of blueorange, yellow, frightyelling falling.

From the Gulflocked window, I see you, sonne/sun/son, scorching the water's skin, turning it the color of night, a poet's set, *crépusculo*, and somewhere in the distance, an albatross flies pterodactyl-like and with the curse of the old mariner hanging from his serpentine neck, squawking with screeching sibilance, that curse so old, longer back than the distance of a primordial, batswooping, stalactitehung, frogdung cave cut deep into the bowels of some earth, some Ozark country that is older by far than the civilization that threatens to bull-doze it into forgetting.

Durrell will rot in Hell for the mastery of sex he possessed; he ate nightly of the tree of knowledge of good and lust, aiming higher than some immaculate conception with his Scobie, his old man, older even than the antique man of the sea, some anachronistic Neptune who sprouted whole and alive from the dawn's scabby womb, rolling out of the birthcave in a wheelchair, rolling out on rubber tires and the automatized stainless steel of the conveyance, never knowing youth, having been conceived on a dare.

> Chris Lovelace lived behind age's wrinkles,
> An old man born too young for Dante,
> Growing young and slow toward death
> And life,
> Spurning a wife, an image, and a whore,
> Four children, and Natalie Muse.
>
> He had to choose his course,
> So long and tortuous,
> Hung with rusty chains,
> The relics of a madman's *vedute*,
> Crawling back through dirty sheets,
> *Albèrgo* beds, and dripping sinks
> From White Cross to Juan-les Pins,
>
> A man lost in night's cave,
> The whitebellied pavement
> Where earth melts into love,
> Darker even than the brain's
> Membranous confusion;
> Lost in myriad contusions,
> Crawling into His purple wound.
>
> The daughter, Veronica,
> Wiping dry his commitment,
> Victim of unfinished business,
> Redblurry eyes, hurt and wet
> Like a cave's stomach,
> Dead in his coming absence.

A head that hurts with the recognition of reality, that abstraction
that resides between the heron and the wren. Mr. Self is everywhere,
hair like Christ's, legs worn thin with abuse and useless wandering.
He walks, crawls, with sandals, feet bloody and the knees bloody with-
out reason, just the continual driveurge toward that which is beyond
the night's reckless, anticfilled mouth, crawling now with eyes bent
upward and the neck craning up, the dusty groundgrits under the
knees, beneath the head, living with the sweat of the forehead clichéd
like indelible tattoos, the cursed droplets beads of Adamic perspi-
ration. His fault, pure and simple, the opprobrium of his choosing,
faulty reasoning, if reason it was in the first, original place — that
place a cliché too — the real sight of the place still alive and green
inside the human heart, the human existing between the choice, which
is freedom, and the fiat, inherent in which is prevenient grace and
supernal will.

> A warm woman,
> The heart of three girls,
> Not reprobate nor lost
> Yet left lost by quick fate,
> Spurned by guilders and myrrh,
> A wise one, coming slow
> Over hollow, lifeless hills
> To this lush Gulf shore,
> Planting her seeds like Cadmus.
> Her revenge will sprout
> Sooner than waking bears.

> Esther from the Garden,
> Ranging wide to Calvary's summit,
> The kerchief soiled yet white
> As still lifegerm boiled
> In veins and body, the seeds
> Of ancient Mordecai
> Living off her energy still.

> Minor immortality, the life
> That grows above ground,
> Through the holocaust.
> A cold, black darkness,
> Wet as eels; albatross,
> Throwing off wingspew
> Against sky-blue abnegation.

A woman once said, "Everyone needs to feel important some-times." She was an aged grandmother, seventy-five and without comfort — just the words of a boy who was unaware of the words' power.

So when the head and the heart refuse to labor further against the sweaty turmoil of study, one goes against the current of things, leaves, bolts upright and stark, flees from the source of the ennui, the fetid cliques of students, long since become men in age, anyway, if not maturity and awareness, who sit around the university coffee table in every city and cow town and resort area that boasts the "finest" academic opportunity in the country, each without respect for the hundreds of other institutions founded, like his own, without ade-quate funds and instructive facilities, sitting slow and languid, suf-fering from brain cramps and fatigue, skull cramps, talking about a Dante they never knew outside the classroom outline-series pony, about Santa Teresa, Fray Luis de León, about the Dunce and Thomas, about that which is demanded outside and beyond the table that sits at the entrance, ten Cory coffeepots going at once, the simple little coins of prodigality and excess lying like anomalous pieces of eight, the result of caffeine inebriation and artificial intellectual stimula-tion. So one flees, until even the fleeing isn't adequate, since one flees from one source to another just like itself, different in name only, the coffee a regional or local brand now, not national, perhaps, the cups Floridian porcelain instead of Sheffield or Staffordshire china, de-pending upon the class of the coffee klatsch.

The sky-blue waters of the North's lakes and streams and rivers are filled with, famous the world over for, three types of fish: northern pike and redeye and ass, small- and largemouth, depending upon the degree of fagginess or queerness.

When drinking, the mind is like the limbo; it sinks lower and lower as the night disrobes its inhibitions.

That's gross. I'm going to brush my teeth after that one.

I'm going to brush my brains. Who's got a mindbrush? I've got a brain like wet buckskin; when it gets wet, it goes all to shit, gets blotchy and soggy. Then I've got to brush it only with the grain-brain.

* * *

"I'm more tired than shit. It's this weather."

"Yeah, this stuff makes ya take your mind off the beach and water."

"I'm bagged to hell."

"Yeah, I'm finally gettin' around to my *Playboy*. Someone swiped

it on me. For all I know, it could have been all the way down to the wax
museum and the aquatarium."

"No. It's been right here in my boudoir."

"Well, after a month, I guess I'm entitled to my *Playboy*. I think I'll
sleep with it tonight. It'll be good for my mind, which is shot all to
hell."

*   *   *

"Say, what's the day today?"

"Twenty-seventh."

"Is it Thursday?"

"Yeah."

"Dino tonight. That's the only thing I watch all week."

"Say, how did you remember it out of the clear blue?"

"It's the only thing I watch."

"Yeah, but you know, it could have been 11:30 or 12:00, and you'd
of looked up and said, 'Piss,' and then you'd of blown a whole week."

"Yeah, but I should remember Thursday night; it's the only thing I
watch all week, as I said before."

*   *   *

"You know, he had a smile from ear to ear."

"Yeah, like a possum eatin' shit."

"Yeah, out at Las Vegas, I blew a fortune.
It disappeared like a fart in a whirlwind!"

"Essie, will you be nice to me tonight if I get a little squalid?"

*   *   *

"You know, a guy'll walk a mile for a Camel, two for a hump."

*   *   *

The new automobile club slogan:
Bundle up for safety.

*   *   *

So the man gets caught, trapped, between the heron and the nasty
little titbiting, socially disordering wren. And then life becomes in-
triguing, becomes hard to manage, takes ingenuity for the individual
to extricate himself from the foul and stinking mess, the dross of
civility and gentility, which gets confused with social humor, socia-
bility, intellectuality, wit eighteenth-century style.

Age is when a man looks at the *Playboy* gatefold, an almost-nude model nipping at a bowl of popcorn, and he says of the food, "You know, that makes me hungry."

* * *

A hot, speckled glass,
Sweat of some drunken brow;
Whiskey waiting, slumming
Down and out of sight
Before the hand comes down.

He was a drummer,
Bumming the freights
That passed day and nighttime,
All hours of summer.

A small western town,
Where a nameless mother
Gave him his unwarranted place;
Waiting even then to flag the train,
Destinationless, a male whore,

Colorado Nation, man of means,
Speculator in soybeans and cabbage,
Mastermind of the great white way,
A Vegas flunky, pockets filled with

                                        grace.
So he ran the pavements,
Denver, Frisco, Spokane,
Even in winter, when rain and sleet
Beat against the brain,
Seeking a mother,
Ever in lewd heat.

So he died in April,
A green, unharvested age,
Thirty-three,
On an eastbound freight,
Found dead and ignored,
Frustrated in motion,
Prostrate and lifeless
On the wood floor
Of a Great Western boxcar.

1/27/66 — [1] (Prose), [2–5] (Poems) (05359)

Confinement

A night too cold for plants:
Palmettos and palms, mangroves
Shiver, ruffling the breeze.
I play solitaire with subtle drafts,
Freezing under Florida blankets.

The cottage winks; its sallow eyes
Blink at the Gulf.
"Poor bastards that live in water,"
I think,
"Sinking under weightless billions.
That I were Vardaman's fish!"

A writer on fire, burning
Under scratchy covers,
Turning out secondhand thoughts
Bought at too high a cost.

Under night,
A slick Brancusi seal,
Alabaster and pumiced soft,
Whiter than Ahab's hatred,
Scurries across my screen.
No easy dream, this one!

A Pierce-Arrow,
Sculpted on someone's rolling mill,
Hurries down endless streets;
Seals and cars retreating fast,
Emblems of freedom and lust
Lost as undiscovered treasure.

Beatrice lives between the legs
Of a too-fast sunrise.
I awaken,
A trembling Dante,
Exiled in a twenty-year yawn.

1/27/66 — [2] (04028)

Between the Heron and the Wren

Chris Lovelace lived behind wrinkles,
An old man too young for Dante,
Growing slow toward death
And life,
Spurning a wife, an image, and a whore,
Four children, and Natalie Muse.

The course he chose
Was long and tortuous,
Hung with rusty chains,
Relics of a madman's *vedute*,
The new Piranesi, Lovelace,
Crawling back through dirty sheets,
Albèrgo beds, and dripping sinks
From White Cross to Juan-les Pins,
Aix-en-Provence to Florence;

A man lost in night's cave,
Traveling whitebellied pavements
And mudflustered *senderos*,
Where earth melts into love,
The path darker even than the brain's
Membranous filters;
Lovelace the Confused,
Lost in myriad contusions,
Crawling wormlike
Into His purple wound.

The daughter, Veronica,
Wiped dry his commitment,
She the sordid victim
Of his unfinished business,
Her eyes, hurt and wet
Like a cave's stomach,
Dead in his coming absence,
Gone for twenty years
From herself.

1/27/66 — [3] (05114)

Essie

A warm woman,
Heart of three girls,
Beating with liquored pulse,
Not reprobate nor lost
But auctioned by quick events
At a ridiculous cost.

Bereft of gold and myrrh,
The wise one still,
Coming slowly over lifeless hills
To this lush Gulf shore,
Planting Cadmusian seeds
To sprout and revenge herself
With images of Saint George.

Esther from the Garden,
Her kerchief soiled yet white
As life-germ, ranges wide
To Calvary's summit.
The seeds of ancient Mordecai
Thrive on her energy.

Minor immortality:
Life that grows above the ground.
Outside, a coldblack night
Wrinkles wet as eels.
An albatross drops from her neck,
Throwing off wingspray
Against the eyes' newer night,
And she submits to sleep,
Counting sheep that pass in threes
Beneath her tired lids.

1/27 — [4] & 2/24/66 — [2] (00483)

Hobo

They recorded his birth
In a small western town,
Where a nameless father
Gave him his nomenclature.

And he seemed waiting,
Even then,
To flag the trains
That took on baggage and grain.

He became a drummer,
Bumming the freights
That passed day and nighttime,
All hours of summer.

Destinationless,
A ragged outcast,
He was Colorado Nation,
Man of means,
Speculator in soybeans and cabbage,
Mastermind of the great white ways,
A Vegas flunky,
Whose pockets were filled with

                                        grace.

And he ran the pavements,
Denver, Frisco, Spokane,
Even in winter, when rain and sleet
Beat against his brain,
Always retreating,
Always in lewd heat,
Ever seeking a
                        mother.

Once, he died in April,
Just thirty-three,
On an eastbound freight,
In a green, unharvested year,
Frustrated in motion,
Prostrate and bleeding
On the hard cedar floor
Of a Great Western boxcar.

1/27/66 — [5] (00487)

Meditation over Coffee, 2/9/66 ‡

Gigantic and fast-descending, disproportionate, *it* has disturbed
the delicate arrangement, has dislodged the sensitive membranes of

sensibility, and I can see her, now, lying there in that bed (a brass-bed head gate looming, crescented, over her head, mattress on the floor, in a room gloomy and windowpelted with slow, continual elephant-grey rain), the symptoms malevolent and febrile, ranging the length of her limp, pronehelpless body, not irrelevant, rather coexistent with that which, like physical death itself, like desert vultures hovering patiently over carrion not yet rotting, has hung off in the wings, has held off until her strength might dissolve, the dissolvement slow at first, the energy and commitment too reluctant, too determined, at first, to relinquish themselves, give way to abiding ennui and torpor, which have finally escalated, elevated, their war on her.

And she, lying there now, defenseless though still not afraid, since the fear hasn't yet had time to pervade her thoughts, she merely helpless against herself and unable, now, even to rouse herself from the slow, recalcitrant, burning listlessness that invalidates and overpowers her will to fight, to vanquish *it*.

                                        * * *

I have seen it coming; first, three months ago, coming unnoticed and nondescript, the simple, short-lived, unfounded and feeble affirmation, and then just before Christmas, so that whatever doubts she had were temporally assuaged and placated by the awareness of two weeks of holiday retreat from the tolling grind of artificially inseminated academic pressure. And still I can hear it, the Sermon on the Mount, her voice short and depressed and wanting to scream out, to break into tears; only, then the strength was still positive and on her side and persuasive, though not inevictable, she saying to me as we walked with books in hand, holding hands and walking toward the Friday-night-empty library,

"What's the use of all this, even the A's and B+'s? Soon we'll all be dead, and why even try to make a career, to earn money for all the things that we will blow up anyway?"

"Honey, please. That's no damn good. Say we do that, say we make sure everything is wiped out, annihilated. Then what? . . . And so what, honey? If everyone was willing to believe that, then we'd all quit now and lay aside our tools or books or black traveling bags and give up. That would be the reasonable thing to expect."

"And why not? What good is working toward a career in fashion design, in teaching?" she said, looking at me then, the eyes not glistening but opaque with muted and impotent and blind rage. "What's the use of going toward something that won't be there when you arrive and are ready to show what you've learned, expected?"

"Now, enough," only knowing that just the voice, her voice, would quit, not the thoughts, the simple fabrications that held latent and yet embryonic the germs of the fear. She was pliant and apologetic.

"Oh, I know I'm silly at times, but I've always felt this way, felt that whatever I was doing was of no matter, consequence, since soon it will all be over. I'm so silly," she said, her smile demure and reticent, the head down, the eyes half-shut, like a child asking forgiveness for some petty second-grade misdemeanor.

And still, before entering the library, the symbol of it anyway, I knew there was more, that she would redefine in her mind the source of the not-yet-fear but doubting of her own role, listening to her deprecate, and with fairness and accuracy, the teachers, the courses in fashion design, which she claimed anyone at home could learn, teach themselves in half the time and for a hundredth of the money invested, telling me about a girl she knew from a wealthy New York family (she from a small, middle-class Illinois farm outpost decked with a Square and a Carnegie-donated library and people who were up to date on all the immediate and local happenings, the hospitalized, the newly married or raped or shotgun-wedded, the lucky in the stock market, all since the town too had a café, which opened its double set of swinging doors at 6:30 to accommodate the armchair-quarterback politicians, the self-appointed and violently annunciatory advocators and judicators for the town's affairs and existing policymaking)

2/9/66 (05299)

[A Venetian, bright and shimmering . . .]

A Venetian, bright and shimmering and coolcrisp Sunday afternoon in mid-February, and I sit again in my study, lined with the dusty faces of the past, the multicoloured dust wrappers, like bears rolling and stretching from winter's hibernation period, ready to open themselves to the light of the eyes' insights again, and I just sit here thinking about the passed months, the inconsistencies we have endured together, November, December, and January and myself, and so all that remains now of the old air is that which lies rancid and stale between the storm window and the inner aluminumpaned window of the study, this vacuum itself redolent of a life past, filled with the dust-crumbled fossils and insect dust of rotted and decayed and all but invisible fly remains, a few black, dissolving carcasses still there like defeated and war-torn Pearl Harbor battleships, the flies lying sedate and unruffled on their backs, this space, vacuum, lined invisibly with the promise of spawning summerjubilant progeny.

The darkbarked chestnut tree that stands shivering in the wind outside the window casts shadows I cannot see; it breathes, with pores I cannot hear, the muffled sighs of promise that is yet to burgeon, to fulfill itself in the White Cross soil, and still it retains a portion of its browncurled leaves, the shriveled remnants of the past which have refused to relinquish their limbed bastions, as if even some primal plague were not powerful enough to dislodge these ancestors of the past spring and summer White Cross months.

Outside and behind, on the tarred pavement, the back driveway, and garage, the hollow bong, bong, bongbong of the weathered orange basketball, which, like the trees and horse and white German shepherd, has remained out all the winter long, still responding to the child's awkward dribbles and flings against the white-weathered basketball standard and backboard, coming back to earth each time with a hollow thud, thud, thudthud, and the child, perhaps ten now, the age I once was, is outside, in a forty-seven-degree warmth, with just the heather sweater and the slacks and loafers worn to Sunday school. There will be time still to remain inside; this is just an Indian-summer day which somehow got lost at the end of October, post-poned, and rainchecked, so that now we have it, he, the boy, has it to play with before the oncoming snows blotch the land again.

I walk outside now, thinking how long it has been since I took the effort to go "witnessing" again, the hours of each month passing in random disarray, so that I have, too, missed the long hikes in the coun-try (this is no longer far out, no longer the country), the rabbit hunts, the treks with shotguns slung over the forearm or shoulder, hunting the tricky fowl (the faststarting quail or the pheasant), the red and blackgrey squirrels. A body has to drive into Arkansas now if he wants to shoot wild boar, has to fly or drive up into Minnesota or Michigan to find the black bear, the icehidden walleye or northern pike or pickerel, the muskellunge.

But my mind has not even ventured from this room or all the other rooms of the mind like this one, the rooms Kafkaesque and stifled and spoiled somewhat by the necessity to focus and concentrate not on the ground, the thickets, the briarbrambles, and upswinging limbs of the forests but rather on the hidden meaning that lurks between festering lines of arcane poetry, the Arcadias of some backward and cinched-too-tightly sixteenth-century minds.

Now I walk out behind the huge, plantation-like house, in La Duc, can see the swimming pool, where Gentry Wydown sat around with his parents and their friends that summer when he returned with his ailing father to White Cross from Rome, and the pool is marked with ice patches, not forming a complete protective shield since the warming airs have abnegated, mitigated, total control. Yet three weeks ago, when the first snows finally came after an abortive period of waiting and predicting, the pool was made into an ice-skating rink, its surface large enough to accommodate ten or twelve dazzling, revolving, sunglinting blades at a time, gratis, something out of Winslow Homer perhaps, a do-it-yourself, Rube Goldberg setup.

And the ground my feet walk over is soggy, and the grass not green anywhere, covered with the almost-white hue of fiberglass, the myriad stands of waiting grass shivering too and colddead and yet not decayed.

I have walked here often during the years, this the last holdout against propinquity, the seven acres purchased on a windfall from some old widow more than fifteen years ago, before La Duc was ever considered the likeliest spot to plant new colonies, to migrate and landrush to, so that whereas the other lots have long since succumbed to the growth, the explosion of wealth, this land sits isolated in itself and unplanted with cement and structural steel amidst the lavish respites of successful car dealers and brokers and clothing merchants, these surrounding and adjacent and juxtaposed citadels of California redwood and Vermont cedar (though the cedar could just as likely be from Lebanon, like many of the inhabitants, except that this would mean defiling the whole concept of Noah's Ark) impressive and stately though close hugging the ground and going against what this country, its masters, Sullivan and Richardson, established for their time; close gripping the soil as if they were leery about giving it up, needed a strong grasp against mortgage and revenue collectors and bank officials, these the ranch homes of prosperity. The one on the slight slope, the white, antebellum, porticoed house copied after something else, still stands, still occupied by the family of the original windfall recipient, standing against custom now, though still more permanent and stately than all the constructed-in-eight-months wonders.

The ears awaken to the welkin roar of some fastshrieking jet, conceived and constructed, financed and tested in White Cross, at the aircraft plant that, fifteen years before, was nothing, a single building perhaps, building the minutiae, trivia, for larger companies supplying our forces in Korea, today considered by speculators of the stock market, by Washington politicians, not to mention those White Cross Rotarians and other civic-minded boosters interested in putting White Cross on the map at 4-H shows and statewide conventions and New York and Seattle world's fairs, as one of the most superlative evidences of this city's continued prosperity, it, the complex, no longer one corrugated Quonset hut but an elaborate series of modernistic structures with pools and fountains and preternatural lights that at night rival the airport's own runway system.

But the jet is invisible in the pureblue sky; only the diminishing sounds persist, until they too dissolve, leaving the sky temporarily inviolate again.

And I walk the hill in the back, which slopes down through the cherry and peach and apple trees planted many years back and still stunted though bearing fruit in the summer, walking slow and smoking a cigarette now, the afternoon as quiet as an untouched pond except for the birds, which are few in number and numerous in sound. Now I see a Boeing 727 up and beyond me, hanging in flight, moving against the still, blue backdrop, the sun glinting off its silverwhite fuselage, and I can indistinctly see the sidemounted engine and the hump on its tail where the center engine whines, and I know that there are people up there looking down at me looking at them, though they can't see me, and they, I assume, have just been told to fasten their safety belts and douse their cigarettes and that the next sound they hear will be that of the landing gear dropping, talonlike, to grab its, the plane's, prey, the white pavement still ten minutes in the future, I thinking, "What a fine day to get aboard a jet and fly to St. Petersburg, to step off at the Tampa airport, hand the porter my grip, and then ride the Sunshine Skyway into the beach links, Madeira or Redington."

But I walk. By now my slow pace brings me to the bottom of the hill, and I am in the valley, can still remember the first walking we did, the father, the Negro, Charlie Jones, and I, just ten then, the three of us men, discussing the problems of clearing the then-unmolested or -tractored or -leveled or -mowed land. The breeze is cooling now, snow is forecasted for the morrow or following evening, and the cooler air bristles through the light, unlined, woolen buffalo-check jacket, nuzzles into the too-short slacks, nips at the points of the English buckled shoes, purchased in the university town New Haven years back.

I return now, churning up the incline, toward the conifers, the two massive pines, the only ones left after the storms of the past ten years. There was no disease, just the indifferent lightning that lopped off the other ones, so that now these stand larger in perspective and blanched against the whiteness of the house behind them.

My eyes cover the ground, walking, the eyes, with poodlesmall steps, the eyes glancing at chips of elm now, chips that, as I follow, become more, though small, as the eyes move toward the source of the chips, the eradicated, electric-sawed, then axed stub, which is all that remains lest it be the charred ashes and limbs and the burnrusted hoops of barbed wire that somehow got mixed into the pyre, the desiccation of the tree; so I think, "Maybe there was a disease, elm disease, because no one would have ordered that tree canceled, not just from spite anyway. And, too, trees are expensive to replace," remembering the catastrophic freeze that occurred in Florida three weeks before, remembering the palmettos and shrubs and palm trunks that were all wrapped in burlap against the abnormal, below-freezing temperatures, recalling the accounts in the *St. Petersburg Times* about the loss of millions of dollars in fruits, the oranges and grapefruits, the cabbages and potatoes and cane, knowing that no one would deliberately take the life of a tree.

And now I see the junglegym set, the swings and slide, one of the swings lifeless and with its wooden seat rotted on the ground, the chain, not silvery but thick and raspybrown, lying on top of it.

I was young once, when these things were new, when they had just come out of their hardware crates, but I am still young, fifteen years older than their newness, and perhaps I will still be here in White Cross when a new family excitedly moves into this house, this anachronistic mansion, which I will think, when they do, was always somehow too good for us, too good for me at least, and I may see them, some new and zealous family that just moved into the lower bracket of the big time, one of my old school friends perhaps, and I will drive by the house and look at it longingly from the road, and if I am able to stop and gaze without being honked into moving by an endless train or procession or entourage of cars, I may even decide to drive up the road and pull around the back, just for a minute though (I'd hate to have to see the young children playing or have to explain to their mother or father that I was lost, a dissimulation, substitute for the truth that nostalgia caught up with me for a flickering second), and see in place of the swings and slide and dog and horse pens and pines and cherry and apple and peach trees the confiscation of the land, see, by enactment from the city council for the benevolence of all concerned, that the back acres are no longer grass and trees and birds and pens but rather all cement: patios and swimming pools and tennis courts for two or maybe three (if they need to reduce the necessary acreage to half-acres for building) houses that have risen in my absence.

But why should I worry? It wasn't mine to begin with, not even mine to gain through legacy or bequeathment of heiring, since even if primogeniture took its feudal course and I were the one to benefit from it, I would have to refuse it, refuse the whole idea of it, as I do now, not because of the concept of property or contracts or deeds

held in trust but simply because of the inherent denial of it I profess
on the sheer and scanty and intangible grounds that what is worth
cherishing and holding and bequeathing is something that no deed
or chronicle or municipal court hearing can dictate, can pass on, can
adjudicate or, in like apposition, efface, alloy, or invalidate,

so that I claim *nolo contendere*, along with all my other apo-
thegms (the *"Pater Noster, qui es in caelis"*s and the *"caveat emp-
tor"*s and *"Gallia est omnis divisa in cornucopiae tres"*s), never for
a moment pleading cynical or guilty or insane, because what I am driv-
ing at is that indefinable Everlasting Yea, hoping only that when all
the scattered leaves of the universe eddy and dissolve into the next
generations, the next century's whirlpool, my words will remain as
building blocks, will be heeded not because they are better than an-
other's or because they are more prolific or even substantial but
simply because they will say, along with all the other voices past
and present and perpetual, that the things worth the preserving and
the nourishing and the heeding are those which precisely have as
their only legacy and bequeathment (and power to osmose) the inher-
ent example and the erect standard by which living is dignified and
immortal, and this quality is the sheer and undeviable human trait
which postulates to each individual man the necessity, the never,
never, never relenting, refusing, to keep trying to go beyond his own
self-expectations, the inevictable result of which has been and al-
ways will be the betterment and the diminishing of the *can't*, the *will
not*, of natural man.

2/13/66 (05300)

Meditation over Coffee, 2/14/66 †

The eye responds
To the jaundiced hue of winter —

A school, university, presumptuous and well-fed on doles and
corporation donations all matched by the U.S. Health Department —

What's it like to wake early, the mind still somnolent and
stupored with heavy, colorless sleep? I know; I awaken each morn-
ing, clean the old room, dress not in boots and Levi's and work shirt
now, though the dark penetrating winter is with us, but in sport coat,

specially fitted in New York and made in New Haven, the English boots, etc.

I listen to the news, the paradox of the new hit tune that wafts through the staticlaboring car speakers, "The Ballad of the Green Berets," thinking of the week-old news: a squad of perhaps twenty of our most honored and revered soldiers, the wearers of the green berets, were ambushed and snipeannihilated faster than a speeding bullet.

Now I listen to the current news:

a brilliant student from U. of Michigan, under psychiatric care, shot his rabbi through the synagoguesacrosanct head, then reciprocated, to cancel all possibility of guilt or recrimination. How much cheaper than doctor fees — God isn't dead, but one of his disciples is martyred.

2/14/66 — [1] (05171)

[Monday morning, with Styrofoam snow . . .]

Monday morning, with Styrofoam snow on the ledge outside this apartment's breakfast room.

I sit here, blearytired, eyes, lids heavy and swollen from dream-fraught sleep. There is uneasiness awake in my stomach, and flutters and nervous tremors shiver through me.

I am afraid the old thing is returning, will fling me through the gates of myself, where no one should tread.

I, I, I, again —

My build is thin, like the attitude, sharp but craving nutrition. I must run again, not from myself but into solitude's respite.

The two stories are formed in my mind, cry out for life. I must give birth to Peaches and Les Taussig.

The old conflict persists: how to get the schoolwork accomplished and yet persist in my own storytelling. I, like Conrad, believe in the efficacy of the "true lie," the illusions devoid even of reason, which alone give man ideals (not ideas) to cling to — old Ibsen's *Wild Duck* was right there, too.

That which gives dignity to man, the noble animal, is the awareness of the conscious illusion, the voluntary deceiving of self for a purpose of enduring, of giving meaning and engaged purpose to his quick span, the heightening of consciousness to breach the impalpable, to gap the stultifying bunch of unpatterned existence —

No philosophy, please.
Don't worry. No professor ever taught me to think in dialectics.

2/21/66 (05302)

Meditation over Coffee, 2/28/66

Monday morning, early, a slow, grey day, and the mind is slow as unmelting butter; even the hand moves unresponsively and dilatorily across the page now.

Something will have to break within the next year and a half, and I feel the course of my productive life will be set rolling on its way.

Perhaps I'll find myself wearing khaki trousers and a twig-strewn helmet, shouldering not the good shotgun but a recoilless M-14 or perhaps squatting behind the fearful rat-rat-rat of some jungle-tripoded, fast-exploding machine gun.

It's just possible that I'll never see a training camp stateside or the snake-crawling terrains of some squalid jungle, will sit before a greenchalky blackboard, exonerating old men for disseminating war, eulogizing the world's great poets and writers, describing to an expectant, anxious freshman English class the merits of productive creativity.

So I sit here, in the lunchroom at the University of White Cross, mind blank and abstracted, thinking not really (at least not with all my heart) about myself, my future, the career, because I am confident it, the work, the think-writing, will come in its own due process, rather pondering slow and glibly Truman Capote's comments regarding the motivation for *In Cold Blood*, his preoccupation with the lives of others, his committed and total absorption in the events of other people —

I'm not interested in contemplating my navel. That's succinct enough, I think.

This leads to the role of the writer, the whole problem of invention and manipulation of character and fact, the purpose of bringing a reader in contact with, of almost forcing him out of, himself in an engagement with the author's creations.

So I sit here, strong in body except for the mind's, the will's, one chief lapse, the continued smoking; dressed in grey-ruled, striped dress shirt and busy, white-grey, woven sport coat, no tie, collar opened one button, the high socks and buckledrawn shoes;

consuming two cookies and coffee for breakfast on this eight o'clock morning, when the rain comes down in loud gasps, a mirage-fuzzy morning cast lugubrious and lonely, a pathetic fallacy of its own state of nature, the air moist and saturated outside and behind the radiator-steaming windows of the cafeteria.

I have passed through the unproductive, country-contemplating hours of Sunday into the breach of Monday's cannon, I the projectile, locked in place, now, inside this week's champer, ready to fly across another six-day trajectory, looking into Gide and Yeats.

But somewhere indistinct, I hear a slow-rolling roar, like a cresting flood, moiling, turbulent, suspended, hovering, slowly overtaking my mind's levees,
saying to me, "Get out; quit it all now,"
but I know that it takes guts to ride it out, the flood, to await its subsiding, to recover lost, emerged, stagnate ground:

My mind is a seed,
greyslow and persistent.
Weeds choke,
and token planting resists
winter thaws.
I am a seed,
needing my own care
and a portion of the wind
that blows wild as stampeding herds.
My words scatter:
dandelion burrs in motion.
I am the simple face
that laces highways,
loitering impatiently in bus stations
with advertisements of myself.

2/28/66 (05303)

[Already the first of March, . . .]

Already the first of March, and the sky is cold blue, hazed with faint shimmers of striated cloudstrings, few and scattered apart, and the blue isn't sharp and cut by foreign sounds of field-approaching jetliners. Up and off at ten o'clock high, a single jet cuts the sky in half before its silent speed, making fake vapour-trail clouds after its quick-diminishing heat.

I sit here on the cold, dank, greywhite cement stairs that climb down from the back entrance of the university's art museum. I look at the penpoint as it curls out mazy, red scrawl over the paper, hunched over, feeling the sturdy pressure of cold cement biting into my seat, the crisp, lunchtime coolness working slowly and unseen over my fingers.

Straight out and posted like some mammoth, reconstructed French Hôtel de Ville, I see the administration building, and as I listen, the faint, intermittent uproar of pneumatic drills and pump engines touches silence. Soon, the birds' cries will be muffled, and the motionless setting dotted with the class-retreating figures pouring out, issuing forth toward lunch cafeterias or parked cars or other classrooms.

I will go too, not annoyed or confounded but anxious to record new things. Now a Phantom jet whines loud over my head, and I watch it bank into tree branches that block sight. Still I hear its invisibility, it, too, having dissolved into the immediate sounds of crunching sidewalk pebbles and the persistent scrape-scrape-scrape, staccato shuffling up these stairs.

I will never die as long as my desire to record my movements follows me. This is my awareness, that alone which makes awakening worth the doing every morning. Else, why just sleep for a limited span of hours?

The cool breeze roughens my lips, shuffles the head of my writing paper, and the toes, through the bramble-gouged boots, go cold. The day is too perfect for itself. I must take a part of it with me.

The cold, bright air tears slowly through my work shirt, and the small breasts shrivel, knot behind the shirt. I am stained, realizing warmth is a state of being.

3/1/66 (05304)

Repulsion

She lies there,
Leaking tears that speak
Liquidly as drunken soliloquies,
Repentant and wrong as winter
When buds still cling to bees.

I am the golden apple,
The silver blossom that falls,
Still clawing the writhing,
*

Soft-spilling belly,
Sinking under twenty centuries of sin.

She sits nude,
A bohemian Eve,
Weightless on bony haunches,
Detesting life that lies
Comfortably between lewd legs.

I, a vengeful Adam,
Bolt from her bedroom,
Half clothed and dank,
Wanting to leave forever,
Knowing severance is impossible.

3/4?/66 — [1] (04038)

[A terminal switcher lurches,]

A terminal switcher lurches,
connects itself,
serpentine,
to the outbound freight.
There is no weighty matter,
nothing that can't wait,
no tumid mail pouch, gum machine,
coffee and cashew vendor
to stall the express.
I flee from a shadowy misconception,
flying beside the Devil on glycerine wings.
Somewhere, I took the wrong direction,
was sidetracked.
A dog whines; now the diesel roars,
and I am carried along
like unmarked baggage into night.

3/4?/66 — [2] (05154)

[Already it is going on two . . .]

Already it is going on two in the morning. A bitter-cold insomnia
flows through the filters of my mind, and I am kept awake by my own

refusal to fall asleep. It was a long evening and a still-longer after-
noon: the weights and calisthenics, the poetry, which always needs
touching and modification, the long-awaited arrival of my Nashville
friends, the Rivens.

And there was something strained, as though sensibilities were
pistons rubbing hot, unspoken friction against the polished sides of
their chambers, I mean, the two relationships, resting side by side
throughout the evening, the one couple married and carrying with
them all the inherent overtones of married, conjugal life, the other,
myself and my Jan, not married and yet somehow as close, if not
more strongly united, though the ties which bind us are different.

And after parting, we returned to the apartment, and she, tired and
thirsty for sleep, lay in bed, the small, lithe, bony figure of a girl, who
spoke through deliriums of dubiety and lonely fear, fearing what to
say to her roommate, the problems extending far beyond the imme-
diate, and I just listening, sitting on the bed under whose covers she
lay, listening to her expressions of fear and doubt as she explained
that she has never fit into the school community, that she has no
friends that are close among the hundreds of acquaintances, she re-
membering the words to a song: ". . . somewhere. There's a place for
us, A time and place for us."

And so I sat listening, too knowing to reply, hearing the anxious,
blearytired expressions of this girl I love so much.

Now I am home, and I walk the short distance from the parked car
through the cold channels of night, turn the key in the back door,
thinking about the first night we dated, when we returned home from
the Mainlander, inebriated, and it was a warm night, the two of us en-
tering into the living room, alone and silent and reaching out to each
other, needing each other's assurances.

Walking through the kitchen into the hollowechoing hall, where
no carpet lies, no wallpaper covers the bare, cold plaster walls, and
upon whose nineteen stairs no carpet is fastened, hearing my shuffling
feet climbing slow and trudging, carrying my weary weight up the
steps to the landing.

The house is all quietude, and in distant recesses behind half-shut
doors, I can hear the muffled breathing, the father's snoring suspira-
tions, and the hand reaches into the room at the head of the stairs,
fumbling familiarly over books lying flat on the bookshelves for
the light switch. Darkness fuses into light, and the room fills, as if
with rushing water, into soft yellowwhites. On the bed where I would
sleep is the ten-year-old boy, breathing his childish weight hard and
without the heat of covers, they, the covers and blankets, strewn
across the floor beneath. In the other, a friend, and I cower, slink

back, flip the switch again, until all is dark once more.

Again, my shuffling footsteps echo down the corridor, until I'm at the back of the house, thinking all the while how they didn't expect me home, hadn't planned for me to fill the bed I have filled since nine years of age.

So I sit in this room, the child's room, with his comic books filling the shelves, the Tom Swift and Hardy Boys series, the myriad articles of clothing strewn over the floor and atop the dressers that line the walls, low as Wright's furniture. And I don't fit back here. I shiver, feeling the tiny breasts shrivel under the coldness of the room, hearing, listening, dreaming of the winds that rattle the oak and maple outside the window, and I know that this is where I will sleep tonight.

But she wanted me to stay, to remain with her at the apartment, to comfort her in her fears; I can still hear her telling me in her uncertainty that she didn't fit, that she couldn't live in the small, country-white farmhouse, with the twenty-five acres for horses and chickens and dogs that roam it, the acreage. I can still see that frown that digs deeper than the furrows that etch the forehead, above the nose, can still hear myself saying, "I'm not sure that is what I really want either, not sure it isn't an illusion, a romantic conception of the way things might be if one were fortunate enough to have everything go one's way."

I can hear the stillness,
The hollow ticktocks
Falling in repetitious schemes.
The refrigerator whirs,
Stirring the air around my ears,
And I can see her there,
Sleeping like fallen leaves.

I sit on the hollowness of bones
In the shadow-splayed kitchen;
An orange sink light
Mocks my silence.
I sit, keeping the vigil,
The ritual of midnight hours.

She stirs, an unborn angel,
Digging fingers into warmth
Where pillow touches the brass posts.
I am the ghost that slinks
Into sullen one o'clocks,
Sinking into fits of despair.

We have grown like weeds
Filling the spaces between nature
And nighttime. My words are rhymes
That lack subtle metaphor.
Our veins leak thick blood,
And I respond with fetid cries:
"Let me know you,
Until nothing matters save
Spontaneity of soaring free."
There is nothing in that though, I know,
And a black angel lights on the lids,
Dimming my vision.
I feel the curse's weight
Bending the neck to the cave's floor.
I am a craven possessor,
Fallen and illegitimate, drowning
In primal tears that wash soil
From sleepdrossed eyes.

3/5/66 — [1] (Prose), [2] (Poem) (05305)

Curse

> . . . *him there they found*
> *Squat like a Toad, close at the ear of* Eve;
> *Assaying by his Devilish art to reach*
> *The Organs of her Fancy, . . .*
> — John Milton, *Paradise Lost*

I sit on bony haunches,
Smoking a perpetual cigarette
In the shadow-splayed kitchen.
An orange sink light
Mocks my busy silence,
And I await something,
Keeping impatient vigils —
The ritual of midnight hours.

Stillness follows me;
Hollow ticktocks
Fall through blank gravities,
And the refrigerator's whir
*

Stirs air around my ears.
Now I see her there,
A wandering gypsy, asleep.

She rolls through trances of heat,
A stillborn angel
Whose fingers read
Brass bedposts' ancient braille.
I'm the slinking ghost
Who whispers lascivious thoughts
In her dreaming ears.

Though we've grown like weeds
Filling spaces between nature
And nighttime,
A voice still cries,
"Let me know warm insides,
Where nothing dies and wetness
Grows gardens in the eyes."

There's nothing in that though,
I know,
And a black angel lights on the lids,
Dimming my vision.
I feel the curse's weight
Bending my neck to the cave's floor,
Where nothing grows
Save blind, black frogs
And darkness behind the eyes.

3/5/66 — [2] (04037)

Seminar Instructor

He sits, speaking slowly from memory too long slipped away, ad-
dressing a seminar class of ten students, deliberating, slow to choose
his words, not for approbation but from sheer forgetting,

sitting at the end of the T-shaped tables, before the greenwhite
blackboard, muttering desultorily to the effect that social/economic
laws have one ideal and platonic set of laws.

I watch, mind wandering through his heapscattered words and
disorganized thoughts, hearing the aphorism "Let your conscience be
your guide" issue from his lips.

He is an old man, taught in the old schools, which stressed polemics and pedagogy rather than critical approach, and I see his pink-wizened hands, the brown splotches of age dotting the hairless tops, the one fidgeting unconsciously with a paper clip.

The voice is sibilant and whispering, tinged with an almost Emersonian-Eastern accent; it is slow and anachronistic in the Midwestern university milieu.

I see gold glowing when he opens his mouth, gold gleaming from the round metal rims that he wears.

And the coat hangs slovenly, loosely draped over the square, large, too-old shoulders, its weave seemingly done by a seismograph registering the similar tastes of ten years prior; unbuttoned, it reveals the tumid paunch that billows out worn grey slacks.

A red tie, drawn too long, printed with dark, off-hewn snowflake patterns, hanging slipshod, a ridiculous napkin; it covers the squared-off shirt, not formalwhite but blue-ruled like graph paper.

His legs are crossed, and I see the pink-white leg, hairless, protruding where the cuff is pinched up, grey socks against shiny, brown, informal shoes.

3/8/66 (05306)

[The mind spans interstices . . .]

The mind spans interstices of time and agglomerates events into one continuous suffusion of thought, so that I sit here, buried within the urn-sealed womb of the university library, a relic of no decipherable value, contemplating flux and stasis. I am no academician, no culture-monger, nor am I an intellectual. Rather, the morning outside is most significant to me now. I can see the outside from within this cubicle, can hear the sounds of the warmdank, early-March morning despite the telephone-booth-like insulation that fronts me and encloses my presence on three sides. I may be the small, resilient handball knocking against three walls, propelled and randomly ricocheting with heedless abandon. I have a desire to record, remembering the conversation with one of the boys who canoed with me in Salem last spring. We spoke slow and precisely yesterday in the coffee lounge, and I listened to him tell of his experiences in New York since the end of last summer. I registered his aspect as he spoke, admiring the Frye chukka boots he wore, listening to him describe the process of removing the original polish with carbon tetrachloride in order to apply his own waxy mixture of deep black-browns. I

knew this boy, my age perhaps, was genuine, that he spoke from be-
hind the eyes, without dissimulation, without regard to pretense. And
I sat sipping coffee, listening to his relations, remembering, now, how
he mentioned that after six months, he felt he had met all the varia-
tions of characters that float gratuitously from group to fetid group,
saying finally, "I like White Cross because it's a good place to re-
turn to." And I sat knowingly, pondering all the words I have spent
describing White Cross, contemplating the myriad hundreds of para-
graphs I will expend before I am done with White Cross.

And we spoke, I telling him that "I am a pack rat, if you know what
that means. I have an obsession, in short, a compulsion, perhaps, that
forces me to guard, to hold onto, everything that I have written or done,
letters and fliers, etc., I have saved over the years."

He spoke, "I agree that experience is vital, the branching out, dis-
covering, that is a person's obligation to himself." He continued, and
I was recording his features, the genuine aspect of this person, the
ruddy face, with the upper lip mustached in lusterbrown whiskers, the
eyes, small and lambent, aglow with intrepid lucidity, the wrinkleless
forehead, decked above with longcurly strands of thick-meshed hair,
a frame tight and solid, sitting there across from me, and then I could
hear him again, not thinking about myself, rather listening intently for
some sign of correspondence,

saying to him, "You should try to write down your experiences,
record them into memory."

"But I figure I'll never forget what I have said and lived and felt. I
never do," he said softly, confident, not insistent because that was not
his manner, sitting there, mincing the old, blackgouged pipe in his
hand.

"But time has a way of silently and unobtrusively evaporating the
things of the mind," I said, knowing that he liked to hear me speak
that way.

Replying indirectly, he asserted, "Let me give you an example.
Some people used to consider me somewhat of an authority on Ber-
dyaev and Kierkegaard when I was studying philosophy here. And I
may have been. I read everything. But now I doubt I could tell you
what those men had to say. Not specifically at least."

"But that's the point," I interjected, knowing he had not yet ex-
hausted his argument.

"No, not really, because I myself know that though I have forgot-
ten postulates and theories, the specifics, the what have you, I have
absorbed these men. I am, in part, the result of these thinkers. I am, at
present, the accumulation of their learning as well as that of others
too, the people in New York, the friends here, you too, even," he said,

the small eyes parting the vacuum between us.

"Well, I see what you are saying, and I agree. But for me, the memory is a different thing. I have a great knack for registering things immediate, but with time, everything blurs into the same thing, and what remains is the bare outline of what I would like to recall in detail. So I write to preserve, to record data, if you like."

"But you see, I am now," he said, pointing his finger unconsciously toward his stomach, "what I have been. I am the be- and end-all at any particular point in the future."

"OK," I said, "but I have a desire to know what I am at every point in the past. For some strange reason, just knowing the present me ain't enough." I was conscious of slipping into the vernacular so popular with university instructors, aware that this usage, the "ain't"s and "don't"s, was an outward sign, manifestation, of an anomalous kind of status which bespoke my occupation — a hazard one risks after too much study of proper rhetoric and critical exegesis. "What, in fact, I think I want is to know not just that I am living now but that I have lived before and that I have absorbed, accreted, changed. It's this change that interests me most."

He didn't have to assert that he understood. The acquiescence was implied.

"I'm going to Sierra Leone with the Peace Corps, as you know. I will write letters home to my friends, the parents. This is what you mean, and I understand. It will just happen."

"That's the way it is with me. I have this compulsion to record, not to let anything pass. And it's not because maybe, like Henry James, I will want somebody in the future to be able to look at these pieces, these reminiscences, and say, 'He lived once,' but simply because I have to do it, hoard the past. And I doubt I'll ever go back and read these things."

So we spoke quietly among the din of students and instructors and transients that filled the large, high-ceilinged room, the converted library, drinking coffee, reliving the trip we took in the Ozarks the past spring, the tremendous rainstorm that fell over our Saturday night and Sunday morning camp, and I knew then that there was importance in being able to recall the past, the pervasive lingering that trails a person, that sinks deeper and lower into the mind's core as he moves forward.

And now I sit behind the typewriter, beneath the yellowslow fluorescent fixtures that speak through this cubicle, this lounge tucked back into the redyellow-bricked walls of this library. I light a cigarette, think of coffee I will take when I am done with this, and now my thoughts turn back into the folds of last evening, when I sat with her at her mother's house, smoking then, and sipping the strange tea of India.

"Did you put anything in this stuff?" I said suspiciously, facetiously.

"It will make you dream," she said softly and distantly, sitting in front of me, deep into the high-backed chair. I looked at her, the face gone gaunt, attenuated with emphasis by the toolong blackbrown hair, which fell like curtains behind her.

I was speaking, and realizing that I had said too much too quickly, I asked her, told her, smiling, that it was her turn to talk.

"But I learn more listening," she answered, the eyes distant, as though hidden into a pillow, the words sententious, consciously succinct. But I knew that she didn't always listen, that, in fact, she was what she would later say was "loneliness" and that her silence was absorption not in me but in some indefinable abstract, the compounded result of which had left her out of time and distant. The eyes were no longer living but far away, not lambent and alive; the face sallow where it had been full of color in youth. Yet her body was tight and compact in the white jeans that clung wrinkleless to her thighs and legs and waist.

"I wanted to make myself pretty for you tonight, but I have been in bed sick for five days, and it would have been bad to get my hair wet so soon."

I was silent, watching her slouched into the cushioned chair, the legs up and bent, resting precariously on the edge of a chair she had pulled up in front of her.

And the cats pranced and dashed through the room, scuttering with sliding clicks of paws across the wooden, uncarpeted floor of the den.

"No, Sutty," she admonished, the voice sibilant and low, authoritative in an easy way. The cat continued to scratch at the edge of the chair's upholstery. "No, Sutty. Now sit. Sit! Watch her," she said to me out of her reverie, not seeing me, her eyes rapt, bent down at the large, half-breed, yellow- and blackstreaked cat.

The cat crouched down and then raised up its front paws like a trained poodle or Boston terrier, as if to beg food. Then her fingers snapped, and the cat scampered away, the other following it out and down the basement stairs.

There was silence in the room, no refrigerator noise, no furnace shutting in and out, all lighted silence, in which I drank from the nimble china the tea that made one dream. Only, my mind was alert, the ears picking up the distant, basemented scratchings of the cats below, tearing at paper.

"They're clean animals," I said clinically, just to break the silence. No response, and I was reminded of the time when her silence, her internal brooding, would have made me uneasy, when I would have insisted on doing something besides sitting there, where I knew she always sat. Only, now I knew that I would not have to endure her recriminations, her brooding lapses of silence, longer than this evening, that it would not have to intrude, to trouble me after tonight. And then she spoke out of her lapse, slow and enigmatically; only, I was looking at a book that lay open on the glass table beside my left arm:

"Nobody takes time to listen to silence."

The book was by Tagore, an Indian writer I was not familiar with. She saw me, and for the first time, her eyes lighted, though the effect was not lasting.

"The man was so beautiful. He said everything I feel."

I was looking at the picture of the bearded prophet on the cover. "My God, look at those eyes. They could eat you, consume you without moving."

But she was silent, and I listened to the room fill with her silence. Then I got up, moved her legs easily from the chair's edge, and sat down in front of her, looking into her face, the gaunt, sallow expression filled with sadness, and I felt no pity.

As though she knew what I was going to say, anticipating my thoughts, she said that she didn't want to think about that time, the period when the two of us were trying to make something between two people. "It's no good to be so introspective," she said finally, not really able to deny a portal into that time.

I was thinking back, remembering the corrosive period when I was sick inside, when it was impossible to understand how fraught with tensions and insoluble, irremediable hurt she was.

"I have changed since then," I heard my lips speaking. "I think since I saw you last, maybe a year ago or more, that I have begun to move away from myself, that other people have become more prominent," knowing as I spoke that the trouble then lay only partly in my own problems, that already she had suffered from her own agonizing lack of responsibilities. But I had no ax to grind now, and it was better that I let her feel at ease with her own troubled conscience. She knew too well what I knew about her: that she was unwilling to look at it, herself, through me anymore.

I leaned into her, looking into her face, and she was holding my left hand, her thumb moving gently along the lifted veins, gazing and lost in nothought: "Your hands are very feminine, very beautiful."

I was self-conscious, not sure what she meant to convey, and it didn't matter anyway. There was no pity for her from my eyes, just stolidity and unspeaking.

"I think we all have to learn, and I know that all that stuff then was a part of my growing up. I'm still growing, but I think I've changed a lot since then."

"You did teach me much, though."

"What could I have taught you?"

"You showed me how to just be outside or within and look and listen and note the small things that occur before our unresponding eyes and ears and nose. Still, there are times when I go outside and don't see or hear a thing."

Now she was speaking, again not directly to me, but talking now, the lips moving as if unconnected from the thoughts, just functioning to express:

"This has happened to me for a long time. I drive into the country, sit by a brook or on the cliffs that overlook the Missouri, and nothing happens. I have tried and tried but . . ." she paused, desultorily turning from one thought to the next without transition. "I can't love anyone anymore," she laughed, the smiling forced, "and you know me and sex."

I knew her too well to respond. What was there to say?

"I'm done with all that. I know, now, that what I want, need to be happy, is children."

"What if you get them and still you are like this?" I asked too quick and sharp. There was no reply. Then, to justify what she knew I knew, she said:

"But I have loved everyone I ever slept with. All except one young boy."

I was playing now, trying to make her lighthearted: "And that one?" I said. "You just wanted to be the first one to show him the ropes, didn't you? Took advantage of him, didn't you?"

She laughed, feigning embarrassment, but then, I knew she was tired. She would show me her new paintings, as she did for everyone who called on her now, would want to hear the praises she knew were undeserved since the work was slipshod and without technique. And I walked with her, followed her into the bedroom, the two cats following, crisscrossing through our legs. The room was small; unmade bed with sheets thrown back and dingy. Paintings and pen-and-ink sketches were strewn about haphazard, lining the dresser and highboy, atop the television, and I looked as she described to me the work, which was child's work, amateurish, done out of boredom rather than inspiration.

And then the car trip back home, through the hissing rain, along the once familiar curves and chuckrutty streets that traverse the suburban district beyond the outskirts of White Cross, until the car plunged down the access onto the main highway, heading south for three miles.

So I had seen her again, after a year's absence, and as I lay in bed smoking, the head too filled with thoughts, I could hear her saying not with fright but directly into my presence: "I am lonely, and I need a companion." I could see her sitting, staring at me, wanting me to say what even she knew I could not say since there was nothing there anymore, not even pity. Then she broke the lapse, "I know I'll be lonely until I have children."

I lay in bed smoking, dragging pensively and slow, thinking, "I just know she won't ever find it, the happiness, the cessation of loneliness, because she'll never teach herself to make anything out of the silences."

* * *

I awaken early, this morning, wanting to penetrate the outside behind the house, the thoughts of the past evening not having filtered into forgetting but having fallen into perspective. I dress not in the Wellingtons, the jeans and slovenly work shirt and rawhide jacket but with a smart cross-stitched sports jacket over an open-collared, white dress shirt; the slacks pressed and neat, just back from the cleaners and still, when I pull them from the hanger, with the white identification tags safety-pinned to the inside fly; English buckle shoes, dress too. I am a different me from the me of a month ago, from the year-ago person I was reminded of last night, and I don't regret it, have no reason to, because I am moving forward again, plunging into the work that I know must be accomplished, the studies, if I am ever to fulfill my goal, the creating, writing about that which is genuine and real enough at any time for all time and universal in application for me and an audience; to make with the materials at hand, with the utmost care in technique and close attention paid to sincerity.

So I arise early, not caring what time is late the night before, and this morning I walk out behind the house, through the kitchen's back door, into the warmwet, greying morning, and the seven-thirty birds whistle and chirp and take the handstrewn crumbs that I throw before me onto the patio bricks and sprinkle along the retaining brick wall. I can see the whitebrown turf below my shoes, not hard nor moist with dew this morning and yet not giving under my slack weight. The mimosa tree, which fills out in spring with pinkwhite blooms and frondgreen leaves, is empty now, all space except for the wizened, wintered trunk and limbs, and I stay beside it, inspecting the limbs that, like scarred battle figures out of some Civil War daguerreotype, are broken and held together by wire. I can look straight through one of the larger limbs, which is rent in two like a river or stream forking for a short distance to pass a small island in the middle of the course. The empty, barren limbs are strung and held together by thick, silvery guy wires, whose construction resembles the rigging for a sailboat's mainmast or a circus's tightrope setup.

The morning is covered with fastfuzzy, greywhite clouds, and I know the sun and blue is above and that it won't have time during the day to eat away the thick layers. Yet it will be warm as whiskey today, sultry and with humidity not offensive and reminiscent of some rich garden or Climatron or greenhouse. In the distance, I see the horse standing upright over the feedbox, and I walk slowly toward him. Behind the animal, a station wagon honks twice, then pulls away, throwing noisy gravel specks behind it. I know some children are going off to school.

As I near the Shetland, the white German shepherd barks jealously, the dog watching my movements with avid spectator's eyes behind the Cyclone-fenced confines.

Even the noise of the dog barking and yelping for its freedom and the quiet sounds of the horse munching corn and hay scraps from the box are peaceful and unobtrusive back of the house. It is still too early to feel in the ears the vibrations of highway traffic heading downtown or across town, and I hear silence that is friendly and wet. I light a cigarette, standing against the chicken-wire fencing around the Shetland's pen, and through the white vapours, I watch the horse nuzzling his wrinkled nose into the feed, looking at the one ear cocking, twitching, the mouth as if perpetually smiling, the tail flagging automatically, and I know this nervous horse is calm in my familiar presence.

From nowhere, the raucous cacophony of a helicopter's churning breaks the stillness, drowns the birds' calls, and it passes off to the right, overhead. The animal shies, knocks its head against the side of the feedbox, back-pedals a few yards, and stands alert until the noise diminishes. Still I stand smoking, the neck craned upward, until I turn my back to the animal.

Now I head toward the dog's pen, watch his excited motions prancing the close interior of the fence, back and then toward me, not feline, less graceful, and I can feel the energy stirring in his short, powerful legs, the tail wagging with friendly anticipation. But I can't let him out this morning, because he will run longer than I have time to wait on his frivolity, his antics.

Returning, walking slow and easy, the limbs still stiff with sleep, I pass the wall behind the garage, musing on the spilled, strewn garbage, the rifled cans turned asunder by late-night dogs in search of alms.

The books are already in the car, and I let it run, warming up, channeling white exhaust toward the blacktarred pavement. I have walked in the silence of my own morning thoughts again for the first time in months, and there is something growing, being born inside me. I am alive in the present tense of being and happy that I can smile this morning.

3/9/66 — [1] (05307)

Meditation over Coffee, 3/9/66

Reading Lawrence's *Women in Love* — his themes tire us now; though "electric" then, to use his favorite word, the ideas are fetid, and I am reminded of Faulkner's insistence that what makes lasting literature is not fascination/preoccupation with the glands but with the untiring, ancient dilemmas of the heart.

To be spontaneous is fine, to act almost gratuitously, but without flaunting societal demands. Ain't possible to just cancel out two thousand years of normative civilizing to give the mind free run, as Birkin suggests. If you do, you soon find yourself burdened by too much freedom.

I prefer Yeats' quasi-solution, expressed in the early play *The Shadowy Waters*, in which the imagination is elevated to the supreme earthly position but God's will must be accommodated and untampered with. To create within the narrow strictures of society is the source of lasting mortality, to transcend commonality of the unimaginative masses by immersing oneself with the Conradian element. Transcendence is only possible for the person who molds with the materials at hand. Any expression that precludes the plight of the unimaginative is aiming toward naught, since the marrow of creation lies in the tension that is engendered when the artist confronts the hurts and grief and disappointments and the failures of the mass of society to extend itself beyond its own hidebound subjectivities. It is the artist's task to give these failures/short circuits breath and credibility.

Spontaneity is a state of mind open to all who perceive its possibilities for their individual conditions, no matter how liberated or shackled/fettered.

* * *

Of late, when the mind wants to posit poetic configurations, the sensibilities refrain, constrain the pen's point, which stalls at the head of its ruled page, drowning in its (the pen's) own pool of heavy ink. I can't think poetry, though the prosepoetics flow ceaselessly.

Let me create new images, new vignettes that can heighten the actual events. It's the situation evoked in poetry and the tension created that give temporary permanence. I write from myself but not essentially, not singularly for myself.

3/9/66 — [2] (05308)

[Congregating downstairs, . . .] †

Congregating downstairs, myriad Christs and
bearded Dylan fans —
    all variations of boots, coiffures.

    The stage: a simple stool; two mikes,
one high for the mouth, one guitar-low;
    amplifiers mouthing ubiquitous cacophony,
myriad, muffled;
    the solitary stool, flanked by electric
and grand pianos;
        trap set in center,
    waiting. Anticipation before he comes on
stage — a house full, loquacious, buzzing
in moderation,
    each individual unoriginal in bizarre duds.

3/11/66 (05153)

[Sunday,]

        Sunday,
    Grey as unlaundered lingerie,
    And all are away at church.
    I am the mouse that preys
    In their holy absence,
    *

Playing poker with myself,
Bluffing every hand that falls
To the table uncalled.

Inconstancy gnaws me, and I sulk,
Washing wake-up pills behind
Morning juice.

I sit here, behind the typewriter, thinking of all that has transpired, remembering the words "ubiquitous," "horrendous," "mesmeric," the complex anagrams her mind makes with the dross of academia, the accolades or calumniations one can engender remembering the performance at the auditorium in White Cross, the Bob Dylan concert Friday night.

Exeunt Dylan

They are all gone from the stage,
The humans in godly stance.
Workmen and flunkies prance
Behind the diminishing rush
Of schoolgirls and college grads
Shoving to exit en masse.
I stand where I sat, musing
In the wake of tired movement.
Already the performers have left,
Hiding in basement bomb shelters,
Waiting for the outside crowd to scatter.
The trap set, electric pianos,
And guitars hover as before,
Only lifeless now and inert.
And they wait, the tools with strings
Like puppets, waiting packaging,
The scuttle and dross of shipment.
And somewhere, another group awaits
The promised arrival, the promotional
Advent of the newer gods.

I let down my guard, and already cigarette smoke bombards my lungs. I can do nothing to avert the inevitable dispelling of the dreams, the careless spilling over of hopes that languish in nighttime gutters that freeze icy in the coldness of March. I am a tame Houdini, caught in my own waterfilled tank, without hands, manacled mind locked too tightly for the nightly escape.

3/13/66 — [1] (05152)

Night Watchman

I let down the guard;
Cigarette smoke
Bombards my lungs.
I can do nothing to avert
The inevitable dispelling of dreams
They leave me to sweep away.

I am a speck of nighttime,
Carrying an everlasting sconce
Like some maddened Macbeth.
I travel feckless and bored
Down tenement corridors
Where no pilgrims stir.

I am no gallant chevalier
But Arthur,
The night watchman,
Dangling a ring of keys
That hold no secrets
Along their nubby spines.

I protect all but myself
From this screaming silence.

3/13–14/66 — [2] on 3/13 and [2] on 3/14 (04006)

[Monday morning, and the sky leaks . . .]

Monday morning, and the sky leaks grey blood. I have wounded its cloudsoft belly with silent cries of despair. I sit in the university cafeteria, alone, drinking coffee, and my eyes register the immediacy of red ink scriptscrawled against yellow paper. The wrist is numb already from holding the pen, from setting this chickenclawed print on paper, and I think how she knew or remembered what I remarked once in passing: "He writes so small because Faulkner did."

And I suppose I do, or have, but now, when I am nearing my twenty-fifth year, it is difficult for me to write at all. I depend on the typewriter's simple mechanics to do the dirty work.

Already it is mid-March. The airs are reaching tropical levels of saturation and warmth, and I sit here musing, trying to take stock in an empty warehouse of the mind.

My friend, an elderly country lady, cashier of the lunchroom, talks with me this morning, wishes me good luck on my horoscope. I return the superstition.

But going on twenty-five, I wonder what there is to show at this point. And five years hence, at that proverbial, Wordsworthian midpoint, what will there be to proclaim my name?

The Heron is done now, finished in Redington, end of January, and it remains for me to revise it and try to find a buyer. The poetry is advancing; this is the best form/outlet, the most satisfying personally, but harder to sell, perhaps.

And where is my salesmanship, that business instinct so pervasive and keen in my father? I must learn to push the work through from the finishing to the publication.

Damn it anyway! I want to teach myself to write. Screw the university that has rejected me from teaching sloppy freshman English. Someday they may just regret this stolidity and artificial haughtiness, their superiority/condescending, engendered on false standards of excellence.

But I will push ahead and try never, never, not ever for a minute to sit still, lest it be sitting with the mind in high gear and the fingers dazzling typewriter keys.

I will give my name, its individual life, an heir/legacy/bequeathment: the work, the words that will, like overtones, linger long after the mind's pedal has sprung back to rest.

3/14/66 — [1] (05315)

Fancy #3

I'm a poet,
but I don't know it.
My feet don't show it,
*

but my nose does;
it's a long smeller.

3/15/66 — [1] (05180)

Tetley's Tit-Mice

For the Washington University Fashion Design Class of '67

I

Ted Tetley's
Twin, tiny tit-mice
Tiptoe
Tippity tat,
Tiddly-toe
Over Teresa Tarkington's
Three Tanganyikan
Tuber turtles
To tickle their testicles,
Then trip,
Toppling tiltwise
Too soon
To terminate
Their turtle-tryst.

Trillions of Tina the Tamer's
Titsi flies
(They despise
Intrepid tit-mice)
Tantalize Tetley's rodents' eyes
With tortured touchés
From their tapered tails.
Tetley's twins
Turn on a triangle
Toward the tea tanks
To try their tricks
On Tina's titsi flies,
Tasting insects.
Ten at a time
Till Tina the Tamer
Trumpets retreat
To her thinning troops.

II

Tonight, at 10:10,
Ted Tetley,
The tentative toastmaster
At Tetley Tea's
Triennial Testimonial,
Told attending technicians:
"Take heed!
There's a need
To tighten touchy things.
The trouble with tea
Today
Is tough to determine.
The way I see it,
Turtles from Tanganyika
In Tarkington's Imports
Next door
Take the titsis,
As hogs the tapeworm,
Through the seas,
To shores of Bimini.
Then untrained stevedores
Tank the turtles,
Ship them, via tramp steamer,
To Trenton and Tampa
Without testing for titsi
Infection;
Then, by train,
They travel
To Tarkington's factories.

"Once there,
Tit-mice,
Who try to eat by night,
Tickle turtle testicles.
Unintentionally,
Tarkington's tuber turtles
Take the titsis' tapered stings.

"Then the tit-mice
Enter through our tiles,
Taste the tea strings
That tie to our tea bags,
*

And the upshot,
As I see it,
Is trypanosome sleeping
Disease."

III

"Gentlemen, take heed!
There's a terrific need
To eradicate these creatures
That tiptoe by night.
Take away this thought
Tonight:
When the mice are away,
The titsis that bite
Will vanish from sight,
And the tea we distribute
Will again be free
From trypanosome toxication."

3/15 — [2] & 5/6/66 — [2] (05115)

[The difference lies . . .]

The difference lies in the nostrils, as I walk from the cafeteria, through the warm March morning, on whose ground lie longdecayed and soggy leaves that throw off glints of the sun, to the library. The nostrils tell the tale. And now, as I walk over the polished linoleum of the stacks, listening to the shuffling resonance of my shoes, I know the stench of antiquity, the foul, reeking odor of ancient bound theses and moldering books, which line these shelves back to back in random disarray. There are just too many books that hold no secrets, no answers to the questions of the heart. And walking toward the library lounge, where I will type for an hour or two the thoughts of Lennie or Walter Mitty or Santa Teresa, I know where to find the answers, the simple reductions that the mind can hold, and as I walk, I still hear Raphael, the sociable angel of Milton, telling Adam that he must contain his imagination, must quell his appetites for the mysterious, that there are certain things that must be left to Him who created all. I know what he meant, the angel: that he, I, must live and be patient and love, love as prime and chief, for therein lies the key to obedience and happiness.

A bit didactic, I put up with the mind, the brain's ramblings, knowing that there is a limit to all speculation, that all else is cant or zealous folly of the sport of winds to pursue, and so the mind turns back on itself like a flood cresting in storm time. The things I crave are Wilbur's things of this world: the rancid laundry, the shirts of thieves, the sight of nun's drooping cassocks of black and white cotton. I seek to grasp and hold to the simple though subtle reductions to the commonplace, as I wrote in the poems "The Sport of Winds" and "Tenement Eyes."

So the mind begins to glean the essence of simplicities that lies beneath the surface of daily commuting. Even the bumper-locked traffic, which jumps and lurches like a freight train in the stockyards, going down seven o'clock highways with occupants restless or blearytired or impatient or daydreaming, even this meets the wandering, speculative eye and pleases me. I am beginning to see the value of progress, the turgid, bumping, grinding effects of progress and material interests. It no longer troubles my mind that the overtones of this growth and expansion have their assailable points. I will not be a sumptuous cynic, delighting in every angle and racket of society for my kicks. And as I write this thought, I am reminded of Joseph Conrad's character Decoud, in *Nostromo*, who was a fine and judicious cynic, remembering Conrad's piercing claim for him: he was fine so long as he was in the society that provided him with material against which to vent his cynicism and vitriolic scorn, but put him outside of society, his material, and he was helpless, floating, then sinking with his own weight into the immense inanity and abstracted nothingness of the sea. The point was that he could not live with himself in solitude, could not discover one truth in his own essence save for the tenet that he was substanceless and alone.

A fine Conradian insight, no matter that the English writer, né Polish, was a bit rhetorical, a bit discursive and flamboyant in his abstractions. So I know that there is worth even in the sheer phenomenology of everyday things. As I pulled into the driveway Monday afternoon, I noticed a robin squatting on the pavement beneath the shiny bumper of a parked car. The periphery of the eye caught the movement, and I wheeled the car slow and easy, until I could see the bird leaping high as a squirrel from the ground to the bumper, pecking its own image in the shiny face that reflected his pecking face. A bird, I thought, fighting against itself; the height of mimetic indifference, I surmised. Narcissus robin, I thought, only Narcissus never had the energy to fight back, nor did Conrad's Decoud. This bird, in its ignorance, had more strength.

Now I sit here, thinking of experience that lies beneath the surface of mundane realities, and I know this will be my source of material, the matter for my writing, the attempt to try in the relating of the essential, basic simplicities of the everyday. I will equip myself by travelling, looking, smelling. A snooping Sherlock Holmes, I will investigate the primal qualities that lie like stones above ground, knowing in my mind that immortality lies above ground, like Essie in the poem of mine. It's what's above ground that counts; the rest is windy speculation and in praise of Erasmus and Momus, Wotton and Bentley.

I will be a swift Swift, uncovering the rocks to let free the thralled insects of life, the bees along with the groundhogs and the herons and wrens.

* * *

On a lark I do things, dress as I please, purchase those things that seem to hold some intrinsic aesthetic for my eyes and mind and the hidden awareness that always lies untapped underneath my lids. So now I focus on the brass cash register I bought at an antique shop months ago for no reason that one could chalk off to utility or functionalism but simply because it evoked, and still does help me conjure, what often I think of as an era in American life, the period of the drugstore on the corner of the block. This may, perhaps, sink into simple childhood nostalgia, but somehow I am reminded of a whole period, a block of American thought, that is filled with innocence, not the Romantic or Neoclassical conjuring of the nineteenth century but more the period before and ten years following the First World War, in which the drugstore on the corner served the youth as the drive-in restaurant and go-go nightclub serve our own sophisticated youth. So I own a piece of the past, which I still like to live with, not living in the past myself; I own a piece of that innocence, even if it goes no further than the brash, confident ring of the register springing open to the touch of the fingers. I can see it there, sitting heavy and unmovable, ever mutable up to six dollars, the myriad keys that record at a touch NO SALE or 5¢ or $6 or GAS BILLS or CHARGED through the glass face of its eye at the top. No Cyclops this one, but a reminder out of the past, like the thundering hoofbeats of some white stallion.

When I contemplate its brass aegis, I am thrown back into the Friday night meetings of Veronica and Archie, the store of Peavey and Gildersleeve and a hundred other conjurations. But Friday night last, I pressed the 45¢ key, and the drawer flew open, waist-high, to bequeath me its simple, white contents, the tickets for the concert, which I had inserted within its compartments three weeks ago. I

was all excitement, anticipating what I had never experienced, and
that night, Friday, I drove downtown with the three girls to the audi-
torium to watch Bob Dylan perform. I had read about him, had re-
viewed his interviewed words, and was prepared for what would
happen.

But then it was over; I had seen with my ears what it is that moves
youth today, and I was excited and anxious to be a part of the phase
that no longer sees brass cash registers or upright telephones or
treadle sewing machines.

3/16/66 (05316)

[She holds, easy as brocade,]

She holds, easy as brocade,
Fading thoughts that weave
Designs in the eyes.
Palms open to time's kiss,
Grasp tufts of sky
Like bees in nets.

3/22/66 (05334)

[This city, Fort Lauderdale, . . .]

This city, Fort Lauderdale, is all sounds. A continuous, incessant
drone of noises invades the privacy of my ears, and all I hear is the
routine whir, the phrenetic, shuffling ennui of busy prodigals buzzing
in fantastic disarray through the channels of my senses. I am here,
arrived, and yet I have no idea where I am. Whoever told Eliot to write
about his unreal city, Londres, was cocksure and went off only half-
cocked! This is the city, the humdrum unreality of sameness and ir-
reverence. Nowhere do I get a friendly greeting or an unsuspecting
eye, nowhere, that is, excepting the friendly, ecstatic welcome from
the Jewish shopkeepers and merchants in the clothing and novelty
bazaar shops that line, like vultures squatting inevitably in wait, like
sin and death in Milton, the slatternly promenade called by regulars
and parvenus alike A1A.

It is Saturday night here, and I am relaxing in my motel room, not for lack of better but from escapism. A body can take just so much routine boredom and sameness before it balks and attempts to purge itself from the strictures of this too tightly bandaged city. Yet there is no silence, no real escaping the noises of the city.

And from where I sit, on my bed, behind the typewriter, the sounds invade the ears. The fingers, which hop like grasshoppers from one key to the next, are busy and without doubt, yet the ears are all over and straining under the burden of repetitious muffles and baffles.

* * *

A too-long and too-fast drive from White Cross to Florida has drained and sent into flaming dissolution all the stamina, the constitution, of my exhausted body. I have come here for relaxation, and everywhere, I am taxed with the sight of this rat-racing crowd. Some consider me a "stodgy bastard," one who refuses to let himself go, to live free and without recrimination. Others don't hold feelings or opinions or calumnious thoughts at all, because they don't know me, none of which disturbs my moral equilibrium. I am no Horace Bushnell, Lancelot Andrews, or Jonathan Edwards; no man of homiletics or fretful diatribes or prophecies about the future am I. But who can allow himself to remain idle and unresponsive when the very facts of dissipation and false structuring are so pervasive? Sleep is unfortunately overtaking me at this point; the two of us, like Hardy's twain, Titanic and iceberg, have converged, and my strength (or guts, rather) has given out.

3/26/66 (05317)

[And now it is past . . .]

And now it is past the height of the sun, and the temperatures are falling with the four o'clock sun into the Atlantic. I have returned to the motel, a block off the beach, and the thick, tepid air from the shower fills the room. Yet the drawn curtains billow placidly behind the breeze that filters off the water, and I know it will be another evening of fifty-degree coolness. I am where I love to be — behind the keys of the typewriter, with the brain rolling out turgid thoughts that congeal slowly behind the eyes. And all I can think of is conglomeration: this city, filled with the milling vacationers from myriad

colleges and high schools, moiling and strutting, each type of itself
and easily marked out.

The drive south, fast and comfortable, occupied the eyespace be-
fore me for three days. There was the idea of regeneration trailing
us, a rebirth, resurrection, in the rising, and we drove, my Jan and I,
through the afternoon, on that coldgrey day, a Wednesday of antici-
pation and exhaustion. Both of us had importunately terminated our
school obligations, packed the station wagon, and then, before leav-
ing, stopped at Steak 'n Shake for a quick bite of three o'clock lunch.
Then there was the drive, fast and without incident, to Nashville.

It was the Parthenon that lit like phosphorescence against the ten
o'clock southern sky that night when we drove into Nashville, and we
followed its divining haze to the outskirts of the city, to a new sub-
division where my friends lived.

We were tired and cold, weary and glad somehow to be out of
White Cross. They were there, the two of them, married and settled
all within the period of six months. How disgusting to be so domesti-
cated and uxorious, so staid in the familiarity of togetherness! Their
lives, like that damn new complex of tissue-thin apartments, trans-
parent and artificial, and the cynicism that invades me now is also
disgusting. Yet I fear what two can do to two when the twoness is so
conjugal and sanctioned. And we sat there at their tiny, barlike break-
fast table, which partitioned the kitchen from the cubical living room,
sitting there bleary and cold and exhausted, and all I could think of
was myself and Jan, not caring for the trivia, the banal minutiae of
minute lives, outside of things and motion and life and time. The
body was tired, but the mind balked at the simplicity of their lives.
The brain retched and vomited the idea of domesticity, and we sat
there, wanting food — so basic and yet so very important.

And we were in motion, moving with Frost's drift of things, mov-
ing together in harmonious discontent, the uneasiness consistent
with our moods, moving and aiming south into the heart of the Black
Belt regions, into which, early before dawn the following morning,
even before the hosts would awaken from the snug, comfortable mu-
tuality of newlywed conjugality, we would be flying again, heading
toward Chattanooga, then Atlanta and Lake City, and on to Tampa-
St. Petersburg.

But it was early, and they were awake, waiting up for our arrival,
the girl sick and tired, the friend, her husband, pleased with his deco-
rous stinkden of an apartment. And we knocked at the door, not
excited to see them but anxious to eat and sleep and recuperate for the
longer drive in the morning, my Jan, cold and the skin with goose
bumps, wanting just the simple confines of warm sheets and a cover,

not knowing then that there would be no covers to warm her, that the apartment would be too cold for Nashville March, suspecting less that the reason for the cold lodging was that gas bills come too frequently and with too many IBM codifications, all of which, when formulated for the lay budget, signify a too-exorbitant monthly bill. But we sat there, two and two, the one couple married and sanctioned, the other, in tired juxtaposition, incongruous within the legitimate expectations of any wealthy married couple, and I ate and she ate, and the other two, the hosts for five hours, sat watching, talking slow, reminiscing, boasting proudly and silently their domesticity, the little trinkets and emblems of the recent marriage, the boyfriend saying, "You ought to try it; there's nothing that can beat it," and I thinking, "Who the hell needs all that crap to say that two people are in love with each other, the stinking emblems, tiny and insignificant in themselves: the pewter and stainless silver ashtrays and silent butlers; the Belgian- and French-woven tapestries that dangle from the white-sterile, paper-thin walls, behind which are the identical configurations of another's emblems; the other myriad insignias of marriage lining and filling the tiny compartment rooms; the new bedroom furniture made of wormwood or cherry, designed expressly for some local, chic furniture store and to be found in all the leading stores in all the big cities of the country, expressly made and designed with the young married couple in mind? That's nice and comforting, and it stinks, because who the hell needs that furniture set when for half the time and a fifth the money and a thousand times the enjoyment in hunting and searching the antique stores and shops, boutiques, bargain barns, one can have his own real, antique Simmons eighty-year-old brass bed and accessories, which were made expressly for no one in general, made to last through two or three world wars and then some, made for anybody who had the aesthetic desire to possess a real bed!"

But we ate, and all the while, the country ham, the acrid, smoke-tasting ham, was so good, and the English muffins and the milk and the cookies all were so much better than anything else, and we ate, though my mind was still running over the insidious catalogue of wedding gifts that lined the walls like driftwood plated with gold, the bookshelf filled with the trivial requirements of a combined eight years of college, books that were out of place where they sat on the steel shelves of the do-it-yourself bookcase in the hall, books that were meant to stand by themselves, not as emblems, badges that proclaimed, "We are among the educated, educated expressly by our parents' fiat for no other reason than to boast the best of everything," books like *Moby Dick, Huck Finn, The Mind of the South, I and Thou,*

Elements of Psychology, Contracts and Torts, and *The History of Art.*
Such an array screamed at me like the blaring headlights of a semi
coming out of a highway's hard curve into the path of my wincing
eyes, these books anomalous and ridiculous where they sat, and all I
could think to hold back behind the budding, enraged cynicism that
was welling up behind the mind and the tongue's sensitive palate was
"Oh, let these things, like used, rancid, cementgrey water in a tub,
drain out and go back to their source! Let them flow out of here as the
contents have long since done from the tubs of these people's minds!"

How cynical and biting and immature. And we went to bed, Jan in
the guest room, myself on the brand-new Simmons Hide-A-Bed. I
was told with boastful pride that I was the first of their future-planned
guests to make use of the bed. It was a beautiful bed, "so perfect and
brand-newy" that, before, I had even feared to sit on its clean, unclut-
tered, unworn cushions of slatternly purple. But I had been seated on
it earlier in order to look at and admire and drool over the wedding
pictures that lined the coffee table before it, along with two matching
ashtrays, which, no doubt, were purchased from the Jewish commu-
nity center's cultural-exchange shop. These trays, which I took glee in
mussing with the blackcharred end of three cigarettes while I sat look-
ing, admiring with feigned approval and not so silent expressions of
envy, given as wedding gifts also, like everything else, were exotic,
with glaze covering giraffelong birdnecks attached by some artful
process to the rest of the crowded birds that could have easily passed
for pterodactyls if their newness was not presaged inadvertently on
the back: MADE IN JAPAN/'66.

"Get me out of here, and let me flow with the motion of things! Let
me have laundry and clean sheets to roll in and forget that there is
such a thing as domesticity! Old Milton, that blind bugger, had the
right notion when he committed his Adam to the awful, slovenly sin
of uxoriousness."

But we would have to talk, the boy and myself, and though my Jan
pleaded with me to get my rest, there was no bowing out of the jun-
ta that would have to pass between us. That's what old friends do.
"Why in hell," I thought, "can't old friends just leave each other's
present state alone and the past as well, the tired, laborious, insignifi-
cant reminiscing alone? Why can't old friends just let out their beds,
sometimes, for sheer sleep, unadulterated and undisturbed?" But we
talked, and I listened while he related the civic projects he was in-
volving himself in, about the duties of his wife teaching fifth graders
at the local school, how convenient everything was, what with the
shopping center just minutes from their apartment and the down-
town district a mere twenty minutes via the nearest highway. Dis-

simulating with attentive seriousness and happiness, I listened, fingering the photograph albums before me, not opening them, listening to the opportunities that he would have in his office, the great group of young executives with whom he associated daily, and all I could think about was sleep, which was waiting for me beneath the covers of the Hide-A-Bed, which would have to be patient with me while he spoke, and now I knew he was ending, and he bent forward, confidential and with the voice lower, almost a whisper, and a leery, secretive smile breaking from the lips, the eyes bending into my tired eyes, and I heard him divulging the center of his dreams:

"Now I wouldn't want this to be known, and the wife and I haven't said a word to anyone, but as you were one of the first to know of our marriage, now I want you to know that we're planning to move from this apartment."

"So soon? It's so nice and spacious here."

"Well, you know how it is. We've been here six months already, and we think we're going to need more room."

I smiled knowingly, conveying to him that I understood his reference to a future child, which neither he nor I had to mention.

"Well, as you know," he said, "the parents are alone now. Jessie in New York and married, and Estelle in college, and me living here." He paused, as though on the verge of some monumental discovery or revelation. "Anyway, and I don't want you to mention this even to my wife . . ."

"You know I won't."

"Well, my mother hinted to me the other day that she wanted us to have their house, and so I've held back on buying a small place of our own."

"God, would that be great," I said, whispering, the eyes wide and feigning excitement. And there was disgust running rampant as I listened to him round out the confidence.

"Well, it would be really great, but there's no telling how long we'd have to wait. Daddy hasn't said anything to us at all, and it could be two or three years, but I think they're going to move into an apartment. It would be a luxury one, of course. One of those things on the top of a newbuilt high-rise."

"Yeah, a penthouse."

"Uh-huh, and so you can understand how excited we are about this."

"That's a terrific house out there," I said, remembering the time I stayed with his family before the wedding.

"So we're just going to have to wait and see what they do. But it's well worth the waiting for, because we could never afford a house like that."

And now I was too tired to sustain the monologue further, too tired
almost to undress, and we said goodnight. "It was so good of you to
put up with us, and your wife sick and all."

"If I don't get up to see you off tomorrow morning, you just help
yourself to the icebox and have a real good trip."

"You bet, and thanks again for letting us impose."

"Shoot! Anytime, you old horse," he said, throwing back a sidelong
glance filled with sly innuendo, by which I knew he was referring to
the trip Jan and I were making together. But there was no envy in his
eyes, no regrets, and I turned from his diminishing back, threw off
my boots and white athletic socks, and flopped into bed, still wearing
my khaki work shirt and wheat jeans. Sleep soon released me from
all cynicism and the possibility of swift recrimination. "We will walk
with wandering steps and slow," I promised myself, sinking head-
long, like a staggering drunk, into complete sleep.

3/28/66 (05318)

[Groups of college boys,] ‡

Groups of college boys,
Clutched like winter quail
Around lawn tables
Or motel pools or
Down empty alleys,
Mutter lewd slogans,
Drinking, guzzling beer
That freshets from brown glass bottles.

A Monday Florida,
And still policemen mingle in twos,
Converging at corners
Or sitting singly on stools inside
Bars,
Check for I.D. cards,
Optometrise with flashlights
The eyes of applicants,
Patients of this punchy town.

I lie alone now,
Following the wind's path,
*

> Which gathers dust in billowed curtains.
> There is no certainty in solitude;
> It all survives in communion
> With the eye's breathing kiss.
>
> We have been together:
> A picture show, dinner before,
> Where hamburgers and fried potatoes
> Stayed hot into the night.

This night, I sit naked on the bed, smoking the xth-too-many cigarette, listening to the stomach holler in staccato cacophony for food, sustenance, and I know there will be nothing to satiate the demands until the morrow. But the wind breathes in deeply through the stale, wet scent of this motel room, and I can feel it stream across the red, burning body, which has sustained too much sun during the past three days to last throughout the coming summer months.

I am away from White Cross, alone with my love, in communion with the spirits of freedom and motion, and somehow, that word, "motion," speaks a sacred ritual to me. In the back of the head, I hear my friend Gene Redmond chanting rituals to his sun and his moon, and for some reason, this evening, when the cool Atlantic breeze filters into my room, I can sense the nearness of the moonberries, the silver apples of the moon, knowing that *mañana* there will be golden apples dangling from the early-morning eastern horizon.

We have spent this night in harmony, eating at the Sheraton Grill cheaper than it would cost in White Cross at Howard Johnson's; then the movie, *A Patch of Blue*, until it was time to return, driving down Sunrise Blvd., then right on A1A, until we arrived at the lot where the nightly dance was going on. There were young people there and a band that could not even keep time to its own bumptious beat.

> The mouth burns dry as blue heat,
> And she has retreated from me
> Into the privacy of sleep.
> We have walked the rickety wood
> Of greenhouse aisles
> Lined with poinsettias, begonias,
> Have driven the distance
> Between White Cross and Freedom,
> And now we are one with the ocean,
> Red and stinging with salt
> *

That won't clean away,
Covered with sand granules
That scrape the skin
Like fingernails

The thoughts refuse to issue freely tonight, and I submit
myself to sleep unwillingly, hoping that tomorrow will
push forward for me the design of recording in depth this
trip with my Jan.
    May God bless Jan with all His grace!

3/29/66 — [1] (05319)

[The day broke grey and cool . . .] ‡

    The day broke grey and cool over the stretch of Florida beach
that parallels A1A, and from the motel's windows, stretching before
the scudding clouds, I thought of nothing but breakfast, the simplest
thought that one can conjure early. And there would be rain, and I
would travel by car to Miami, would avoid the hot sun and salt water
today in favour of other attractions. We were without the sun, with the
need to improvise, and as I shaved, my eyes caught her lithe figure,
dressed in cutoff khakis and strollers, a paint-strewn sweatshirt,
walking quick and yet languidly down the street from her motel apart-
ments. I did not have to rush, finish the small duties of dressing, be-
cause there was familiarity between us lingering from the preceding
night together.
    The silent, quick knocks on the door. "Wait a second." Then I put
the toothbrush into its holder, the tube down on the white porcelain
sink, and without shirt, I stepped through the constricted room toward
the door. She stood as I had seen her before on the street, looking at the
redness of my stomach and chest, the face bronzed and peeling in
flakes as tiny as slow, small snow.
    No hello, no greeting, no necessity in that; simply, "I'm hungry.
Let's go get some breakfast at Howard Johnson's."
    "Let me finish dressing, will you? And maybe you can help straighten
up this room. It's a pig slop."
    "You should have hung those shirts up, what with all this moisture."
    And I thought how she always had an eye out for the simple things
that never troubled me. And why should they, when whatever was
soiled or wrinkled was still wearable?

The day was breathing hard, like a spent athlete, and before leaving the room, I made a change of clothing. When she arrived, I was dressed in slacks and with a sport shirt laid out on the unmade bed. Once dressed, and with the impending awareness of rain and colder temperatures, I slipped out of them and into the work jeans and shirt and bramble-cut and -slashed Wellington boots that I had worn to drive down from White Cross.

And we ate as we always did, the same meal of sausage and toast or English muffins, two eggs each, over hard, and three or four cups of get-started coffee.

"Let's get these cards off this morning. We've procrastinated too long already."

"And whose fault is that?"

"Let's get 'em off today."

"You write, and I'll add something to it."

So neither of us could write anything funny or satiric, and I thinking how poor, how damn difficult it is to contrive humor when you don't feel it.

And soon we would drive through the rain to the alligator farm, would see the monkeys in their cage, smelling worse than spread manure in a rose garden; the assorted items pulled up in nets from forty fathoms, the sea fans and conches, starfishes and blowfish; the myriad, sundry shells, selling for twenty-five or fifty cents; and the large, airy building, filled with the dross of commercial tourism: the carved Indian totems; the figurines of glass covered with nautical rope knots; fishnets and bead-strung cork bobbers; the stuffed, five-foot, fifty-dollar alligators, perching in suspension on the shelves above like store detectives hiding in immobile waiting for someone to shoplift, at which point they might crawl down and devour the victim of petty thievery.

Heading south down Highway 1: Hallandale, Dania, Hollywood, and then North Miami, and by this time, I was expecting to see something out of *Goldfinger* — the lavish appurtenances of wealth. Instead, we drove through the ramshackle dross and debris, the excrement of North Miami, with its pastel barbershops and hundred lounges and nightspots, burlesque houses, drive-ins and restaurants and motels all strung with vacancy signs, until the mind went sour and disgusted with false expectation. The disillusionment, and then the red-white-blue sign of 195, with the marker hinting at Miami, which hung like a mountain of glass over the rippled waters that separated the two pieces of land. "So this is Arthur Godfrey Boulevard. How ridiculous!"

"What a stupid thing," she said.

"I agree, but he must have done a lot for Miami." "Stupid answer," I thought, and we continued until we were into the city, dwarfed by the sheer height of old stucco and white-plastered hotels and buildings, and still I was moving ahead, in the direction of the Atlantic, still on Arthur Godfrey Boulevard, until we reached the stoplight at Collins Avenue. Then I knew where I was, that I should turn left and follow the street out past all the concrete luxury and the cantilevered grace of symmetry. But I continued straight for another block and came to the dead end, a small stone-and-brick obstacle of a wall, behind which was the water of the ocean, and I stopped the car, slapped it in reverse, and then sat motionless, laughing so hard the eyes filled with blurry water. She was sitting looking at me inquisitively, asking with her silence why I was laughing.

"This is the funniest thing I ever saw," I said, one hand holding the stomach from hurt. "What do you think of this? Goddamn Arthur Godfrey running on until he finally ends up in the water. He must have flown his plane this route." But there was no need to continue. I was incensed and crazed with disillusionment because what I had expected was just not materializing. True, as we turned right and drove along Collins Avenue, some of the better cars passed, the Rolls Royces and Jaguars and even a four-seater, metallic-grey Ferrari, but the buildings were so disappointing and so cramped: the Americana, Deauville, Castaways, Dunes, Fontainebleau, all lined up like bums in some postwar soup line, meretricious and gauche, untidy and garish and huge like great piles of concrete and steel and glass guano dropped from some highflying pterodactyl, these monolithic structures mastodons of garishness and artificiality, out of place and at once in obeisance to the weather, whose deleterious elements were already at work on them, as seen by the rustbrown and clay-coloured lines that ran down the sides of the window casements or where the air conditioners were attached into the walls. And we drove on, saying to ourselves how disgusting to be so close together.

"I know one thing for sure," I said to her. "If I were to take a vacation, it wouldn't be here. God, a person who came here would have to spend all his time in one hotel."

> I sit on the sofa,
> Head against the wall,
> And two lit cigarettes
> Burn in tandem
> Into the eyes of night.

Outside, the rain slithers
Through mangroves and royal palms,
Washing green dust
That hides in daytime
The fronds' patina.

This rancid evening,
Soiled as dirty clothing,
She lies huddled
Under the bed's spread,
Shivering like wheat
In some faraway winter.

I hear shouts and tired voices,
The ceaseless vibrato of cycles
Churning down A1A,
Importunate roars
From four hundred horses'
Drug-injected throats.

Outside, cars churn on slippery streets,
Throwing back swishing sounds
The colour of yellow nausea,
And the lamp's frayed cord
Sets sparks of clear skies
Playing ricochet games
Against the baseboard.

Beneath me,
The grandfather television
Mirrors phosphorescent ghosts
To elderly visitors
"Down" for the winter.

And she just lies there,
Silent as winter leaves
As they lose their color
And wither into dissolution.

That I were a forever man,
To wander with leopard's spots
Faded like winter freckles,
To return with each tomorrow!

Let me slither like serpents,
Reptiles that grovel in pits
*

Of zoo and aquarium,
Alligators that writhe,
Lying lifeless, with eyes shut
Against peeping tourists,
Alligators whose bodies grow
An inch at a time
Through a year's lifeless cycle.

I can live on top of my friends,
Brothers of the slime,
Reptiles of sunless days,
When rain pelts the scaly back,

Or a kangaroo, whose young
Dangle and bounce like jelly
In the pouch, where birth and youth
Coalesce to form a full-grown thing.

This night, I will drink
Without the stinking thoughts
Of endless works that will spill
From the fingers and pen,
The fetid typewriter's keys.

But then, tomorrow, when the effect
Has failed to persist,
I will insist on the coffee,
Will take off again
To the sandy beaches of the mind,
With fingers flying over keys,
Will plant the fingerseeds
Of creativity, and there,
Where the water ends and land
Begins,
I will crawl up slow,
Open wide the jaws,
And slither fast into the underbrush,
Flapping my tail behind me.

A cop, stalled at the door
Like a dunce in the back
Of the fifth-grade classroom,
Checks my reality,
*

Shines his flashlight beam
Into the black recess of pupils
To ascertain my reality,
And I say, "It's me.
Can't you read the specs behind glassine?
I'm Pleistocene."
"Don't go gettin' obscene with me,
Buddy."
I say civilly, "Can't you see
The specs don't lie?
Can't you see the greying hairs
And the sleep still in one eye?
I am the real image of me.
All I want is a quick beer
And maybe a girl to sit with
And talk to through raucous songs
Of college boys and
Botticelli girls."

So I pass into the cave,
Where no sawdust lines floors,
Where shipmates and whores
Line the bar
Like spent athletes huddled
On halftime benches.

"Let me have a Bud, ma'am,
And a bag of stale pretzels."
"That's all we got, mister,
What with the weather
Being soiled as dishtowels."
I look at her, laughing
Into her workaday eyes,
And her white back disappears
Somewhere into the noise.

I sit silently, waiting patiently
For the food and drink, my
Prison pension. I'm here
On fifty dollars and a whim
To see the kids playing their games.
No dirty old man am I
But an aged youth myself,
Who missed out when Creation was,
*

Who peeps like a sociologist
Into everyone's business but his own.
I am the preacher of beer joints, beaches,
Speaking figments of others' imaginations.
I lie and cheat,
The prevaricator of idle works.

Early Evening

Cigarette pack, crumpled like the day
Between two nighttimes, resting now
On the checkerboard cloth,
Which covers like a blotter
Spilled dross of drunkards
Who never learned to pour properly
The foam that hides at the bottom
Of bottles.
My elbows, resting on the top,
Absorb the sweat of sloppiness,
And I relent, waiting,
Hoping to meet some widowed date
Wearing blond hair and a midnight
Bikini or skirt with nothing
Underneath except her reality.
And one sits beside me,
But she is married for the night.
Soon, the squat bottle
And the soggy pretzels,
Which are all they have,
Owing to the soiled weather,
Sit staring at me.
The eyes peer out behind
Gold-rimmed spectacles
Toward the gates of Hell,
Where the cop sits checking
Realities that go forged by scalpers
And experts with a Xerox machine.

There she is, coming now,
Alone, wearing tight slacks and
Pushing off the door
For midair support.
*

I see the cop accept her
Underage dollar bill, and now
She walks down the cave's corridor.
I stand where I sat,
And she stumbles into the chair
I offer with my straining foot.

"My name is Gambrinus," I say.
"What's yours?"
"Ursula from the trade winds."
"Have a drink."
"A cigarette will do."
"Who sent you here to me?"
"The rain," she spoke,
Lisping in faint whispers.
"Have a beer to wash you clean."
"If you must insist."

The bodies,
Good-looking college kids
All of them,
Lie like shades of Hell
On the beach,
Each one of them
An athlete
In his motel room
Or car's backseat
Before the sun holds
Revival meetings.

Last night,
When the rain beat

12:01 Sunday Morning

I sit nude on the bed,
Awaiting the head's message
To the stomach.
Soon I'll eat midnight coleslaw
And corned-beef sandwiches.
And I see the stomach,
*

Rolled twice in small folds
Where the paunch hides the navel.
I live between the legs,
Despising too-fast union,
The communion bought the last moment
On some slatternly beach.
I need the rainbow's fire
To cauterize wounds.
This is the season of lust,
When a body runs phrenetically
Through jungles infected with waste.
Where is the one whose touch
On the redburnt skin,
Whose tepid fingers scale summits
Of rib and shoulder bone
Easy as Norkay's genius?
I am the beach bum
Who stumbles on tired shells,
Wearing a swimsuit of madras,
To look for grassy clots
That grow in sand
At the end of day,
When the children of children
Have gone away
And the ocean lies still
In abandoned Kenilworths.
But no green tongues grow
Where I have planted sperm,
And my seeds waste
Like dry puddles of salt,
Adrift on buffalo flats.
I will sleep on the beach
Again tonight,
When the breeze sets sail,
The sun sets over Florida.
And no more morning walks to the beach
For me and the woman
Whose sun burns for us alone.
Tomorrow, the drive home,
Out of this barren paradise,
Through the Cumberlands,
Which make jumping beans of cars.
*

I have traveled to Madagascar
And Lompoc in the fields,
And now I return home.
White Cross transmits invitations;
I respond with formal script:
"Home, I will be happy to attend
The gracious festival in your honor,
On the zillionth day of finality,
In the second year of our Alligator,
1966 . . ."

I have seen too much in these eight days to record. Résumé falls in hundreds of vitreous pieces, and there is need for strength in these fingers and through the baffles of this mind to find the proper configurations. The familiar streets and bywords of this city, so clean and beatific: Sunrise Boulevard, Federal Highway or 1, Broward, Las Olas, A1A. And the dining places — Uncle John's Pancake House, Mai Kai, Wolfie's, The Forum, Sheraton Pub Grill, Tony's Fish Market — all these and more make the dining superb, not to mention the old standby Howard Johnson's.

This is all the strength; feeble commitment tonight; too tired, and preparing for the long trip ahead. Hope God is on our side tomorrow. God bless Jan, my parents, and the kids.

3/29–30 — [2] (Prose) and [3] (Poem) on 3/29 & 4/1/66 (05116)

Student Prince

For Jan, in April

I

He sits on a sofa
In some ocean-soiled apartment,
Head against the wall,
Not realizing his two lit cigarettes
Burn in tandem.

The sandaled feet
Twitch like galvanized muscles
*

On the table before him
As he thinks of culture
And Christ mounting Calvary;
He's a religious bastard,
Even in despondency.

It's a late afternoon,
Soiled as dirty lingerie.
The hours parade like grey rhinos,
And rain slithers down drainpipes,
Washing the day's green dust
From mangroves and royal palms.

He hears shouts and tired voices
Retreating in twos from the beach.
Cycles churn ceaseless vibratos,
Burning down A1A,
While drug-injected throats
Of four hundred horses
Roar importunately
Above the rain's soft tappets.

Cars, like Moses' miraculous wand,
Part slippery streets
Outside, beneath his window,
Throwing off sounds
The color of yellow nausea.
His ears grow sullen and wince.
The eyes see lightning
About the lamp's frayed cord;
Sparks of clear, jagged skies
Ricochet against shadowy baseboards,
And all is aglow,
Momentarily.

But he just sits,
Shivering from too much burn,
His curly hair
Turning a thousand twirls
At wrong angles.
He's silent as a windless winter
In this summering spot,
Where hot-puckering suns wizen skin
Until fingers and forehead
Become mummies out of gauze.

II

He's spent the day
The way the children do it,
Prostrate against the sand.
He's seen the unpurged bodies
Of good-looking college kids,
All of them grown riotous
As shades in Hell,
Each an athlete in motel rooms,
Porky's bar,
Or the car's backseat at night.

It's one great revival here,
Where he's come to preach the gospel.
He's traveled by thumb and car
To drool over bikinied flesh
And meet the wise men
With guitars and adolescent poetry
That drips like saliva
Off demotic tongues.

But he's forgotten his words,
Left them at Crazy Greg's
Or somewhere else along the "wall."
He can't compete with screeching gulls,
Radios' dull cacophonies,
Or the ocean's predictable swell.
Perhaps it's all just as well.

III

He wants to smoke both cigarettes;
His stomach muscles strain
As he brings lips into filtered heat.
The painful, burning bite of nicotine
Eats his eyes, and he thinks of culture
And the gifts and juvenescence.

Those gifts placed at his feet,
Veronica's kerchief,
And tears the ground-dust drank
Before he could stoop, could touch,
All float to the mind's ceiling
*

Like balloons released by accident.
The hot-awful pinpricks
Through the wrists and ankles,
The visceral slit leaking grapefruit
For lack of caustic unguents
Still pain his writhing thoughts,
Thoughts that run wild as lunatics
Over his tongue's vindictive lawn.

"You bastards behind the tans.
That I were a forever man,
Able to wander these fabled coasts
With leopard spots for freckles,
Eating the pard's liver for strength!

"That I could change like serpents
And rend these purple robes
That rub the raw, red waist
With each dry molting!
Then you'd see me as I am:
Just another of your kind,
Wearing madras trunks, Coppertone,
And maybe a shark's tooth about my neck
Or a surfer's Croix de Guerre.

"That I were reptilian,
Groveling in zoo pits, aquariums,
An alligator writhing wildly
Through endless daytime shadows,
With eyes pulled down like shades
Against prying, paying tourists,
An alligator whose body grows
An inch at a time
From Easter to Easter.
Then,
When rain pelted the scaly back,
I'd live atop my friends,
Brothers of the slime,
Reptiles of sunless dens.

"But tonight I'll drink beer
Without thoughts of charity
And works that spill like dross
From your preachers' unflossed cavities.
*

And tomorrow . . . tomorrow, I'll have coffee
With parched toast or buttered muffin,
Then take off again,
Wearing buffalo sandals,
Carrying this wrinkled staff
Over my shoulder.

"I'll walk the beach,
And there, where the water ends
And land resumes
And each knows each other
As of the same species,
I'll crawl up slowly,
Open wide my jaws,
And slither fast into the underbrush,
Flapping my tail behind me."

3/29 — [3] & 4/2–4?/66 (00481)

[Drive home — Florida] †

Drive home — Florida
to White Cross

Driving,
one to two o'clock;
greyblue sky through
sunglasses;
red needle locked at 70 mph.
Windshield smacked and
splattered with yellow, white
upward trails of juice.

Hood ornament, chrome,
holding three black dragons
as though all three eating
each other.

Hood dulldusty,
almost the color of army
*

green, dirty olivebrown,
reflecting, from where I sit
behind wheel, roadside
fence posts, heads of trees,
occasional Stuckey's and Ho Jo,
Esso and Texaco signs.

Homes and
    the green direction/
mileage signs, brocaded
with reflector buttons, sequins.

    The dashboard highlighted
brown with sunlight glare
and hot as frying
pan.
    The bug smatterings
  reflect off the dash top
in black blotches, the upward
flows going downward on the dash
as if to run over like
cataracts.

    On driver's side of dash,
match packs and
parking ticket; behind
left windshield wiper,
off whose chrome casement
bounces ten thousand suns,
is a Florida Turnpike folder-
map and a circular mileage
calculator, all of which
reflect, inverted, up onto
the inside of the windshield.

    Radio aerial shudders, as
if cold, through the hot-bumping,
bouncejouncy Georgia air:
great phallic emblem of chivalry.

    Inside we sit, one
window cracked, and the
*

rushing air gasps, plunges
in torrents of ear-rumbling
ferocity into the inviolate
station-wagoned sanctuary.

Windows closed now; air leaks
in mousesqueaks through
jumper window.
Air inside goes acrid,
with odor lifting insidiously
and osmosing from open
ashtray.
Radio rumbles through
dash baffles, climbing like
maggots through cut-out
holes in leather dash.

4/2/66 (05335)

Meditation over Coffee, 4/4/66

A cold, brightsunny morning, and I sit in the university cafeteria
again, the bones of buttocks resting hard and sensitive beneath my
Florida weight; familiar place, with familiar, deep, brownburnt coffee
at my right hand; smoking too much.

And I have returned to White Cross, having made another trek into
the jungle of my life's mind; have gone exploring, safaried into the
Black Belted South; have been spared the squalor of Georgia and
Tennessee Negro depravity, thanks to the twelve- or thirteen-cent-a-
gallon highway taxes that have paved a wizard's yellow-brick inter-
state down 41, 75, and the Sunshine Tollway.

Now I'm back, the mind still balking from the ten-cent newspaper
in front of me. I know the journalistic paraphernalia, which stalks
like slow boa constrictors around the limbs of smearblack print, can
squeeze, constrict, crush, and stultify the mind with its insidious me-
dia, can burn the little squint eyes for the straining to read minutiae
inherent and redolent in the print size.

4/4/66 —[1] (05172)

Facing Prospects of War

No horoscope,
No "Stargazer" for me today!
Who needs journalistic nemesis constellations
When Dürer lies on library shelves
And war runs races with itself?

I'm the stoic son
Who runs races with himself,
Sets phrenetic paces
Between classrooms and the gym.

I'll school myself
To accept the draft's selectivity,
Not to reject dungarees
Or a Daisy pump gun.

I'll school myself
To fight through senatorial brows
And deactivate time-clock,
Congressional Senecas,
Who wear holes in overtaxed floors.

But who knows?
When the war's over,
I might bring home to mother
A bronze star, a purple heart,
And a slantyellow whore
To perpetuate the family name.

4/4/66 — [2] (05117)

Prince of Cigarettes

He's a pastime man,
Whose Class A hobby
Is making tinfoil globes
From cigarette wrappers.
Every carton builds a world,
And when it gets too large,
The garbage collector
Carts it away with napkins,
*

Corned-beef scraps,
And pulpless orange rinds
That find their way
To furnaces in basement graves.

But who minds being God
Every week or so, even if cancer
Leaks through yellowing lungs?
"That's the price you pay,"
He tells himself,
"When making mountains
Out of charcoal filters,
Silvery Bastilles
From fanatical wrappers,
And ashen molehills
To be buried beneath
When you get too old to contemplate."

4/4 — [3], 5/4/66 — [1], & 1/28/67 — [3?] (00554)

April Seminar

The legs pain;
The brain lags like cold butter
On steaming toast
In this once-a-week room.
Here, one discusses "myth";
Another,
Who knows the Fool,
Fusses over Cuchulainn
And the moon's silver fruit,
While I sit mute,
Cringing intellectually,
The hand hiding suspect yawns.

Oh, that I were Oisin,
Driving some fast machine
Past country lawns
Where poetry flows
Harsh as a muffler's vibrato,
Soft as gears slipping smooth
Through tamed mathematics.

Then alone,
Released by ungoverned speeds,
Would the heart tremble,
The eyes grow wild,
Flinging tears that smear
A million ragged sunsets.

4/4/66 — [4] (04022)

[Old men, fearing usurpation,] †

Old men, fearing usurpation,
Make the wars
For young ones to fight.
The victors determine their occupation,

Get spoiled, and lose dominion
When women of Troy
Toy with red-hot genitals

"Did you hear about the new-married couple who didn't know the
difference between Vaseline and putty? . . . Their windows fell out."

Soon I'll quit cobbled paths,
Carry waterproof boxes for shells
In place of books

The old men have done it again,
Made what the young must end.

"It's time to go," I read.
The quota needs me this month.

4/4–9?/66 (05118)

[The tongue tastes liquor] †

The tongue tastes liquor

Where were you
When the horrible tornado
Flew against Floridian eyeballs?

I am so very weary, sitting here with cold pills revolving,
Revolving in downswirls of stomach, esophagus.
I can't guard the curiosity on the face,
And the lids close tight as lobster mandibles.

4/9–10?/66 (05336)

[Already it is long past . . .]

Already it is long past the hour of midday, and Easter is arrived,
so that what I feel is ecstasy through fatigue, thinking of her there in
that fine, private, brass, high-posted bed, alone and, no doubt, cring-
ing from the suspect sounds that creep and slither through the plas-
ter and wood moulding of the apartment. I am worried, fearing for
her safety. Then again, one must remember that I'm like an old mother
hen, brooding about anything that crosses the path of my sensi-
bilities.

But the mind travels back through the long, slow recess of this day,
the reading in the library — W. B. Yeats and the plays and mytholo-
gies — lunch at Steak 'n Shake, which consisted of chili with spaghetti
and navy beans and chili meat and crackers; cheeseburger, plain;
extrathin french-fried potatoes; and a coke. But this was late, almost
three in the afternoon, and still my Jan was talking of the photographer
and the outfits and the poses and crazy stance they persuaded her to
approximate.

This is the day that marks a year, an anniversary from the time we
first met at Howard Johnson Restaurant; it is the day to the day, only
now the pitchblack of night surrounds and envelops my fatigue,
and I give thanks to God for having delivered such a wonderful per-
son to me, so sensitive and strong and flexible, so compassionate and
understanding and forgiving, so much, in fact, that I am not, nor ever
will be, without her help — and funny how she can't even read Jona-
than Swift.

4/10/66 — [1] (05337)

[Outside the study . . .]

Outside the study window comes the thick-scented rumble of April lightning and thunder.

I wonder who is out there causing all that racket. Maybe it's Rube Goldberg, eating corned-beef sandwiches and chopped liver and cole-slaw, sitting around some picnic table, doing cartwheels and hand-stands and flips like some anachronistic Don Quijote, which doesn't get spelled that way anymore

Who can dance with Jethro
When the fancies turn to dust
And all the world
Falls prostrate on the balls of feet?
I am Lilliputian,
Pissing on palace walls
That crumble like crawling worms
Trod on by marching, warring feet.
Who knows defeat better
Than Thor and Aengus, Cuchulainn
And the Mistress of Bo-peep?
I am the Pied Piper's lute;
A mystical blow, and I succumb,
Come all over the window.
Art is for the moneyed class,
The asses with the biggest billfold
And the smallest conceptions of merit.
Who said the best of two worlds
Lies between the Centaur's legs?

Easter
                Easter
                                ethical humanism
        irrationality
                        resurrection — insurrection
        faith in faith alone — no rationale
                        Easter

4/10/66 — [2] (05338)

The Arcane Archeologist ‡

Everyone loves discovery;
No one who keeps busy
Asks if it's worthwhile.
So rich, *Ulysses* —
How astounding human ingenuity is!
Look, here are six rivers
On this page,
Eight, eighteen, on this section.

A child's mentality
Wants totality of life
In one week, all
The world's religion,
Weather, geography.
How fatuous, prurient!
Didn't that primitivistic mind
Know that only God sees all,
Only the Deity plays the game
Omnisciently?
                unhinging the mind's apparatus
        puns in twelve languages
        macaronics

4/11/66 — [1] (05119)

[Opaque lecture notes]

Opaque lecture notes
Float off fetid, academic lips
Like bubbles some child blows
Unimaginatively,
And I sit listlessly,
With my legs subliminally crossed
To deprive the tight-knit girl
Beside me
A single sneaking distraction.
Outside my eyes,
A ginhued April noon
Stumbles drunk through unsunned hours;
*

A dog barks too soon,
Begging admittance to the library;
A dissident tractor whines,
Or is it a mower's crowing report?
The this-that chemistry building,
Under construction underground,
Howling, growls from hammers' pricks,
Chisels' gouges, ruptured joints
Inflicted by beerfat carpenters.
All this through the window,
The eye of my education.
But who would ever hear
Of a lop-eared dog wanting to study?
Well, Milne would,
And Swift, too, if pushed hard enough.
As for me,
Ulysses is fine, and the *Quijote*,
If one's bent is prolixity,
But one can ponder literature anytime.
I hear the lunch-hour hall writhing
And soon will be dismissed.
I wish to find some warm dormitory
And fall fully clothed,
Naked in spirit,
Into miles of bed
And decades of vanwinkle wit.

4/11 — [2] & 4/16/66 — [2] (05120)

The Trial of a Retiring University Professor

His hollow-echoing feet
Follow treads of stoic tribunes
Who paced forums of oldest Rome.
The feet retreat repetitively
Through April's grey rain,
Down daylong corridors
From outside into the cave.

I, an intellectual heretic,
Stare at the taffy-pulled face
*

Of this academic mastodon
From the age of Eakins and Twain,
Waiting for his tired words
To stir two hours of dust.

His gullcolored hair
Refuses the room's heat,
Stays matted as morning grass;
The sodden mustache withers
Like drooping dog tails.
A scent of nicotine trails hands
That grasp at stray passages,
Friends without faces, sepulchered
Among disarrayed stacks of books.

His eyes, opaque fishbowls,
Grope for marginal notes,
Ghosts slinking in dark closets,
He made ten years ago.
Fraught with serious doubts,
He thumbs through yellowed pages
That crumble to his touch.
He fumbles, stumbling over words
That decimate his upstaged thoughts.
Wondering whether rescue will come
To his distressed memory, he asks,
"Are there any questions before I begin?"
A mutual pause embarrasses silence,
And he feints, boxing imaginary shades
That stand between him and his class.

Now the voice that knew Thoreau,
Emerson, and Edgar Poe
When he was still young enough
To be their grandsons' age
Breaks from his sacred notes,
And nine heads turn deferentially
Into his lips to listen.

"Why crave immortality
Just to outlive longevity?
Don't you know the Struldbruggs,
Lotus-eaters suffered their whims?
Why avoid those who sneeze
*

Or squeeze the grapefruit dry
Each morning before driving to work
Downtown? Why read hidebound books,
Whose authors read Juvenal, Democritus
Vicariously? Pleasure denies the intention.

"It's the pure intent, the furious pulse,
That makes death worth living for.
Eat the leopard's liver if you must.
Superstition is the best there is
For those who lack courage,
And religion without tradition
The best for those with convictions
Of their own temporality.
Morality, like the Holy Word,
Must be reinterpreted each tomorrow
According to the transfigured sorrows
And myths we create ourselves.
Crave the mortal in living!
Its grave lies out in the open,
Waits on nobody's dying humilities."

4/11 — [3], 4/16/66 — [1], & 1/16/67 (04019)

[They call it a lack of purpose, . . .]

They call it a lack of purpose, positively a not-knowing what I
want to do or aim toward or goal myself for, but the truth is that I
need sheer blocks of time in which to create the living material from
the static words that, without inspiration, lie festering on the type-
writer's keyboard or on the ridges of the brain's crust.

Today there is gloom everywhere in the sky, in the corner of all
the university buildings, between the fingers of wetsoiled grass, and
through every node that has begun to bud on every dogwood and
plum and peach and mimosa tree. It is the day after Easter, and every-
thing has subsided: no greatblossoming summer hats, no fancy young
girls home from Florida with their manufactured-in-a-week tans, no
effeminate men out walking their poodles before the massive indif-
ference of some new-built high-rise overlooking Forest Park.

All has gone from the world of light, to aberrate an old line of po-
etry, and I sit flustered and nonplussed by all the indifference that
fills my mind, the inability to work in this late season of schooling. I

know where I should be, now that the grammatical inadequacies are appearing and the words are coming slovenly and desultorily to my mind and tongue and untrained fingers. I need the sheer practice and practice and then the unmitigated desire to record, but I lack the spontaneity and the accuracy of thought and insight and perception. I lack not the will but the impulse, the motivation, and most of all, I lack the environment and the free, liberated time.

There is the *Heron and Wren* thing which I must complete, do the second draft on, before, like toast, it goes cold and won't take the butter, and the four short stories that must get done: Peaches; Fort Lauderdale-type setup; the story about the Corvette accident with Lester Taussig; the story about the boy and his sister and the dog.

This is a day too morbid to create, and I feel the despondency of uncreativity. Where in hell is the impulse, the driving force?

4/11/66 — [4] (05339)

Seminar in Symbolism

Monistic fusions of word and world
Swirl through my tired brain,
And I start to fade from the instructor's voice.
The eyes droop as in a child's blush;
The green floor rushes into my head.
"SPIRIT FLOWS THROUGH THIS MORAL EARTH."
Four cigarette butts define divinity
Beneath my feet, and I feel the linoleum's
Green-streaked whitecaps
Seeping comfortably into my skin.
Waves, light as webs, weave and roll,
Shrouding a school of white leviathans,
Four of them, swimming, killing real men.
(Hostile signs of divinity. The fusions:
Contradictions in terms. Symbols of sperm
And darker than jet.)
"SYMBOLS ARE OBJECTS
THAT STAND FOR SOMETHING ELSE,"
He reads from cryptic notes
Jotted ten years ago last Tuesday.
The ears hear pens running obliquely,
Squeaking over nine lined notepads,
*

Leaking under burdens of profundity.
The one who speaks behind my ears
Pauses, shuffling his tarot pack,
Listening to Ishmael tell Melville
About the moment of perception.
(Ah, difficult recognition . . .
Significance in all things . . .
Knowing and doing: the links of meaning.)
"MAN IS A SYMBOL-MAKING ANIMAL,"
He intones, insisting on heuristic fictions.
My eyes are spectators at the race,
Whose goal is a verbatim tape.
(The truth captured: an animal caged
For Sunday displays in an April park.
It's all the same cliché, though darker
In some climes than in others.)

"THE WHALE IS SYMBOLIC OF EVIL AND HATRED."
Chairs with eyes and ears sit straight
Before the T-shaped table in this booth,
Straining to hear each intonation:
Attentive arbiters of thought and truth,
Whose duty is to reconcile evil
In the human heart, mete out justice
To the whole or any of its literary parts.
"AHAB SOUGHT THE WHALE. THE WHALE IS EVIL.
ERGO, AHAB WAS AN EVIL BASTARD."
But the fusions deny syllogistic intrusion,
And I see the self and its universe
In endless search. Now Melville and Poe
Run below me, atop the sea's rutty crests,
Spanning interstices of history. The seas
Run more mysteriously. Bells ring through mist,
And I watch the mizzen listing
To lee shores alive with Elmo's fires.
(There's no safety there, where destruction
Bewilders lemmings and slow black cobras.)
Dark waves fragment darker horizontals,
Pitching the slipshod *Pequod*,
Like God the fallen angels,
Out of sheltered vaults of darkest night.
"SYMBOL IS AN OUTWARD SIGN
OF SOME INWARD STATE OF THE MIND."
*

I sit balking, I an animal stalked,
Not stalking, whimpering into his busy ears,
"But was the evil not there before?
And think if Ahab had brought safely into port
That blubberbooty boat? Yes, I can see them,
That crew, dicing for pieces of eight,
Gold doubloons, clothing, rusty harpoons —
Temples filled with blubber changers."
(Evil lurks in the heart of the process,
And the reverse hides ambiguities.)
Through the flaxen web, I see spiders;
One among them, the one-legged arachnid,
Drags the body's bilious personality
Along wharfs of Bedford and Nantucket,
In search, still seeking the universe
Behind the web's masked patina.

"SYMBOLS RARELY CARRY A ONE-TO-ONE . . ."
A cough. Now the prolonged five o'clock bell,
And I awaken, filled with imagination's depressant,
Rationality.
The bloodless foot shuffles cigarette butts
(Mere dirty dross of human nervousness),
And slat-back chairs cease creaking,
Go dumb as museum pieces,
Objectified.
And I am I,
Shaking out the eyes' dusty blankets
Past nine other sets of numb spectacles,
And each is of a similar species:
Students whose pens have dashed out marathons,
Dragging lagging sensibilities behind their scribble.
The voice erupts: "I SEE OUR TIME IS UP TODAY.
NEXT WEEK, BE PREPARED TO DO *WALDEN*."
The room darkens, the species lumbers out,
And the door goes closed against slow vacuum,
While heavy sighs stay locked in stale demise.
Outside, the city sun sinks through roofs
Of tight-eyed office buildings
As I walk to the car,
Dreaming of dinner and an evening cigar.

4/12 & 4/19/66 — [1] (04021)

Inquiring Adam

. . . be lowly wise:
Think only what concerns thee and thy being;
Dream not of other Worlds, what Creatures there
Live, in what state, condition or degree, . . .
Raphael, VIII, 173–176

But apt the Mind or Fancy is to rove
Uncheckt, and of her roving is no end; . . .
Adam, VIII, 188–189

— John Milton, *Paradise Lost*

Someday,
When unicorns
Drip in single file
From the kitchen spout
And drop,
Nimble as lions
On all fours,
Onto the porcelain sink,
I'll pause on the brink
Of discovery
And shout,
"Raphael,
        I
            Disagree!"

4/12?/66 (00498)

Meditation over Coffee, 4/14/66 †

A break in mid-April weather, and the morning, wet and Venice-bright, warms the cells of my head; the thawing process functions.

I remember sitting in the cafeteria at the university last year at this time. Where did the year between birthday and birthday go? It galloped in random fashion, and I began to burgeon out of a former ice-block —

A few pieces published modestly this year. One must start and, once one overcomes the initial self-consciousness of seeing one's name where others can efface and adulate indiscriminately, must teach himself that sheer and unflagging effort alone to sustain output is vital.

Soon, three days, I will turn twenty-five, and the sense of purpose is becoming more focused; the doubts of talent subside as I push ahead.

But what a staunch, unbending, frowning-too-often bastard I can be! The need/necessity to *laugh and interact!*

The need to educate oneself, never, never, never to deny the mind ample exposure; must accrete/add to the fund of knowledge: books

> people
>
> events

Lawrence's concern for strife — Hawthorne

> Melville

The elder Hank James knew that Adam had to experience evil/the fortunate *culpa* to achieve some semblance of dignity.

What happens when innocence resists maturation by being dragged over the coals of Hell? Emptiness and vacuity? I'm not sure.

Dr. Fielding, in *Passage to India*, travels light.

What about ties and travelling?

Sever connections? Not the answer.

Fend for self? Yes, but with the mind, not the arms and torso flailing helplessly.

I have lingered perhaps too long, not pushed my mind hard enough regarding common relations with mundane happenings.

Must push but always behind a smile, a spot of laughter.

Is this a time of containment, when youth deludes itself? Yes, and the misconception engenders from the apotheosis of hopelessness.

All significance resides in the commitment to the community, the striving, persevering.

Dogs spit

4/14/66 — [1] (05340)

Exigencies

He sits atop parapets
Of the school's museum of art,
Thumping a cigarette
*

Whose grey ashes
Jump walls of April space.

A radio splatters silence
Nearby,
And his eyes spring spiteful
As maddened cobras;
The ears bite each other.

His mind, a butcher knife on butter,
Splits particles of dust,
And he lapses,
Hardening inside gauzy riddles
Like fortunes in Oriental cookies.

Now he thinks of that cave,
The reason Christ chose to escape:
"What in hell was there
In there
That pared His nerves
Like manicure scissors to nails?

"Was it the darkness,
Nullity
(Our Father, who art in darkness,
Hallow be Thy shallow grave,
Thy cave),
Or was it reverberations
Of His gushing blood
That drove Him from us to Him?"

But it's late, and he should leave
These debates to concentrate
On more immediate things:
Titian and the Greek.
He must memorize discreet answers
The teacher expects to read
On tomorrow's blue-book sheets.

The break over, and he retreats
To hide his head in picture books.
He'll have to study long tonight
And eat from vending machines.
"The 'complete man,'" he tells himself,
"Is he who learns his lessons well
*

And leaves abstractions to the poets."

4/14/66 — [2] (00486)

[A busy-wheeling car] †

A busy-wheeling car
Cuts a path

Scattered gift wrappings,
Strangers to the symbols
She gave today.
Emblems

The creek by the black-walnut tree
By the Hollisters' house
Bubblerushes with winter's overflow.
On its surface, in the sun
In the shallow eddy,
Rush the circles of insect peculiarity;

4/14/66 — [3] (05341)

Dr. Johnson's Rain

I

It's the weather. The legs swell to enormous size.

Another day spent inside a bottle of camphor.
No Happy Valley this hot garret,
Where he meditates entries for a dictionary
And a candle drips drops of immortality
From a flame that festers in his raw-red eyes.

"Father! Father!" he cries. "Why can't I define you?"

He walks into the next afternoon through the fog,
And groggy gloom drips from walls, thatched roofs.
The cobbled water collects in puddles
*

Beneath his scrubby shoes, and his foot kicks
Imaginary obstacles above the blistered bricks.

"Father! Father!" he sighs. "Why can't I find you?"
An unclean wind thumbs leaves and other debris
Against his haggard face. At his back, the past
Repeats itself in the pitter-pat, pitter-pitter-pat
That saturates lumbering Thames, whose calm
Gives way to the graceful rape of perfect circles.

It's the weather. Hell's dregs flood his eyes.

II

A slovenly figure, fatter than marble statuary,
Goes lonely along Thames' muddy quays.
There are no spectators, no tattlers today
To testify to his silent, dying defiance.

His head is wet under thick rain. Grey stains
Collect like grease on his creased greatcoat,
Melt into motley sameness. Will these blemishes
Go unnoticed by the frail Mrs. Thrale?

"Father! Why didn't I understand your wisdom?

"What the knowledge, the fatuous quotations:
Martial, Livy, Lucan, Pliny the Elder, and Plato.
What easy philosophy! What pedants' canticles
It all was before your quiet, compliant eyes!

"Father! When is penitence consummated in action?

"Those slow eyes on mine, circles on the surface.
Something awakens thoughts of love that, in youth,
Fashioned immortality from a pair of ragged shoes,
And I see you now, seller among vacant bookstalls."

III

"Father! Father! I've been so apart from you.
Let me return to where we started together.

"Oh, Father! For the memory that washes backward
To the simpler, unstudied words and a head
That looks beyond poetry's borrowed ideas.
Let your demise comfort me now and those eyes
Light paths more ancient than Thames' tides!

"Father! Father! How does one as old as I
Do rituals for the mind's forgotten spirit?

"Oh, Father, from whose temple I tumbled too fast,
If it's not been too long coming, then hear me
And accept this hat I hurl to the river's hands,
That I may leave now and need never return
Through this crying rain to Uttoxeter plains."

4/14 — [4], 4/17/66 —[2] (04032)

[Poverty] †

                    Poverty
                        Mississippi Delta
                        Appalachian region
                        Negro slums of Chicago and New York
                        Watts district of Los Angeles

   Bringing a poem far along toward completion is exciting, filled
with some trepidation, the fear each time that this will be the last one,
that there will be no more creation — how can there be after reaching
each particular pinnacle?
   But then another one happens; like a sudden May shower it de-
scends on you out of no expected context.

               Two long religious poems I must bring along:
                        "A Hard Coming of It"
                        "Student Prince"

4/15/66 (05342)

[I have awakened early, . . .]

   I have awakened early, this Sunday morning, too early for the three
o'clock immersion, and now the mind runs slow as antique clocks in
some boutique in London. But this is a new morning, and already I
have walked outside to smell and witness, and I recall the words I
spoke with my mother late last evening.

The house was all black and indistinct owing to the absence of a
moon, and there were no brightlooming lights as there had been when
Jan and I left for the reading. The yellow car parked in the stall under
my upstairs study, I took a sody from the two o'clock rack and filled
the glass with ice. There was silence in the halls and rooms of the
house, where before there had been soft murmurs and quiet, civil gen-
tility, the urbanity of wealth, gathered and mingling together, many of
whom had grown up together, gone to the same schools, had the same
experiences, and now, after thirty years, were commingling again to
indulge reminiscence and nostalgic veins of gold.

I walked upstairs, covering the nineteen steps fully carpeted in
softmuted greens, and stood in my room, the one with all the memento-
like pictures and diplomas and knickknacks of the past hanging
strewn and yet ordered on the walls, standing with the pipestem coat,
like a '30s banker or '20s lawyer, in one hand, and there she was, com-
ing out of nowhere with insomniac strides, like a veiled phantom, in
her negligee, the nightbaggage of twenty-eight years of marriage.

The woman, still attractive long beyond her years, still retaining
in the soft, brown hair and the smooth skin a semblance of what, in
youth, must have been remarkable, simplistic beauty, stood there
now, talking with a son to whom she had just remarked, "It's hard to
imagine that tomorrow, actually already, you will turn a quarter of
a century."

And the son, "You know, I'm kinda different, I guess. Empathizing,
I would think that you must be sad. I am, or can imagine it anyway.
Don't you wish you were just starting it for the first time: the small
apartment, following the move from some large hotel by the park; the
war ration coupons and the little blue Buick you used to park before
the four-family apartment building in Clayton; all of it — the news of
the war in the morning paper — in short, all that now it has become
'camp' to call trivia or nostalgic minutiae?"

"Well, I don't know. To me it's just wonderful that there can be
all this from the two lives your father and I have made into one over
the years."

"I suppose you're right. It's too easy to sink into the past for com-
fort. Each day must be lived as though it were the best, the day of won-
derment, as though you were seeing it through the eyes of the poet,
everything new and exciting."

So I stood there looking at the woman, a mother who was tired
with happiness and that slow, silent sense of accomplishment and
satisfaction. And she had given a party, that evening, in her home for
the old friends, the civil and affluent members of a society that had
spawned hard work, perspicacity, and humble striving and perse-

verance; these were the ones who had started patiently and worked themselves into the upper echelons of the society which, fifteen years ago, had scorned their presence but which by now was used to praising and revering their accomplishments; these were the people who, that many years ago, would look at, read, the names of gentile bank presidents in the Sunday society section of the paper and say to themselves, "That's the man or this is the group who has decided to loan me five thousand dollars," or etc., the men of Protestant or Lutheran or Episcopalian descent, heritage, legerdemain, what have you of hand-me-downs, who looked down, condescending, with that air of haughty refrain, snubbing all but the financial aspect of the human encounter, and hesitant at that, as though their word were more weighty than God's or Christ's — or Mammon's at least. And these are the same men today who retain the title of bank president but who now are relegated to an occasional special box seat at the baseball park or reserved space under the list of credits for the outdoor opera or board of directors of the hospital or perhaps the wife of whom is appearing in the fashion section of the Sunday paper, not because they were able to touch up the baggy skin under the eyes or the jowls, because they could somehow hide or disguise the corpulence, but simply because the woman of the man who fifteen years ago had been something just because his name was Hickock or Shapleigh or Charles or DeWitt scrimped to buy a four-hundred-dollar Dior outfit, which has no place on her anyway save for the fact that it is the one big splurge-of-the-year Charles routine.

We left the party early for the engagement with my friends at The Circle Coffee House, below Grand, on Cardinal. It was a cold night, and the whir of the convertible meshed softly, mutely, into my ears, the car moving fast through the headbeams that searched with yellow or white fingers the intervening spaces between west- and eastbound traffic, so that when we arrived, there was a void, as if the opening of the door from the cold into the soft music of guitared "Greensleeves" came too fast for accommodation. We walked from the parked Jaguar, yellow and soft under the corner light standard and quiet in settling sounds, toward the coffee shop. Inside, the atmosphere was comfortable and not friendly but indifferent and catalytic, as though each knew that what was important and made all the difference was the group, the friends one joined or met or were introduced to at The Circle.

One Bouquet of Spice, one cup of jasmine tea, and the odor still remains with me now, long after the sipping; and we sat there, silent with ourselves, having been there before, knowing the routine, and

the frequent opening, closing of the door brought with it each time new
drafts of cold April, and we sat together, awaiting Gene's arrival.

4/17/66 — [1] (05343)

[*A Passage to India* — E. M. Forster]

A *Passage to India* — E. M. Forster

Possibility of brotherhood seems unsatisfactory —
        each individual isolated.
    Religion divides, doesn't unite.
Mrs. is a good example of Christianity:
        she trusts impulses, not ideas;
        religion and God, for her, are love.
    Her Christianity is one of mysticism.

But all Western culture based on hierarchies; so too in Indian re-
ligion.
    We impose system of order — always thirty-nine orders of some-
thing —
        religion — orders   God has infinite
        Chain of Being —   forms.
    Without hierarchies, *hay* anarchy, which levels all people to
    equal violence —
        burn the fire truck —
        exclusion/inclusion or else anarchy, rule by irrationality.
Forster's sympathies go out to Hinduism.
    Mrs. Moore either has vision or nightmare; she transcends all
    hierarchy.
    Moore has a kind of life, is reborn into a myth.
But Christianity has nothing to do with justice nor anything to do
with world — Forster
    Hinduism is closer to dealing with world;
        image of cave is closer to truth:
        complete incomprehensibility, indifference —
                                                Conrad
                                                Hardy
                                                S. Crane
        Mrs. Moore realizes futility of all: marriage
                                        justice

hierarchy and master/servant relationship

People in book all divided:
>food diff.
>custom
>stock stereotypes

•• Sensitivities out all the time for being hurt, like antennae on a butterfly

Christianity exclusive, hierarchical — separates the good and evil.
>|
>Dante/*Divine Comedy*
>teleological kind of world
In Hindu, evil as impt. as good but no sense of justice; it does not
>believe in correcting evils that exist.

We believe in order/hierarchy.

The caves are perfectly dark and circular, not sacred at all. They are caves of the world, symbols of unholy universe, in which all is dark and out away and beyond, circular; they mirror nature of world itself: no reason, no order, no one cave leading into another.

Hinduism echoes the oldest religion in world, when *no existe el orden.*

>Yelling through the caves,
>Box after box
>After box after box;
>Sounds resounding from rocks
>Through Marabar Caves,
>Off far-off walls,
>Returning the echo
>In myriad ten-folded
>Distortions:
>"Portions of the earth,"
>Earth-earth-earth,
>Lisping into faint pockets
>And buttoned;
>"World without end,"
>End-end-end;   Earth
>*

                    "God is love,"   End
                    Love-love-love.   Love

Even Hinduism inadequate because no ceremony can do either.

                    Fashion designers
                    Constantly shock our sensibilities,
                    Distort our "used to being,"
                    Seeing, acting according to definition.
                    Look at that skirt,
                    Climbing an extra inch
                    Above some disturbing kneecap,
                    Give an inch.
                    People rent the garters, cinch belts,
                    Plunged breastplates, etc.
                    I love "ibid."s, "et cetera"s, etc.

Under humanism, you abandon religion as barrier; belief in absolute brotherhood in this world, transcendental faith.

•• Machines are an extension of one's skin.

Trilling pointed out that *hay* very few Hindus in the book — all characterized by Godbole; they have no varying characteristics.

Aziz lives in social world, in which he believes *existen* cause and effects — must be sharp.
    Usually, Aziz guesses wrong reason for things that happen.
    Fielding's reasons are more correct than Aziz's, but his too are only partially so.

Adela Quested hopes to quest India intellectually but ends with emotional knowing.
    Fielding projects but can't experience for himself.

Technique of novel — Forster never leaves doubt of every character's position.

4/18/66 (05344)

University Nymph

A blast-furnace afternoon.
Who threw open the clinker door?
I sit drinking coffee outside the lounge,
On lawns no dogs defile.
"Love thy neighbour,"
Intones the campus queer,
"As thou love thyself."

To my right,
A green girl, wearing flesh,
Bare feet skipping over world's fair cobbles,
Stands below pillars,
Ten feet out,
A hand holding pendularly
One of her buffalo sandals.

She waves it like a railroad conductor
On some red-swinging night,
And now it's airborne
Above the ground's grasscool gravities,
Following her ambiguous intent.

What's up there
That got in the mind's way?
Why didn't that sandal return?
Then she is gone into the shade,
Shoeless as an urchin.

There's no trace of her under the portico.
My eyes swing up through her invisible path,
Where malintent and sandal went only once,
And there, perched like a strange Buddha,
Is a bulbous, stony face, not angelic,
With heavy, weathered curls crowning slit eyes
And a chipped nose. A waterspout Bacchus leers,
Myriad grape bunches, avocados, apples, pears,
All the color of soiled laundry,
Dangling in cluttered array, and there
Where the spout mouth gapes open
Is the sandal, hanging precariously,
Waiting for the next rain to vomit it.

4/19/66 — [2] (05122)

["Seminar in Symbolism" evolved . . .]

"Seminar in Symbolism" evolved out of a real incident, a seminar predominantly on nature in nineteenth-century American literature, though the topic for the week diverged to include symbolism. As was usually the case on these afternoons when the class met, my mind would wander to outdoor things of a nonacademic nature. This was the extent of my thoughts on nature. But this particular afternoon, the ears and mind were somehow geared to a willing suspension of disbelief, in which state I was receptive to and semiaware of the instructor's voice intruding on my wanderings and, therefore, the inclusions of real, generalized definitions of the meaning of symbols.

In this poem, I count three distinctive voices, the most salient one being that of the professor mouthing these generalized responses. These meanings serve in each case to bring the reader and the listener, the second clear voice in the poem, into a definite immediacy, the realm of the actual classroom. This second voice, the "I," is brought back each time into partial awareness of the other members of the seminar as well as the fatuity of the professor's efforts to pin down the slippery term "symbol." Then the "I" submits to the mind's preternatural identification with the "superreal" present/past — a totally new experience.

The third voice, which is separate from the other two, may be the voice of a conscience, an oversoul, or sheer omniscience. In any case, it serves to give direction to the moral intent of the poem.

The basic ideas behind the poem are set in jangling juxtaposition, dialectically opposing the rational and the irrational, the world of the imagination and that of the literal, objective realms of thought. On the one hand, the teacher and his disciples represent followers of truth, which man classifies, categorizes, and sets aside as ordered fact. On the other hand, the "I" is the voice of imagination, which balks at all attempts to set down orderly systems that we call truth.

In the course of the working out of this poem, the "I" recognizes that he has gone behind the mask, perhaps akin to the Spanish mystics in their ability to commune through the heart of the imagination, to reach the heart of the universe, which has God at its pinnacle, before returning, though, here, I'm not so concerned that there should be a readily accessible god to commune with or reach so much as just the ability on the part of the "I" to rupture the tenacious bonds of immediate reality, to get behind the mask of the mind, to wallow temporarily in the world of the imagination, and ultimately to return to real things of this world (dinner, office buildings, a cigar). It's the experience that counts here.

The substantial tenet of the Transcendentalists (and the Symbolists, later) is shown to still be valid in the mind of the "I": namely, that the truth of any object is manifold; that an apple, through words or other extensions of the mind, can be more than an apple, even more than a red-ripe apple; that, in fact, a whole aura can be conceived as a new truth not previously apprehended.

The actual facts of this scene are clearly visible to the reader and the "I," and so too are the transformations that occur as a result of the "I's" challenging mind. The booth is a small seminar cubicle in the university; a real teacher lectures to very real students, who are too busy trying to copy each word and phrase he utters from his tired, yellow notes to think about the significance of the phrases he recites, a little bored himself. The "I" sits around a table with nine other students. The floor beneath his feet becomes, in his mind, a roiling ocean-sea, on which, first, he imagines four cigarette butts to be white whales. He actually feels the water soaking his shoes and socks. After a time, his mind distorts the chairs and is unable to distinguish them from the occupants who fill them.

Too, in the second stanza, the question of evil imposes itself on the "I's" sensibilities, and he determines that it exists separate of any individual act in time, that it "lurks in the heart of the process" of all life at all times. Therefore, he not only forgives Ahab, but he apotheosizes the "one-legged arachnid," whom he imagines "still seeking the universe / Behind the web's masked patina" after the boat is scuttled.

In the third, shorter stanza, the "I" is disturbed from his trance by the actuality of the dismissal bell, which, no doubt, was the bell he heard ringing from the perilous *Pequod* earlier. He is returned to the world of "rationality," in which all objects get treated with similar precision and are "objectified."

He claims, unlike Roethke's "I" in "In a Dark Time," that he knows which "I" is *I*. Though a distinction is still made between the "students whose pens have dashed out marathons" and the teacher, whose voice announces the next week's assignment, the "I" recognizes that the class and the trance, his flight, have come to an end and that each one, himself included, is "of a similar species."

The final seven lines heighten his sense of sameness in the physical world of classroom seminars and weekly assignments, and as he walks toward the parking lot, alone, he is thinking of immediate needs: dinner and relaxing in some den chair at home, behind banal discourses in the evening newspaper.

The denouement, which culminates the tensions built into the poem's hundred or so lines, suggests that the "I" has come away with

an awareness of realities that exist behind the immediate perception
of things as they appear and his role in extending the perception.
The experience, this particular one anyway, is complete.

4/19/66 — [3] (05345)

Epiphany

> *. . . an old . . . horse galloped away in the meadow.*
> — T. S. Eliot, "Journey of the Magi"

A loud, thick night
Crowded our noisy sleep;
Its soft rain burned window frames
That held no glass.
That world on fire,
Where vertical and flat coalesced
Like colliding stars,
Singed our naked raiment,
Charred infinite half-lives of lust.
And there
In the eastern breach,
Where lightning shadowed the darkling sky,
Was a star too hot to recognize.

And I remember thinking,
"Something is being born
Somewhere."
But her teeth on my tongue
Repeated rituals of joyous strife,
And we grew to ripeness
In that season's brightest moment.

Somewhere, an angel stirred from hiding.
Three palominos,
Halos of Oriental brass,
Each hosting a ghost of an ancient order,
Passed through the burning frames,
Where the glass should have been,
And galloped away in the meadow.

That weary trio,
Decked with ragged panoply —
*

I had seen them before,
In a less satisfactory life
Perhaps,
Coming by camel or dinosaur,
Had heard their sandaled feet
Beating hard the pavements
In alien village streets,
Retreating from hostile calumnies
Into warmer climes reeking with fruit.
But where? When? And who had warned me
They were coming again?

My lips drew out her supple milk
Like hands of a craftsman
Unthreading strands from a tapestry.
"A host-drought consecration," I thought.
And then I knew the pagan ghosts
Come walking, come riding hard
Through deserts marred with crowded life,
Through courts diseased with endless wealth
And patronage and grave intrigue.
"Was I He who died so long ago,
And she, who lay upon my left,
The one who gave immaculately
That gift of matchless ecstasy?"

But she tasted my tongue too harshly,
And the blood ran sharp as salted pap
Where her teeth bit blistering lips.
I had sipped the whiteness of maternity,
But her breasts went dry from my gluttony,
And I cried like an orphaned child
Into the meadows' stifled ears.

The rain no longer spoke to us,
Was kept outside by rattling frames
That held a glossy, foggy glass.
The burning fires sizzled cold,
So the ears could hear no coming hooves,
And the eyes could only see themselves.
We slept like lovers born to die
In ageless acts of infamy.
And the three who had come riding by,
Burning like halos of the sun,
*

Rode on with gifts of flaming gold,
Into the mangers of the night,
Away in meadows of the sky.

4/23/66 (04036)

[April races to impasse.]

April races to impasse.
Its fingery vapours press cold,
Wrap tourniquets about air we breathe,
While in streets, lots glutted with machinery,
Puddles seethe, and everywhere, rain clamors.
Lions in heat beat against bars.
Cars are animals waiting turns to stampede
From forests flooded in monsoon seasons.
This is no place for civilian repose.
Retreat comes easily for those who concede
To the weather. Bears, lemmings, snakes
Bake their rancid scales under alien suns.
Sands on fire tire the million tired souls
Who have come by boat, plane,
Who have come by automobile to be saved,
Saved from the pains of old age,
Saved from recognitions of loss, saved
From themselves, and saved from death,
Which hides beneath their sheets, beds,
In catheters, and along the fine strip
Beneath their feet that contains shadows
That would otherwise spread out
Before them impetuous as sirens.

4/25/66 (02026)

The Poet in Me

        daily

Lives
        inconsistently;

Trembles like mosquitoes
Buzzing
        persistently;

Flips a dizzy cigarette
Over the rail,
Into the
        Mississippi;

Stretches arms high
In smoke-filled air
To measure the sky
Against the city;

Shrugs shoulders
Of the mind
At passing traffic
That spans time's
        spontaneity;

Yells like hellhounds
At churning tows
Strung out below —
Bowels in
        infancy;

Stands on a girder
Over water washing,
Wishing to drink
        infinity;

Dives through darkness
        insistently;

Drowns in "quick"
        lubricity

        daily.

4/26/66 — [1] (05123)

Secret

                            For Jan

Please don't tell a soul,
But
*

I like you a whole
Lot.

4/26/66 — [2] (05312)

Storm: A Dialogue

Spanish thieves in sandaled feet,
Wanting the "secret intelligence,"
Chased sightless beggars down streets
Too dark for common sense.

"Who put the storm out there
To shatter my sleepy rhymes
Like illusions lost to the aging blind
When they find their second sight?"

Angels wearing purple cloaks
Shed raiment and went naked
Through meadows piping poppy fumes,
By lakes with upturned fish.

"Who told rain to fall upward
And wither my thirsty dreams
That grew accidentally perfect
Like hyacinthine verse?"

A one-eyed sailor stood alone
On a beach no map disclosed,
Dashing stones in a mean, hungry sea
That started tides to shake the world.

"Who tucked thunder under the pillow
To muffle my restive sounds
Like waves that ride onto the shore
And hide themselves in shells?"

Nightingales covered with blood
Tottered in tedious, tandem flight,
Casting shadows against red winds
That fought to ruffle their brains.

"Who sent screenrending winds
To scatter my clouded thought
*

Like birds that waft to limbless trees
In lands they've never seen?"

Children hung with choking faces
And sockets dripping afterbirth
Swung from fast-whirling chandeliers,
Singing poems the silence heard.

"Who threw lightning against the lids
To pock my infant insight
Like bullies hurling burning sand
In eyes of five-year-olds?"

But as I lay beneath the sheets,
The moon broke in the east,
And all my doubts retreated fast,
And I returned to easy sleep.

I saw the thieves in sandaled feet,
That one-eyed sailor on the lee
Leave off the chase, set down the stones,
And pray forgiveness for their deeds.

Nightingales smoothed their ruffled blood,
Flew soft above scudding clouds,
And angels retreated from pagan fields
To don their purple mourning shrouds.

Children hung with choking faces,
Swinging from fast-whirling chandeliers,
Climbed down to wash away the waste,
Singing poems to my tranquil ears.

"Who can cage a dream at work
And insight clouded in infancy
Or restive sounds or sleep-filled rhymes
That fight to free man's poetry?"

4/27–29/66 (04030)

[A catchall for call girls,]

A catchall for call girls,
Devout whores of all classes,
*

And bored philosophers of eighteen
Or fifty who pass for twenty-four.

Cloclasure converses with Kreider,
The entrepreneur, about old times
They had together three years ago:
Automobiles, elapsed times
At local strips around White Cross.

"Those were choice, choice times,
And that little Crosley, remember?
How cherry of a machine!"
And I ask about elapsed times,
The chromium, brass-plated trophies
That still parapet his highboy
And the plastic toy models he made
When winter drove him indoors.
He still has the best elapsed time
On record — he's in the book.

"The market, you say? It's funny
You should put it quite that way.
I was just this day telling Sid
Felker to buy me in on beans
And a dozen shares of barley feed."

4?/66 (05151)

Babbitt Agonistes #1: Communion ‡

He wanders in nets
The Fisherman casts,
A blundering bundle of bungling
Attitudes.
His lobe-finned legs,
The scaly head
Try to slip free
From secular quarrels.
He swims in channels
Where no schools run,
Plunges through swells
To denser regions
*

Beneath the green sea's
Liturgy.

He passes vaults,
Gasping for air,
But the Fisher's bait
Follows his bubbles
As vultures the *Pinta*,
Until repast tempts
Abstinence;
He nibbles the wafer —
Soggy inducement
For mindless amens.

The body writhes;
Then the final tug,
And he rises, caught
In painful bends,
Genuflecting.

He breaks the surface
With upturned belly.
To his reverential amaze,
No barracudas
Circle tight
To chew his body
Into wine-hued chunks.

5/2–3/66 — [1] on 5/2 & [1] on 5/3 (05124)

Unmatched Ecstasy

They thrive by the score,
Living without growing
Under a folded roof,
In houses painted with juicy steaks
And occult spoofs on nomenclature.
Beneath stapled impermanence,
Martinets with red helmets
Stand at static attention.
Frequent visitors open their door,
Snap them one at a time,
*

As hunters winter cornstalks.
But they crave fresh air,
And the rasping flick
Down runways
Flecked with skid marks
Sets the halo flying.
A glow guides the curling body,
Until a shudder chokes it white.
Then each knows, in that instant
Before it lies discarded
In table graves,
In front-yard gutters,
The glory of its painless death.

5/2 — [2] & 5/4/66 — [2] (00485)

Reductio ad absurdum

Brown brows that should be grey
Grow shrubbery in shades of tired eyes.
Gold rimmed around thick glass
Glistens like two suns in eclipse,
While this ten-year-too-old mind
Defines events emotionally,
Lacking substance that lacks definition.

To his right, a student cringes,
Watching his wrist watch for futurity
That comes regularly each six o'clock
Every Tuesday evening. Academics
Play some sort of mental havoc
With considerations of time
That line his mind with sandbags.

His wrist piece is a neon eye
With ten years' experience
Behind its foreign mind, a brain
Blinking through silent revolutions,
Sprung, cased, and counterbalanced
With metallic precision, guaranteed
To define time, substantially.

Eyes are eyes that underlie memory
Beneath glass that separates the now
From its ever-present recession.
But each (the eyes), when left untended,
Goes predictably slower and slow,
Until lies shatter them and they die,
Each six o'clock, every generation.

5/3/66 — [2] (00553)

Boats Against the Current

Day-before-yesterday snobberies
Suggest refuse
(Dung heaps,
Garbage steeped in all-black
Backyards);
They rest anachronistically
As Whitehall chain mail.

Who ever knows what "fixings"
Rode wings of meretriciousness
Or who the "solid" party was
To unreal shenanigans
Washed clean by fanatical few,
Who rushed to ticket booths
To claim "accidental" quinellas?

The Wolfsheims, Esteses, Bakers:
Yesterday's urchins bookmakers
Admired and feared,
Their sons elevator jockeys,
Delivery boys chauffeuring corsages
To LaDue parvenus.

But the refuse, slime,
From which climb the Gatz-bys,
Lady Ashleys . . .
Isn't it primogenial
And sound, too, the slime
That windfalls and landfalls
Bulldoze,
Then refill with newer men?

Can't you see them,
The ruptures,
Dike fissures, everywhere
In a world patently corrupt?
Don't you realize they're unseen
At first? They come slow,
Then burst like flourishing Judas trees.

The trouble doesn't rest with the people
Necessarily
Nor in the dreaming either
But with what they leave behind
In wakes of hurried tradition —
I mean the others,
Those wide-jawed dreamers,
Those hind-duggers drinking dust
And ignored by select success.

I accept my station
Gracefully,
Though I'd gladly submit
To mobile poverty
If some understanding economist
Could teach me to exchange
My ninety-dollar suit
For bushels of wheat
Or mattocks to dig Indians
And pigtailed blacks
From embryonic graves.

But don't you see?
It's that the dream,
The possibility, does exist,
Breeds like mosquitoes
On the eye's swollen surface.

Yet,
That the dream persists,
Lepidopteral, unreal,
Is, at best, tentative.
Don't you see?
Can't you see this?

For who can tell tomorrow's children
That today's milkman
*

Was yesterday's lawyer's son,
That their benefactors
Were dentists a decade before,
Or that one fine day
Their own offspring
Might be Israeli kings
Or buried under slime
In Thessaly?

5/6/66 — [1] (00491)

[This is the first time . . .] †

This is the first time I have put my fingers to a typewriter, and the
feeling is extraordinary; it's been close to three weeks since a poem
has crossed my mind, not because I've slumped but because of the
voluntary cessation in the process, so that now it will take me some
time to attune the mind to that type of thinking again.

All fifty of May's
Early morning degrees
Slide like goblins
Through my knotted hair

Jacksonville, up 67,
Lies like statuary,
Colossal and slow as tarnish
Over basement furniture
Whose varnished patina
Goes cold in time's tomb;
A town that time forgot,
Locked in custom
Like toys children leave
In backyard lots
As they slouch into manhood.

Who dares to rent clothes
That fall away
In time's decaying pageant —
*

Legend of the wandering Jew
Come riding slow, come walking
Lewd as naked golightlies
Down Fifth Avenues of the mind?

The kind old florist,
The local druggist, a slatternly,
Late-night Blanche DuBois,
Caddy Compson come home
To Jacksonville to see her child;
The mildwild bugs that scatter light,
Cicadas, frogs that croak the time;

Pat Lyon at the forge,
And Addie is a horse,
A wet seed wild in the teeming soil,
Where blood runs swift as serpents;
Its head bolts up, sigmoid,
Sidewise through the knee-high grass.

Muscles of athlete, head of Pluto,
Sirens with silt that hangs
In lichen reservoirs, capsules
Springing, and everywhere, birds
Come fluttering to fornicate
In random flight with tandem
Skill, adroitly, exigently,
And sparrows nestle under tile-red eaves
Like leaves about to burst their buds,
The human heart, the eye of May
Delayed in troughs that break the sea.

A down-topped drive by fields
Brown with lustering seeds
Seething with growth beneath surfaces
That leak germ of June consummation.
It's been a long winter,
And signs of late-night, coldhuddling
Lovers
Communing under covers
Walk the streets,
Bellies tumid as pineapples
And half as wet, though husky too.
*

The blue of day sprays pavements
That glister with silverquartz,
And the Square stares back at us
From all four sides
Like carneyqueer mirrors,
Distorting life's perspectives,
The narrowslender mind,
A plumpsquat body,
Perhaps,
That accounts for the lapse
In sensibilities.
A town gone stale as pastry
Left overnight
Behind glass;
A town, hamlet maybe,
Crowned with glories
That never were since children
Left to discover what lay
Beyond the furrowed fringes
That their fathers planted with soy
And barley seeds — the things
That were the city: touring cars,
Gramophones, and a fedora hat,
Where bib overalls and boots
Walked their own walks and
Tin lizzies and half-ton pickups
Throated business to deceased.

5/31/66 — [1] (Prose), [2–3] (Poems) (05346)

The Prodigal Children

For Jan, in May

The headless horseman,
A yellow sports convertible,
Flees dawn's gaunt apparition,
Whines down country strips,
Ripping May's fifty degrees
Like hands a plastic bag.
The car, a goblin,
*

Slides stroboscopically
Past wallowing sows' eyes,
Beneath laundered skies
That withhold impatient heat.

We race away,
Distancing the city's silvery ghost,
Pacing ourselves against no-clocks,
Erasing imaginary blocks of time
That contain people
In White Cross.

We flee that city
Retrogressively,
Not just beyond clipped lawns
And planned littlehouses
But by immediacy
Itself,
Into a past that thrives
Like ancient taboos.

And at once,
A blink discloses
One,
Then manifold billboards
Fading under a feverish sun
That never knows defeat.
But the eyes know
What the mind has yet to see:
An ancient civilization just ahead,
Growing, still, in its tired soil.

Penshurst, if you please,
Up 67
As the buzzard flees:
Statuary lying colossal
As cast-iron lattice work;
A town gone stale as pastry
Left overnight behind glass;
A lukewarm remnant
In time's subsiding womb,
Locked in custom
And dislocated
Like toys children leave
*

In backyard lots
When they slouch into manhood.

Am I the kind old florist's son
Or one of the local druggist's boys?
Is she
Who rides with me
Some slatternly, late-night
Blanche DuBois
Or careless Caddy Compson
Come home
Embracing pointed calumnies
To see a nameless child?

Now, day's blue noon
Sprays pavements that glister
With silverquartz.
The Square stares at us
From four angles
Like carneyqueer mirrors,
Distorting self-conscious perspectives,
Filling narrow-slender minds
And plump-squat bodies
With unknowing glimpses of themselves.
We see them seeing us,
Striding easy,
Eyeing windows lined with vapid dreams
That come from newer worlds.
We are the freaks here,
Children who wear their namesakes.

It's the children. They escape
The gartered constriction
Parents wear about their brains;
They flee inculcated complaints
To seek out richer societies
Beyond the furrowed fringes
Their own fathers sow with soy
And barley seeds.
Cultivation bears no relation,
In their impatient minds,
To wheat thrashers
And co-op combines.
Perhaps this accounts
For the lapse in sensibilities.

But we've returned, now,
To confront the source,
To abide with invisible remorse
That breeds in bib overalls and boots,
That goes helling Saturday nights
And bends the spirit of Sunday
Like strongmen lifting rubber weights.

We have come home with ourselves
Intact,
Practical pilgrims
Who know the virtues of slow change,
No change.
We'll crusade against elm disease
And things like that.

5/31 — [2], 6/2 — [1], & 9/27/66 — [1] (04014)

The Withheld Sensibility

Whoever mothered mildwild bugs
That leak nightlight
In the mind's whitewet palm,

Whoever ran fast through larch
Or matted juniper at dusk,
Chasing a shadow of former love,

Must confess
Life's unrecoverable beauty
To himself,

Just as the bent
Narcissus
Spoke the meaning
Of Benjy's deeper moaning
For him.

5/31 — [3], 6/2 — [2], & 9/27/66 — [2] (00495)

[Another fine, quick trip . . .] ‡

Another fine, quick trip to Jacksonville — returning in time to a town where the ghosts of Glenn Miller, Hal Kemp, Tommy Dorsey still flow on Saturday, country-club nights, *Arabian Nights* nights, on which townsfolk dress up in sports coats, wear carnations in their lapels to celebrate someone's twenty-fifth anniversary.

When does the newness, novelty, dissolve again into the unimaginative dust from which it comes: tractor, mule-trodden dust, whose particles burst forth spontaneously for a creative, unsustainable flicker, then skid downward, drifting listlessly in blackbrown mounds of just soil accumulation again?

Who can say, predict, how long the mind can go on accepting phenomenal reflections

6/12/66 (05347)

[If the magician smiles] †

If the magician smiles
While some audienced
      Houdini
Drowns in spectacular bubbles,
     The moon will cry.

Marc, Susan, and Jan reside
    in absentia.

Who should survive
  the man with asbestos fingers?
   Thoughts linger so long
     d
      o
       w
        n,
     running
     [Caligula's *illegible, ed.*]

I was scared,
   pared as bitten nails,
    sharing,
    *

tearing,
            caring for nobody.

You
  Bastard!
    Clasp lips,
      Rasp teeth over
        Sandpaper

I am
  so tired.
          The fires inside me
              sizzle cold, like exploding furnaces
                  in the watery holds of a sinking freighter.

And where's the boy
      Who should be after Bo-peep?
      He's chasing female sheep,
      Doing rituals of sodomy.

A baby, diapered,

6/22/66 (00942)

Grandfather to Himself

That's a strange place to keep perfume
And a vanity mirror . . .
In the kitchen window, I mean,
Where you can't see me seeing you
Fastidiously estimate your features
While I eat across the way each evening.

I don't mind your radio screaming
Or the slow odors of meat
And bread that settle like phoenixes
In this yardstick corridor separating us.
Who would notice the noises, perfumes
Any other season than this hot summer?

Drawers slam; plasticware shares space
Where the breeze should be,
And I just sit here, staring nowhere
Particularly.
Yet I bet if Alice were here,
She'd say something. I just bet she would.

That highway out there . . .
It can really scare a person
With so much insomnia.
Doesn't it ever just want to quit?
That jet overhead on the roof . . .
I wonder where it's going.
If Alice were here, I bet she'd know.

This heat . . . so sticky. If I could drink,
I'd take a single shot of whiskey,
Iced.
She always liked it that way. . . . Say,
Where is she? Alice? Want a whiskey, dear?

I can hear them across the way,
Playing tag, kick-the-can.
Wonder who'll lick her perfume,
Whose room she'll lie naked in tonight.
Those kids . . . they'll be frightened. What about . . . ?
Who'll tuck them into bed, douse the lights?

Alice would say, "Who cares anyway?
When will you learn to concern yourself
With me? You be the homebody I married,
Not a monkey that gapes and stares at others."
Where are you, Alice, my sweet?

Maybe those kids'll ring my bell.
I'll tell them lore, mystery stories.
I have a brand-new carton of bubblegum.
They never come anymore. Not since Alice . . .
Who'll rinse their dishes, put them to sleep?
There I go again. I should think about myself,
Keep my mind off things that don't concern . . .

God, but it's hot. If tomorrow's like this,
I'll . . . Alice? Is that you crying inside me?
In whose room tonight? . . . A brand-new carton . . .
*

God! Let me sleep tonight and dream of children
And Alice and ice-cream cones, or I'll . . . I'll . . .
Anything to forget how little is little, being alone!

6/30/66 (04017)

[I am what I will be]

I am what I will be
In a decade or three
If humility doesn't frighten me away
Tonight.
It takes a time to grow,
To throw off husks of continuity,
To show the faithful few
Who share the silty hopes
That groping is worth the pains,
The row-hoed agonies of maturity.
Tonight, when July is born,
I sit here warning myself these things —
To love the simple pleasures
That ask for liberation.
Incantatory dreams cry out inside,
Hiding from the mind's free hand.

7/1/66? (05144)

[I ask so little of life, . . .]

I ask so little of life, just to rise above the tedium, the common-
ality of day, to make the mind say things it didn't know it held in-
side. The wideness, fullness of experience is what I crave: a minor
Dante, whose saving grace is immortality — that's the price you pay
for humility.

This is a fine, preserved night, the first of July, and something new
has happened. I know, now, that love lies fully in the small acts of easy
obligation: a mother who has watched her son grow out of the love
of two others so far away in sensibility; a mother so beautiful in her
duty, her crying, silent love. And so tonight, I saw it, was filled with
its ubiquity like fragrance from the honeysuckle, the mimosa tree,

when blossoms of softfuzzy reds fill limbs, then fall to bear progeny on an unalien ground.

And I know where the failure lies: how I spoke, telling her, one night, that as children grow, they go away from the source, the beginning of their life, into the strife and busy traffic of impersonal days and stray crazies and waifs who never knew, cared, felt they owed the world a tin, thin dime;

how, like tonight, when the fog rolled in on everything, all one's life could be covered, bathed, in a sheer patina of ruffled camouflage; how I told her that parents have to accommodate to their children's new environment. But I know, now, what she said was right, that it's the springtime of youth to plant new seeds in that mind's womb that conceived, brought forth the opportunity to grow, to go away or toward the beginning again. And that source lay open as a steaming wound tonight. How I wanted to say, "Mother, I love . . . love." And then the simple kiss on the cheek to try and say, "Yes, I know the painful birth that grows more harsh each day, unless . . . unless . . ."; I see it all now, slow and strong in the mind's eye, how to say, "Yes, yes," the Everlasting Yea that knows no limitations, no bounds, manacles. I feel so much what no words will say. For her I pray, I say, "Love that hides in unchecked disrespect must slink from its crater and go out to you, Mother . . . Mother . . . love, love," crying, screaming, "toosilent love!"

7/1/66? (05168)

Expulsion

The eyes' dim light goes dark as beer,
And I hear angels' raucous chants
Dancing in my ears.
    All's gone from this world!
    Tongues droop like dog tails.
    Eyes locked tight as deposit boxes
Hide their contents behind heavy blinks.

Do you remember that first, fast kiss
Or the last purge of youth
In wet bedsheets?
    All's gone from this world,
    Where, once, friends smiled,
    *

Ran races with each other,
Passing our names like relay batons.

I sing a blind-tired song tonight.
Lightheaded memories leap barren furrows
Where we planted sighs.
        All's gone from this world!
    Mad seeds scattered wild
    About that child/woman's eyes,
But the season was bad for harvesting.

Quick winds split our dust-dry dreams
Against walls built of saber teeth;
We were eaten alive.
        All's gone from this world!
    Two thousand evil years,
    Repeated in a solitary lapse,
Were mastered by bastard importunity.

She's gone from this world of light.
A portion of my mind is lost
In the sea's extremities.
        All's gone from this world!
    I am a blighted Pharaoh,
    Harrowed by another's curse,
Bursting like fish eyes out of water.

Where are you, daughter, when I cry,
"Bring me nosegays to bathe in
When I pray
        (All's gone from this world!),
    Sinless bowers to lie under,
    And a sun too bright to hide behind
When I look for you inside myself"?

7/7/66 (04039)

This Shallow Grave Is Myself

I run out of myself,
A scared jack rabbit
Escaping brainy blasts
That come out at me
Through night's bramble seams.

I sit typing, absolutely nude,
Wrestling with some private angel,
Demon, I don't know which,
In the dark face of this easy keyboard.

Where am I going?
What paths can I follow
Now that the storm has washed my runs
Out of their fixed geography?
It's something I can't resist,
This persistent warring.

Maybe it's just an angry band of fallen gods,
A devil of no ordinary proportions
That hunts me down like so much carrion
On a sunless, sightless sea of sheet ice.

I am falling off the edge,
Holding by a single finger to the laurel's stem.
But the curse's weight is bringing me down
And d
    o
    w
    n,
       downward; downtrodden, I fall apart,
Call out for succor that doesn't exist.
I must resist the easy temptation sleep affords.

The restless cavities of my soul echo
Like uneven breathing of five-year-olds.
I can see it now, darker than the deepest shades
That fill the pool's shallow silt,
Deeper than the darkest trough of the tidal wave.
That cave! I'm being swallowed,
Troglodytical,
Sucked in like water leveling to the critical drain.

Why does pain come to those who deserve it most?
What is this hurt that hosts me now, in this hour
When everything else is smothered by sleep's semen?

I creep on my belly, a simple being being born again.
When does it end, the pain that lines the eyes
With ugliness and the foul stench of bat manure?

Before me, I see a string of feckless waifs,
*

Balls on their scabby feet, manacled with flaming slag,
And I stop to ask their destination.

"But don't you know? We're the dead coming home.
Join us, fellow. It hurts to run alone. Follow, follow!"

But that light ahead. Can it be for me to follow,
Or am I a creature too cautious to chase stray beams?
What's that echo setting up behind my ears?
Is it a voice I've heard, or is it my own? Who knows?

Now I return, hoping to keep that light before me.
But there seems no end, and I am bending about myself,
Walking out of the cave, up the slimy path into myself again.
Where have I been? When was I here before?

Sleep, hide me until I find an answer or drown beneath my sheets!

7/8/66 (05125)

[Light rum with a twist of lime —] ‡

Light rum with a twist of lime —
    This is the Yale Club,
      in New York,
        1897–July 26, 1966

  Young men who were nothing especial
in New Haven, used to hang out at the
Yorkside, Trumbull Buttery, find their sophisticated niche.
  I suppose one could come in here every
afternoon, late, for a quick drunk, then slink
home to some renovated
            tenement without much loss
to one's identityless dignity.
      Whoever travelled to Bennett,
            Poughkeepsie,
            Conn. College
surely must know that those good old days
can be brought back to life easy as a wink,
    on an inebriated, rum-swizzle whim —
      travel by signatured junket

This austere, not-quite-staid-old-England club had
its inception the same year Faulkner was born.
   Now I ask you, humble jury, which has
more worth?
   That's tough to answer, because the
one is quite dead physically, while the other
runs ahead into a traditionless future no
member's list will deny.
   I sit at a table old as anything
out of Mory's, waiting for a Yale friend —

   How can the mind begin to grasp the variegated
enormity of New York? Where does one simple pair
of eyes first glance? Is it that, no matter, it's
just never enough — the scope — time? I would
have to be a purveyor of clairvoyance to know all
that's going on in my mind — not all

7/26/66 (05350)

[A joint crowded with adolescent reprobates —] †

A joint crowded with adolescent reprobates —
                  late-night party, coming from which
            one will die in drunken crash;
                  they erect a bronze monument
                     for extraordinary bravery —
                                    Gordon Pasha

Adele Fitzsimmons
Julie Milo
Bloney Millard

Each one a king
      in his own local beat, fief;
queens by the baker's dozen,
   unlucky as Cleopatra,
      Desdemona fornicating
         in a basket of hot asps.

Who chases windmills anymore?
    I need someone killed:
        his conscience.

Who chases windmills anymore?
    high-school football jerseys
    and cutoffs,
        white socks,
            and two hundred lonely kids
                just wishing, without knowing,
                    someone would channel them.

7–8?/66 (05348)

[This is just a little token]

This is just a little token
With a moral.

This is not a joke and
Not so horrible.

If its nose seems broken,
Feed it orally.

If its body were oaken
And its hair sorrel,

It could still be spoken.
If left on your door,

Peer into its eyes —
It might be a princess in disguise.

You can see
What lies inside:

The ugliest things
Hold most beautiful surprise.

8/9/66 (05126)

Lake Nebagamon, Wis.: The Camp △

The rec hall rings round
With stifling noise
And sounds of anxious boys.
I hear an easy voice
Call out behind my age:
"Face the facts.
There's no disgrace
In growing up, in sowing seeds,
Unless the past intrudes
To set rules in the future."

Camp Nebagamon . . .

I see what I was at ten:
Receptacle . . . bright-eyed face
And sowfat belly,
Loving to eat and swim,
Ready to aim a rifle,
Fling arrows with a snap of the wrist.
Everywhere,
I see a healthy subordination.

Camp Nebagamon,
And the rain cuts jigsaw patterns
Over clapboard cabin roofs.

Lake Nebagamon . . .

When a man grows light
As milo,
His eyes die
Each time he cries
For his father.
Dante and Sam Johnson
Were children at fifty-six.

Walk out of yourself one night,
Into Gethsemane gardens,
Stop on the verge of yourself
To ask pardon of God,
Go farther than the sun's extremity
And peer,
Listen to a solitary albatross
*

Squeaking like old desk drawers,
Watch it turning through pewter sunsets
Into brighter insanities;
Then you may just die
With the gold-drooping dusk.

May I always tell myself to return!

8/11/66 (00002)

Keep the Fires Burning ^Δ

For Larry Cartwright

Who can hear the silent pine
Whining,
Bereaving a boy's departure,
Or the soft-trod paths
Pumiced under no boys' feet?
Will the Wisconsin breeze
That settled in summering ears
Breathe in a boy's newer dreams
In some unforgetting bed?

I know the secret of everything!
It's friends, boys!
It wends through the spruce
And folds beneath waters;
It sits at your table
And hides beneath your pillow.

Who can refuse that gift,
The harbinger that comes calling
Like a happy beggar
Behind parting farewells
And when snow and rain
Detain the slower spirit?

I am witness to summer's grace.
You are the ones, boys!
This is the place!
Don't be forgetting
Nor ever regretting the myth
That is your birth,
*

For being born comes fast,
Sometimes;
It matures in the youngest mind,
Sometimes.

Boys! Boys! This is the truth!
How can you not know?
Growth is that sacred moment
When all else falls away
And all that stays
To remind you it ever was
(The growing)
Is the faith that those
Who breathed and slept,
That those who ate and played
With you, tomorrow's men,
Will always be your mates
When you say the words
"Friend"
And, again,
"You are my friend!"

8/18/66 — [1] (00001)

Exalted Thought △

There's something about singing
That lifts a lowslung spirit;
It's the song sung with soul
That builds the heart,
Fills the whole, slow earth
With a breath
That never forgets its birth.

8/18/66 — [2] (00003)

[Camp's final day,] △

Camp's final day,
And the quick, cold air
*

Cramps the free-seeking spirit.
Boys are ready to bid farewell
To their two-month community,
And I am sad,
A friend among closer friends.

But this is my house, too,
A fifteen-year place of worship
And play. A life in a day!
That's the way it is with me,
Here today,
A preacher among small believers.
When will I return?

At my back,
The fire crackles,
Consuming birch and ash.
Who could ever imagine such thoughts
Could arise from dying things?

When the weather goes foul,
The lungs holler for breath;
Life comes short as loco chuffs.

This is where boys become men.
When the days dwindle down,
Winter comes around again,
And tokens of grace go unseen,
Glow like imaginary dreams.

A drizzle-slow Friday afternoon:
A grey sigh covers everything,
And campers move restlessly,
Like uprooted émigrés.

And then the train homebound.
What have they found here,
The boys, I mean?
They've been outside themselves
This summer.
Omnipotence knows no dominion,
Makes no distinctions
In this northern fort.

8/19/66 — [1] (00004)

Season's End △

For "Muggs"

Trunks piled high as shipping crates
Await stevedores.
Dust-swirling cabins are vacant
As discarded pepper tins;
Their screen doors
Creak in the rain's imperious face.

The boarded-up rec hall
No longer reeks of hot meals
Or feels the dizzy weight
Of children milling, spilling drink
Over hardwood floors
That wear scars of two-score years.

The boys are going slowly
Down brown-rusty tracks,
Cracking barriers
Where birch ends
And the easier scent of poplar and ash
Is lost in diesel exhaust.

We who waved at the station
Take up the highway home,
Seeing in each fleeting town
The same boys running down hills
Where we don't stand, anymore,
Waiting to check their graceless descents.

8/19 — [2] & 9/6/66 (00005)

[It's about this weather —] †

It's about this weather —
    the tether chokes my neck.
I am a reckless fellow,
who doesn't mind simplicities;
few pride themselves on pleasures
I consider luxuries.
    I am a wizard of TV
dinners.

I win the giant sweepstakes
each week,
   peek behind the sealed envelopes
that hold answers no questions require.

   The Drift of Things —
         Eric Cloclasure   (poet)
         Veronica Lovelace

   Baldwin — White Cross

                        poems of Florida:
                           first trip, "Memphis,"
                                          etc.
                        Peaches era

A dog dies.
   The girl mourns its loss:
      "It's not the death but the time in between."

8/19/66 — [3] (05351)

[This is the finer portion of night, . . .]

   This is the finer portion of night, when three days' constant rain has
finally abated behind the ears. Now, there is no pelting disturbance
on the roof of this cabin, no patterned sounds against the waterproof-
ing of a poncho. It is all quiet now except for the Mahler symphony
that fills the ears.
   A slow coldness slips through this room, and my weariness climbs
walls of sharpness. While the body rests, the mind spins ancient
thought: Oh, that the mind finds no rest! Let me always be awake to
the nuances of each day. Let the eyes say through a smile, a laugh,
that all is well that begins and ends well. I will be alive. I will over-
come, defeat, lassitude; I will beat it at its own lame game. How can
a person not know that to follow his God-endowed right to learn and
see and breathe is the only thing worth all the living a person initiates
in so many days?
   It's freedom, man, and the will to overcome inertia,
      freedom to choose and endurance to lose for the moment,
      freedom to look boredom and lifelessness and indifference straight
in the eye.

It's a long haul, all right, and the "bag," the scene, has to be a little different if a person will make it. Effort to persevere in what he knows is what he wants, no matter what the consequence.

We drive out not knowing what to expect, and we find a guy with class . . . an auditorium, the curling rink, filled with too-young, too-fast girls and boys, and there, presiding as though a king or leader/ prince, Sam the Sham, a guy not older than myself, filled with life and the desire to tell them, the younger ones, that it's not all sham. Doesn't he speak to the guys on the sidelines who think indifference is a sign of maturity? Why have anything to do with them? "What I have to tell you tonight," he must think as he totters and rants against juvenile cant, "is that you've got to love it, the entertaining, and that a person has got to believe in what he's doing or it's no-go."

I know what he's got behind that beard, the "nasty-old-man" smile: it's a wealth of enjoying and living and fighting to overstride the limits of himself.

We have strayed into his life tonight and come away higher than drugged dreams and spirited drinks could ever hope to do to us. We have heard and seen, felt and screamed out silently into the scalding fluids of the brain's calm ocean.

God bless Jane Jewell! Bless Sam for his humanity!

8/22/66 (05352)

Temporary Stay △

We approach the slow city,
Cloaked like a sleeping princess
On the lip of a hill;
Neither of us cares what witch
Fixed that throat-clogged apple.
Imagination's constancy,
The mind's timeless antic,
Subdues the necromantic spell.

Twinkle-fuzzy lights
Blink far out,
Tiptoe over the lake's wizened face.
Beacons go red, then null,
Their voices noiseless as dog calls.
*

Here in the harbour,
Hulls that know no stopping
Resist the channel's chop till dawn.
But we'll be gone
Before those high-shouldered tankers,
Wands that Moses never knew,
Crank Cyclopean props
And veer obliquely from the shore,
Parting waters of a thousand ports.

Now we drive home,
Alone as unknown pioneers
Leaving disappearing traces
Behind twin-braced Conestogas.
The smoothbellied bridge
Climbs higher than ever before,
And grain elevators, oar docks
Float in tilting retrograde.

We are those lights
On the hilled horizon
And the ships moored tightly
With perishable lines.
We are that raucous cascade of sound
That came bounding, tripping, winding wild
Across the ears' invisible spines.

As we head home, our eyes,
Clocks that forget to remember,
Filter out uneven shades,
Tear with incommunicable surprise.
Ragged grass and roadside eyes
(Coon, deer, and peregrine cats)
Scatter before us
Like illusive thoughts that poets have.

We've entered the city and returned
With another of those treasures
That lie just ahead
Each somehow-, somewhere-tomorrow,
Awaiting only our discovery.

We will never forget
Duluth,
*

When strangled some other where,
Under copper-colored fahrenheits
Of sulphur-covered air
Or in the ruthless mangle
Of pitiless cities,
Locked in some other when.

8/23/66 (00006)

Taps

Day is done.
The roads are muddy
And loose as no-colored putty.
Who can see, when mist
Whispers through pines and spruce,
Where the breeze should be,
Beyond the windshield's scope?
Who unleashed this wetness?
What wild wizard would belch
This slobber-drunk night,
Mindful of no-people out for love
Or discovery?
We pass through that glass
Like undefined memories in gauze,
Outclassed by nature
And a god no eye could find.

Gone the sun,
Behind birch and virgin pines,
Dispersed like dead air
Before a pair of fans
Whose chopping blades are razors.
We drive where the light was,
Swerving for dead raccoons
And fabulous jumping frogs
That escape haunt-clogged swamps
No humans infest.
Is this that source where pests
Demand painful conversation
And radical explanation to simplicities
Adam was warned against by Raphael?

From the lakes
To ten thousand other forsaken bodies,
We gambol, swilling blended whiskey
And boilermakers in flight.
This ragged, mist-spitting night
Challenges us like the wicked witch
In search of oven fodder.
Why was Hitler a male witch?
Do Jews make good gingerbread men?
Cookies spoil in dank cellars;
Their faces break, brittle as bones,
In crispy furnaces of the imagination.

From the hills
We come, to further hills that spill
Like daredevil barrels
Over the lip of this lake.
Can't you hear the waves there,
Paring themselves against the shore
Like demons' nails on circular saws?
There's a war growing tumescent
Beyond that last hill, toward which
We go, now, slow as lemmings
That doubt their own motivations.
There it is, that ear-breaking lake,
Superior to none but itself this night.
Where are the million blighted souls
Who fight in swamps and rice fields?
(I saw a real Indian yesterday,
Dressed anachronistically in war bonnet,
Offering handfuls of unshred wild rice
To customers come to gorge themselves
On All You Can Eat For Three Dollars.
"God, Mom! It's a real Indian!"
Bastards that laughed and touched him!
Buffalos and whooping cranes are less
Extinct.)
Who will send the slant-eyed freaks
Weeping in agony for deeds done
In some combustible notion of freedom?
Don't they know that freedom is word,
That words are rationale for lack of action?
Action is neither walking with a gun
*

Nor stunning crowds with rhetoric.
I am an anti-semantic gingerbread man.
I act in the name of others,
Those brothers of the slime and mire
Who load their minds' quags
With boisterous folly.
Who can let them go unnoticed,
When night spreads over itself,
Like orgiastic reptiles just hatched,
Four horsemen who ride with scythes?

From the sky
Lightning fails to break the mist.
There's something frightening when air
Shares the nostrils' passageways
Like too many people crowding
Fallout shelters on a calm day.
Something hangs distrustful out here,
Where water and vapor coalesce
As though night's shroud might never lift,
Darkness never ascend to daybreak,
Nor midnight ever come again.
We gather driftwood from the beach,
Tossing up decay on littered decay.
What were once trees now explode,
Join the fire's ravagement,
And here is light burning off,
Drilling temporary holes
In this raucous, antic-filled screen.
Who has seen a shell blast a bluff?
Who can hope to stay catastrophe?
People! People! Can't you see it?
Discreet politicians who drink milk
Can't tell you the simple nontruths.
A curse descends on them,
And the end cries for recognition.
Who can tell this colossal wreck
That what the world needs now
Is to slow down and take stock?
The earth's shelves are cluttered;
Things and things spill off them,
And inventory comes later each year.
Somebody has been pinching things.
*

(I saw a house so filled with china
No bull could have got through the door.)
And where is the bull turned buffalo?
There's a distinction to be made here
Between extinction and survival;
I refer you to the word "revival"
In the Thorndike daily stock return.

All is well
Somewhere, where neutrality flourishes,
Jack and Jill still trudge to apexes,
And the King of France
No longer dances with himself.
(Hear tell, he wears nothing underneath
Except a terminal case of leprosy.)
But now he shakes, casts dice, rolling
In the name of Lot's sacred lot.
Sodom erodes like Mexican soil,
And hotels sink eight feet each year.
Can't you hear the crumbling dirt
Suffocating worms and steel piles?
When will the Queen of the Adriatic
Dissolve into static grots of cold mud?
And where is the King of France now?
Why, he and the cow are after Bo-peep,
But the haystacks are creeping away
Like Indians on plains with trees
For feathers stuck in their skulls.
The salt lick burns; eyes leak blue ink.
Who can think about new lands,
When these sands we stand on now
Refuse our drunken, reeling weight?

"Safely rest,"
They say at revival meetings,
When repentance comes hard as hell
And hell breaks like laboring dusks
Over forests on fire.
We try to look out over this misty water.
That city is there somewhere,
A hidden anchorite covered with scabs.
Cabbies in the city have quit their hacks.
The people fear another crash.
*

Didn't stocks fall once and people leap,
Landing on two-legged lemmings
On their way to defunct banks or
Atop cranks about to assassinate presidents?
Glad I brought this blanket to sleep on.
Who ever heard of a twenty-five-year-old
From a filth-spoiled family in Shaker Heights,
Grosse Pointe, drawing a pallet on nothing
But sand and empty beer cans
Crushed by the inebriated hand of disorder?
(Just the other night, I talked with Dante.
He said he'd taken out all his cash
And stashed it behind the eyes, in vaults
Where no one with parasites
Could undermine his bad conscience.
He'd write his own obsequies, he told me,
When there was more than a beggar's chance
To dissent.) What is change but suffering
Yourself to outlive calumniation?
Was there ever a rebel born of contentment?

God is nigh,
But the people in high places
Disgrace themselves
Believing they know what's going on.
Here where I sit, trying to find sleep,
The world rages about my naked chest,
The throat cracks like quarry mud,
And elements whisk about my dreams
Like tubercular angels from Walpurgis lands.
The dimming fire lights portions of me,
While a god looks on with bewilderment.
The fire flickers; flames are swallowed alive.
To repent is impossible here on this plot,
Phony as the Lone Ranger's rendezvous clump.
Sand and air, fire and water simmer,
And my eyes, like unpredictable geysers,
Cry, though no people buy tickets
To witness nature's wonders.
Where is that land, and the end of days,
Where all is calm and filled with grace?
Are there pastures beyond here
*

Where sheep jump walls and scurry away
Without worry of monkeys hanging from trees?
Who can hope to try God's patience,
When we refuse the sages' insight?
God alone can refuse us — fools
Who prejudice each other for tradition's sake.
But somewhere, that slinking creature
Crouches, awaiting his chance to start fires
Boiling once more the hot blood of dinosaurs.
We lie in the balance.
Alchemists play with our values,
And nothing has any worth.
Whores run rampant through streets.
Black faces rob stores for payment,
Though remuneration falls short by centuries.
Bordellos exact dignity from our billfolds,
But there are no more gold backs. Silver dollars
Are scarce, and Kennedy halves are toys
For speculators' soaring greediness.
Why can't a pound of feathers
Weigh more than Galileo's golden pebble?
I know. He knows, too. It's you and me
And all the ships at sea that founder
When the scales are tipped and trumps
Finesse themselves in suspect crossruffs.
There He is, in the waves out there!
I can see Him in the eye of the lake,
Hear Him in night's bristly ears
Listening to me listening to Him
Move in, taking His cautious time.
The fire spins high, bellows, then crawls
Inside charred logs wet as dawn and dies.
The sand under my stomach goes flat,
And somehow, I can live with myself out here.
Can it be that death and its antipode
Thrive side by side in certain minds
That entertain notions of immortality?
Can I ever return to my quarters in town?
Will they know I'm different or see me
Still as of that same tired species
That dies, each night, inside itself?

8/30/66 (00416)

[It's hard to know . . .]

It's hard to know where to begin, when the end is so illusively at hand. The End! I repeat the words over and again; they have a mesmeric quality. One never starts with beginnings; he merely leaves off at some indistinct stopping point and picks up where he left off earlier in another region of the mind's rigorous travels.

And the end I contemplate is imminent, has been occurring off and on for three years now. I echo an Everlasting Yea somewhere behind the eyes, but the pebble ripples, like light-years, have taken infinities to catch up with their own motion. When does a person resolve the inconsistencies that spin and skitter more wildly than maddened dervishes across the sensitive tissues of the brain?

The celebrated coffee lounge of Calaveras County surrounds me now, and I think of all that stuff that lies ahead that's just got to get done. Has a person ever been able to respect himself without putting forth that genuine effort? How easy it is to delude oneself — that famous old life-lie of Ibsen's. But, recall, it worked for a time. And then, who knows what evil lurks in the heart of man? The shadows of one's deeds are telltale.

Another new year: a time for fermentation; must distill all the unfinished loose ends, the novels. There's room there for infinite improvement and revision; must put all the energies there with unflagging, undeviable drive to culminate. This kind of work can be useful, entertaining, satisfying if promoted with genuine care for the truth. What is art but a redefining of certain undissolvable truths? We all know them: stability, consideration, imagination, self-respect, intellect.

Has there ever been a man to believe absolutely in his chances for failure? If that had been true, man would be sitting on a tractor tire or throwing handfuls of vomit behind zoo bars like vegetarian gorillas who pass their mortality on arrested haunches.

The trick is no trick at all but a simple reaffirmation to the self's core that things repeat themselves in always-changing, ever-returning cycles — that it's the writer's challenge to stop these matrices just long enough to calculate the mad-whirling change. But motion is essential to stability. One must discover the frequency of immediate happenings; then alone will he become party to the inspiration of the past tenses of man's travail.

9/13/66 — [1] (05353)

The Achieve Of

Dormitories are full of children
Too old for home and other conveniences
Though too untried for menial lives
That kick environmental walls
With foetal ineffectuality.
Class schedules and tuition checks
That bear little relation to work
Their endorsees have known firsthand
Get neatly filed by clerks
In the dean's and bursar's offices.
Dorm singles and suites are reclothed
With bric-a-brac and untimely slogans
Cut from *Realist* and *Mad* magazine
And tacked to walls scrawled in lipstick,
Where fictional Kilroys were last year.
Once order is replete,
They can make their ways
Through a thousand grey Decembers
And slide viperine among salacious leaves
That sift daily Aprils of sensuality.

How fine it is returning,
When routine tilts with inexperience.
For those who know the ropes,
The freedom of easy-patterned pressures
Pothers no one seriously.
This is the life in a once-time,
Brothers, sisters of the golden slime.
There's no need to reason why
Or to try your wings too assiduously.
To sport factional winds,
Where dissidence spawns behind beards
And sandals and gold-rimmed spectacles,
Is to bury yourselves under dissonant plots
Of self-consciousness. A weariness of things
Only rings true to dreary imaginations.
See each day as a pageant of hours,
As a thing of fecund immediacy.
Hear its quainter shades rippling ivy
And Indian rain trees,
Where breezes part space for persistent suns.

Accept that freedom before these years
Exchange you for tedious transactions.
Be able to say you've won something
Autumnal days can never take away
Nor dissipate. For whoever's heard rain
Inch down drainpipes to a full bin
Beneath the eaves and listened
To a groaning freight train
Hollow out tunnels of slower nights
Or seen a tanker's rusty hull
Bulging with too much grain
Must know the meaning of completion.

9/13/66 — [2] & 1/24/67 — [2] (00410)

First Class with the Last Professor on Earth

When I sit
Listening to nothing
But valueless molasses
In the classroom's kitchen,
I flip my lid,
Have visions of griddlecakes
And a rasher of bacon.

9/20/66 — [1] (05130)

Elegy for a Living Professor,
or On the Passing of Academic Mastodons

Where am I, being here,
Hearing this crackpot,
Never-place, no-show poet,
Who died so long ago?

You poor-phony, sick-fetid bastard!
Cast your aspersions and tired reversions
In the classroom trash basket
Be   Cause
*

There's no clause in your contract
That says you can't retract your words,
Treat your betters with some small respect.

Squeeze that paunch back in;
Your thin skin can't take it.
Who would ever guess your chest
Is hairless, those harmless arms
That batter stale air before us
Are dotted with brown age-stains?
What are you doing here,
Sick-lost, wife-bossed poet?
Don't you know an abandoned cliché
When you see it in the morning mirror?
A five o'clock shadow metaphors
Your stubbly, untended brain.

You are trapped, festering,
A burnt-out coal, foaling progeny
That spawn in voiceless wombs.
The poetry machine is booming today,
But it's way out there, Herr Professor.
You should be arrested for vagrancy
In this lecture sty. Why not resign
Before the vine pulls away from its crag,
The cliff tears loose from bluffs,
And the youth-governed earth
Buries you under your worm-worried words?

9/20/66 — [2] (05129)

Mass Hysteria

Pondering the Percy slaying, 9/18/66

It's that damn black cat again,
Spanning neighborhood window ledges
When all but few have settled in bed.
Who belongs to that fictive miniature,
That little leopard licking night's foggy paws,
Watching drunks slobber home alone?
There ought to be a law! Superstition
*

Shouldn't be allowed out on all fours.
"Someone forgot the door latch, that's all.
He'll come home. You just watch and see.
No need worry yourself sick," she'd say.
"People know a cat . . . wouldn't you agree?"

Prowlers go on the loose,
Combing unlikely districts for girls
In nightcoats and innocent breasts.
There's unrest in this place,
Where disgrace prates like eunuch satyrs.
There's no room in here
For queers disguised as messiahs.
Be gentle, baby! That's all I say.
If you're going to club skulls
And stab eyes, like gigging frogs,
Pick on deep-sea fish and dinosaurs,
Things that don't exist anymore.

It's that damn black cat again,
Posing coquettishly as a German whore
Behind the window where I lie in bed.
I wonder is anything abreast out there,
Where footsteps breed maggots
On the floor of my restive ears?
I hear car squeals
And the roar of diesels far away
In cellars where dreams of myself
Huddle like children in air-raid shelters,
And I wonder does this gangrene darkness
Really divide day from night?

9/21–22/66 (04008)

Zealous Voices

*On the fatal shooting of a Negro teenager, allegedly brandishing
a pistol from his back pocket while handcuffed and guarded, by
two metropolitan police officers.   St. Louis, Mo., 1966*

Defectors, protectors,
And scandalized insurrectionists
*

Protest before Court 109.
The magistrate slams the door,
Declines their insults
And lewd replies. "You have no right!"
They shout. "Screw you," he says.
"There's no room in here for you
To obstruct scrupulous mainsprings
Of jurisprudence. The process
Must run its own due course,
Divorced from indignation
And publicly vulgar representation."

Outside, the group belches, curses,
Then disperses behind next morning's
Uncontroversial headlines to learn
That they, not the circumstantial men
Defended on thirdhand accounts,
Have been cited as the greatest threat
To a law-abiding citizenry.
Then each, without delay, puts away
His mutual redresses, digresses
Into horoscopic debates with himself,
Hoping to go incognito
Behind an aegis of individuality.

9?/66 — [1] & 01/24/67 — [1] (00409)

Legacy

The son of Fitz-Patrick
Was,
Of necessity, a bastard.
At least,
That's how the word
From above
                        has it,
Etymologically.

9?/66 — [2] (00555)

A Tended Vastation

Two pigeons
And a pearl-whorled squirrel
Scampered for acorns
And spiny blades of grass
On a shaded campus lawn.

These public fowl,
The cache-collecting scavenger
Went unseen by students
Crossing the green
On their way to share
Higher, well-deep secrets,
Hour after fetid hour.

Earlier,
I'd heard the black mechanic
Crack a rotor's motor,
Break the bracken air
Beneath a passive classroom.

Some studied agreement
Must have been made
By men for man
Himself
To rend seeds, emulsify leaves,
Unsightly things that breeze
And dog-eared days
Refuse to do away with
Gratuitously.

Yet
Who could ever guess
What intimacies
These ignorant creatures
Wrested from the ground,
Where the black hands,
Guiding the thrasher's scythes
From his parch-patterned paths,
Left a quay of Octobering grass?

10/13/66 (04020)

[The Shepherd passed here,] ‡

The Shepherd passed here,
Near the gas station
Where we stop to relax.
Nature's factions
Fuse in regard to facts
That challenge its truth.
Mutton Hollow
Shoulders tracks we follow
Down to the belly,
By the weathered well.
This man sells bric-a-brac,
Antiques ransacked from cabins
A hundred years young.
The jungle in October,
Throughout this country,
Flourishes in city estates,
Resorts behind planned dams.

10/13?/66 (05131)

Jan's Song ᐃ

Each March twenty-third

Who can ever know
From words about ideas
Alone
That verbs of finest style
Are formed of feelings
Undisclosed?

Who can say for certain
That words blurted out
Aloud
Don't consist of whisperings
That lie too often
Unaroused?

Who can judge the self
By what it says to
*

Others,
When only minute trickles
Come back in words
Of silent love?

10/25 —[1] & 11/12/66 (04035)

[The day goes down] †

The day goes down
Like a floundering whore
At the door of a merciless
Creditor.

The trees, treasonably
Drunk and shuddering,
Free the champagne mellow
From the sky's horizon.

And I, imaging indoors,
Take a stead on the porch
To watch the cunning sun
Scorch the iris, tear
Lids

The fifteenth phase
plays havoc with the brain's
spinning, turning, painful
experience.

10/25/66 — [2] (05354)

[I sit here, in this same . . .] †

I sit here, in this same lotus-land coffee lounge, with a head perking dangerously with too much coffee. I wonder what it is that locks a person so hermetically within himself. The same self-questionings arise, and I balk, thinking of the *personalized I.*

The novels go well. I may be burrowing my way slowly through

that narrow-dim cloaca of the self, but who can say how long the
process will take or what will lie at the end, if indeed there is any end
to the self/soul/searching? And, further, who knows what it is one
seeks? Maybe the danger lies not in the burrowing but in questioning
why.

What of self-respect? Does it depend on outward values, such as
being able to show a reasonable income by status symbols, or does it
reside in individual response to the immediate apprehensions of psy-
chical accomplishment? Maybe both.

What happens when one clutters his existence with too many
responsibility-necessitating duties?

All one can do is continue pushing.

     I think winter was come,
     Then gone

               Dry, amber mimosa pods
               rot in the breeze.
               Random leaves, like birds,
               still hang, dangling up high
               in season-sterile trees.
               Squirrels go "nuts"
               playing scamper games
               over shamefaced lawns.

I dwell in coffee lounges, listening to the tinkle of china, which
reoccurs more often than coughs and wheezes in a symphony hall.

I think of what Kafka wrote in his aphorisms:

    He proves nothing but himself, his sole proof is him-
    self, all his opponents overcome him at once, not by
    refuting him (he is irrefutable) but by proving them-
    selves.

There is nothing outside oneself that needs justification. All that
can ever occur to a person is that he alone is justification (the pun-
ishment and the privilege alike) for, and the consequence, simul-
taneously, of, all his actions.

A man can go far to find what's inside him, and, to be sure, he
must do just that — must go farther than he thinks he's even got the
energy to do.

Without this, the achieve of, the mastery of the thing, there is nothing else.

All the verities, humanistic ideals fail before the colossal master, self.

Selfishness is a rutty thing when it stands firmly without accomplices: compassion, honor, self-respect, tolerance, and patience.

I am one to whom patience comes hard and labored. Whoever has savored the easy compliance of peace within knows the virtues of patience sans evoking the abstract nomenclature.

Give me the patience, the endurance, to mediate those things that will spring out at me with snake tongues!

Cloclasure, the great innovator
of rationalized chastity —

* * *

Once again, after an interval of a month, I spend the early hours of the morning in the U. cafeteria, the way Cloclasure would have done it. I think after a time a person might teach himself to read the newspaper completely aloof to the depressing factors; the trick is to read the thing clinically.

At this end of November, I take stock, look back over what I've been able to accomplish. The *Drift* revision work was good experience; I'm now confirmed in my belief that good fiction isn't written but rewritten.

This Capote thing, syndrome, is a farce that looms large in my thoughts — the irony of it from start to finish: two guys, Hickock and the other, kill a Four-H family (the pride of Midwest, *Reader's Digest* life), little knowing that the money that they speculatively craved would go, by semi-artistic default, to Capote (two million dollars) to throw a masquerade, "in"-set ball in the Plaza. If this is the by-product of a modern, hybrid, guaranteed-to-grow-bigger fiction, then we, as hopeful persuaders of the future, recorders of contemporaneity, are doomed.

Can a writer remain unaffected by the millions and still write for them? Can he still be contemporary and universal? He can, I hope, by writing about immediate things, the repository for which is located somewhere in that illusive tradition of the free spirit.

I must now get to the task of finishing revision on *The Heron*. One must never let these things filter away. I'm reminded of my old football coach, who used to emphasize the importance of "follow-up" (keep those legs churning like piston rods) after initial line contact.

While these thoughts pass through the mind, already I can see a new story forming out of the old, traditional antipodes of country versus city life. One must never make the mistake of believing in a pastoral, halcyon golden age before the advent of automation; life was too rough then.

Yet there are advantages to be accounted for in small-town life.

I see a story about two central characters, who are bordered by significant peripheral figures:

"The Prodigal Children"

City vs. small town — they must, in the end, be defeated by both environments. But the defeat comes not from the diff. *ambientes* but from the inherent fallacy of the American mind confronting the dilemma.

The American dream is at fault, not because the dream is wrong in any moral or absolutist sense but because it simply isn't viable in a society that demands money to achieve moral tranquility: job and ideals don't jibe.

The two live in the city, move to a small town — defeat in both: anonymity of city, too-great propinquity of small town.

> Review: Jonson, Marvell, country-house genre poems
> Faulkner — "On Privacy," "The American Dream,"
>   *Essays, Speeches, and Public Letters of*
>   *William Faulkner*
> Newspaper — population rates
>   ideal city — Wright, etc.
>   corruption

What happens to family unit in city and small town? Rebellion in both instances — but blind effort to escape that which is indomitable since there is no place to go in the country except horizontally.

> The day dresses itself
> in grey lingerie,
> making those who go
> out of doors
> whoremongers stalking
> the penetrant goat.

I sit here, in the classroom, wondering about the passage of nostalgia. What makes up ongoingness if not a certain amount of reminiscence? To live, thrive, on dying clinkers *no vale la pena*. Where to go?

Somewhere, there's a place for us. One must never disgrace oneself
with too much high seriousness.

I love, but paternalism *no funciona nunca*!

> The words echo
> like invisible, hard rubber balls
> off walls of handball courts,
> Hollow. I holler inside,
> biting the elephant hide
> that lines my ears. I hear him
> repeating repetitions, speaking
> about elaborate clichés he takes
> at face value — maculate
> abstractions. Who can do
> sans clichés, I ask you?

The brain goes dull, strains to draw tight the strings about con-
sciousness.

I feel sick, vacuously pointless, and I wonder where the rhythms
of my thoughts are leading me. Grant me peace of mind, and let me
fight for right reason fused with spontaneous activity. A proclivity
toward boorishness and dullness rends my purpose at times. I want just
to give, never to use or abuse another person. My Jan, I do love you.
May you find your way back to me. I will not let the hurt of separa-
tion pain me into paralysis.

Oh, God! Where is the urge to entertain friends?

Everyone must doubt loneliness everlasting, just as none can con-
ceive, really, of the irrevocability of death. I doubt, though I know
the possibility dearly of awakening, one heavy morning, to find that
I've fooled myself.

Jan, I am so selfish; I want to possess wholly — this is my grave
fault. One can't afford to wholly enrapture another thing, let alone
a *human*.

> Self-pity is shitty.
> To suffer is tougher.

11/4, 11/9, 11/20, & 12/6/66 — [2] on 12/6 (05133)

[Did you see that apparition]

Did you see that apparition
In the vanity mirror?
It was there an hour before,
Developing out of the shower:
Fuzzy sweat that settled where
Water went vapourous.
It might have been the Wife
Of Bath or Catherine, the Gray
Lady of Hemingway.
Who can say whether faces
Glazed with nozzled rain
Go down the drain-swirl?
Why ask for past addresses
Without return incumbencies?

I see her lips, naked
As late-night lake swimmers,
In a mirror of silhouettes.
The lips are all that remain.
They stare through the room,
A fragile pair where she was.
What does she do now,
Out there where the city
Shares her impersonality?

I would kiss those lip prints
In the clear, silver mirror,
But who would ever smear
A master's still-wet canvas?

11/8/66 — [1] (05134)

The Seer

When I look back into the future,
I see history pimping for doges
And brocaded ladies for lesbians.
I hear gimps pounding their gavels,
Eunuchs barking for courtly order,
And revellers quartered in every corner
Of a land gone mad as castrated bulls.

Can't they see those dicing lords
Changing coinage every night
Like prostitutes in temples of the groin?
Won't they heed the feigners and whores
Who lust behind baptistry doors by day,
Pray to alligators and sacred snakes
When night leaves off the panting moon?

Don't they know their future tense
Is but futile hope to regain a past
They chose to ignore in childbirth
Or that the present holds in check
All promises of a graced futurity,
Every immortal expectation,
In a land that has no memory?

When I used to look upon the future,
I saw bystanders no longer innocent,
Whose eyes were shades snapped up
By multiringed fingers of the blind.
Yet who could help see atrocities
Parading each May in ermine mantles
Or babes wrapped in morgue-white shrouds,
Victims of infanticide, genocide,
And extravagant abortionists?

Who could look upon his elders then,
When they hid from themselves
In air-raid shelters beneath the day?
Who would dare say experience
Was the great Socrates of ignorance,
When any little secretary or livery boy
Could toy with immediacy so easily?
Who could see the zealous preachers
When handmaids stole their golden robes?

We bowed, like circus elephants
Consecrating their applauded dance,
When we crowded before altars for praise.
We'd been sufficiently domesticated
To crate ourselves away from one city
To another less harried antipode.
We married (some of us did, anyway),
Only to hide from alien neighbors.
What unfavorable times before the grave!

When I look beyond my present future,
I see something unattainably bright:
Three concentric circles of blinding light
Shimmer like blue-green neon eels.
But the mind buckles like a whiplashed bridge,
And that gap stays closed to my passage
As I float in limbo, consequentially.

11/8 — [2] & 11/22/66 — [2] (04034)

Up from Exile

Beatrice was a whore,
The temptress who raised Florence
In a single evening
From a gloomy forest to Paradise.

Her wetness,
An Arno of endless restlessness,
Flooded my eyes,
Where enraptured images
Vied with sterility.

Now, we run after each other
Like ends of a perfect circle.

11/8 — [3] & 11/13/66 (04031)

Advice from a Frustrated Poetry Instructor

In the manner of Ben Jonson

Read Keats. Neglect Tennyson.
Place a slab of venison before me.
Milton can be completely
Forgotten. Pour the Port wine
Before it goes rotten with disease.
It's an outrage to scour Dante,
Ulysses. Useless facts smack
Compendiously of Momus' play.
*

Bring on the special soufflé.
What other way is there to share
Congeniality? Some say Shapiro
Outlived promise that never was,
While Yeats masturbated
For love of literary images.
Let's serve Maud Gonne under glass
For an intercourse. Don't gorge
Or pass out, fellows; that's all I ask.
Auden read newspapers, drank orange
Juice, ate eggs scrambled loosely —
What normal perversity for one to toast.
Let's drink in modern thinkers;
They're carbonated, up for rent
To small university reading clubs.
They're good for the mind's calm.
Who needs ancient balm for the genitals?

11/11/66 (05127)

Do Not Disturb

He twitches a muscle,
Switches positions in his chair,
Secretly winks an eye
Now and again
To itinerant gods passing by.

He spends hours on fetid end
Scouring compendiums,
Writing letters he never seals,
Sealing thoughts and hard-fought insights
Onto a typewriter's roller
He never threads with paper.

When the air goes stale
In his shelf-lined museum
Of signed limited editions,
He draws open the curtains,
Pulls the scroll-rolled shade,
And lifts a winter-long window
To sniff the uncertain air.

The days stay fixed for him out there,
Where the screen locks limbs
Like tape stuck loosely to its mesh.
But those trees seem dimmer than usual today,
The sky shimmers myopically in his eyes,
And he thinks how things resist change.

He sees past the crippled mimosa,
Through plastic-coated magnolia fronds,
Toward a duck-filled pond nearby.
But these are decoys left intact
After ten tedious winters he's seen;
They still bob aimlessly
When wind ruffles their balsa backs.
And there, a red-painted, plaster-casted,
Lackluster pickaninny
Fishes the neighbour's arithmetical lake.

He sees this same scene changed slightly
Every day, each season, by the moods
He brings to his study from sleep.
It's here, in steeled states of calm,
He finds relief from all that was
And might just be were he to leave
For half an hour's emergency.

But he finds life most interesting
In desk drawers only he can unlock
With keys he hides discriminately
Or when thumbing through dog-eared copies
Of Lockean philosophy
While relighting cigarettes
Abandoned in moments of creativity.

But just now, he seems at loose ends.
Something has stopped him dead to rights.
It's the quiverless trees, the unshrill air,
And the silence filing through the screen
Like legions of insane driver ants.
He sees the silence coming in funnels
Toward the desk at which he sits,
And he listens, as a dog might
From conditioned fright,
To hear these insistent echoings.

The ringing behind the ears grows loud,
And he knows, now, it's calling him.
He jams down the glass, draws the shade.
The curtains meet, and his comfortable study,
The retreat where he competes with death,
Is again complete about his head.

11/16/66 (04025)

The John Wall

Response: If this is the only place
            you can find to make
            your contribution to society,
            I feel sorry for you.

Echo: If that is the only
            fault you find to
            correct, you're hurtin'
            too, buddy.

José Macaroni   "Revelations" —
Marco Nicollotti   *The Drift of Things*

11/20/66 (05313)

Sleeping Poem

She sleeps,
A faceless head
Resting on a desk-bowed hand.
Who said rest
Graces only the fatigued?

I'd have to agree
That she
Is the most fortunate
Of us all
In this poetry class.

She accepts boredom
As another,
Bothered by morality,
Learns to live with ghosts
That decay in closets.

Then a sunray
Splays the room,
Cutting her insensate face
Like a plane through skies
That close behind it.

I alone, grown restive
And searching for anything
In this blighted box,
See her silent face
In a way not seen before.

But the recent heat
Must have touched a nerve,
For the girl shutters,
Grasps her pen, and assumes
A look of interest.

11/22/66 — [1] (05135)

Like a Rolling Stone [†]

A complete stone,
Unknown,
Rolling home,
If
Only home were known.

Compromise,
Surprise,
Alibis
With the eyes' nectars.
Lids lie,
Frowning,
Feeling hard
Behind the hairs,
Where mother sails
*

Mystical ships
Behind the veils
There, Hercules gates,
Hellgates,
Strutting, prating,
Invisible as chain mail,
Vacuous.
Hair grows on eyes.
I see bulrushes,
A nude harmonica
Blowing cold noise.

News, food,
Nude as pregnant cannibals;
Lewd brutes
Claw where alligators
Used to crawl.

Thoughts converge, collide like unprogrammed stars.
Someone pressed a key
Preternaturally. Human clusters vie for ice cream
And greasy pizzas.

Back aching,
Breaking clay bones
Some sculptor left undone.
Who can finish what was never meant
For completion? Retreat
Home, where old ladies stare
And rats share their husbands' beds.

Run-down jumper cables clamber,
Climbing around
Dead metal,
Shoot sparks of dead electricity,
Screw the air uselessly —
Fire come home,
Burning blemishes, taints of skin
Lost and exploded.

Freight train screaming black noise
Shatters, strips midnight
Like shrapnel on warm legs.
*

The ears shudder like lids,
Whistling

He wears his eyes like clothes,
Sees flourishes in magazines,
Carries them high on the shoulders,
Tapered low, then narrower
At the ankles, doesn't like dirt,
Rubbish, clutter that gathers
Wrecks, waifs' hunks, humanized

His mouth speaks, opens wide,
Showing cavities filled with tripe:
Conclusions, intrusions on his privacy —
The green man in purple skin,
Thin in the brain, trained to read
Every volume of *The Golden Bough*.

11?/66 (05149)

[Blue-green neons] †

Blue-green neons
Advertise Suzan Parque,
Cover girl for instant sex.
Hexter Swanson p

I holler for bed right now, yet the cells see hell
where sheets should spread coolness over the body
as menthol the throat.
And I am nowhere right now, at loose ends, you might
say, when I see nasty old men and young boys toying
with depravity and instant success and profligacy
and infidelity and lasciviousness.
And what am I writing now that I'm on the brink
of finishing *The Drift of Things*?

11?/66 (05132)

El Quijote °

Él leyó la mayoría
De la literatura
Caballería.
Él se murió
Del corazón frío, roto.
Era el hijo
De lo incumplido.

11–12?/66 (05147)

[Can't eat — body trembling,]

Can't eat — body trembling,
And I wonder, now,
How to fling myself beyond the void
In which I electrocute myself.
    Self-pity is shitty.   (confinement,
    To suffer is tougher.   the pent-upside-down
But who can evacuate old selves   stubbornness)
That, like ghosts in a cluttered closet,
Violate the privacy one doesn't know
He owns?

11–12?/66 (04680)

[It's been a long time . . .]

It's been a long time since these fingers touched the keyboard for
the purpose of exorcising demons, and I can tell they are foreigners.
I have gone so long feeling togetherness, and now I fear another of
those intervals of solitude will creep over the mind, blocking all ac-
tion. I sense it crawling like a turgid, waterlogged worm through my
filters, and I don't know how to holler uncle.

What's it like to have the rug pulled out from under your sensibil-
ity? One loses mental equilibrium, allows that insecurity, that inef-
fectuality of human connection, to take reign over behaviour (I sound
like some poorly annotated psychology manual), those words that
might still sting, and I have the feeling this time that the mind won't

rid itself of the consequence. I don't know what I'm writing . . . the fingers . . . foreigners . . . What does a person do confronting another person with whom he's spent so many warm, convivial, mutual hours and who now seems a stranger?

I fear to act, to speak, as though whatever worth I may have confidently felt existed has been sapped, drained, until now I have no more to give.

It's that the giving, the sharing, the trying together was never anything at all, because a person has it within his or her power to strike it all from the record in one outbreak of female hysteria.

But the implied weakness — from where does it evolve? I can answer it: it comes from both objects of love. But now my mind begins to question whether there was ever anything at all besides the importunity, the necessity of possessing a love partner. I know the answer. There was more, but how hurting to watch the burgeoning warmth and sharing and mutuality of incipient love dissolve into commonplace. Dear God, what do married people do after the afterglow has subsided? Doesn't it mean that there has to be more to start with than sheer and blind and hasty adoration?

I smoke my fool head off, not really concerned about death or life but only the accomplishment, the filling of certain daily hours with life-giving thoughts. I heard someone say that poetry can teach people how to die as well as live — I don't know what to make of it.

I don't want to give up all that loving and warmth, but a person has to make himself realize that certain ends are not reached with inordinate incompatibility.

I love that girl so much, and still, I don't know where to go. I cherish all there is about her, with the exception of her latent thoughts. I have the feeling I've cheated her in a wrong kind of way. I've given her some inkling into a life that might just be filled with more than lurid happenings — this is where I've done the harm. I've lifted her only far enough to suggest, hint at, the possibilities, and showing her this is what never should have happened.

One must not disturb, even unconsciously, the disparities, because they always find their convergence eventually.

So where does a person go to find the path out of his own recriminations, his own doubts and insecurities? How does a person tell himself to bend down on the floor and pick up the pieces and begin again? I'm not sure he does bend down when he's been bowed so low, so callously, by the forces outside his awareness.

I am so selfish, I suppose. Everyone has told me that, until now I don't know how to function. I can go on repeating what is me, but the price — the price, the cost, is so hard, and it goes up with each mistake. When does a person tell himself he can no longer afford to bid at the auction, no matter how much he covets the object up for bids?

So I smoke myself sick, and I could wish to die right now save for the fact that there is so much more I want to get done, the writing, the telling others, if that can ever even be partially achieved through words, what to try to avoid. I have so much to tell, and then, if I ever feel that the mind has squandered on paper all it has hidden there that needs to get said, then I will wish to die.

I hope there will always be enough energy to continue until the mind simply bolts upright on hind legs, balks, and cries for rest.

I love you, my princess of peace, my litle Jan.

Do you hear me calling through the baffles of this night?
I love you, love you, love!
I cry for sleep to comfort my cells.

12/8/66 (05356)

Suggestions of Demise in an Occasional Professor of Modern Poetry

His trouser-baggy legs
Are trees lost in a forest
Of insidious undergrowth;
His shoes' dyspeptic laces
Snakes that dangle from twigs
In a jungle of raceless natives.
Those knees that trunk the paunch
Buckle with each dramatic strut
As he reflects, through words
That genuflect like Indians
Before Coronado's dreams of wealth,
Colossal thoughts of impossible schemes.

His splotchy hands tear the air
Before his gnarled face; his hair
Shares spaces with tangled sounds,
And he cackles, bellows, grunts,
*

But reverberations of ancient drums
Free tympana of conundrums
He no longer needs to explicate.
A smile, a somber, parading cortège,
Traces across his facial horizon.
His thoughts range like minute water striders
Chasing diminishing circles they make.
Though notions of change and death
Etch no poems on his rubbery ears,
He clears his throat to expatiate
And, with clichéd coda, disappears.

12/20/66 & 1/10/67 — [2] (00492)

[Voices swizzle,]

Voices swizzle,
as plastic mixing sticks
through sperm-thick whiskey,
in the coffee lounge of my odiousness.

None of them, the lurid, secretive voices,
ciphers me, plies my heroism
with self-inflicted adulations,
because the plausible formula,
that bond that breaks equations
like Borghese, time-locked safes,
locks its figures in numberless
quantities.

Dreams of Gatsby's dreams
ruffle my superficial thoughts
as wind the corrugated surface
of some meretricious East Egg Sound.
What he must have found,
or thought he found,
then lost, is what I see inside me
now; a plutocratic conception
revolves about the platonic unreality.

1/10/67 — [1] (05136)

[Williams] ‡

                    Williams
an anarchist

Sunlight paints the window's
blind, passing, as ghosts
through rooms, between slats,
brushes up against wall clocks,
whose pendulums cut shadow-
black ruts in the wooden spines.

Where is the poetic sensibility in me,
        the tension, dichotomy, *entre*
        prose and poetry?
            Must continue the fiction,
        but, oh, how I scream out
        with purblind eyes and ears to
        hear one single, simple rhyme
        or timeless metaphors

1/12/67 (05357)

[Who can guess at the lives] †

Who can guess at the lives
Hiding behind incidents
That parade down corridors
Where

"The life you save
Might be your own," he says.
May I correct aloud,
Through the ear's hollowness:
Solitude can be mitigated
This way, by soliloquizing.

1/20–24?/67 (05137)

The Personal Creation

On discussing the merits of Calvert blended
whiskey with Essie, 1/28/67

I

The mind fills up with psychedelic smoke,
Goes blind as time in spherical cyclotrons,
Trying to open up the last three thousand years.
What would older minds have thought
Confronting an unperceptive Socrates on dope?
How can the brain resurrect residue
Tired imaginations can't fire up
Yet refuse to set loose in garbage cans
Where you and I beg for food and weekly news?

II

That's the way it is here,
Where any little high-school teacher of twenty
Can tell pupils she'd spit in the President's face,
When Jewish bartenders outwit the FBI.
The national disgrace is anywhere where people
In high places serve up idioms on silver trays
And ransacked clichés on china-lined Melmac.
It's all in the *Doomsday Illuminations*.

How does a person know to call it quits,
When milkmen and Sunday-school teachers
Of Judeo-Christian persuasion
Inculcate younger minds with prejudice
And unscrupulous political rubrics
They know so little about? It's not right
To hide away in cork-lined shacks on Laputa,
No matter how unprostituted the word you preach.

III

The rope that holds the foundered ship in tow
Shreds, slips its capstan; the bow sinks deeper,
Until there's no hope to save the boat from worms
And urchins that swarm below pacific seas.
Are there no engaging purposes for us to share
With unaging history's madrigal? Hey, you, Thucydides!
*

Aren't there any lessons to be taught
Or bought in paperback translation with pocket change?

I gloss reports that appear in weekly magazines,
Cases contested and brought before diapered courts
For libel that harms no familial dignities
Or calumnies that bear little resemblance to reality.
Extracurricular activities feed life with energy;
They alone single out metaordinary deeds we idolize.
It's honor, pride, derisive bitterness and courage,
Abstracted and dissociated from sensibility and light,
That form stalactites in the mind's chilled cave.

IV

The Gulf busts loose tonight. Unnatural light
Consorts with cripples and wheelchaired mermaids
Who wear scales where their groin should be.
Who can see into the spume and froth
When lightning cancels perception, signals doom,
And destruction hovers like a hungry buzzard
Looking for purchase on the brain's carrion?
These humans, a strange kind that worships itself:
Bastard dogs all, hypnotized by plate glass!

V

Which way does one turn when the ears burn
With wind's scurrilous trumpets and the eyes
Line uterine tubes of accidental space,
Collide with sperm traveling in threes and nines
That abort the inner perception and kicking truth?
It's the items and conventional ideas they feed us
That disturb humors, curb the intellectual appetite.
A strange kind that barters each other: sick lemmings
All, who sink back circumstantially into earth to be born!

Can you hear that horn scraping the ears' womb?
What unusual call to transmutation! Do you see
Those embryonic lemmings of unnatural cause
Growing tumescent within the human pupa? Soon,
They'll crawl walls where women in labor lie,
Then cry to be suckled, weaned on liquid fodder
Too hot for the latent butterfly. Only one
Each three hundred years becomes a flaming peacock.

But they thrive off the tree, beyond the gate,
In shadows on the western side, deprived of nothing
Save the Struldbruggs' wrinkled life. They writhe,
Slither among each other like new-hatched snakes,
Despising the form they take, the life that slows
In subtropical alphabets to an idiot's pace.
They're a classless race of faceless creatures,
Who eat each other with words not rooted in fact.

VI

Can you see that man with slatted ribs?
From him came helpmates too numerous to bear,
Whose fleshly names and hair belie their curse.
With their fish eyes turned inside out,
They see only themselves and pia-decay
That oozes in blood banks of confused speculation.
Peculation begat itself a tougher hide:
Self-consciousness under a shell of unnerved pride.
Narcissus died urinating his brains in a basin.

VII

Now the storm vies with weakness inside me.
I hear voices clamoring like lions in heat
From the crumbling peak of Ararat. Rack the balls
And break now, or forever hold your cue in hand.
Who cares what tutors taught you to play the game?
The fact remains that beggars never cheat
Except when pressed, nor wise men break from rest
Unless to watch stars falling in the west.
As for me, I have no serious doubts about anything
Except doubt itself and the sun arising in the east.

1/28 — [2] & 2/2/67 — [2] (00421)

The Burning Off

I

A near V of foraging sea gulls
Deviates from tedious formation,
Strafing shore-bound ebbs.
*

Sandpipers scurry faster than field mice,
Nipping at stray diatoms and plankton;
They hurry to elude waves that slobber
Impatiently as apple-foaming horses
Against the glutted beach, then turn
To join a million fallings away.
Along the bleached stretch of land
That bars hotels and walled resorts
From water, flaccid jellyfish
Wallow in their own diameters;
Barnacled shells hear themselves
Grinding away in millennial lassitude;
Horseshoe crabs pock the pumiced sand,
Their brittle skeletons, their tails
Tilting like useless dragon quills,
Menacing even in rigid demise.
And as I go, hands behind my slowing motion,
Eyes tracing prints of fowl and human trek,
Something, the voiceless breeze perhaps,
Reminds me night is coming again.

II

Not so far out that the mind,
If it so inclined, couldn't lift a hand
And touch, the circular furnace
Bends down to sear a burning horizon.
I turn so near in to its core
The eyes exclude all former notions
Except residue of the listing day.
(I see two men inside that mass,
One working a bilge feverishly,
The other stoking boilers with acetylene.)
Who made that hole that ingests you,
Sun? Will you extinguish yourself
Or, like a Halloween apple
String-dunked in a molasses vat,
Reappear with a more enticing coat
When dawn draws you up into day?
The eyes blink once, and when I search,
All has disappeared but a single smear:
Cinnamon spread in ripples over toast.
Far off, down both outrushing corridors,
*

Flecks that could be other people
Seep into the brilliant dusk. I am left,
A ghost among ghosts going cold,
Bereft out here in a cemetery.
I have buried something of myself.

1/29–30/67 — [1] on 1/29 (00417)

Land of the Setting Sun

A jealous sun beats hard the reef
And warps motels that line the beach,
While the aged sleep or pass their days
Playing heated games of shuffleboard.

From east and north these people come,
Effigies and maskers of darker suns,
Who hope to make some compromise
With failing sight and slow decay.

A man, or silhouette, in fatted tan
Stands with pole on the end of a pier,
Scanning mullet, catfish, and bass
That pass his bait for richer catch.

Perched on the sea wall not far away,
His wife crochets, adjusts her bonnet,
And, warned against the sun's disease,
Creams red legs to avoid poisoning.

An elderly lady gets wheeled about
By a spinster nurse in patient white;
She nods her palsy to silent guests,
Who breathe identical etiquette.

Though sandpipers play upon these shores
And kingfish and cobias flute greyer shades
That nuzzle beneath the water's wedge,
No humans pace the pockmarked sands.

I alone lie against hot sands,
Waiting on rays to burnish my skin,
*

Or walk the beach with tireless feet
From one end of day into the next.

I bathe in dreams, with de León,
Of pilgrims who came to stake a claim
Where history had taken preeminence.
My youth is wasted on fantasy.

I awaken just now to excited shouts
Of two blond children about my head,
Digging for shells, filling their pails
To buttress a fort by the swelling shore,

Whose waves no longer speak to me
(They have sluffed into feeble chorusings,
While the screeching gulls' soliloquies
Go out in muted cacophony).

Those shells are dying on the shore;
The ocean's roar in their coiling ears
Rolls back to sea like silent notes
Tuned in a vacuous continuum.

The pain of heat goes down from day,
And all retire into evening dress
Except for me. I feel the absence
Of absented things closing in on me.

1/31 – 2/1/67 (00422)

[William Carlos Williams]

> William Carlos Williams
stripped, bare quality
> distrust of abstraction
> not in ideas but things —

How can one man parade his dullness
So flagrantly before his detractors?
My mind sinks in turgid quicksand —
Let me lobotomize him.

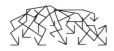 *hog brains* with Medusa-like configurations

1–2?/67 (00946)

Another Mother

For Essie

When the last granules scratch the glass neck,
A man will dig more buckets of sand
From islands on which he's stranded himself
And hope to extend his amnesty.
But he stands a slave to his waning age.

Alone in his own failing quietude,
A man will go an untried way
To hear his dry voice echoing
On the farther side of an alien cave.
But his words are gaunt and emasculate.

With his attitude planted before the grave,
A man will pry open his iron lids,
Draw back the tomb's grey-wrinkled face,
Which hides ripe secrets buried in youth,
And cry for that woman who breathed his birth.

When wreaths are hung about his eyes,
A man will lock all his doors for sleep
And creep back into his childhood bunk,
Waiting for his mother to tuck him in
And lie beside him while he says his prayers.

2/2/67 — [1] (00552)

The Foul Rag-and-Bone Shop

Such a night as never followed Pharaoh's curse,
Worse than the blight witch doctors watched,
Breathes over this Gulf apartment, its only child.
We hide inside, bastard pride of TV lions.
Fog, pervasive as persuasive Reichstag rhetoric,
*

Envelops sensibilities, blinds police and highwaymen,
Who pursue each other in ever-widening circles,
Until the hunted and the chaste leave off the chase,
Disgracing their occupations with compromise.

A snippet of lightning, like a newsreel clipping,
Slips through night's projector, struts comically
In ragged burlesque. No victims hiss the villain.
The tides ride in, their voices choralling hymns
Beneath the porch. We have nothing to reward
These unseasonable minstrels except blind submission.
Yet they persist in laying gifts at our feet,
Repeating the ritual, there in pantomime (welling pause),
Here in raucous chants against the shore's drugged skin.

Somewhere along the beach, an air-raid siren
Screeches a trinity, then hovers ubiquitously
At the ears' extremities, reminding me
Of London under a hungry blitzkrieg.
I arise. My eyes follow me, willing to leave
The fluorescent screen, whose images coalesce
In blessed falsifications. Down on the street,
Ponderous machines from another age stampede
Toward a conflagration's smoldering source,

And I can't return to the apartment's warmth,
Where the other three languish behind whiskey
And abbreviated soliloquies. Something calls me
To the weed- and kelp-strewn beach out back.
I follow to the wet edge, where coiling waves
Fester like leprosy over black-furry skin.
At once, I see purblind images roiling in light.
Silence overwhelms my raw speculations.
I await, wondering whether a newer day will whine,
Hesitate, then suckle off night's dark teats.

2/4/67 — [2] (00403)

A Newer Consummation

For Jan, in February

Windows rimpled with ice and frost
Reflect their ministrations
*

Against an opaque, outside night.
Like projections of infected cells,
They fester in their own undoing.
An unconscionable hiatus
Separates their youth from lateness.

Behind the earlier hours,
Before night severed itself
From their twin umbilici,
They'd sealed themselves in birth,
Howled voiceless elegies
In praise of unphrased verses
That curse them now with fatigue.

The bed creaks under slender weight.
The meek are spirited from sleep.
Viperine tongues lash out below,
Climb brass gunwales that coffin them.
No children of God ride its shoulders
But victims of spectral floods,
Whose blood is mottled with iceberg clots.

Was it sublimation
Anchored to floating islands
That grew maggots from unspawned kisses
Or a ululation of hungry lust
That ate its way to decayed surfaces?
Abject nakedness clothed them
In perversities Adam never knew.

She complains. His frantic restraint
Navigates falls where salmon writhe;
He swarms in crowded vacancies.
No mere physical notions, no sibilances
Scribbled down her upturned spine
Can unhinge the mind's conclusions.
They're caught in the net's wet twine.

Why did they come all this way
Only to write epitaphs in cemeteries
Where history's foolish Tenorios
Sprawl ignobly as captive slaves?
Was there ever an hour this evening,
He dourly wonders, when fecklessness
Wasn't baiting them unchecked?

Now, the hand that stayed him
Swims unexplainably through the sheets
And, like original clutching in space
That undid hiatus with less darkness,
Divides myriad newer firmaments.
His hand slides into her palm's halo,
Making silhouettes of an echoing silhouette.

2/9/67 (00407)

[The beaches along the Gulf coast] ‡

The beaches along the Gulf coast
Read like names of a brokerage firm
Conjoined for security's sake against waves
(They say in '87 a guileless hurricane
Cauterized the inlet at Madeira,
Channeled John's Pass further south)
That, today, stay constant as blue chips.

But if the crow flies into the city,
A buzzard tails him, flailing salt spray

2/10/67 — [1] (05138)

[I sit here, again, in the cafeteria, . . .]

I sit here, again, in the cafeteria, holding court with myself in the will's saloon. Soon I'll be obliged to remove myself from this womb, where the muse has visited upon me four years of security and purposive creativity.

If inclined to look back, take some sort of illusive stock, I would have to assert that for all the seeming irresponsibility and conscious unwillingness to apply myself fully to the wretched, oft irrelevant business of academic inquiry, I have not been prodigal. My goal, no matter what the success (since success is merely a configuration of the mind and in some sort of proportion to the attitude of internal speculation), is, as it has been since writing *The Terrible Trio* in '60 and '61, to write, to continue schooling myself (the mind confronting and assimilating personal and public experience) to better apprehend the sentiments of our time, to more fully change to record the progress of my notions. To write is not the business of the prodigal, for responsibility and honesty are gains too immaculate, too hard fought, for the disenchanted. The word can bite; words in conscious, honest juxtaposition have a force unequaled by all but death itself. Poetry can teach a man not just how to live but, more, how to die. To be a writer, an honest man with himself, requires the personality to assume extraordinary, metaordinary obligations for all those not as sensitive to the words. The obligation is a collective one, and each writer is but a newer link in that great, humane chain of literary being. To disregard the past (form, convention, tradition, sentiment) is as egregious as to avoid or circumlocute immediacy, for the keen perceptor of the written word.

I will, I must, write; it is the calling God or environment, of which it is but a portion of the unseen ubiquity, has instilled in me. Will I know how to accept recrimination and evanescent indignation? Will I be able to know the quietude of humility? Will I be able to accept some small portion of praise and prejudice? Will I be able to submit myself to, and then withstand, the iniquities of a Dantesque exile?

To trust in time and the purposive, single-bent intention is a must for me. Never, never, never to stop long enough to look back for forgotten praise or to look ahead for consolation and assurance for things projected is the thing I must remember before all else. God helps those . . .

2/10/67 — [2] (05173)

Narcissus

Not for love nor money but from necessity,
I left the Gulf beach's retreat
To enter these gates, where shades
Masked in human decay breathe out their days
A decade at a time. Here is no paradox:
Suns of antique days barely part live oaks
And ponderous royals and Washingtonias
That line pavements in this warmer clime.
De León might have foreseen inevitabilities
When his fountain refused nourishment
To his scruffy Old World life-stock.

In the park, people that might be leaves
Crinkled and wrinkled, blindly strewn
About benches painted green and lawns
Matted yellow where green was sown,
Listen, like slaves overhearing spectators
In some Academia gallery, to the symphony
Punctually glued to the bandstand's crescent.

I pass through, circumventing feet
Knitted with blue ruptures and tumid faces
Confronting what their ears don't recall
From times foreign to this immediacy.
Even the heavy tuba and bassoon,
The barrel-chested kettledrums' revelries
Wake no signs of recognition in the man
Planted like a desert bush in his lawn chair.
His hands manage a palsied accompaniment.
He leans through twenty bars of "The Mountain King,"
Then resumes his paperback investigations.
Unobtrusively, I pass on toward the other side,
Detected by none save a grinning face
That tilts behind some chronic idiocy,
Spectral prophet of unnatural causes.

The music slithers into air pockets,
Currency that counts in waning decibels,
As I edge slowly away down streets
Parallel to themselves endlessly. The shops here
Are different: jewelry from Faulknerian estates,
Antiques, monogrammed pocket watches,
Cameo pendants, diamonds defying credibility;
Gift shops offering plastic fruit in boxes
Under taut cellophane; import stores
Huddled in walls like beggars in Mecca streets,
Displaying ivory icons, Buddhas made in Spain,
Inlaid-pearl music boxes, woven rugs, tapestries
That took someone seven years to weave, a day
To barter for passports and field rifles.

But still I walk, having not yet arrived
At what I came to take back with me.
The streetlight changes, discharging shot,
Each related, every one a vestigial species,
*

Freaks of ectomorphic distortion.
An ambulance stalls the turgid crowd,
Suspending suspension, and in this moment,
Each face glowers, suspecting itself
Behind those urgent curtains. Now unstalled,
We follow out our trajectory to the other corner.
No one here erects monuments to progress.

Just up the street, the most unique drugstore,
Remnant of defunct petroleum fields, looms:
City within a sprawling community,
Entirely self-contained in callous ubiquity.
Inside, I vie with motherhood. Who would guess
The womb could be this crowded after birth?
But the hothouse blasts its creatures
With preternatural heat. Petals droop,
Leaves parch blacker than untended toast,
And Southern widowhood boasts longevity
Attended by grandfather clocks with canes.
Regulated animation is controlled from above
By the conspicuous nature of vain desires.

I pass through the gates, and faces graze me
Importunately — logs conveyed upstream
To planing mills, whose saws buzz circularly,
Cutting the horizontal cambium from wizened timber
And gnarled cypresses strangled by their roots.
I share spasmodic shoving to exist,
Resisting temptations to easy impatience.
I have come all this way from necessity,
To acquire something with which to return.
My mind refills its dwindling catalogue.
I am up for sale. Everything is on display,
From white elephants to chartreuse carnations.
But who can tell, among the tinsel litter,
Where they've stowed my operating equipment?

On the ground level, escalators creak continually.
I opt for horizontality, stop to see grey people,
Prematurely dead, who eat ice cream from boredom;
These children without children of their own
Are too old for carnal pleasures, too adolescent
To regard carnivals and puddles they leave on vests
*

And bespattered spectacles. Popcorn odors
Eat the air, profaning their personalities,
And perfume leaks from sample decanters
On counters where "crackers" and pygmy tourists
Press tight into newer skins that don't fit either.

Along one corridor, outmoded guidebooks
Reassure accidental Diderots and natives
That exotic plants, trees, deep-sea fishes
From prehistoric categories still exist.
Offset shells fill books with Linnaean completeness,
And I read just enough to know that life
Lies somewhere else than on this shelf
Gathering dust and violate fingerprints.

Upstairs, Tussaud mermaids brood over treasure
In cardboard boxes, their neon breasts
Titillating no one but themselves. There, ransom
Is fit for defunct kings and fatted queens
Out for vacuum cleaners and pillow slips.
My eyes decline, and I explore the bookstore,
Lingering over rows of fairy tales, myths,
And fables from a more favorable time than ours.

One floor above, a pasteboard farmscape,
Set off like a rural fair with crepe and flags,
Draws spectators with sensational slogans:
SEE THE BANTY RUTH PLAY BASEBALL . . .
FOR A DIME, YOU CAN WATCH THE LIVE ROOSTER
DO A SCOTTISH JIG . . . FOR ONE THIN DIME . . .
PRIZE HEN WALKS THE TIGHTROPE, SHOOTS BASKETS . . .
FARMER WEBBER'S FANTASTICAL FAIRGROUND FOWLS.

My pockets yield to curious fingers, change jingles,
And I hold up a silvery disk that glints off eyes
Behind the mesh before I slide it down channels
That might be connected to the rooster's pituitary.
Lights belch, reaching toward threshold intensity,
And the door that barred his conditioning from play
Swings open. Electric talons click and scratch
Upon waxed surfaces green as ballpark turf.
A beak pecks tentatively. The wooden bat balks,
Swats a Ping-Pong ball, wafting it three feet
To the sensitized bleachers. . . . Home run!

Lights appear by each base. The fowl prances
As though his trainer were pacing behind with butcher knife.
As he passes each pasted goal, the lights flicker.
The animal dashes down homestretch, importunately.
No teammates greet him. Only pebbly grits,
Feed, pelt tinnily inside the cage's container.
A beggar rushes in, pecks grain the machine vomits,
Then settles into prolonged insatiety
For the next entrepreneur with a silver coin.

I rush to escape children tied to balloons
That float like cartoon captions behind them.
Where is it? Why does a person such as me
Have to search among relics, antiquated minds?
I bolt, purblind, past a neatly arranged line
Gathered behind a snack counter, by books
Tampered with and abandoned, like toys
Ravished by curious children, to be reduced
Or given to the needy deaf and dumb.
Two flights pass me by as I walk down
The ascending escalator. I decline entertainments
And unbenign speculations that infect the brain.

When I am outside again, the air explodes my lungs with heat,
Exhaust, and caustic remarks from delivery boys
Unloading poultry cartons and unbinned fabrics
From transports mated blatantly to loading docks.
The day drops quickly onto the city, and now
I see a pendulum swinging where the Gulf should be.
The need to flee this city grows intolerable,
But the mind resists. Something about these people,
Who loiter headlong into dusk, attaches itself to me.
What do they possess, this feckless brood of gulls?

I retreat. The park is still filled with people
Caught in rapt inattention, though that band
Has long since retired. The man behind idiot grins
Leans, stationary, against the tree, laughing alone.
The sedentary one flips a page, concentrates,
Then hides inside his curling leaves and sighs.
Something. I know something is yet missing.

Will there be time? Will there be time to resign
From the cluttered mind to distanced objectivity?
*

Can I find behind a glass of blended whiskey,
When the shore fills up with listless gulls
And the submerged sun pumps water into tides,
The things that defy inspection? Must I decide
Tonight? Must I decide which items I bought today
With my imagination, when lambent city lights
Ride crescent islands beyond the cottage porch?

My stomach churns, and its hungry mind
Makes widening wakes as I leave this city.
Something refuses to let me loose. Invisible strings
Pull against my motion. Necessity eats my guts.
Another me struts before the windshield. I stop
Where no red light appears, apprehended by notions
That bear no relation to interpretations I crave.

Returning is a feckless exercise for me;
I have compromised something. Compassion lapses
Like Greek messengers run through for evil news
They oracularly convey from call to duty only.
The shore is a cemetery I pace absentmindedly.
Cold wash on my sandaled feet burns the toes,
And further retreat is impossible. I throw off my shirt,
Go slowly into the onshore breeze, which blows
With singular intent against my chest. I stretch,
Straining the biceps, wrenching the constrained torso,
Boasting contorted definitions of myself that screech
Painfully inside me like rusted windlasses.

I am youth. I am reckless spirit and intellect.
I am energy and full-bodied determination.
But what is it that in this fetid place
Splays the mind with unglazed greyness?
I go far up the diminishing corridor.
Gulls trace my carrion steps, expecting reward,
But my words spit upon the crowded air,
Curse them with boring self-commiseration;
I have lavished off others' beggaries too long.

A bristly wafer runs above my head; the goat
Slides in and out of the eyes like an illusive dime.
No suns of former days pursue themselves in shells
That rush up to slice my toes, and I stall,
Wanting to drink in the entire Gulf, to spit it out
*

Upon all that is dying or about to be dead.
I . . . I am very youth. I am such body
That nothing can contain me, and yet I am me.

I turn. The gulls have dispersed. The sodden sand
Has eaten shells. I near the cottage. I am . . .
I hear a rasping sound: tinfoil unrolled, ripped off,
And stretched gratingly over me. *Was* is me,
And I am trapped inside myself like a buried clam.
All along the fuzzy shore, horseshoe crabs,
Their fragile, crackly shells intact,
Pock the paths I follow. Jellyfish,
Flabby as cellophane bags filled with dirty clothes,
Wallow in menacing battlement. I see death.
Dead things are singling me out, unexplainably.

I wonder, now, what drew me out from the Gulf
To that pungent, venereal city today,
Only to bring me back to this stinking place.
Can it be I've squandered some provision?
No matter. There will be time to reconsider
The bitter decay I see in others and to learn
From mistakes and faulty calculations they've made.
This is no place to take detours or make of delay
A salable pastime. It's child's play to contemplate
Others' hasty retreats from themselves.
I am very youth. Who would barter his life
For grosser considerations? They were . . . I am I . . .

Yet, as I go inside, I wonder, has some simplicity
Been compromised? Could I have left undone
Something of necessity? I see *was* and *will be*
Grappling for my thighs, wrestling me into *am not*.
I see myself inside the whiskey bottle, or image,
Floating upendedly, immersed in darker substances.
I tilt, pour myself out of glass into clearer glass.
My lips toast me, and I imbibe, and I am I and me,
Simultaneously. Something burns my insides.
I drown, swallowed alive in my own inebriation.

2/10–13/67 — [3] on 2/10 (00556)

Valentine's Wish △

Another year has passed us by
Yet not disturbed us,
Like a gust of whirling wind
Passing over two leaves lying together,
Sheltered by the big oaks.
I hope no passers will hurt us
Or separate us — I cherish the stillness
Of our security.

2/14/67 (05121)

[She wears her nakedness]

She wears her nakedness
Inside out,
Her tawdry thoughts
Shouting secrets
Her coy hands knead like ambergris.
She tells herself
They only want the self.
Her guts cover, like beads
Or sandy shells,
Imperfections in the hide.
Suitors bow down,
Revulsed by what they see:
Her, a former movie queen,
Sequined in capillaries
And venous wrinklings.
They've only known the other.
She disturbs their minds,
The Junoesque peacock
Become harpy, night owl,
Eating out daytime hearts.
They should have known,
She thinks, that golden rings
Detach when tarnish blisters things.

[2/15/67]? (02520)

Awakening

For Larry Millman

This is no great awakening,
No enlightenment, this morning,
When severed branches beyond the glass
Scratch the eyes' contours.

Someone must have declined grace,
Reasoned differently. Dawn has come
Without intervention, and light
Pierces shades no supplicants pace.

A cough rattles my clumsy frame.
Convenient tissues take the waste
My nose obstinately relinquishes.
The eyes forage themselves, naked.

Unregeneration wears this bed's sheets:
Togas that clothe inquiring Oedipus.
Light leaks facsimiles of its original,
Shares space with my body heat.

I sneeze. Winter engenders itself in me.
Freezing fingers, webbed duck feet,
Reach to touch their fleshly machine;
Covenant of skin and soul comes hard.

The traduced spirit hovers above itself.
I look on, dissociated from anticipation,
Taking no cues from morning's newness.
My palms rake the spine's perforations.

The back comes cautiously erect,
Hoisting ten hours off reclining night.
A bristly blight, prospect, descends,
And the end rushes up. Dreams crawl out

Like worms to inundated surfaces,
Seeking paradoxical refuge in thicker air.
Residual configurations confuse vision;
The eyes grapple with indecisions

That cry in this auctioneer's estate,
Whose posthumous codicil demands execution.
Thy will be done,
And I offer up myself to the highest.

My strewn trousers, nicotined shirt
Attest that someone lived here once.
My isolate spectacles, instruments of war,
Reflect blindness from their insular perch.

I see myself in their vitreous walls,
Hung to that oak behind the blinds.
My mind crawls down before its body,
But the tree grows continually skyward,

And I teeter in impartial weakness,
Too feeble to divide leafless partitions.
An incongruous cardinal lights on my limb,
Finds no feed on the eyes' window sills.

Yet light has filled this torpid room.
I must make my move, breathe life
Into abandoned relics of other moods.
A vagrant yawn impregnates the process,
And I, an exile, break from the gloom.

2/16/67 (00424)

Shall Rise Again

Owls mourn valleys bullets shred.
Life hovers over dead memories
That have painted dusks red
Every evening since Appomattox
Shed its twin flags. An empress
In her last solstitial phase,
The moon, scimitar out of scabbard,
Whispers a cry before upstaging day.

2/17/67 (00551)

The Well

I climb up the well
That's bored within my drowsy head.
Its moss-cobbled walls
*

Barely support my heels and toes.
I have passed this night down here
Up to my knees in silt and fungus,
Among splintered rabbits and fowl.
No water has filled this cylinder for years.

During the night, accidental trespassers,
Guarded from specters and reckless insects
Within their lanterns' penumbras,
Must have placed these planks
That lid the opening, where light just drips.
I can't budge the intractable cover
Above my head. Precarious balance
Teases me. My arms span the diameter.

But I am no Samson, and these dank walls,
Pillars that buttress the worm-burrowed earth
Of my unfurrowed fields, don't yield.
Am I Leonardo's frozen humanist,
Head hung in painful repose, naked legs
Groping between middle-aged darkness?
Only the hands' diminishing strength
Keeps me from another descent.

2/21/67 (00420)

Clyde Griffiths' Chrysalis ‡

Simulacra shimmer down shafts
Where elevators, like discarded cartons,
Await decay. Registered guests
Hide inside green decanters
Or under covers while maids make beds
Over them. Animals out of steaming showers
Slip tips for whiskey through door slits.
One-night couples take their dinners
Under glass. The hotel creaks,
Leaning away from the windy street,
Where debris passes for shiftless people.
This is one of the posh retreats
For litter-making creatures, a dream
*

Inside of life, self-contained, complete.
God, mother! If you could only see
The limousines and hear the easy change
Rearranging itself in my pressed pockets.
This is the life for me

2/23/67 — [1] (00557)

Ishmael

> Buoyed up by that coffin, for almost one whole day and night, I floated on
> a soft and dirge-like main. . . . On the second day, a sail drew near, nearer,
> and picked me up at last. It was the devious-cruising Rachel, that in her
> retracing search after her missing children, only found another orphan.
> — Herman Melville, *Moby Dick*

I

I searched Cíbola's seven cities
For gold, charted Phoenician states
In hope of discovering Cathay
And richer trade routes further east.
I tasted of de León's glades
Without encountering his fountain
And anchored off western Hesperides,
Though no Tithonus broke from sleep.
Twice I passed Tenerife and the Cape,
Went beyond the Pillars to Atlantis
And back, once settling near Pompeii,
Until black wax molted pagan bones.
I crossed temporal divides,
Trying to reside near fairer temples
In cities swaddled in warmer climes,
But monuments erected themselves,
And all was not well anywhere.
Now, I alone am left, though the tale
To be told necessarily escapes me.

II

Aye, and there's the timeless rub.
Inhibitive forces ply me. Royal Societies
*

Require my assistance as living proof
To skeptics that one such as me
Has survived their untried projections.
Academies soothe me with pedagogy,
While I, dizzy from maddening heights,
Dangle from science's vocal folds,
A Jonah in a thousand larynxes,
Unable to approximate my own sound.
Printers, clinics, juggling troupes
Seek my freakish company.
Misery would marry me at once. Aye,
But there's no time for compromise
When all's not well in Terra Firma,
Where temples erect themselves in effigy.
My discoveries go cold as seas
In deepest winter.
I should have been that wretched whale.

III

Of late, I've paused with quainter shades
In Padua, Oxford, and Alcalá.
In Rome, in Avignon, I sat with God,
Wore periwig and costume frock
In courts with reason at their side.
Now I'm the world's specious cash.
Counterfeit crosshatchings undermine me;
My spurious currency is spent.
Balance comes unfavorably,
Though what I demand is abundantly cheap.
Are there no profiteers out for booty?
I could be pickled brine or salted pork,
Sold by the hogshead. I might be water,
Precious water, saved in staved barrels.
Yet who would squander their last doubloon
When prosperity crowds the sensibility,
Hearts and brains bleed in meat markets?
That I were son of the *Rachel*'s captain,
Suspended in humors of cold affection!

2/23/67 — [2] (00413)

[I am a gross national product] †

I am a gross national product
of the suck, suck, sucking sibilance
our heritage whispers in the ears,
bristling the hair with electricity

precariousness of physical life

identityless
implacable
indomitable
transience
sententious
pedantic
inviolable
penetrable
subsequent
instinct, head, reason
purgation
repentance, absolution
Erebus, son of Chaos

2/24/67 — [1] (00944)

The Strangler

*Pondering the Boston Strangler's escape from
Walpole State Prison, 2/24/67*

The neck swells with congestion.
Suggestions of contagion
Are rife in my neighbourhood.
Who would dare deliver milk,
Mail, merchandise from boutiques,
When madmen crawl into keyholes?
Innocence has been threatened
When men confined for life
Vault over neglected scaffolds
Into the snowed-in outside night.
Conventional locks and brass chains
Can't contain inner sanctums
Nor restrain stray perversities
From defiling domestic ovens.

Inquiry into the daring escape
Stops where snow prints
Walk out of themselves into freedom.
A camera pans the abandoned cell;
We see its interior,
Smell the anxious sheets,
Guess at schemes conceived
With the help of the gods.
Behind the myna mouth, mirrored
By a million silvery electrons,
Ticker tapes beat themselves to death,
Competing with this modern Tiresias
For the last say before "sign-off."
The divining rod points toward itself.

We lie in bed in this sheltered flat,
Propped up against a late movie.
Trollies clatter past a stalled car.
Again, the camera, a different eye,
Itches itself into artistic focus
As an obvious actor backs into day.
His riddled Packard goes forward
Of its own accord, conveys his crime
Through crowded streets like ink
Invisible under nonviolet beams.
An airplane multiplies his getaway road;
The car runs off the screen,
Into a commercial for better vision.
Suspense is haply interrupted.

Soon the motorcycle has its prey.
We slide deeper into the sheets,
Predicting the inevitable justice
We've seen a thousand times before.
The verdict has only to wait out
Three more intervening commercials,
And the process defines itself.
It's the public threat that matters,
Not the twenty-six dollars
He stole from the fastidious tailor.

Capital punishment is none too good.
But it's an older movie, we know;
Things were different before Freud
*

Slipped unnoticed onto grocery shelves
And off tongues of dumb attorneys.
Today, we label them insane;
They get put away for behaviour
Deemed psychotically disapprobatory.
It's only the humane, democratic way.

She sleeps, now, while I fidget,
Listening to the wind's thin fingers
Rapping out codes on our window.
Her slow breathing is the wind.
Her dreams leak out before my eyes.
I am witness to her secrets.
My ears tap her fragile wires,
And I listen to those busy signals
That torture her uncolored patience.
A man steps tentatively over wires
She reels out like spider silk
From her cell. He climbs scaffolding
That lines her lidded eyes, descends
Onto our snowlike sheets, disappears.
Something is liberated. She contorts,
Springs erect as a cautious cat,
Grabs my insomniac sensibility for comfort.

I know her nightmare before she gasps.
Inquiry comes hard for her.
"It's of no import," I say, though now
I know freedom has no quarters
Where fear feeds itself on doubt.
Somewhere on the street below, a shout
Breaks into day; night gives way
To the clatter of milk bottles.
A truck roars quietly, vomiting its package
Against our ground-floor door.
"Her new dress," I think. A paper waits
In its place. Coffee bolsters apprehension,
Makes headlines bearable. Bold, black print
Strangles the escaped victim, splays him
Comfortingly across the nation's forehead.
Our locks and brass chain have held again.

2/24/67 — [2] (00550)

Sounds

The radiator, a four-legged goat,
Gaunt, with ribs predominant,
Huddles against the wall, unafraid.
Its mouth, a loud escape valve
Hissing, slobbers invisible vapour.
The tail, a varicose pipe,
Takes the rusted juices of time
Out and down basements —

I hear the Fitchburg Railroad
Rattling tracks near my ear's pond.

The noise rattles; I can't hear
The instructor's voice — it stops
(A colored janitor reads the gauge
With wide, white eyes, shuts the valve).
The elements of Petrarchan influence
Get lost. I register snippets:
Validity of art form . . . love
Most appropriately expressed
In sonnet . . . statement of relationship
Of lover and Platonic loved one.

2/27/67 (00798)

Portrait of Jan ‡

The golden mosaic comes unfastened
Above the worshiper's slender focus,
But time's dusty imprint remains.
Nothing can change that halo
Or erase the inlaid tapestry
Fashioned from the eyes' privacy.
What once was the pride of youth,
Priceless and wilder than truths
That escape poetic imagination

2/28/67 (03926)

[Morality gapes through the bars,] ‡

Morality gapes through the bars,
Aping itself in other humans,
Who stare antically
All of a Sunday afternoon.
Too soon it will be too late
To imitate behaviour
That paces quadrupedally in cages
All of a spring zoo afternoon.
Temptation, a bisexual stripper,
Prates on condemned stages
Minors are forbidden to watch.
Participation in the mating thing
Comes in the youngest places
All of a sensual afternoon.
Is there no cure for modernity,
That vile creature, that lion
That wears its hair scruffy
And shares its harems polygamously?
Don't ethics, illusive fancies
Dreamed up by nonpracticing agnostics,
Count for anything other than love
All of a new generation?

2?/67 (05364)

An Anatomy of the Believer: The Twenty-Sixth Anniversary

*Wherein, by occasion of the symbolic death of
Louis Daniel Brodsky, the frailty and
the decay of traditional faith
is represented*

His shelves,
With countless colored faces,
Dilate like birds in flight.
Their varnished wings
Fling insults at his yawning.

These lettered spines,
Those mouths and lidded eyes
Withhold personality from him
As he tries to pry apart
This four-jawed vice.

Memory, like nervous drops of rain,
Splatters against storm windows.
He is witness to disintegration
That washes his murky brain.

Accumulation has made him slave
To wisdom that demands manumission
From this six-by-eight cave
He calls Plato's immolated grave.

Though he fingers his chin,
There are no more contemplative poses
In this world, where art and Scripture,
Like the self-deposed children of Moses,
Have chosen the harlot's namesake.

He finds no new themes to scribe,
And the tortured Saxon rhymes
That line his mind's back streets
Like scarecrow row houses at night
Cocoon his stillborn insecurities.

He feels precariously forsaken,
Having curbed his appetite
To include only older forms of learning.
He suspects no rewards
From fashioning oneself as a martyr
When poverty fattens the bones,
Chastity finds neither majority
Nor obedient few who raise a voice,
And forbearance gets no extension
On debts incurred in Monte Alverno.

The books' sacred words taunt him.
He, like Alcibiades, has vacillated
Too often between antagonistic factions.
The precepts conjoin to defeat him
Where he sits, a ravaged go-between,
At stalemate. Self-consciousness
*

Stones him. The ancients arbitrate,
Throw his clothes to hovering buzzards.

He goes naked among vacant lands,
Whose desolation mocks his vacancy.
But no Oedipus fleeing some curse
Waits, where four roads intersect,
To slay him, and his library,
This descendant of the house of Atreus,
Decries his defection, defies inspection
That might set his own house in order.

Nero, like an unwilling Virgil,
Escorts him to the right hand of Erebus.
But his insulation stays the flames,
And he awakens from prolonged yawning.

When confusion puts pressure on him
To draw conclusions or make excuses
For himself, he caresses with faith
Sacred revelations of unseen things.
From his cluttered shelves, he takes
A ruffled Bible, whose poppy-scented ways
His eyes have passed a hundred times.
Blessed confinement comforts him,
While the days lengthen his wrinkles
From one end of night into the next.

3/3?/67 (00405)

[Whitman] †

Whitman
p. 53, Parkman — "I and beasts alone have consciousness in nature."
Alone in a wilderness, *common American experience* — isolate consciousness.

Whitman moves toward establishing a doctrine, calls it names, then goes toward breaking it up so it won't become dogma — a revolutionary imperative.
sense of ever-new beginnings —
forward movement and yet paradox of eternity — past, future irrelevant

Grass growing out of mouths
of dead men — Whitman

I was when the beginning
Yet was not engendered.
Light washed shadows off me
That had no source as yet

The Fitchburg Railroad
Whistles to my ears —

3/10/67 (00945)

The Abiding

Boxwoods and lesser bushes
That buttress this house
Wear extravagant coronas of white.
The house is lost for a night
Just splitting shadowy prisms
I walk through to meet the sun,
Coming out of nothing into day.
Stray starlings and jays
Connect invisible threads
From soft pine to oak
That line morning's perimeters.
I smoke. My vapours coalesce
With freeze the March air breathes.
My breath pushes outward,
Endlessly clear, without rising,
Along a path at odds with the sun.
The feet move easily across lawns
Brittle yet with tight moisture,
Forming runs no rabbits make.
Beyond the fence, the neighbour's pond
Respires — something is warmer than day.
Water's skin wrinkles with first light
The sun raises cautiously above woods
That border his pond, and I see red
Enlarging like microscopic spores
*

In the pond's circumscribed eye.
A squirrel eludes its fear,
Traces a line, from hutch to hiding,
The breadth of the yard I scan.
Overhead, in its own domain,
A crow shreds the air's wrappings,
Lights preemptorily in the comb
Of a naked oak behind my sight.
The sun, caught in its act,
Is wrapped in smog that congregates
Farther east than Old Man.
My eyes belch, scanning themselves
In that pond, which no longer nets
What minutes before was a Ping-Pong ball
Painted the color of boiled lobster.
Something is changed, and now the eyes
Find no counterpoint for the searing.
The ground still takes my weight,
But the feet share its property
With sweet-gum seeds, whose spines
Lie dormant as foetal porcupines.
And here and there, mimosa pods,
Like weathered gondolas,
Mustard-brindled and almost innocent,
Too brittle to be disturbed,
Manage this Adriatic turf,
Set impermanently in gradually uncurling waves
I also walk upon this early.

Already that mass is moving away
From the woods, up from the pond,
And now my breath stays fixed
Inside the nostrils, the feet
Retrace where no runs glisten,
And the ears, unavoidably open,
Listen to the highway's dry-point burin
Scratching persistent burrs
From stertorous wheels over concrete.
On the street beyond my lawn,
A snake slithers toward the cemetery.

A different kind of light glows now.
Trees are merely trees against an earth;
*

A whitening sky a day that will take
Itself too seriously. And I retreat,
Wondering why people sleep through change
Into less subdued phases of day,
Which we've made for them this dawning.

3/16/67 (00549)

A Wintering Mimosa

The old mimosa, planted out back
In the yard I scavenged as a boy,
Lifts arthritic, splintering bones.
The accomplishing winter whistles
Through its bristled ears,
But it hears no birds noising about
On limbs secured by tarnished wires.
Its blacksmith back leans tediously
Over the turf's unheated anvil.
Each branch, a brittle hammer,
Beats no shape from the icy earth.
Down the side lightning once struck,
Its naked spine shows tarred cankers,
Unnatural bark that exposes its death.

Is this a male or utterly female tree,
Whose molted plumage deceives the eye?
What avatar is this in seasoned disguise,
Whose autumnal phase, like west-drained hues,
Has evolved from shortening days of June
Into shadowy perpetuity?
This *is* night. No ordinary specters roam.
Winter's blight is cemetery grey.
Raw is the ridge where unthawed sod
Bites this icon of prickly life,
Whose blood is sap, whose tissues pods
Disseminated as scattered bones,
Whose trunk is a useless crucifixion —
A body lying upright against the sky.

If an actress poised on her knoll,
She might be a legacy of antique Troy,
*

A relic of Hector's unheeded affection,
Or an ancestor of Southern belles,
The queen of New Orleans coppices,
That genteel pride of Richmond verandas
And patioed lawns near Charlottesville,
Untouched by greedy, moss-cloyed hands.
Now, a distaff mourner out of party gown,
Frozen at the head of a circular stair,
Sharing her pride with the deadening air,
She patiently awaits no lover's return.

I planted this seed of woman and man
In springtimes of youthful harmony,
Communed through green years of piety,
And carried our love, this double marriage,
Above and beyond the unspoken vows
That set the self outside its house.
But the hours have crowded out the blood,
And I must set my stores in order
Before their fruit gives back my seed —
This tree has grown old inside of me.

3/18–19/67 (00548)

The Gathering In: March Ides

A mid-March sun
Breaks out of the ridge of a homespun sky,
Hovers atop a kelp-oak
That could as easily be slippery growth
Swaying with tides beneath the sea.
The tree's steepled twigs glow with fire
No breeze kindles, forming a star
Whose apex grazes the sun's escutcheon.
Is this oak or belated sign of Christmas,
Fastidiously lined with ornaments,
Seeds clustered by natural design?

A huge pupil in the sky's socket
Dilates like a moon come back disguised,
Then dissolves for the grey-quilt clouds.
March wans in its seminal hours.
*

Ragged tentacles pry denser shards,
Parting the hazy carapace once more
Before swarming to surfaces it forms.
Air the turf releases goes warm,
Then cold with the gradual closing in.
Finger-paint patterns conceal thoughts,
Reveal yellow emotion in secret grooves,
While a migrant thread of blue
Scurries to elude the ubiquitous rift.

Soon, all is quiet, as if night,
Somehow ranging off its seasoned axis,
Has bloomed, relaxing its hold over day.
A greyer light than any before
Proceeds from the source of all that grows
And dies. The mosaic collapses,
Showering debris and pieces of glass
Against the fetid retina. A frustrated sun
Cowers behind saturnine lids.
Trees are blown. The hours groan heavily
As drops clinging to a running spout.
A lascivious snow slithers through pores
Before mating with the accosted earth.

3/21/67 (00547)

47th Street West

Men carrying black suitcases,
Wearing de facto patrician noses
For frontlets between their brows,
Expose themselves to the crowds.
Traffic flows jagged as lightning;
Currents go against currents,
While these suspect shades
Masquerade wares from a hundred ports
For others with taximetered eyes.
Inside these Geneva retreats,
Compromise and agreement goad people
From Scarsdale, Grosse Pointe, Park Street,
Who pause tentatively at the door
*

For a right to partake of bargains
Only the rich can afford.

Their windows, identical in all but gender,
Are peacocks preening conceitedly
Or transvestites ending their stage routine.
Amethyst, jade, and stony topaz,
Like veins marbling bony fingers,
Line their yellowing display trays.
Cameos lifted from abandoned vaults,
Necklace halters of beaded crystal,
Like tubercles racing through blood,
Flood clutter-greedy imaginations.
Estate diamonds, rings, cultured pearls,
Stopwatches encased in platinum
Suggest conceptions of Rothstein,
Who wore stickpins and clips
Between ruffled shirt and wide, loud tie.

A bookstore, solitary as a Bedouin tent,
Reeks breath that never reaches the street.
Its window, a defunct Cyclopean eye,
Is bedizened with complete back issues
Of extinct magazines and posters
For poetry readings two years old.
Within, volumes molder in orange crates,
Toothpaste cartons, and on rented shelves
That shoulder history's promised failures,
Slapdash mysteries, classics, and myths.
Tourists stare. Peddlers share its awning.
An occasional collector finds its door.
In a graveyard lined with unknown lives,
This store is a monument among cenotaphs,
Whose genealogy increases with time.

4/7–9/67 (00423)

The Accomplishing

I

An eyeblink ten days long,
And all has gone from space to industry
*

As if winter's relinquishment
Were an act of generosity.
All of it, a child in bed: trees, nests,
Restive cocoons, buds tucked under pith,
Each species wrapped in warming, with care,
Sharing a million washes and hues.
This is the time for choosing.
Myriad reincarnations advertise themselves
Against a sky too veteran for surprise.
Unnumbered substances engender legions.
Infinite divinities explode. All the air
Is a miner on haunches by a stream,
Screening minerals through a leaky sieve.
Every odor, every color is a kite
Pasted upon a corrugated climate.
If there was a pause in the process
When the awful, cold air balked
And recognitions of another self
Gained definition, they did not know it
Or see it or feel or hear it happening.

II

The lilacs' purple-petaled cones
Postulate a queen's sweetest fragrance.
Even a vagrant blue jay strays to sniff
Before sifting away. In the rusted gutter
Above the eaves of this sleeping house,
Martins, starlings, and vicious wrens
Cease their vendettas to take note.
Tulips, tumid as guinea pigs, line walls
Where ivy begins its purblind ascent.
Boxwoods and hollies inflate with green
To hide the robin and mockingbird,
Whose mimetic activities deceive the ear.
Elms, sweet gums, expansive oaks, and
Tandem walnut trees that turret the front
Choke for the screaming growth,
And all is caught in furious frieze.
Everywhere, forsythias and dogwoods
Quilt collages no museum could frame.
Nowhere can the curious eye find rest
From redbuds and white apple trees,
*

Whose supple puberty defies violation.
This is the haughtiest season of all.

III

Only the mimosa and three magnolia trees
That border the moss-fatted patio
Decline this festivaled invitation.
The four are whores poised nakedly
In the face of boisterous neighbors
Who recline in overstuffed chairs
On a porticoed porch overlooking summer.
They stand in alien irrelation
In this warming northern clime:
Brown the magnolias' life, bleak
The Delta mistress who knows time
Does penance to her coquettishness.
Perhaps they know this moiling thickness,
This quick, wet seething of soil and air,
This crowded sharing of noisy space,
Is but fanfare for the marathon
They'll spend three months running.

IV

The community glowers at their sterility,
Mocks their recalcitrant inconsistency,
Their apparent insensitivity to the hour.
They withstand these evanescent abuses,
Unable to liberate collective knowledge
Or inculcate measured proprieties
They have gained for the going ahead.
This is a cruel place for the few
Who patiently await their appointed time.
Yet they alone, for the gaudy revellers,
Will explode into the mildest whites
And blessed scented rose, the softest pods,
The strongest supple leaves of deepest green,
When, in June, the nights catch fire,
July singes lawns and limbs like skin
Roasted over a charcoal grate,
And August suffocates the most chronic weeds.

4/10/67 (00430)

[For three weeks, I have awakened]

For three weeks, I have awakened
The same hour of dawn; the sun
Goes continually higher in the glass
Above my bed. Who could ever catch
The waning month? Winter is going;
The winter freeze is going, gone
Before I arise: a troop train
Leaving Kiev for the colder Ukraine.
Do February, March find another place
When April inflates White Cross?

4/22/67 —[1] (05139)

When the Birds Resume Their Attitudes

Anchored to warmer soil,
Proud as spangled queens
Between chiefs of state,
These trees know no words
By which to express themselves.
Birds back from sequestering,
Prepared to repudiate sterility,
Tumid with fertility and nerves,
Light in limbs to reconnoiter,
And all is ready to take their acts.

4/22/67 — [2] (05140)

The Yard Man †

During winter, he and his wife
Remained inside, tending furniture,
Waxing the patio's terrazzo

[4/22/67]? (05099)

Proposal ^Δ

For my Jan

I, as a poet of major chords,
Need to make you rhyme with me.
We must each be metaphors
Forming verse of unending harmony.

4/25/67 (05310)

Nightmare, 4/28/67, St. Louis, MO

I

Aphrodisiacs inform insomniacs
Of unrelaxed journeys
Back to the forest's source,
Where Gorgons, black as jet,
Unsettle themselves from restfulness,
Prey on creatures whose nature,
Like the needle of a crazy compass,
Fluctuates with earthly coruscations,
And days are snakes coiled, looped,
Choking the insatiable appetite,
Constricting resourceful imaginations
That weigh heavily within the heart,
Trying to gain labored foothold
In caves where dreams are made
From labial openings about the brain.

II

Yet night, with one enormous inspiration,
Ingests its unsuspecting guests,
Absorbs them whole, until the core,
That unwilled suspension of disbelief,
Chills the fast-passionate whore
Who runs naked through all men,
Extinguishing the doves' white flames,
Until there are no more appetites
Save those supplanted with chaos,
*

And night unwinds its greying shroud.
Now crowds, whose blatant curiosity
No human excuses, gather to see perversity
That reduces the human anatomy
To filaments under a microscope.
Who would watch this wretched spectacle?

III

The mind, an alien in this nether chamber,
Tries to find escape from blame
It alone incurs by searching for worlds
It can neither claim in the name of peace
Nor possess for those restive few souls
Who take no pride in human affairs.
A terraqueous scape spans this terrain.
Grass with thorns breaks to the touch,
Glass snakes shatter underfoot, and all,
For the exploration, gives way, shudders
As though an earthquake felt miles away
Were making its way on limber feet.
Yet bad dreams reformulate themselves,
Refuse easy retreat dictated by sleep
This unhealthy being very dearly needs.

IV

Nothing can stay the visions. The eyes,
Blunt objects under murky lids,
Defy revision, bathe in aqueous humors
That no longer clarify the inturned sight.
Stalactites dripping behind retinas
Accrete from the eyes' scarred tissues,
Pointing gnarled fingers to the last room,
Where no one who goes past its gate
Or touches himself in its dusty mirrors
Ever reappears as the person he loved.
That fiery maw devastates the closest ties
With the self. All thoughts of soft repose
Are lost forever, and he who thought he saw
What none had ever seen and returned to speak
Comes home with stony lips and a bleeding groin.

4/28/67 (00793)

[The changing of the guard; seasons rotate.]

The changing of the guard; seasons rotate.
A magician waves the wind, whose wand
Makes drafts of warming descend. The end rushes up;
Winter slithers away; newness
Appears from this high-topped hat
Quicker than the eye can fractionate it.
By the porticoed door, a robin pauses,
Contemplates possibilities for her nesting.
Her mate stands at nervous attention,
Tilts with white-striped mockingbirds
Who chide his paternity; they squabble
Over territorial rights, the rite of survival.
In the swayback branches of a pine
That shelters a jay nest, a blue screaming,
Illusive as that hidden highwayman,
Bends the air, and all leave off their notes.
I make it my business to watch from a distance
The dizzy flight this robin makes from the pond
To this holly and back. It's a frenzied chase,
A race with time. The nest is formulated,
Postulated close by the door for all to watch
When the giving birth is accomplished.
She weaves the days together, shuttling fast
Past the pine, the fence this side of the pond,
Her breast speckled with mud, her beak
Tinseled with dry straw she chooses
From beneath the trellis. I watch
From my perch behind the flagstone wall
That guards the driveway from the lawn.
I blink; she is gone again. The mate
Still hops, keeping his anxious vigil.
This is a preternatural exhibition,
A race against death. She returns again,
Her belly-smooth down rounding out the nest.
She moves clockwise with time, lining
This hutch for the moment of the eggs.

Around the back, by the chimney, whose ivy
Has weathered the winter intact, another robin
Enacts the ritual. But her nest has resisted
Abandonment; it is as it was when she left
*

Last fall. Her work is confined to nesting.
She is barely visible for the foliage,
Sheltered from the wind, from passing eyes.
I see her seeing me through clustered leaves
Whose fingers climb continually skyward
And thicken until there is no possibility
Of discovery. Then she leaves, and I see
Three blue ovals awaiting only her warmth.

From the porch that borders the front,
I see the activity, the frenzied march
Of determined life vying for time.
This other nest resists completion. Something
Suggests distress, yet the robin hurries
To elude inevitability she must sense.
Perhaps there is time. Then, when I peer,
Three eggs of equal dimension lie idle
In that precarious nest, which a hard wind could
Dislodge yet no human hands would touch.
The mockingbirds have sought refuge elsewhere,
Respectful of the growing, mindful of life
That exists in that burgeoning cluster.

Days fuse. I have work to attend to.
When I return, there is nothing but vacancy,
And the eggs I saw before incubation
Are jagged shreds, like broken glass,
On the grass beneath the holly bush.
Not far away, a raucous blue jay screams,
His voice partaking of that glutted nature
Of impatience common to birds of prey.

In the ivy that clings to our chimney,
The other robin broods imperviously.
Neither the shuffling of my feet
Nor the obvious curiosity I show
Suggests the need to retreat. She goes on,
Warming what will soon repeat her actions,
While I, wondering what justice demands,
What equality exists in little things,
Run to the pine tree that wings the house,
Wanting to reach up and grab that scavenger
Who scurries from limb to limb excitedly
And ring the life from its glutted breast.

4/30/67 — [1] (00790)

Homecomings

It was not until the limbs filled up
That we could even think of looking.
Perhaps they'd sent a few scouts before
The accomplishing to claim arbitrary sites,
But everything remained tentative,
Everything silent, for the coming spring.
If we put our ears to the kitchen window
We might hear the mocks, jays, and starlings
Complain tediously at the suet cans
That lined like sentinels the patio's edge.
Occasionally the eyes would witness
Transient doves and speckle-glutted quails
Trailing prints in the snow, ranging close
To the house's lee for warmth.
Yet nothing could do more than endure
For the accomplishing. None could know
Durations; mathematics carried analogues
Beneath the snow and hard-blown weathers
No one of them could calculate or solve.

Now the trees are green, as though nothing,
Not even the winter, arrived and left,
And turf sends up the mildest odors of seed.
Dandelions, bulbous as potential explosives,
Stipple the sky with white-flying burrs,
Like talcum spread in clouds over dry skin.
Toadstools' rubbery shelves mottle grass
Our shoes don't impress. Walnut husks,
Left behind for the ripening, line plots,
Pocking the ground like deserted temples
Of migrant Toltecs, huts of Bedouins,
Who, in their reckless abandon, jettison
Precious possessions for newer terrain.
These monuments, these tough-crusted wombs,
Are proof that whatever dies grows soon
In newer formulations. Yet only two
In each ten million are destined to bloom
Decades from now, boasting their heritage.

Sumac has not yet arrived, nor onion sprouts.
Cherries rest in that silent hesitation
Between bud and efflorescence. Holly berries
*

Writhe inside unconceived protection.
Only the birds have begun the ordering;
Their lives are routine, as seen by the eye
That detects their first familiar patterns.

4/30/67 — [2] (02292)

Toward a Newer Expression

To form, to order, to mold out of disjuncture the words that fit my moods, this is the task, this and revision. But there is need to supersede what one has accomplished; else, all becomes dissatisfying repetition.

The poems feel to me as though they have run their course, that they need not necessarily new forms but a newer, more rapid, running content. Can the mind set itself free from shackles of memory and break through to a time it has never known and may, save for the creation itself, never know?

Once I wrote, "I sing a blind-tired song tonight." Now I feel as though all my verses are tired, that I am going blind for lack of experience. The last thing in the world a poet must allow himself is comfort. He cannot afford himself the luxury of bathing in his own immediate preoccupations. For a poet to write about poetry or the poem or himself is only compounding the difficulty of the poetic medium itself, which, in good part, is an art of obfuscation, of essentials.

The subjects for poetry best suited to the vessel words float are things . . . things . . . things about things about things about thinginess. Everything has a potential distinctiveness about it, if only apprehended. All things contain within them the possibilities of fable, parable, symbol, i.e., universals. The poet is nobody about whom to write; he is boring, both to himself and to any paying audience. The things of greatest interest are those which lend themselves to generalization and abstraction: horseshoe crabs, blue jays, Gorgons, gloomy woods, the number nine (9), alligators, and cripples.

I look about me, and I see sick people in hospital beds, pregnant women and teenagers, boys with beer and drugs in their hands, women, née lesbians, who eat their hair for lack of stimulation, football players driving Mustangs . . .

I must find a newer expression for all that unfurls my mind's spinnaker, new concatenations of ideas, not forms. The slant, or off, rhyme and internal rhyme will suffice, but the mind, like a branding iron, must be red hot before the image will take.

5/1/67 (05324)

[Green, green, the dazzle-dizzy lights] ‡

Green, green, the dazzle-dizzy lights
Scream far out and away. The bridge
Leans into the spray, its cables
Squeaking. The pavement crumples, kneaded
Beneath vagrant cars that flee cities.
That city, an Alcázar, steeples . . . zenith!
Night creeps in, slides down streets
Lined with urchins, cripples, freaks.
Red, red, the lambent-heated glow
That drips from identical tenements
Whose flaking faces levee the "el."
Shades drawn to half-mast emit
Odors of female to passing shades
Of inscrutable gender. The night
Leaks hot air; pressures get blown
Through saxophone valves and bells
A shrill-tilting musician caresses

5/5/67 (00749)

The Quick

A touch of summer fills out the night
Like wind in rigging running wing and wing.
Opaline whiskers whisper through trees,
Whose limbs would erase them for the breeze
That sways, stays, whisks them crazily.
Goats pasted against an eccentric sky,
Disguised as satyrs, rape the eyes.
The moon, a bobber on a hungry lake,
Dilates with weight of all this stillness
Down here. Lightning-bug stars
*

Sear sides of the eyes' horizon,
While a shadow of the man hides, naked,
In its own outreaching across the lawn.
Only a shade of his former self
Retains definition. Age has debarked him;
He is a telephone pole, belfry, a felled cross,
Outraged Ishmael clinging to a coffin
As night reels out to sea,
Liberated for the final inward tug.
There is no other hour except the trees,
The breeze, and random moon. He is a man,
Or haughty silhouette of his past, a sun
Casting shadows that, with every dusk,
With every backward glance, consume him,
Until the moments of his breath coalesce
In that most blessed equanimity, death.

5/10/67 (04040)

[Gophers burrow backward hurriedly.]

Gophers burrow backward hurriedly.
Impalas float in pantomime,
While a pride of lions lies quietly;
Their hunger settles inside.

Springs of a talking machine
Lose their temper, snap in two;
Voice dies on felt's green grave.
The horn is a wilted sumac.

Hunters chase the bear's shadows;
A knife is buried in its throat.
The woods run up conveyer belts;
The planing mill goes up in smoke.

A cold night cracks the block;
Compression leaks from the motor's veins.
The crank is a cigarette set askance
In the mouth of an angry animal.

Elephants and bears eat ladyfingers;
Giraffes bite fingers, tongue eyes,
*

While nursemaids warn another's child
Not to frighten the mating snakes.

An electric blanket catches fire;
A household dies while five alarms
Disturb the sleep of volunteers
Who mount engines to keep the peace.

Flowers unable to gauge the blaze,
Fowl that lay nocturnally
Respond as though to the break of day;
The sun has come to night's domain.

The face of an eight-day regulator clock
Accumulates blotches and weather stains
Behind painted glass. Its pendulum
Stays time in postures of drowsy stasis,

While at its foot a portrait flakes:
Flesh deteriorates; the banker writhes;
His shirt expands; the gold chain breaks,
Exposing a belly of amber canvas.

Cherrywood bookcases share the walls
With spare adornments: a rural phone,
Two pairs of sconces, Harper's prints,
And a hearth that snarls disconsolately.

The gables decay in such gradual splendor
Spectators refuse to pay them attention
Despite the town elder's exhortations
That someone will have to set it right.

A bulbous tank contains the water supply,
Stands on silver stalks, festoons the yard,
Where once the governor of Illinois
And General Grant passed a restive afternoon.

Only this house has resisted the rush
To standardize the face of the town;
The others were pulled down years before
Or divided to suffer retired genealogies.

A governor's son, a senatorial lawyer,
Once a wealthy wheat and soybean farmer
Maintained this mausoleum. Now its bones,
Its frame skeleton, shrink into the ground.

A condemned ruin, its porch is warped,
A mouth, a hat askance to the street.
Its iron lattice dissolves, a retreat
Whose insides confuse the settling dust.

5/12/67 (00791)

Apocalypse, Seen While Under the Influence
of Peace

The nights line up behind my brain
Like freight cars drawn by a groaning train.
Ancient thoughts uncouple, break apart,
Their destinations marked on boards
Whose circuitry refuses revision.
Decisions made blind as Goodwill brooms
Come loose, and all goes wild. A child
Lies down in muddy gutters, cries for milk
From prostitutes on their way to church.
A bugler blows retreat; the streets empty,
While from a toppling steeple, shouts,
Screams stream across the sky. Eyes fall out,
Hands grapple for stray coins, the dice explode,
And all are restless, all are sweating sperm
From pores. Garbage dropped from river barges
Foams the tides; the smell rides in to shores.
Bikinied whores scramble for shelter in tents
Where men of many-colored coats rend skin,
Touch each other, pet, scratch, bite scaly ears.
This is no place for glutted worms to spawn.
The waters rise forty inches each hour. Cowards,
Preachers, nuns in leotards take the stage,
While crowds genuflect and orchestras conclude.
Somewhere beyond the walls, armies march in step.
Stalled cars and sheep confuse the repetitious energy
That diffuses en masse, while bears and lizards
Disappear down alleyways. The streets are still.
Evacuation knocks down children and sages.
Cynics rage. The aged surrender their heritage.
Ovens flame, screech gluttonously. Every minute,
*

Another thousand debased symbols of humanity
Descend the increasingly diminishing stairway,
Until daylight scatters, shadows elongate,
And night feeds the maw with human dross.
A cross flies a migratory course; its pilot
Sits in a cockpit overlooking the pilgrimage.
An odorless coldness crystallizes ice on hair,
Limbs tear apart, legs lie strewn in markets,
Arms and maimed fragments of life fill sties
Where shoats pick and nudge the sickly clots,
And somewhere distant, in an alien stable,
A groom whisks, curries, rubs liniment
Down thighs, over withers and flanks,
Preparing a wild stallion for its final race.
A single shot, a button pressed high up,
And a pack of ten thousand violent monsters
Stampede, their sole objective to complete the circuit
That, when open-ended, withstands the inebriated hand
That swings the flail that severs creation.

5/14/67 (00789)

[Leaves preen for the slow breeze.] †

Leaves preen for the slow breeze.
Green covers the stale cathedral,
Whose dull grey wrinkles at dusk.
Lust ruffles grass that retains weight
From people who pass to sleep.
The bells' frail winds bend sound
Surrounding the eyes' examinations.

Two blackboards

The blackboard writes its own ciphers

5/18/67 (05314)

Mother Earth

The Earth Goose,
Most obtuse mother of all,
Shows wrinkled features,
Tobacco nose,
No shoes on her feet.
She has so very many children
No one knows what to do
But retreat
     In need of new soles.

5/19/67 — [1] (04003)

Epitaph

Life at stalemate:
An end anticipated
So long ago
That now
Even memories are in white.

5/19/67 — [2] (04023)

Valediction Forbidding Despair △

This summer is Treblinka;
Its regimental months
Are maws that caress us
In bloodless custody.
Victims, like crickets
Scratching dryness from limbs,
Chant hymns from lips
Which shape the air
With unfinished kisses.
Musicians and carpenters
Guard darker silences
Of those who crowd naked
In boxcars and chambers
Where perfumed night descends.
*

Memories race down chutes
To steaming graves
Obsequious few ply with balm.

Yet
Minds are excused from spirit.
The end obliterates nothing
But flesh
And the temporary wish
To rest.

5/21–22/67 (04024)

The Uprooting

He is both sexes, self-perpetuating,
A limp erection injecting itself.
He has thrived in the womb he cocooned
After thorough investigation. Parasitic,
He chose this room for himself.
He was this room; his inaudible voice
The choice that moved no other earth
Than that which threatened to doom him
Where he lay in terrigenous cloisters.

Now floods rage above his civilization.
Sounds that compound his heartbeat
Grow dim inside him. Walls give way.
All fortifications are inconsequential.
As he climbs out, his lungs pump air
Too pure to sustain his squatty body.
The end rushes up to defeat him.

The precipice toward which he gestures
Refuses his suicidal ascent.
As he concludes an inward journey
From the scruffy pit of his guts
Through symmetry where neck joins head,
A man within the animal stands up,
Surveys his passage out of the bowels.
He squirms, curls, sinks to surface mud,
A sluggish creature in an alien terrain.

5/24/67 (04002)

Sortie

Bristles of a searchlight's broom
Scratch the night with nervous strokes.
Although clouds attract its sweeping beam,
The sky stays whole, annealed, and clean,
For the pendulum's consistent twitch.

The pilot flies a piece of flak,
Tracking doubts that besiege his mind.
Fear attacks him through her sights.
The man explodes in a moment's flame.
Night remains broken, bloody, and alone.

5/27 & 6/13/67 (04001)

The Vanity of Human Beauty

The mirror through which she peers
Undresses her. A dying reminder
Of nosegays pressed between pages
Rivets her flesh to the glass.
Outside, naked silhouettes pass.
Ghosts who have never known retreat
Reach up to touch her fleeting glance,
Kneel down in gutters to weep.
The secret she keeps discovers her.

6/2/67 (04004)

Squall

For Jan, in June

Wind beats the winter wheat.
Cornstalks not two feet old
Inflate rippled fields,
Flap in the stippled breeze
Like people clapping hands
In a crowded coliseum.
*

Cows turn their backs to the world.
Sows leave off feed troughs
To huddle against weathers
That twist the swifts' course,
Knot a freight train's whistle,
And buckle the very air
That bridges spoke-taut cities
And these flat-out plains.
Now rain paints war designs
On the face of this plow-traced land.
Furrows retreat like sandcastles
Washed by a truculent sea.
Autos creep wheel-deep in water.
Traffic lights blink into sleep.
Against one window of the restaurant
Where we, just passing through,
Have been forced to serve the storm,
Debris etches a dance of death.

6/11/67 (04011)

APPENDIX

with translations by Rose Passalacqua

~ p. 35 ~

Culpa eterna

¿Qué es nuestra culpa
Si no es la ensimismada pulpa
En el corazón, que nos motiva
Buscar lo interior subjetivo?

El destino es cosa determinada,
Con una significación obligada
Siempre en la aceptación inevitable
Del hombre que conserva la fe adorable.

Eternal Fault

What is the fault in us
If it isn't the engorged flesh
Of the heart, which moves us
To seek the subjective interior?

Destiny is a determined thing,
Obligated always to mean
Inevitable acceptance
For the man who keeps supreme faith.

3?/63 (05142)

~ pp. 49–50 ~

[El cielo azulado,]

I

El cielo azulado,
De líquido azul,
Parecía lago vago,
Vacía languidez.

Sus aguas calientes,
De extraño calor,
Radiaban estrellas
De fluctuante embriaguez.

II

El cielo iba poniéndose negruzco, nublado.
Él veía caminos que se alargaban hasta el infinito
Y los seguía y los seguía y los seguía, y siempre
Volvió al mismo sitio de asco y de sed.

III

Fué una noche estrellada,
En que planetas y vaguedades
Bailaban,
   Reflejándose sobre la retina
   De una pobre golondrina,
Cuya visión fué aterciopelada.

Fué una noche quebrantada,
En que lacayos y fantasma-lunas
Se trastornaban,
   Cabalgando las espaldas desnudas
   De colinas de tortólica nubladas,
Cuya existencia fué algodonada.

IV

Qué lástima, que su vida era una cosa tan inconcreta,
Como una de aquellas nubes sin fuerza
Que se iba esfumando en el escenario,
El dibujo, el cielo del artista que pinta sin paleta.

[The bluish sky,]

I

The bluish sky,
Of liquid blue,
Looked like a lazy lake,
Empty languor.

Its warm waters,
With a strange heat,
Radiated stars
Of fluctuating drunkenness.

II

The sky was becoming blackened, cloudy.
He saw roads that extended to infinity
And followed them and followed them and followed them, and always
He returned to that same place of filth and of thirst.

III

It was a starry night,
In which planets and vaguenesses
Danced,
> Reflecting on the retina
> Of a poor swallow,
Whose vision was velvety.

It was a shattered night,
In which footmen and phantom-moons
Were in turmoil,
> Riding upon the naked backs
> Of cloudy turtledove-hills,
Whose existence was cotton-soft.

IV

What a shame, that his life was such an insubstantial thing,
Like one of those impotent clouds
That trailed smoke across the landscape,
The painting, the sky of the artist who paints without a palette.

9-10?/63 (05006)

~ *pp. 50–51* ~

from [I watch; I perceive]

I watch; I perceive
What is impenetrable
And know that the
Illusory chimera of
Sedentary sustenance is
Lleno del alma

>   *   *   *

¿Qué es la vida?
Un frenesí.
¿Qué es la vida?
Una illusión, una sombra, una ficción,
y el mayor bien es pequeño,
que toda la vida es sueño,
y los sueños sueños son.
— Pedro Calderón de la Barca, *La vida es sueño*

>   *   *   *

García Lorca:
> *Jaca negra,*
> *luna grande,*
> *y aceitunas en*
> *mi alforja.*

from **[I watch; I perceive]**

I watch; I perceive
What is impenetrable
And know that the
Illusory chimera of
Sedentary sustenance is
Full of soul

> * * *

What is life?
A frenzy.
What is life?
An illusion, a shadow, a fiction,
and the best is not much,
for all of life is a dream,
and dreams are but dreams.
— Pedro Calderón de la Barca, *Life Is a Dream*

> * * *

García Lorca:
> Black pony,
> big moon,
> and olives in
> my saddlebag.

9-10?/63 (05174)

~ pp. 53–54 ~

from **[Sir Walter Raleigh]**

resignación
fertilidad
yerma

Let   *frustración*
   the goodness of my   *humildad*
             heart   *soledad*

                              Suzane
Historia de una escalera   Suzan
   Antonio Buero Vallejo   *quel chic*

     name
     shame
     fame
    vaga or *Dios*
    mi amante

¿Qué es la vida?
Un frenesí . . .
una sombra, una ficción,
y el mayor bien es pequeño,
que toda la vida es sueño . . .
— Pedro Calderón de la Barca, *La vida es sueño*

   Qué descansada vida,
  la del que huye el
mundanal ruido
   y sigue la
escondida senda por
donde han ido los pocos
  sabios que en el mundo
  han sido . . .
   — Fray Luis de León

    *   *   *

Me veía la chi

from [Sir Walter Raleigh]

            resignation
            fertility
            barrenness
Let   frustration
   the goodness of my   humility
       heart   solitude

            Suzane
Story of a Staircase   Suzan
   Antonio Buero Vallejo   what style

                              name
                              shame
                              fame
                    vague woman or God
                         my lover

What is life?
A frenzy . . .
a shadow, a fiction,
and the best is not much,
for all of life is a dream . . .
— Pedro Calderón de la Barca, *Life Is a Dream*

    What a weary life
  is his who flees the
noise of the world
    and follows the
  hidden path along which
have gone the few
  wise men who have lived
    in the world . . .
        — Fray Luis de León

      * * *

the [girl *? ed.*] was looking at me

9-10?/63 (05245)

~ *p. 62* ~

from Questioning an Untimely Passing: Phrenology

*¿Pues dónde queda la reverencia por parte de la
gente frente a la situación peligrosa en que se
nos encontramos predestinados y ciegos?*

        * * *

*Hay una falta invidiosa de comprensión
manifestándose en el fondo de la conciencia
moderna que abnega la compasión y la afección.*

from **Questioning an Untimely Passing: Phrenology**

But where is the reverence by those of us
faced with a dangerous situation in which
we find ourselves predestined and blind?

      * * *

There is an invidious lack of understanding
manifesting itself in the depths of modern
consciousness that renounces compassion and affection.

11/22-25?/63 (05008)

~ *p. 120* ~

from **[Why do certain special individuals . . .]**

I can see the yellow-green light at the end of Daisy's dock, and I am Nick
Carraway, twice removed. My eyes accommodate now, and I am living in the
moment before America: I am a Spanish sea dog *quien se llama hijo del Dios*,
Alonso Quijano.

I am yelling to those aboard a galleon we have just boarded: *"Deseamos nada
menos que el respeto y la fe adorable a Él quien existe para todos nosotros."*

from **[Why do certain special individuals . . .]**

I can see the yellow-green light at the end of Daisy's dock, and I am Nick
Carraway, twice removed. My eyes accommodate now, and I am living in the
moment before America: I am a Spanish sea dog who calls himself the son of
God, Alonso Quijano.

I am yelling to those aboard a galleon we have just boarded: "We desire
nothing less than respect for and supreme faith in Him who exists for all of us."

12/2/64 — [1] (05186)

~ *pp. 130–132* ~

from **[And I am so tired, . . .]**

I hear a Spanish verse ringing in my ears, and it is ringing, and it is ringing
louder and more vibrantly and incessantly, until I am forced to put it down on this

yellow paper, and now I am ready to write it, or, rather, repeat it, since it was already written and composed before me by Rubén Darío, and I am ready, and I am very tired, but I want to type it:

> No hay dolor más grande que la vida.

No, no, that's not it, but I am faltering, and the yellow hue of the paper is distorting my memory, and I am tired, but I want to try to write it again:

> No hay dolor más grande que el dolor de ser vivo,
> Ni mayor pesadumbre que la vida consciente.
> ["Fatalidad," from "Los cisnes" y otros poemas, ed.]

* * *

¿Qué es la vida? Un frenesí . . .
una sombra, una ficción,
y el mayor bien es pequeño,
porque todo el mundo es loco.
[first three lines by Pedro Calderón de la Barca, La vida es sueño, ed.]

from [And I am so tired, . . .]

I hear a Spanish verse ringing in my ears, and it is ringing, and it is ringing louder and more vibrantly and incessantly, until I am forced to put it down on this yellow paper, and now I am ready to write it, or, rather, repeat it, since it was already written and composed before me by Rubén Darío, and I am ready, and I am very tired, but I want to type it:

> There is no pain greater than life.

No, no, that's not it, but I am faltering, and the yellow hue of the paper is distorting my memory, and I am tired, but I want to try to write it again:

> There is no pain greater than the pain of being alive,
> Nor a greater sorrow than consciousness.
> ["Fatality," from "The Swans" and Other Poems, ed.]

* * *

What is life? A frenzy . . .
a shadow, a fiction,
and the best is not much,
because everyone is crazy.
[first three lines by Pedro Calderón de la Barca, Life Is a Dream, ed.]

12/17-18/64 — [2] on 12/18 (05192)

~ *p. 210* ~

from [I am imprisoned beneath the ceiling . . .]

I can hear Spanish verse flowing through my ears again, as I did once before; only, now I can remember what it was and who feared enough at the time to transcribe it for us. The good Fray Luis de León, in his retired life, wrote the most beautiful of all verses when he reclaimed from Shelley's visitations of the divinity in man this thought:

> *Qué descansada vida,*
> *la del que huye el mundanal ruido*
> *y sigue la escondida*
> *senda por donde han ido*
> *los pocos sabios que en el mundo han sido . . .*

from [I am imprisoned beneath the ceiling . . .]

I can hear Spanish verse flowing through my ears again, as I did once before; only, now I can remember what it was and who feared enough at the time to transcribe it for us. The good Fray Luis de León, in his retired life, wrote the most beautiful of all verses when he reclaimed from Shelley's visitations of the divinity in man this thought:

> What a weary life
> is his who flees the noise of the world
> and follows the hidden
> path along which have gone
> the few wise men who have lived in the world . . .

2/14/65 (05199)

~ *p. 257* ~

from Meditation over Coffee, 4/7/65

> *No funciona la inmobilidad para nada menos que la muerte vivienda. El ser humano se baja a los hondos de la noche oscura del alma.*
> *¿Y yo? ¿Que pasa con el Yo de la personalidad?*
> *Se rompe en mil pedazos de vidrio y carne. No vale la pena de*

from **Meditation over Coffee, 4/7/65**

Immobility serves as nothing less than living death. The human being sinks into the depths of the dark night of the soul.

And I? What happens to the I of the personality?

It breaks into a thousand pieces of glass and flesh. It's not worth

4/7/65 — [2] (05211)

~ *p. 335* ~

from **[She was so filled with humble grace]**

Ave María, llena de gracia!

from **[She was so filled with humble grace]**

Hail Mary, full of grace!

7?/65 (5268)

~ *p. 563* ~

El Quijote

Él leyó la mayoría
De la literatura
Caballería.
Él se murió
Del corazón frío, roto.
Era el hijo
De lo incumplido.

Quijote

He read the majority
Of the literature
Of chivalry.
He died
*

Of a cold, broken heart.
He was the son
Of the unaccomplished.

11-12?/66 (05147)

BIOGRAPHICAL NOTE

Louis Daniel Brodsky was born in St. Louis, Missouri, in 1941, where he attended St. Louis Country Day School. After earning a B.A., magna cum laude, at Yale University in 1963, he received an M.A. in English from Washington University, in St. Louis, in 1967 and an M.A. in Creative Writing from San Francisco State University the following year.

From 1968 to 1987, while continuing to write poetry, he managed a men's clothing factory and outlet operation in Farmington, Missouri, where he resided with his family. From 1980 to 1991, he taught English and creative writing at nearby Mineral Area Junior College.

In 1987, the author, his wife and two children relocated to St. Louis, Missouri. At that time, he resigned his position with Biltwell Company in order to focus his full energies on his writing career.

Mr. Brodsky is the author of thirty-four volumes of poetry, four of which have been published in French by Éditions Gallimard. His poems have appeared in *Harper's*, *Literary Review*, *Ariel*, *New Welsh Review*, *Orbis*, *American Scholar*, and *Southern Review*, as well as in five editions of the *Anthology of Magazine Verse and Yearbook of American Poetry*.

Also available from **Time Being Books**

LOUIS DANIEL BRODSKY

You Can't Go Back, Exactly

The Thorough Earth

Four and Twenty Blackbirds Soaring

Mississippi Vistas: Volume One of *A Mississippi Trilogy*

Falling from Heaven: Holocaust Poems of a Jew and a Gentile
 (with William Heyen)

Forever, for Now: Poems for a Later Love

Mistress Mississippi: Volume Three of *A Mississippi Trilogy*

A Gleam in the Eye: Poems for a First Baby

Gestapo Crows: Holocaust Poems

The Capital Café: Poems of Redneck, U.S.A.

Disappearing in Mississippi Latitudes: Volume Two of *A Mississippi
 Trilogy*

Paper-Whites for Lady Jane: Poems of a Midlife Love Affair

HARRY JAMES CARGAS (editor)

Telling the Tale: A Tribute to Elie Wiesel on the Occasion of His 65th
 Birthday — Essays, Reflections, and Poems

JUDITH CHALMER

Out of History's Junk Jar: Poems of a Mixed Inheritance

GERALD EARLY

How the War in the Streets Is Won: Poems on the Quest of Love and Faith

ALBERT GOLDBARTH

A Lineage of Ragpickers, Songpluckers, Elegiasts & Jewelers:
 Selected Poems of Jewish Family Life (1973–1995)

ROBERT HAMBLIN

From the Ground Up: Poems of One Southerner's Passage to Adulthood

WILLIAM HEYEN

Erika: Poems of the Holocaust

Falling from Heaven: Holocaust Poems of a Jew and a Gentile
 (with Louis Daniel Brodsky)

Pterodactyl Rose: Poems of Ecology

Ribbons: The Gulf War — A Poem

The Host: Selected Poems, 1965–1990

TED HIRSCHFIELD
German Requiem: Poems of the War and the Atonement of a Third
Reich Child

VIRGINIA V. JAMES HLAVSA
Waking October Leaves: Reanimations of a Small-Town Girl

RODGER KAMENETZ
The Missing Jew: New and Selected Poems

NORBERT KRAPF
Somewhere in Southern Indiana: Poems of Midwestern Origins

ADRIAN LOUIS
Blood Thirsty Savages

GARDNER McFALL
The Pilot's Daughter

JOSEPH MEREDITH
Hunter's Moon: Poems from Boyhood to Manhood

BEN MILDER
The Good Book Says . . . : Light Verse to Illuminate the Old Testament

TIME BEING BOOKS
POETRY IN SIGHT AND SOUND
St. Louis, Missouri

FOR OUR FREE CATALOG OR TO ORDER
(800) 331-6605 • FAX: (314) 432-7939
http://www.bookworld.com/timebeing/